The Bible's Foundation

The Bible's Foundation

A Catholic Introduction to the Pentateuch

DR. NATHAN SCHMIEDICKE
Professor of Scripture
Our Lady of Guadalupe Seminary
Denton, Nebraska

ST. AUGUSTINE ACADEMY PRESS
HOMER GLEN, ILLINOIS

First published in the USA
by St. Augustine Academy Press 2021
Copyright © Nathan Schmiedicke 2021

All rights reserved:
No part of this book may be reproduced or transmitted,
in any form or by any means, without permission

For information, address:
St. Augustine Academy Press
12050 Rambling Rd.
Homer Glen, IL 60491
www.staugustineacademypress.com

ISBN 978 1 64051 119 4 pb
ISBN 978 1 64051 120 0 hc

Cover: Rembrandt van Rijn,
Moses Breaking the Tablets of the Law (1659)
Cover design by Michael Schrauzer

This book adheres to Catholic dogma on the divine authorship, inspiration, and inerrancy of Sacred Scripture and to Catholic tradition concerning Scriptural interpretation.

Scripture citations in this work are either translated directly by the author from the original texts; taken from the Douay-Rheims Challoner edition, which is in public domain; or taken from the Second Catholic Edition of the Revised Standard Version (RSV) of the Bible, copyright © 1965, 1966, and 2006 by the Division of Christian Education of the National Council of the Churches of Christ in the United States of America. Used with permission. All Rights Reserved.

Table of Contents

Preface ix
Introduction: Foundational Principles 1

Genesis
Lesson 1: The First Book of the Five Books of the Law 7
Lesson 2: An Important Phrase 17
Lesson 3: A Curse . . . with a Promise 30
Lesson 4: "The wickedness of man was great . . ." 45
Lesson 5: God Has a Big Problem 64
Lesson 6: Abraham Attains Perfection 79
Lesson 7: The Story of Isaac 95
Lesson 8: The Story of Jacob 114
Lesson 9: Jacob's Sons 137

Exodus
Lesson 10: Israel in Egypt 155
Lesson 11: Who Will Deliver Israel? 163
Lesson 12: "The Egyptians shall know that I am the Lord" 174
Lesson 13: Consecrate to Me All the Firstborn 184
Lesson 14: Up and Down the Mountain 195
Lesson 15: From Riches to Ruin 205
Lesson 16: Covenant Consummation 218

Leviticus
Lesson 17: Making Sense of the Central Book 229
Lesson 18: Entering the Outer Court of the Sanctuary 237
Lesson 19: The Code of the Priests 245
Lesson 20: Entering the Holy of Holies 250
Lesson 21: The Center of the Center 256
Lesson 22: The Code of Holiness 262
Lesson 23: The Code of Reverence 269
Lesson 24: The Code of Redemption of the Land 274

Numbers

Lesson 25: That's a Lot of Numbers 283
Lesson 26: The First Census of the People 291
Lesson 27: Worship before War 296
Lesson 28: The First Generation Prepares to Move 300
Lesson 29: Forty Years of Wandering 305
Lesson 30: Movement Toward the Land, Part 2 316
Lesson 31: Waging War 320
Lesson 32: Second Census 329

Deuteronomy

Lesson 33: Introduction to Deuteronomy 337
Lesson 34: Moses Explains the Torah 344
Lesson 35: "Hear, O Israel!" 350
Lesson 36: The Leaders of the People 356
Lesson 37: The Prophet Who Is To Come 364
Lesson 38: Social Life and Institutions 370
Lesson 39: Blessings and Curses 379
Lesson 40: Moses Writes the Torah 384

PREFACE

Welcome to the *Torah/Pentateuch*. If the Bible were compared to a house, the Pentateuch would be like the foundation—the part upon which the whole house stands rooted to the ground. In this course, we are going to be studying the foundational realities of all that God is doing in the world. There is so much wonderful wisdom packed into these first five books of the Bible that we are going to have to do some hard digging so we can see the strength, order, and beauty of this foundation and look forward to the house that is going to be built upon it, which is nothing less than the dwelling place of God with men!

About the first half of the forty lessons of this course are going to be hard work! It will be challenging, but enjoyable work as you both learn about what you are reading and also learn how to read Scripture better. After that you will be able to move much more quickly—so don't lose heart! Scripture is the Word of God in human words. These are the best and most important words you will ever read as God speaks to you about all that He is doing in the world and His plan for building a place where He can dwell in love with the human race:

"Behold, the dwelling place of God is with men! He will dwell with them and they shall be his people and God Himself will be with them; he will wipe every tear from their eyes, and death shall be no more, neither shall there be mourning, nor crying nor pain any more, for the former things have passed away... Behold, I make all things new!" (Revelation 21:3–4).

Introduction: Foundational Principles

Why did God create the world?

God created the world, but He didn't *have* to do it. It does not make Him better or more perfect. It does not make Him happier than He is, in any way. He is already perfection itself and has perfect happiness in Himself. He does not need to create us or anything else. So then why did He do it? In this first lesson, we are going to learn a very important part of the answer to this very important question. But before we get to the answer, we need to learn some basic things about the Bible and how to read it.

The Bible is made up of the Old Testament and the New Testament

The Old Testament tells the story of God's creation of the world and mankind, the fall of mankind, the election of Israel, and the promise of a Messiah.

The New Testament reveals the coming of the promised Messiah, Jesus Christ, and His establishment of the Church, which will last on earth until the end of time, and in heaven forever. The New Testament has two main parts. The first part is the Gospels, which record the life, teaching, death, and resurrection of Jesus Christ. The second part is about the Apostles, which records how the Apostles carry on the work of Christ in the world until the end of time. So the Bible covers from the very beginning of time to the very end of time and the most important times in between!

The Old and New Testament are made up of a lot of books

There are 46 books in the Old Testament and 27 books in the New Testament, for a total of 73 books. The word "Bible" comes to us from the Greek phrase *ta biblia to hagia* which means "the holy books." The Bible is a collection of holy books, also called "the Holy Scriptures" or just "Scripture." They are holy because God, who inspired different men throughout history to write them, is their Divine Author. That is why you will sometimes hear the Bible referred to as "God's word." The Bible is called "Scripture" because Scripture means something that is written down. Today, Bibles are printed in large quantities by computers and machines, but up until the modern era, each and every Bible was written and copied by hand!

Each book within the Bible has its own name

There are two basic kinds of names given to the books in the Bible. The names of the books are either a description of the book or they are the name of a person. Those that describe the book describe:

1. What events happen in that book, such as Genesis, Exodus, or Acts of the Apostles.
2. Or they describe what type of literature that book contains, such as Proverbs, Psalms, and Lamentations.

Of those that are the name of a person there are also two kinds.

1. Sometimes it is the name of an important person in the story, such as Judith, Esther, or Tobit; and
2. Sometimes it is the name of the human author of the book, such as Jeremiah, Isaiah, or Luke.

Each book is divided into chapters

A long time after all of these books were written, people who studied and wrote about the Bible wanted an easier way to find or tell about a specific part of a specific book, so they divided each book up into smaller units called chapters, which contain a large portion of each book. For example, the first chapter of Genesis contains the whole story of the first six days of creation, from when God created light on the first day until He created Man on the sixth day. In this way, whenever someone wanted to tell someone else where the creation story was in the Bible, they could just tell them the name of the book and the number of the chapter and the person would know right where to look for it—in Genesis chapter 1, or more simply, Genesis 1.

Each chapter is divided into verses

The chapter divisions helped a lot, but then scholars wanted to get even more specific, so they divided up the chapters into even smaller units called verses, which might be only a sentence or two long. That way, people could be more precise about which part of the Bible they were talking about. So, if a scholar wanted to refer someone to just that part of the Bible where God first created the animals, he could now give:

- the book name = Genesis
- the chapter number = 1
- and the verse number = 24

This is written like this: *Genesis 1:24*, which means "Genesis, chapter one, verse twenty-four."

To make it even easier to write, scholars would shorten the names of each book. So, for example, instead of writing Genesis 1:24, they would just write *Gen 1:24*. If they wanted to refer to more than one verse at a time, they would write it this way: Gen 1:24–31 which means "Genesis chapter 1, verses 24 through 31." You can usually find a list of abbreviations for book names in the front of your Bible.

So, if you open your Bible up to the first page of the Book of Genesis, the large number 1 that you see at the beginning is the chapter number and the tiny numbers you see written next to the words are the verse numbers. As an exercise, find Gen 1:24 and read it. Find Genesis 1:28 and read it. In what verse of Genesis 1 does God say "Let there be light"? How would you write that? If someone asked you what God says to the man and the woman the first time He speaks to them, what chapter and verses would you tell them to look at? How would you write it? This way of writing the chapter and verse divisions is very simple but also very useful, so be sure to master this before moving on.

Unless you are reading in Hebrew, you are reading a translation

All of the books of the Old Testament were first written in the Hebrew language, but about 300 years before Jesus was on earth, it was translated from Hebrew into Greek (this version is called the *Septuagint*). The New Testament was written in Greek. After this, throughout history, the books of the Old and the New Testament were translated into many, many different languages, more languages than any other book in the world. We will learn more about this later, but it is important to realize that you are reading the Bible in a translation and that there are many different translations that exist, even within one language. There are, for example, about a hundred English translations! So it may happen that the Bible quotations in your lessons may not be exactly the same as the one that you have in your translation of the Bible, even though you are reading the same chapter and verse. You can use the translation your family prefers, but be aware that there are others, and that their reputations for accuracy and eloquence vary.

GENESIS

Lesson 1

The First Book of the Five Books of the Law

THE LAW IS ALSO CALLED the *Pentateuch*, which is from Greek and means "five books." The Book of Genesis covers the story of God and His people from the creation of the world up through the death of Jacob-Israel, with his family in the land of Egypt. The name *Genesis* is a Greek word that means "Beginning." Many of the titles of books in the Bible we have today come from their Greek names. In Hebrew, the first book of the Bible was called *Bereshith*, which in Hebrew means "In the Beginning." In Greek this was shortened to just *Genesis*, which you already know means "Beginning." This is a fitting title for this book because it reveals the beginning of everything that God did in creation.

Genesis 1–2:3

For this first lesson, you will be reading Genesis 1–2:3, which means Genesis, chapter 1 through Genesis chapter 2, verse 3. This covers all seven days of creation. Catholics and the Jewish people before them have always held these first chapters of Genesis to be among the most important in the whole Bible. This is what the *Catechism of the Catholic Church* says about them:

> Among all the Scriptural texts about creation, the first three chapters of Genesis occupy a unique place . . . The inspired authors have placed them at the beginning of Scripture to express in their solemn language the truths of creation—its origin and its end in God, its order and goodness, the vocation of man, and finally the drama of sin and the hope of salvation. Read in the light of Christ, within the unity of Sacred Scripture and in the living Tradition of the Church, these texts remain the principal source for catechesis on the mysteries of the "beginning": creation, fall, and promise of salvation. (CCC, 289)

In the first two chapters of Genesis we learn that the good God created a good universe for a good purpose. He called everything into existence so that it could share in and enjoy His own life, goodness, and beauty.

God created everything

You have studied in your Catechism that God created the universe out of nothing (*ex nihilo*). It might seem like Genesis contradicts this by saying that there were waters already there "in the beginning," but this is not the case. The waters are there in Gen 1:2, but they don't exist apart from God's creation of them, which is what Gen 1:1 makes clear—God created the "heavens and the earth," which is the Hebrew way of saying God created everything because the heavens and the earth encompass all creatures that exists. The author also used a special word for what God does when He "creates" something. The word in Hebrew is *barah*. In the whole Bible, this word is only used when talking about what God does. Many people in the Bible will "make" things or "build" things or even "start" things, but only God "creates" things, because only He can bring things into existence out of nothing. And nothing can exist apart from God's creation of it.

God parts the waters with a simple command, and orders them to stay in their place. He is very much in charge of the waters. For all of the living things on land, the great waters are a threat. God's word brings order to the universe and pushes the waters back so that life can exist on the earth. The waters represent the "formlessness and void" which God's command pushes aside and replaces with order and fullness and good things. We will be seeing the waters again in the story of Noah and in the story of the crossing of the Red Sea in the Book of Exodus.

Genesis 1 is very orderly and so is God

The God revealed here is a God of order. The life, goodness, and beauty of the creation come from the order God gives it. When things depart from God's order (which we will begin to see a lot of in Genesis 3) they become evil and ugly, and they experience death, not life. This is especially true of man who is made in the image and likeness of God. Orderliness is next to Godliness.

After Gen 1:2 the story follows an orderly pattern. God will command something to come into being and then it does. God does further work on the thing that now exists, sees that it is good, names the thing, and then each day of creation ends with "there was evening and there was morning, the second (third, fourth, fifth, and sixth) day."

The orderliness is also seen in the order in which God creates things. First He deals with the simplest non-living things: light, the sky, the dry land and water. Then He goes on to living things: first the simplest of living things (plants) then later the higher living things, animals, and lastly, the highest living thing in the material creation, Man, made in God's image and likeness. God is a careful worker, and yet nothing is hard for Him! He speaks and it comes into being. Before He creates Man, He creates a world in which He can live, and in which He will rule all lesser creatures. Before He creates the animals, He creates the plants that they need for food; before He creates the plants, He creates the earth, air, water, and light that they need for *their* food.

Another way of seeing this is in the following chart, which shows how days 1 and 4, 2 and 5, 3 and 6 match up. The first set of prepares for and is completed by the second set of three days. For example, day 1 tells about the creation of day and night while day 4 tells about the creation of the "rulers" over day and night—the sun, moon, and stars. Day 2 tells of the creation of water and air while day 5 tells about the creation of the "rulers" over the water and air, that is, the animals that live in the water and air. And so on.

THE DAYS OF CREATION			
Day 1	day & night	Day 4	the "rulers" over day and night = sun, moon, and stars
Day 2	water & air	Day 5	"the rulers" over the water and air, that is, the animals that live in water and air
Day 3	dry land & plants	Day 6	"the rulers" over dry land and plants = animals that live on land and eat plants/fruits, followed by Man, who has dominion over EVERYTHING else that God has created before (Gen 1:28).

You will also notice that Genesis 1 repeats the phrase "and God saw that it was good." In fact, it repeats it seven times: the first six times it says that God saw that "it was good." But then the seventh time it says God saw that "it was VERY good." Take a few minutes and find and count all of these in your Bible and if you want to, underline them or highlight them with a marker. There are many other "sevens" in this story. For example, in Hebrew, the first sentence has seven words and the second sentence has two times seven words (14)! There are also the seven days.

The reason for all of these sevens can be seen if we learn a little more about Hebrew, which, as you remember, is the language in which the Old Testament was written. In Hebrew the word for "seven" and the word for "perfect" are spelled exactly the same way, so "seven" is a symbol of perfection or completion. But all of these sevens help to make the same basic point: what God has made is so good that it is perfect. When there are seven of anything in the Bible, it can be a way of saying that it was perfect or complete. So, saying that the creation in all of its parts was good six times and then adding the seventh saying "it was VERY good" was like saying that this creation was so good that it was perfect—God's world was complete—there couldn't be a better one!

The seven "goods" help to show two very important things:
1. Obviously, they show that *Creation itself is GOOD*.
2. But more importantly they tell us that the God revealed in this book is a GOOD God; *GOD IS GOOD!*

You can't give what you don't have and everything to which God gives existence is good, therefore, since God's creation is perfectly good, God Himself must be even better! God, who is so good, sees and loves His good creation.

This is the first part of the answer to our opening question: Why Did God create the world? He did it because it was good, and very good, to do so. God is so good that He wanted to share His own goodness and blessedness with others outside of Himself. He creates because He loves. He gives of Himself, not because He needs to, but freely from love. (We will read later in the Bible that it can even be said that God IS love!: 1 John 4:8.) In showing this fact about Himself in the first pages of the Bible, God already shows us how we should act, without even giving a command. If we only have goods without sharing them, then we aren't acting like God does. It is in the nature of true Goodness that it shares what it has with others freely and generously.

Man is created in the image and likeness of God and completes God's creation

When He created everything else, God simply commanded it to come into existence: "Let there be light! Let there be land! Let there be plants! Let there be animals!" And they all were. But with man, God does something different. He says *"Let us make* man in our image, after our likeness." This indicates that God takes especial care with making man and that man, in a special way, comes out of God's own being, His own inner life, similar to the way children come from their parents and are "in the image" of their parents. Later on in Genesis, for example, we will hear about Seth who was "in the likeness" and "after the image" of his father Adam (Gen 5:3). It is only after

God has created Man that He looks at the whole of creation and sees, for the seventh time, that "it was very good." Man brings God's work of creation to completion.

However, this does not mean that there is nothing else left to do in creation. There is in fact a great deal of work to be done. God appoints Man, male and female, to do this work by giving them a command: "Be fertile and multiply; fill the earth and subdue it. Have dominion over the fish of the sea, the birds of the air, and all the living things that move on the earth" (Gen 1:28).

This is the FIRST commandment given to mankind in the Bible. It is very important because in it God calls man to do the two things that we have already seen God Himself doing:

1. To share their goodness with others = "Be fertile and multiply and fill the earth."
2. To bring order out of disorder = "Subdue it. Have dominion..."

We are called to act like God acts! Some people think that the perfect world would be one where we didn't have to do any work, but this isn't what Genesis says. The perfect creation for man, who is made in God's image, is not a world where man sits idle and is entertained constantly. God wants Man to be like Him, to work with Him, not to be entertained by Him. The perfect world for man is one that is not totally done. It is a world that requires work, a world where man can add his efforts to God's. Man is called to take what God has given and work with God's help to bring it to completion. This gives Man the chance of lifetime—the chance to work alongside God in the biggest project of all—ordering the whole creation back toward God!

This is a world with no death

After God gives this first command, He also gives man "every plant bearing seed...and every tree bearing fruit" for food. Then He gives all of the animals "every green plant" for their food (Gen 1:29–30). This talk about food might not seem very important at first, but it shows something wonderful about God and what He wants for the world He has created: There is no death in it! Animals don't kill green plants when they eat them because they just grow back from the roots; Man doesn't kill a tree by eating its fruit. In God's original plan for the world, there was no death, anywhere at all, in the whole world!

The seventh day of Gen 2:2–3 is the goal of creation

God creates order and life in the world and He commands Man, who is in God's image, to "fill the earth" with that image, to make the whole creation something that by its very life reveals and glorifies God. You might think, in reading up to this point, that the goal of the whole creation was Man because everything points to him and it all seems finished with him. But Man himself is meant to direct himself and the whole creation back to God. Even though Man is the best thing in the material creation, even Man has a further purpose—to bring all of creation into the seventh day of God's rest.

This is the second part of the answer to our opening question: Why did God create? God created Man as a kind of priest who is called to offer the whole creation, and his own work in that creation, back to God. This is what the seventh day in Gen 2:1–3 is all about. It is a day which God "hallows" or makes holy. Creation itself isn't the goal—God is! Or, more precisely, God and His creation resting together in love.

How does Genesis tell us that this is the real goal, the real end? When we come to the seventh day it has no "evening and morning," no end or purpose, no further step or goal beyond itself. We already learned that the word for *seven* and the word for *perfect* were spelled the same way. Well, now it is time to learn that there was yet *another* word spelled the same way: the word for taking an oath or making a solemn promise. If I wanted to say "I solemnly promise" in Hebrew I would say, "I seven myself." It sounds funny in English, but this is how the importance and perfection of a solemn promise was made clear in Hebrew. This makes the seventh day a day of perfection, but also a day of promise—in it God completes His creation, but also makes a solemn promise to His creatures, especially Man, that He will bring them into His Sabbath rest if they are faithful to His command. The Sabbath rest of God in His creation, and His creation resting in Him, is the goal, the final answer to the question of why God created. The Sabbath, because it is God and His creation resting together with one another, and because it never ends, is thus an image of Heaven. On the Sabbath, the whole creation becomes a temple in which God promises Himself to Man, and Man, the priest, offers himself and the whole creation back to his Creator in worship.

Other peoples did not understand God or creation

Now, some of these ideas might seem obvious to you if you have studied your catechism well, or because you have read about them since you were little, but they were not at all obvious to the people of the time during which Genesis was written, nor are they obvious to many people of our own time. Many other people around the land of Israel had their own ideas and stories about how the world came into existence. One of these stories, called the *Enuma Elish*, was written in Babylon, a land east of Israel. The Babylonians were the worst enemies of the Israelites later on in their history.

When the story of the *Enuma Elish* was first discovered, some people thought that because it told a somewhat similar story of how creation happened, this meant that the story of creation in the Bible was nothing special—just one story of creation among all the different stories that were out there. But this was wrong. As time went on and scholars began to compare the two stories, they began to see that in every case, even when the two stories seemed similar, they were in fact saying completely opposite things about God, the creation, the purpose of Man in creation, and the relationship between Man and God. The following chart shows some of the most important examples of this.

IN THE *ENUMA ELISH*	IN GENESIS
There are many gods.	There is one God.
Creation happens as an accident because of a war between the gods.	Creation is good and is the free decision of a loving God.
The world is made from the dead bodies of murdered gods.	God creates the world out of nothing.
Man is created to be a slave to do the menial labor that the gods don't want to do.	Man is created in the image and likeness of God to participate freely in the noble work of ordering the world, which is what God Himself does.
The chief god is annoyed when humans begin to multiply and fill the earth because they disturb his sleep.	God commands the Man and the Woman "Be fruitful and multiply and fill the earth." He wants the earth filled with His "image."

These differences point to an important truth. Although the Israelite people were just one tiny group of people among all the many peoples of the world, they were also the most important people because they were God's chosen people. They were the people to whom God revealed Himself and His plan for the world. Every culture in every place and time has had some kind of an explanation for why the world exists and what the purpose of life is. Sometimes, they even got some part of the answer to these questions correct. But Israel had the most complete and best answers to these questions, free from error, because only they had the true God reveal these truths to them.

Genesis 1–2:3 corrects the false ideas about God and the world at the same time as it reveals the fullness of the truth about them. Not only are God and creation both good, but they are called to be together in the endless Sabbath that God will give after Man, like God, has completed his work. And the work which God gives Man is the work of ordering and directing the creation back to God.

Summary

In this lesson, you have learned the major divisions of the whole Bible. You have also learned how to read and understand biblical references and begun practicing your knowledge by reading Gen 1–2:3, the seven days of creation. This part of the Bible reveals how the good God created a beautiful, good, and orderly universe out of nothing. He created Man, male and female, in His image and likeness and called him to participate in God's work of creation by filling the earth with God's image and by ordering the whole of creation back to God in the rest and worship of the seventh day, which is an image of Heaven. In our next lesson, you will learn more about how man accomplishes the work God gave him to do.

DIRECTIONS: Students are required to memorized the material in *italics* below.

QUESTIONS

1. What is the Bible?

   The Bible is the collection of books—inspired by God and written by holy men throughout history—that reveals God to Man.

2. What are the two parts into which the Bible is divided?

   The Bible is divided into the Old and New Testaments.

3. What is the Old Testament?
The Old Testament reveals God's creation of the world, the fall of mankind, the election of Israel and the promise of a Messiah.

4. Into how many parts is the Old Testament divided?
The Old Testament is divided into three parts: Law, Prophets, and Writings.

5. What is the New Testament?
The New Testament reveals the coming of the Messiah and the establishment of the Catholic Church.

6. Into what two parts is the New Testament divided?
The New Testament is divided into two parts: 1. the life and teaching of Jesus Christ (the Gospels) and 2. the life and teaching of the Apostles.

7. How many books are there in the Bible?
There are 73 books in the Bible: 46 in the Old Testament and 27 in the New Testament.

8. How is each book of the Bible divided?
Each book of the Bible is divided into chapters and verses.

9. In what languages was the Bible first written?
The Old Testament was written (mostly) in Hebrew and the New Testament in Greek.

10. What is the Pentateuch?
Pentateuch means "five books" and is another name for the five books that make up "the Law" in the Old Testament.

11. What is the first book of the Pentateuch, or the Law?
The first book of the Pentateuch is Genesis.

12. Why is the book named "Genesis"?
Because Genesis means "beginning" and it tells the story of the beginning of all that God is doing in creation.

13. What is contained in the book of Genesis?

The book of Genesis reveals the story of God and His people from the creation through the death of Jacob.

14. What does God create on each of the seven days of creation?
    1. Day and Night
    2. water and air
    3. dry land and plants
    4. Sun, moon, stars
    5. water and air animals
    6. land animals and man
    7. The Sabbath rest

15. What does the story of creation teach us about God and the world?

The creation story reveals that God is good, that He made man in His image to know, love, serve Him.

Lesson 2

An Important Phrase

IN OUR LAST LESSON, you learned the major divisions of the whole Bible. You also learned that a long time after the Bible was written, scholars divided the Bible up into chapters and verses so they could refer to individual parts of the Bible more easily. These chapter and verse divisions were not part of the original Scriptures and were not inspired by God. They are simply helpful tools.

But there are some divisions that were in the original Scriptures. When the Bible was first written not many people could read, but of course everyone could listen. Because of this, certain things were built into the story to make it clear to someone who was *listening* to it that one part was divided from another part, or that a particular idea was very important. Chapter and verse divisions are *visible* in your Bible, but for the original audience the most important divisions were *audible*. This is one reason why it is still a good idea to read the Bible out loud when you can, as is done in the Mass or the Liturgy of the Hours, for example.

The first of these audible dividers is the first verse of the reading from Genesis for this lesson: *"These are the generations of the heavens and the earth when they were created"* (Gen 2:4).

This may not seem very important at first, but you will see how this phrase "these are the generations" gets repeated several times and is one of the ways Genesis divides up into parts. It's like the refrain to a song that you sing at church. The refrain is the repeated part that comes between one verse and another. The verses tell the "story" of the song and the refrain unites all of the verses together by repeating an important word, phrase, or idea.

The word translated as "generations" in this refrain in Genesis is the Hebrew word *toledoth* sometimes also translated as "history," "story," "origin," "descendants," or even "children."

The meaning of *toledoth*

In the old days, when all liturgies were in Latin, you would have heard or sung this at the start of the Roman Canon: *Sanctus, Sanctus, Sanctus, Dominus Deus Sabaoth!* Which in English is: "Holy, Holy, Holy, Lord God Almighty!" You can see that the last word *sabaoth* has the same ending as *toledoth* = *oth*. This is because Sabaoth is not a Latin word, but a Hebrew word that was left untranslated in the *Sanctus*. It means "armies" and is used to indicate God's almighty power because He is the Lord of the heavenly armies. The ending in both words is one of the ways that Hebrew indicates that a word is plural (*toledoth* = generations / descendants; *sabaoth* = armies).

This word is a noun, but it comes from the Hebrew verb for becoming the father or the mother of a child. If the subject is not a man or a woman then the verb indicates how something was caused by or "came from" something else, like the way a child comes from his mother and father. It is concerned with the origin or history of the thing.

This "*toledoth*" refrain that closes the account of creation in Genesis 1 also introduces the next part of the story. It tells where the Heavens and the earth came from, but it also introduces the story of what "came from" the creation of heaven and earth, namely, Adam, and later Eve, and later still, their children. As a refrain, it is like a doorway—it closes one part of the story and opens into another. This way, you can both see and "hear" the divisions.

In the following chart, the first column shows the twelve parts of Genesis made by the *toledoth* refrain, the second column shows the chapter and verse numbers for each part, and the third column shows who "came out" from the previous part. So, for example, the one who came out of the Creation of Heaven and earth was Adam; the ones who "came out" of Adam were Adam's descendants, the most important one who "came out" of Adam's descendants was Noah, and so on.

Part #	Chapter/Verse	The one(s) who "came out" of
1	1:1–2:3	The Creation of Heaven and earth = Adam
2	2:4–4:26	Adam = Adam's descendants
3	5:1–6:8	Adam's descendants = Noah
4	6:9–9:29	Noah = Noah's sons
5	10:1–11:9	Noah's sons = Shem
6	11:10–26	Shem = Terah
7	11:27–25:11	Terah = Abram/Abraham who by Hagar was father of *Ishmael*, and by Sarah was father of *Isaac*

8	25:12–18	Ishmael = his twelve sons, who with Ishmael are outside the covenant relationship with God
9	25:19–35:29	Isaac = Jacob and Esau
10	36:1–8	Esau inside of the Promised Land
11	36:9–37:1	Esau outside of the Promised Land (outside the covenant)
12	37:2–50:26	Jacob = his twelve sons, the twelve patriarchs of Israel, who are inside the covenant relationship with God

We will be studying each part carefully in future lessons and you will learn all about each of these important characters in detail. For this lesson, it is enough simply to read the eleven *toledoth* refrains (the first verse of parts 2–12) and perhaps underline them in your Bible so that you will remember their importance when you come to them. Be sure to note that the *toledoth* phrases divide Genesis up into 12 parts. Some of these parts are very long (such as part 7) and some are very short (like part 10), but all twelve of them are ordered toward showing God's choosing and forming of the 12 tribes of Israel, through whom the whole world would be blessed (see Gen 12:3). The number twelve in Scripture often indicates something that has universal or cosmic importance for the ruling or ordering of the community such as the twelve tribes of Israel and the twelve Apostles, and even the twelve months of the year.

You should also remember from our last lesson the importance of the number seven, and note that the seventh part of Genesis is all about Abraham, which makes him *very* important. All the *toledoth* refrains before Abraham show how throughout the history from Adam all the way to Abraham God chose righteous men to be close to Him. After Abraham, there are two characters who have their own *toledoth* refrains but who do not have this special closeness to God. There are two other characters who do have this special relationship with God. Ishmael and Esau do not; Isaac and Jacob (and his 12 sons) do.

We also learned in the last lesson that the purpose of Creation is so that Man might be in a relationship of love and adoration with God. In the next lessons we will be reading a lot about how Man rejected his vocation and chose himself rather than God, and how this led to death and destruction of the Good that God had made in creation. This is why the *toledoth* refrains matter so much—because they reveal how even though there is death and sin in the world, God still works out His purpose through those men who do choose Him, despite the sinfulness of the world around them. Foremost among these in Genesis is Abraham.

Thus, the overall structure of Genesis outlined by the *toledoth* phrases is that parts 1-7 show how we get from Adam to Abraham while parts 8-12 show how we get from Abraham's sons to the 12 sons of Jacob who will become the 12 tribes of Israel.

Knowing the structures of Scripture

St. Augustine, in the fourth century, wrote a book about how to use the classical liberal arts to help Christians understand Scripture. The book was called *De Doctrina Christiana*. He had a good answer to the question of why knowing these structures matters.

St. Augustine said that the very first thing students of the Scriptures should do if they want to understand the Scriptures was to memorize them. He did not necessarily mean that you should memorize each and every part word-for-word, though for some of the most important parts you should do that. What he did mean was that you should memorize the whole basic story or outline of the Holy Scriptures. One of the ways we do this is by learning the structures of the individual books and then fitting these into the larger structure of the Bible as a whole.

The reason this helps so much in understanding the Scriptures is that it allows you to "see" the whole all at once. These structures are like a map of a large forest. If you are just walking through the forest on foot, you will surely see many beautiful things. But, there is also a good chance that you will eventually get lost. Even if you don't get lost, you will certainly miss some of the best things that you should have seen. With a map however, you can go through the forest with certainty, not missing anything important and seeing how the parts fit into a beautiful whole.

Genesis 2: Why are we reading about the creation *again*?

Many people are puzzled when they read Genesis 2 after reading Genesis 1. Genesis 1 completed the story of creation and Genesis 2 seems to be starting all over again, talking about how the earth, plants, animals, and man and woman came to be. Why does it do this? This common question has two very simple answers.

First of all, creation is such a magnificent and wonderful event, such an awesome act of God, that we should really be surprised that there are *only* two short accounts of it here in Genesis. We might expect there to be fifty or a thousand! Because creation is such an immense and beautiful and important work of God, it makes sense that there would be more to say about it than simply what was said in Genesis 1. The authors of practically every book of Scripture, throughout history, found in the creation an inexhaustible source for reflection upon the majesty, power, beauty, and goodness of God. There are many things to be said about creation and almost every book of the Bible has something to say about it!

Second, the two most important things to talk about with regard to the creation are:

1. The One Who made it = God
2. The most important part of what God made = Man.

Genesis 1 focuses more on the first, Genesis 2 on the second. Together they give a more complete understanding of Creation than either does on its own.

A focus on man's actions

In Genesis 1, no one but God does anything, except come into existence at God's command. God is omnipotent and transcendent and completely above and beyond His creation. He alone acts and gives commands. This comes first in the Bible because it is important for us to understand that God is infinitely above us *before* we understand that He is also close to us, closer to us than we are to ourselves, as one of the Saints said. As the book of Proverbs says "the fear of the Lord is the beginning of wisdom." Fear comes to its perfection in love, but fear of God is still the right place for creatures to begin. God comes first and is more important than anything He created, even ourselves. God is the source of everything and is infinitely above it all.

In Genesis 2–4, Man and his actions and decisions become the focus, and the emphasis is more on God's closeness to Man. Man tills the garden and takes care of it, names the animals, writes a love-song for his wife, and gives her a name also. God forms man from the clay of the earth, like a potter, and breathes life right into his nostrils. God doesn't command the garden to come into being; He plants it Himself. Later we will see Him forming Woman from

Man's rib, and taking a walk in the garden in the cool of the evening. This does not mean that in those days people thought God had a body, rather, it is the way that the Bible gets across to its human audience that God is close to us. Man is also at work in creation and God is very close to him!

It's almost like Genesis 1 is God's "diary" of creation and Genesis 2 is Adam's diary of the same events, told from his own perspective. You can "hear" this change in perspective in the words Genesis uses in 2:4.

Looking back at the story of Genesis 1 it says,

"These are the generations of the heavens and the earth..."

Then, looking ahead to the story in Genesis 2 it reverses the order and says,

"In the day that the Lord God made the earth and the heavens..."

The one is written from God's perspective—from heaven looking down on earth; the other is written from the human perspective, from earth looking up to heaven.

This change between the divine and human perspectives is important for understanding all of Scripture because it often shifts from one to the other. Scripture, like Christ, is both fully human and fully divine. Just as Christ was fully human without sin, so Scripture is fully human without error. Many difficulties in Scripture can be solved by remembering these principles.

The story of creation from man's perspective has three basic parts

They are: (1) the creation of Man, (2) the creation of the garden, and (3) the creation of Woman.

Part I (Gen 2:5–7): Two important things added

There are two important things Gen 2 adds to our knowledge of man at his creation.

1. You will have learned in your catechism that Man is a creature composed of body and soul. Gen 2:7 makes this very clear by showing that Man's body is formed by God from the dust of the ground and his soul is breathed into him directly from God.

In Hebrew it is even clearer that man's body comes from the ground because the word for "ground" and the word for "man" sound the same!

Ground/dust = *adamah*

Man = *adam*

This is where we get the name "Adam." In English this would be like calling the first man "earthling" because he was made from "earth." So, remember that when you read the name "Adam" in the Bible, it is the name of a particular man, but that this man, because he is the first, represents all humanity, and his name even means just that—Man, mankind, humanity.

2. The second important thing that Genesis 2 adds to our knowledge of man is this: God gives two things to Man: 1. life and 2. friendship with Himself. Friendship with God is a special gift above and beyond the life that God gives to all. And of the two things, the second is more important. In fact, as we will come to see, it is all-important.

Part II (Gen 2:8-17): The creation of the garden

How does Genesis 2 show all of this? Easy—it shows that God formed the man and brought him to life *outside* of the garden. Later He placed him *inside* of the garden. The garden is the place of intimacy and friendship with God. So, first Man is alive and later he is brought into friendship with God. Later, we will see that when man breaks his friendship with God, he will also lose his place in the garden, and ultimately, even the life he was given outside of the garden. We can even say that Genesis shows us that there are two kinds of life for Man. The first is the body united to the soul (God breathes into his body the breath of life.) The second is Man's soul united to God (God brings the man into the garden).

The garden is a miniature creation. Just as we saw the whole of creation in Genesis 1 from God's view, so here we see man's view. God sees the whole creation; Man sees only a part. But that part—the garden—represents the whole. Just as the whole creation is ordered toward the worship of God, so the garden of Eden is the place where man is called to intimate friendship with God.

The next part of Genesis 2 talks about a river. The garden is in the land of Eden. The river begins in Eden, flows to the garden, and waters the garden. Then it does something remarkable—right at the garden it divides and becomes four rivers. The rivers and the description of the lands they flow through are not a geography lesson or a map so that we can go and look for the garden of Eden (though some people have tried!). The point is that the rivers water the earth so that there can be life. When they part and become four rivers right at the garden, right at the place of friendship with God, this means that friendship with God is the real source of life and blessing for the whole world.

The number 4 in Scripture often signifies something about the whole earth because of the four directions that encompass every place: north, south, east, and west (see, for example, Revelation 7:1; Jeremiah 49:36). The description and naming of the different lands that the rivers flow through makes the same point. The gold and gems, which we will see again when we read about the Ark of the covenant, the Tabernacle, and later the Temple, remind us again that the whole of creation is a Temple for the worship of God. Because the rivers flow from Eden to everywhere else, this also indicates that Eden was the highest place, which again indicates its importance and its closeness to God.

Just as the rivers come from the place of friendship with God and go from there to give life to the whole world, so we will see time and time again in Scripture that those men and women who rouse themselves to be God's friends are the only real source of life and blessing in the world. On the other hand, the cause of all the misery in the world comes from people who reject God's offer of friendship, choosing to make something other than their friendship with God the most important thing in their life.

The tree = the test

God's friendship is a free gift that we could never pay for, but that doesn't mean that it doesn't have to be earned in some way. Besides giving man the work of tilling the garden and keeping it, which makes perfect sense, He also gives him a command that doesn't make much sense: you can eat of all the trees in the garden, but from this one tree DON'T EAT.

It is not a test to see if the Man can control his disordered appetites because he didn't have any disordered appetites. Plus, he had all the food he needed from the other trees. Nor is it that the tree was poisonous, since everything God created was good. Rather, it is simply a test. It is a test of trust, to see if Man will trust and obey God even though he doesn't understand the purpose of the command.

God has already given life and friendship to Man freely and without any reason other than His own love and goodness. Even this test contains two more gifts, one having to do with life and the other with friendship.

1. *Life:* God here gives Man permission to eat from the tree of life and so to possess immortal bodily life. So long as Man continues to eat from this tree, he will never experience the separation of his soul from his body (death).

2. Friendship: This "test" is man's chance to offer friendship back to God freely and without any reason, other than his love and gratitude for God and his trust in God's goodness. This is yet another gift: the gift of a chance to give to God the only thing God can't make or take—freely-given love and trust—which is the foundation of any real friendship.

So, the test is not so that God can find out what the Man will do, since God knows everything, but rather to give Man a chance to do the one thing that will ennoble him and make him perfect more than anything else: make to God a freely-given gift of himself and his love and trust in friendship.

Part III (Gen 2:18–25): The creation of woman

As if Man didn't already have ample proof that God loves him and is good and is concerned for his every good and therefore worthy of all trust—God, after giving the command to not eat from the tree, gives him one final proof of His goodness. This one is the grand finale. He wants to make sure that Man is absolutely convinced that God is good, is worthy of all trust, has Man's best good in mind in all that He does. How does He do this? He does it by giving to Man the best gift in the whole created order—Woman.

As you might have guessed, she is the seventh gift that God gives to Man in Genesis 2.

1. He gives man a body from the dust (a body).
2. He gives man the breath of life (a soul).
3. He brings the man into the garden (friendship with God).
4. He gives man charge of the garden to till it and keep it (stewardship).
5. He gives him permission to eat from the tree of life (immortal life).
6. He gives him all the animals to name and be his helpers (kingship).
7. He gives him Woman, a helper fit for him (marriage).

In this way, Genesis 2 shows that Man had a fullness of reasons for trusting in the goodness of God. The Man can obey the command of God without question, even though he does not understand it, because it comes from an authority he knows is GOOD.

You remember from your last lesson how "it was (very) good" gets repeated seven times in the story of creation. Now, for the first time, God says that something is "not good": *"It is not good for the man be alone"* (Gen 2:18).

Why is it not good for the man to be alone? Because, as long as he is alone, the Man cannot fully understand the love that God has for him. Man and

Woman, through their experience of loving each other, can understand how deeply God loves them and wants what is best for them. And just as their friendship with each other is the best thing in creation, so through that friendship, they are to understand that the best thing absolutely is their friendship with God.

This is what the *Catechism of the Catholic Church* has to say about it:

> God who created man out of love also calls him to love, which is the fundamental and innate vocation of every human being. For man is created in the image and likeness of God who is himself love. Since God created him man and woman, their mutual love becomes an image of the absolute and unfailing love with which God loves man. It is good, very good, in the Creator's eyes. And this love which God blesses is intended to be fruitful and to be realized in the common work of watching over creation: "And God blessed them, and God said to them: 'Be fruitful and multiply, and fill the earth and subdue it.'" *(CCC, 1604)*

So, God says "I will make a helper fit for him." But then instead of making the woman right away, He first makes all of the animals and brings them to the man to see what he will name them.

God does this not because He thought maybe Man would find a helper fit for him from the zebras or giraffes or monkeys, but because He wants the Man to experience what God already knew—it's not good for Man to be alone. The animals are all Man's helpers, but none of them is a helper "fit for him." The word translated as "fit" can mean "opposite" in the sense of "corresponding to." Woman will be his counterpart and his complement. They are like two pieces of a puzzle—not the same, but they "fit" each other perfectly, they complete each other.

So the man sees and names every one of the animals, and, in doing so, sees two important things:

1. that each of the animals (male and female), has its helper fit for it and
2. none of the animals is a helper fit for the Man.

God is above the Man, the animals are below him, but no one is his equal.

So, after God puts the man to sleep and forms the woman from the man's rib, the man exclaims, in the first love song a Man ever made for a Woman, that he has found his equal.

"This one at last is bone of my bone and flesh of my flesh; She shall be called Woman (*ish-ah*), because she was taken out of Man (*ish*)."

In Hebrew Man/ husband is *ish* and Woman/wife is *ish-ah* and the part *-ah* can mean "from," so *ish-ah* is taken here to mean "from man." So, *adam* means man in the sense of human being, but *ish* means man in the sense of male, the opposite of female.

Finally, man has found his counterpart, his helper fit for him. She is another person, but is also another self, since she came from his own flesh and bone. She has the same human nature that he has, and yet she is different from him. Just as she was taken from Man, so it makes sense that a man should leave his father and mother and "cleave to" his wife. She came from his flesh and so the flesh that was two becomes one flesh again when a man and woman marry.

This is one of the most profound things that the Bible has to say about marriage. It is so important that Jesus, when speaking about marriage, points his listeners back to this passage in Genesis (see Matthew 19:6).

The vocation of marriage is not only a thing beautiful and holy in itself, but throughout Scripture, it is the primary symbol for understanding God's love for each person and Christ's love for the whole Church, which is called His bride. St. Paul speaks of the "great mystery" (Ephesians 5:32) of marriage because it symbolizes how even the Son of God, in becoming a man, "left his father and mother" in a way, to cleave to His bride, the Church. Even men and women who give up human marriage to give themselves totally to God, such as religious sisters or priests, still use human marriage as the primary way to understand their vocation. A nun is called a bride of Christ; priests speak of themselves as being married to the Church. An attack on the sanctity of marriage is thus an attack upon God Himself and the Church, which is why the Church, from the very beginning, has always revered and protected marriage.

The last part of this chapter ends by mentioning that the man and his wife were naked and unashamed. This emphasizes two very important things that prepare for what is ahead in Genesis:

1. Things were not always as they are now.
2. How they are now is a falling away from a much more perfect life.

The first man and woman felt no shame at their nakedness because they were totally pure and innocent. It is sin that brings shame, as we will see in the next lesson.

Summary

In this lesson you have learned how the eleven *toledoth* refrains divide the book of Genesis into twelve "verses" that can be grouped into two major parts—from Adam to Abraham, and from his sons to the twelve sons of Jacob who become the twelve tribes of Israel. You have also learned how memorization of these structures helps in understanding the whole of Scripture. The second account of creation in Genesis 2 is told from a more earthly and human perspective than Genesis 1 in order that we may understand first that God is infinitely above us (Genesis 1), and then learn how close He is to us (Genesis 2). God's closeness to us is the main point of this whole section. The three main parts of Genesis 2—the creation of Man, the garden, and Woman, all hinge on the importance of intimacy, love, and friendship with God. The primary experience of this, for human beings, is the intimacy, love, and friendship of marriage, which, in the Bible, becomes the most important symbol for understanding God's love for humanity and the love that we should have for God.

QUESTIONS

1. What is the meaning and purpose of the *toledoth* refrain in Genesis?

    Toledoth means "generations" or "history." It divides one part of the story from another, telling how God accomplishes His purpose in history through the righteous who choose Him.

2. Into how many parts do the *toledoth* refrains divide Genesis?

    The toledoth refrains divide Genesis into 12 parts.

3. What is the significance of the number twelve in Scripture?

    The number twelve in Scripture indicates something that has universal importance for the ordering of the community, such as the twelve tribes of Israel, the twelve Apostles, or the twelve months of the year.

4. Why is the memorization of structures important for understanding Scripture?

    The memorization of structures is important for understanding Scripture because they are like a map that allows the student to go through the Scriptures with certainty, not missing anything important, and seeing how the parts fit into the whole.

5. Are there are two kinds of life for Man?
Genesis 2 teaches that there are two kinds of life for Man. The first is the body united to the soul and the second is Man's soul united to God in love.

6. Why did God test the Man?
God tested Man to give him the chance to make to God a freely-given gift of himself and his love and trust in friendship.

7. Why did God create Woman?
God created Woman to be a helper fit for the Man so that Man and Woman, through their experience of loving each other, can understand how deeply God loves them.

Lesson 3

A Curse ... with a Promise

You will remember how in your first lesson you read from the *Catechism of the Catholic Church,* which said that the first three chapters of Genesis were among the most important in the Bible. We have spent one lesson each on the first two chapters, which contain the heavenly and earthly accounts of creation, and now we will spend one more on chapter 3. It records the story of the sin that became the source of all other sin, suffering, and sadness in the whole world. But it also contains the greatest hope in the promise that the Woman's offspring would crush the head of the serpent and bring the reign of sin and death to an end.

All of Scripture speaks about God

It is a great mystery that the greatest blessing is connected in some way with the greatest evil. We can understand this better if we understand something more about Scripture. In your last lesson you learned how Scripture frequently shifts from a heavenly to an earthly, or, from a divine to a human perspective. For example Genesis 1 is the divine or heavenly account of creation and Genesis 2 is the human or earthly account of creation. But even the human account of things is a view of things inspired by God that reveals God or creatures as they relate to God.

There are two things that are not God: creatures and sin. When Scripture talks about creatures, it may be difficult to see how it is talking about God. When Scripture talks about sin, it can be even harder. But if we learn some basic principles for how Scripture speaks about creatures and sin, it becomes much easier.

Scripture speaks of created things:

1. As they come from God. *"The eyes of all creatures look to you"* (Psalm 145:15). Scripture speaks of everything from the lowliest mud and insects to the highest stars, plants, animals, men, and angels. In fact, the author of the Epistle to the Hebrews even says that if something is not in Scripture, then it must not be in the world, because Scripture talks about everything in the whole world (see Hebrews 7:3)! But Scripture is not talking about these things in order to give us a lesson in natural science. Rather, it is taking what we have already experienced in some way from living in the midst of God's creation and showing us that it all comes from God and how it reveals God's power and goodness. A great example of this is in the Book of Job, chapters 38–39. Every creature reveals God in some way because it came forth from God as an artifact from a master craftsman. If you spend some time thinking about His creations in the right way, you will know more about the master craftsman.

2. As they return to God. *"How can I make a return to the Lord, for all his goodness to me?"* (Psalm 116:12). Just as all creation came forth from God, so it is called to be re-united with God in Heaven. As Jesus said before dying on the cross, "When I am lifted up, I will draw all things to myself" (John 12:32). You have already learned that all of creation is presented in Scripture as a Temple for the worship of God and also how man's primary vocation is that of ordering the creation (and himself as part of that creation) back to God. Prior to being with God forever in Heaven, this worship is the primary way in which all creation makes a return to God and is drawn to Him. One of the finest examples of this is the song of the three young children in the fiery furnace, which is sung not to God, but to the whole of creation and all of its parts, telling them to "Bless the Lord!" (see Daniel 3:57–90).

Scripture speaks of sin and evil:

1. As it comes from creatures. *"Through the envy of the devil, death entered the world"* (Wisdom 2:24). Evil comes from creatures when they turn away from God, their highest good, that is, from creatures who, by misusing their God-given freedom, are trying NOT to do #2 above.

2. As it returns to God. *"You intended evil against me, but God intended it for good, so that many people should be kept alive"* (Gen 50:20). God is so good and powerful that He makes even evil "return to Him" in the sense that He always brings a greater good out of every evil. No evil can escape God's ultimate plans for good.

God brings good out of evil . . .

We learned in our first lesson that God is so good that He brings goodness into being out of nothing. What we are going to see again and again in the Bible is that God is even better than we thought! We thought God was pretty great for bringing good things out of nothing. Now we are going to learn that He is so good that He brings even greater goods out of evil.

From nothingness, God brings . . . very good things.

From worse things (evil), God brings . . . even greater good things.

. . . but evil is not therefore good.

To say that would be just dumb. (See St. Paul's reaction in Romans 3:8.) Rather, it means that God's goodness is so powerful that you cannot defeat it no matter what you do. You can choose to be God's enemy if you want, but you will only hurt yourself. Even if the evil you choose hurts other people in some way, God will make from that evil an even greater good for His own glory and the glory of those who are His friends. We will see a wonderful example of this at the end of Genesis in the story of Joseph and his brothers.

It's as if the Church (God's friends) is a big sailboat going toward God, with the wind and the water (creation) carrying it toward God. Since God controls the wind and water, the ship is inevitably going to get to God, no matter what happens on the ship. People who hate the ship and where it is going can jump off if they want to, but

1. that will not ultimately hurt anyone but themselves,
2. they will still be carried along by the wind and water and have to meet God,
3. It will only make the ship go faster.

Three parts to the Fall of man

After receiving his existence, the creation, lordship over the creation, the offer of friendship with God, and full proof that God is trustworthy, Man also received a test: "Do not eat from the tree of the knowledge of good and evil." Genesis 3 records how Man failed to pass the test and what resulted from that failure.

Part I. Temptation (Genesis 3:1–5)

In Hebrew, the first word in Genesis 3 is *nachash*—the serpent. There is no hint of where the serpent comes from except that *God made him*. Here, where evil enters the world, we are told very clearly that it comes from one of God's creatures and not from a rival god or power. Evil does not exist all on its own, but rather only as a turning away from the good that God made, as a kind of parasite on the good. The serpent is just another creature, a creature that God created as part of the good of the whole creation, a mysterious part of God's plan. God did not create the serpent evil, but he became that way.

We find no further reflection on this enemy of mankind and God until later in Scripture, but we know that the serpent symbolizes and is under the power of the devil. However, here he is presented as just another beast of the field, though the most "clever" or "subtle" of them all. That Hebrew word could even be translated as "sneaky." To make the connection between the serpent's cleverness and his evil character clearer, Genesis uses two words: the Hebrew word for "clever" sounds a lot like the word for "accursed" (Gen 3:14). The serpent starts out as the cleverest (*arum*) of the animals, and ends as the most accursed (*arur*).

As an animal, even as the cleverest of the animals, the serpent is beneath mankind and should therefore be taking orders and advice from Man and Woman, not *giving them!* But he is very clever, after all. He doesn't give any advice at first, but he seems to be innocently asking a question about the command God gave the Man. The serpent twists the command just a little, but it is the first calling into question of God's word in the Bible: *"Did God REALLY say that you should not eat from any of the trees?"*

It is noteworthy that the first thing the Bible tells us about the devil is that his first way of attacking humanity is by trying to get them to doubt and be confused about things that are absolutely clear.

Up to this point Man has given unquestioning obedience to God not because he was naïve, but based on his experience and knowledge of the goodness of God. As our past lessons have shown, God has done nothing but good, a perfection of good, to Man from the moment of creation. Everything that God has done for Man has been perfect and good. The most reasonable thing to do is to trust God and obey Him.

And who is the serpent?

1. He's an animal, lower than Man, pretending he has some great secret knowledge to teach to Man.

2. He hasn't done anything good for Man.
3. He has absolutely nothing to back up his authority, which is to say that he has no authority.

The only way he can undermine God's authority is first by pretending that God's command isn't clear, and then by denying that God is good. He can't give any proof for what he is saying because there isn't any! In the end, the serpent is telling Man to trust *his* authority rather than God's—even though Man has absolutely no reason to do so and every reason not to.

The point: sin is irrational!

Before sin is bad, wrong, or evil, it is *stupid*. It is completely unreasonable and ridiculous. The serpent's whole rhetorical argument can be summed up as follows: "Trust me, not God. You should deny your senses and your reason, which tell you in a thousand different ways that God is good. Instead, you should trust me and be suspicious of God. God cannot be trusted to give you what is good; you need to take what you can get for yourself."

The serpent's response to the Woman is the key to the whole story. He says, "You will not die." This directly contradicts what God had already said. So, either God is right and the serpent is lying or the serpent is right and God is lying. The serpent knows this, so he seeks to explain why God would lie. He says, "God knows that when you eat of it your eyes will be opened and you will be like God, knowing good and evil."

In other words, God lied because He doesn't want you to be like Him. He wants to maintain power over you, to dominate you by deceiving you. He wants to keep you under His thumb, so he is lying. But again, this is ridiculous, because Man already IS like God, created in God's image and likeness (Gen 1:26).

Up to this point Man has seen God providing everything good for him and wanting to live in intimacy with him. The serpent suggests that Man should deny his own senses, saying that God really isn't good and really He wants to keep Man from having what *is* good. God is afraid that Man might become like Him. Moreover, God is selfish and cannot be trusted. If Man wants to get ahead in this world he needs to be selfish and start grabbing power for himself. It's Man against God. Man must seize the power so he can use it for himself!

One of the ways the serpent reveals himself to be under the power of the devil is that he only understands power as *selfishness*. He can't (or doesn't want to) understand a God who uses His almighty power totally unselfishly, sharing it generously with all sorts of other beings and using it in love to serve them.

The *Enuma Elish* showed creation resulting from a selfish power grab, a fight, and then humans created to be slaves to do the work the gods did not want to do. On the contrary, Genesis shows God creating peacefully, and freely making Man king over all creation as a gift to him. What the serpent suggests to the Woman is rather that God is just like the gods of the *Enuma Elish*, like the gods of the nations—that God is trying to make man a slave.

Behind this idea is the idea that God is on the same level as man: God is in danger of man seizing power from Him. This idea denies the difference between Creator and created, which Genesis 1 especially made very clear. The serpent's suggestion is thus closely related to idolatry because it says that the God of the Bible is just like the gods of the nations.

"You will be like God"

There are some very important things to know about this phrase, used here by the Serpent and later by God (Gen 3:22).

First of all, the Serpent is speaking to the Woman when he says this, but when he says "you" it means both the Man and the Woman. In English, "you" can be either singular or plural, but Hebrew, just like Greek and Latin, has different words for "you" when it means one person and when it means more than one person. Whenever the Serpent speaks to the Woman, he uses the Hebrew word that means "both of you "—so he is including the Man in the temptation.

Second, "you will know good and evil" *does not* mean that Man and Woman didn't already know good and evil.

How can we know this? The Woman said to the serpent, "We may eat of the fruit of all the trees but God said 'You shall not eat of the fruit of the tree which is the midst of the garden, neither shall you touch it lest you die'" (Gen 3:2-3).

As the Woman's response to the serpent shows, she and the Man knew what was good—and chose it—and also what was evil—and avoided it. They already knew good and evil in that way. Furthermore, they obviously had consciences, because otherwise they could not have sinned or have been punished for it. So, they already did know good and evil in the sense that they knew the difference between right and wrong.

But the serpent isn't talking about knowing the difference between right and wrong because he doesn't care about right and wrong. For the serpent to "know good and evil" is right in line with everything he has already said. He puts it in terms of power as selfishness: "*You* will control good and evil. *You* will get to decide for yourself what is good and evil instead of receiving it from God."

In other words, Man will get to create his own little universe, deciding for himself what good and evil are in it. The serpent says "you will be like God" in the sense that Man, if he decides for himself what good and evil are, has set himself up like a little god, a rival authority, determining what is good rather than accepting it from God. In fact, when he says "You will be like God," the word translated as "God" (*elohim*) can also be translated as "gods" = "You will be as gods." You will be your own god. You will have all the wisdom and power and choices at your command, rather than following God's commands. But again, whenever the serpent speaks about God, it is always God as the Serpent imagines God—a power-hungry tyrant—not as God really is, a generous and loving father to all of creation.

Part II: The Fall (Genesis 3:6)

In a very short description, Genesis tells us that the Woman, instead of rejecting what the serpent said, decided to go and have a look at that Tree again. She looks at it, desires it, eats it, and then gives some to her husband and he eats it too.

Instead of trusting to the authority of God or her husband, which is how the Woman started out (Gen 3:3), she decides to set God aside and become her own authority *apart from and against the authority of God*. With the intelligence God has given her, she first knows it isn't poisonous (so it's good for food) and she can see that the fruit is beautiful (delight to the eyes). Then however, she not only sets God's authority aside, but she chooses to follow the serpent's authority: *she saw that the tree was desirable for making one wise*. Well who said that? That's right, the serpent said that. She actually has no idea whether the tree's fruit will make her wise or not. But she has decided to trust what the serpent said instead of trusting what God said.

As creatures, our lives and our minds are always, no matter what we think, under some authority. We must answer questions such as:

- Is the authority that we listen to going to be the better thing (our reason, our parents, God) or the worse thing (our passions, bad people, the serpent)?
- Will we trust what is best or what is worst?

The first Man and Woman already had perfect trust in God's goodness. The only way they could stop trusting Him was by a free act of the will to kill that trust in their hearts. This is what makes the first sin so horrible. They had no inclination to sin; they had to force themselves to do it. In the words of the *Catechism of the Catholic Church*:

> Man, tempted by the devil, *let his trust for his creator die in his heart and, abusing his freedom,* disobeyed God's command. This is what man's first sin consisted of. All subsequent sin would be disobedience toward God and lack of trust in his goodness. (CCC, 397)

Then the Woman gives some to her husband and he eats it. Sin often seeks to make itself look normal by getting other people involved in the same mess.

The serpent had told the Woman, "You will not die." Well, she has eaten from the tree and she hasn't died, so didn't he tell her the truth? No, he didn't. As we studied last lesson, Genesis shows that there are two kinds of life for Man—the union of his body with his soul and the union of his soul with God. The life of the body is union with the soul, and the life of the soul is union with God. Therefore death of the body would be separation from the soul, and the death of the soul would be separation from God. As we will see, the most important one, the union of Man's soul with God, is lost immediately. The second, the union of his body with his soul, will eventually also be lost.

It was all over very quickly, but the consequences, even so many thousands of years later, are still with us.

Part III: Punishment (Genesis 3:7–24)

In Scripture the number six is often the number that signifies Man and man's work *apart from the perfection of God*. We see this in Genesis 1 where Man is created on the sixth day (so is the serpent!), which is brought to its total perfection IN God's rest on the seventh day. Because it signifies Man apart from God's perfection and completion, six can also be used to signify imperfection, evil, or opposition to God.

It is noteworthy then, that Genesis 3 shows six consequences/punishments for the sin of Man and Woman. They are presented in three pairs of two each:
1. Shame at themselves
2. Shame before God
3. Woman's pain
4. Man's pain
5. Death of the body (no Tree of Life/immortal life)
6. Death of the soul (no life in the Garden/friendship with God)

We will deal with each in order.

Shame at themselves; shame before God

The immediate result of sin, in terms of what the Man and Woman feel, is shame. The serpent had promised that their eyes would be opened and that they would be like gods, "knowing good and evil." Well, their eyes are opened, but all they know is that they are naked. They thought that they could control a whole universe of good and evil, but as it turns out, now they cannot even control how they feel about themselves. They make a pathetic attempt to recover the security and confidence and peace that they had before they sinned by covering themselves with fig leaves.

Surprise! It doesn't work, just like all of man's attempts to recover what only God can give apart from God.

Their intimacy with God was so close and peaceful and beautiful that it can accurately be described as taking a walk together in the garden in the cool of the evening. But this evening, when the Lord comes for the walk, they are afraid of Him. This is not the good kind of fear, of which we hear in the Book of Proverbs: "Fear of the Lord is the beginning of Wisdom." *That* fear draws one closer to God. The fear described here is the opposite. It is just a desire to be far from God, to hide from Him, to get away from Him because you know you have betrayed Him. They are ashamed to be in God's presence because they have broken their trust with God. They don't come to Him in fear and sorrow, rather they pathetically try to run away from Him in fear and shame.

Surprise! That doesn't work either.

Woman's pain; man's pain

God calls to the Man and asks: "Where are you?" This is not a question about which tree the Man is hiding behind, but rather a question about the

Man's state. The walk with God is the symbol of intimacy and friendship with God and the Man isn't there for the walk.

The fact that God calls *to the Man* is also significant. We have already seen the Man receive instructions from God. It seems perhaps that on these evening walks, he was getting to know God more and more and was teaching what he learned to his wife. That is how she knows what to say in response to the serpent's question. God never told her anything, but he did tell it to her husband who in turn told her. As Man came from God and Woman came from Man, so Man learns from God and Woman learns from Man. Man and Woman were created equal, but they have different roles. So there is a beautiful order: God, Man, Woman, and the rest of the creation (animals, plants, and the earth).

With God, differences between beings, such as Man and Woman, or animals and plants, are a source of fullness, order, and beauty in creation. With the serpent, however, as we have seen, differences between beings are a reason for envy: no one and nothing can be happy unless they can "be as gods." If you ever hear someone trying to make the differences, especially the differences between men and women, a reason for discord and envy—guess: *Where are their ideas coming from?*

So, with the original sin, God's good order gets turned upside down: the woman accepts the forbidden fruit on the authority of the serpent, and the Man accepts it on the authority of the Woman. *Woman listens to an animal, Man listens to Woman, and no one listens to God.*

Then, when God starts asking questions, the whole thing happens again: Man blames God for giving him the Woman and he blames the Woman for giving him the fruit. The Woman blames the serpent for tricking her.

But notice that God maintains the original order. He speaks first to Man, then to Woman, finally to the serpent. Then going back up the order, He speaks again to woman, and finally to man (re-read Gen 3:9–19).

It is noteworthy that God does not ask the serpent any questions, but only curses him. He still has the possibility of a friendship with the Man and the Woman, so He will talk to them, but not with the serpent. After cursing the serpent, the Lord predicts that just as the serpent's "victory" came about through the Woman, so his ultimate downfall will come through the Woman and through her "seed" or offspring—again setting up His original order of things = serpent is beneath woman. The significance of "he shall strike your head and you shall strike his heel" (Gen 3:15) is that the serpent will be able to give the Woman's offspring a wound that will cause pain, but the Woman's offspring will give the serpent a wound that will kill it. This looks forward to the death and resurrection of Jesus who suffered and died (a wound to his heel), but who through His resurrection utterly defeated death (a lethal wound to the serpent's head).

Then God says to the Woman that He will greatly multiply her pain in childbearing. Remember that Woman was created to be a "helpmate" for the Man. Well, what does she do to help? The most important way in which Woman helps Man is in the fulfillment of God's first command to Man in Genesis 1:28—to be fruitful and multiply and fill the earth. This means having and raising children to know love and serve God. Only when Man has his wife can he have children and raise them. That is the primary way in which she is man's "helper."

So Woman's vocation is to be wife to the Man and mother to their children. But now she is going to experience pain and hardship in doing the very thing that she is called to do. Likewise with man, who was given the vocation of tilling the garden and keeping it. He also is going to experience pain and hardship in doing the very thing he is called to do, because even the ground, out of which he was taken, is now cursed (Gen 3:17).

You should also make a note of the following:
- To the Woman God says in Gen 3:16, "I will greatly multiply your *pain*..."
- To the Man He says in Gen 3:17, "Cursed is the ground because of you, in *toil* you shall eat..."

Although translations for the two words in bold above often differ, the Hebrew word is exactly the same in both. Instead of experiencing peace and happiness in their vocations, they are now both going to experience pain. Man is still called to do God's will, but now it is going to be a painful and toilsome task. Life will be toilsome and painful generally, but especially in the area of doing God's will. It isn't going to be easy.

Death of the body; death of the soul

It is while speaking to the Man that God first mentions the death of the body: "*In the sweat of your face shall you eat bread till you return to the ground, for out of it you were taken. You are dust and to dust you shall return.*" After this first mention of death, the Man names his wife Eve, because she will be the mother of all the living. Her name sounds like the word "living" in Hebrew. Though she was supposed to have been the mother of all the living who would live forever, she has now become the Mother of all the living who will die. The first sin affects *everything* down to the end of time.

After this, God clothes them with garments He makes from skins of animals. Why does God do this? Hadn't they already clothed themselves with the fig leaves? What is interesting about this is that in Hebrew the word for "skins" and the word for "light" are *homophones*—they both sound like our English word "or" though they are spelled differently. The point is that before this the Man and the Woman were naked, but clothed with light. That is how, once they have sinned, they suddenly know that they are naked because the light, which is the visible sign of the life of God in them, has gone out. Now that they have sinned they are again clothed with "or" but it is an "or" that is lower than them—the skins of dead animals—instead of an "or" that was something above them—the glory of God that clothed their bodies because of the life of God in their souls (see also Psalm 104:2).

Right after God clothes them with skins, He says something that might sound a little strange: "Behold, the Man has become like one of us, knowing good and evil" (Gen 3:22). Does this mean the serpent was right—that eating the forbidden fruit would make Man and Woman like gods, knowing good and evil? No, but the translation might make you think that. Man has only become like a rival or little god in the sense that he has taken his own authority as more important than God's. In all other respects he has actually become LESS like God, as the skins show.

If you read this section word-by-word in Hebrew it says: *the man has become like/as one from us.* Most translations take this to mean "like one from among us" = "like one of us" and that is one possibility. But the word "from" in Hebrew can also mean "away from" or "apart from" so that God could be saying: "Look! The Man has become as one *apart from us*, knowing good and evil."

In other words, the skins that God just put on Man in place of the light that he wore originally show visibly (*look!*) that Man now thinks differently about good and evil than God does. Therefore, he has separated himself from God, especially from the intimacy of the interior life of God, which as we saw in Genesis 1, is when God refers to Himself as "we" or "us." Man used to be "one of us" but now has become "one apart from us."

The next verses also establish this interpretation. In order to keep him away from the tree of life, which gave Man immortality, God drives him out of the garden and places an angel with a fiery sword at the entry to the garden to guard the way. If man really has become like God, why does God kick him out of the garden and not allow him the tree of life? It is because Man has NOT really become like God but rather has become separated from God. He is in a state of sin where his constant temptation is going to be to think that he can "be as god" in the way that the serpent suggested. Remember that for the serpent, knowing good and evil means deciding for oneself what is good and evil without acknowledging God or anyone else. Expelling him out of the garden to keep him from the Tree of Life is God's way of helping Man to see that life without God (life where Man chooses to be his own god) ultimately means the worst sort of death for Man.

From the perfect order and harmony of God and Creation in Genesis 1 and 2, Man has chosen a state that is disorder and disharmony. There used to be harmony:
1. Between body and soul
2. Between woman and man
3. Between creation and Mankind
4. Between Mankind and God

In each of these pairs, the first (body, woman, creation, mankind) freely submitted to and freely helped and served the second (soul, man, mankind, God) out of obedience, honor, and love. The second, in turn, loved, ennobled and cared for the first. Now, because the highest part of creation rebelled against the highest being absolutely (God), the very same disorder they introduced into that relationship has been introduced into all of the others. The work of the Savior will be to restore all four of these relationships to their perfect state.

God's punishments are for our healing

If we were to remain in the state of rebellion from God, then immortal life would be a curse, not a blessing. Death saves man from the illusion that he can "be as a god" without obedience to God and without God's gift and help. So all of the punishments that God gives to Man in this section are punishments that are meant for Man's healing. When embraced in a spirit of *penance*, all of these punishments—toil and labor in having children and raising them and in working, and even death—are seen as gifts for our salvation, to save us from far worse things.

As Job 5:18 says: "Blessed is the man whom God corrects; do not refuse the punishment of the Almighty. For He wounds but He binds up; He smites, but His hand brings healing." In punishing Man, God is just, but even in His just punishments God is merciful and is calling mankind back to Himself.

Summary

In this lesson, which covered the original sin of Man, you have learned some basic principles for understanding how Scripture speaks about God even when it is speaking about creatures and sin.

Regarding sin, you have learned that a major part of the Scriptures is devoted to showing how God brings good even out of evil. You have learned the three parts of Genesis 3—temptation, sin, and the six consequences. The nature of the temptation was that it was a temptation for man to try to be "like God" but without God, a temptation for Man to set himself up as his own ultimate authority. The sin reveals that Man still trusts in some authority even when he tries to set out on his own, but now, instead of the best authority (God) he has chosen the worst (the serpent). The consequences reveal that God is the true authority and this authority reveals not only His justice, but also His mercy. Sin is separation from God and the real consequence of separation from God is death. In our next lesson we will see that this first sin unleashes a flood of sin and death on the whole world, but that even in this spread of evil, God is still working out His own plan for good through those who choose to be His friends.

QUESTIONS

1. What are the two ways Scripture speaks about created things?
   Scripture speaks about created things as they come from and return to God.

2. What does it mean to say that creatures return to God?
   Creatures return to God by love, service, and worship of Him.

3. What are the two ways Scriptures speaks about sin or evil?
   Scripture speaks about sin or evil as it comes from creatures and returns to God.

4. What does it mean to say that sin or evil returns to God?
   Sin or evil returns to God because God always brings good out of evil.

5. Does this mean that evil is good, or that we should do evil so that God can bring good out of it?
   This does NOT mean that evil is good or that we should do evil so God can bring good out of it.

6. What was the temptation of our first parents?
   The temptation of our first parents was to "be as gods," loving themselves more than God.

7. What is the Fall?
   The Fall was the pride of our first parents such that they chose to love themselves more than God.

8. What were the punishments of the Fall?
   The six punishments of the Fall were:
   1. Shame at themselves,
   2. Shame before God,
   3. Woman's pain,
   4. Man's pain,
   5. Death of the body
   6. Death of the soul.

9. What is meant by "Woman's pain and Man's pain"?
   This means that Man and Woman have great difficulty in doing God's will, which is the only way to happiness.

10. What is meant by "death of the body"?
    Death of the body is the separation of the body from the soul, which is its life.

11. What is meant by "death of the soul"?
    Death of the soul is the separation of the soul from God, who is its life.

12. What is the significance of the number six in Scripture?
    The number six in Scripture signifies Man apart from the perfection of God and therefore six can also signify imperfection or opposition to God.

13. After sin, what disharmonies replaced the harmony that used to exist?
    After sin, there was disharmony in all four relationships that had been harmonious before:
    1. Between body and soul
    2. Between Woman and Man
    3. Between Creation and Mankind
    4. Between Mankind and God.

Lesson 4

"The wickedness of man was great..."

You should recognize the following chart from Lesson 2:

Part	Chapter/Verse	The one(s) who "came out" of
1	1:1–2:3	The Creation of Heaven and earth = Adam
2	2:4–4:26	Adam = Adam's descendants
3	5:1–6:8	Adam's descendants = Noah
4	6:9–9:29	Noah = Noah's sons
5	10:1–11:9	Noah's sons = Shem
6	11:10–26	Shem = Terah
7	11:27–25:11	Terah = Abram/Abraham who by Hagar was father of Ishmael, and by Sarah was father of Isaac.
8	25:12–18	Ishmael = his twelve sons, who with Ishmael are outside the covenant relationship with God.
9	25:19–35:29	Isaac = Jacob and Esau
10	36:1–8	Esau inside of the Promised Land
11	36:9–37:1	Esau outside of the Promised Land (outside the covenant)
12	37:2–50:26	Jacob = his twelve sons, the twelve patriarchs of Israel, who are inside the covenant relationship with God.

So far we have covered part 1 of the chart (lesson 1) and part of part 2 (lessons 2 and 3). In this lesson, we are going to cover the rest of part 2 all the way up through part 6.

In your last lesson you learned how the number 6 is often significant in Scripture of man and his work *apart from the perfection of God* or in opposition to God. In this lesson Genesis shows this again by taking us through the sixth *toledoth*-part of Genesis and presenting six individual examples of the statement: "The Lord saw that the wickedness of man was great in the earth and that every imagination of the thoughts of his heart was only evil continually" (Gen 6:5).

This statement is the main theme of this section of Scripture. The first sin of Adam and Eve leads to a world "full of violence" (Gen 6:11) and Genesis 4–11:26 shows five more specific examples of the truth of this statement, for a total of six:

1. The sin of Man and Woman
2. The sin of Cain
3. The sin of Lamech (the descendant of Cain)
4. The sin of the "sons of the gods"/daughters of men (the Nephilim)
5. The sin of Ham (the son of Noah)
6. The sin of the people of Babel

Since we have already dealt with the first one, we will now deal with each of the last five in order.

Killing God's image: The sin of Cain and Lamech

Genesis 4 tells the history of Adam's first son, Cain, down to Cain's descendant, Lamech. Both Cain and Lamech are murderers, which is part of why Genesis 4 deals with them together. Genesis 4 records the first of many genealogies that we will encounter in the Bible. A genealogy is a list of the people in a family from one generation to the next. You may have a great Aunt or an Uncle who likes doing genealogies or "family trees" for the fun of knowing who your ancestors were and what they did. That is all fine, but in the Bible, the genealogies are not just for the fun of recording history. They have a bigger purpose. Most importantly they are a record that shows how certain people and families were or *were not* participating in God's plan for the world, either because they did, or did not, choose to follow the true God.

If we count the number of fathers listed in Gen 4:17–18 we get six people—Cain, Enoch, Irad, Mehujael, Methusael, and Lamech. Cain begins the list of six fathers and Lamech finishes it; Cain does evil and Lamech does even worse.

Adam and Eve begin to have children as God commanded them in Gen 1:28. Cain, the first one mentioned, is a farmer and Abel, the second, is a shepherd. Both bring a sacrificial offering to God, but God accepts only Abel's offering. Why? As we will learn again and again in Scripture, what God wants is not our possessions, which belong to Him anyway, but rather our trust in Him and our love, which is the one thing in the whole creation that we can truly give back to God. This is the meaning of God's statement to Cain: "If you do well, will you not be accepted?" (Gen 4:7).

This is the first time in the Bible that we hear of sacrificial offerings. In God's original plan for the world, Man would have offered the WHOLE of creation in all of its parts as a living sacrifice to God. After the Fall, Man's highest ability—the ability to worship and be in relationship with God—is wounded and weakened, like all of his other abilities. Nevertheless, those who chose the true God, in the small way that they could, offered some part of creation back to God in the form of animal or plant sacrifices.

God did not accept Cain or his sacrifice because Cain did not "do well." The Hebrew "do well" is the same word as the seven-times-repeated word in Genesis 1 "good." There it was a noun and here it is a verb, but the basic word is the same. God is calling Cain to "do good"—to act as God acted in Genesis 1—making goodness a reality in the world. Although sin is now a reality in the world also, God tells Cain that he can master sin and that he doesn't have to be mastered by it. Thus, the reason God did not accept Cain's sacrifice has nothing to do with *what* he offered, but rather with *how* he offered it.

Cain, instead of changing his will to fit God's will, tries to change God's will to fit his. Cain wants God to love him better than He loves Abel and is willing to do anything to accomplish this—anything except the one thing he really needs to do! He thinks that if he kills his brother this will force God to love him. Instead he makes his relationship with God even worse, killing his brother, then lying to God about it. This is another example of how sin is irrational. Of course this ridiculous plan can't work. Even Abel, though he was killed, is still alive in a way: God says to Cain, *"The voice of your brother's blood cries to me from the ground!"* (Gen 4:10)

Cain is the first murderer, the first to shed innocent blood. Man, made in God's image, was meant to have dominion over the earth, but Cain, in killing his brother, kills the image of God and loses his own dominion over the earth: "Now you are cursed from the ground which opened its mouth to receive your brother's blood from your hand. When you till the ground it will no longer yield to you its strength" (4:12).

Cain knows that his sin of bloodshed against his brother is going to make him a target of similar violence from others and he is worried that "whoever finds me will slay me." God, in His mercy, and in His desire to stop the tide of violence that is rising in the world, puts a special mark on Cain so that everyone will leave him alone, along with the statement: "If anyone slays Cain, vengeance shall be taken on him sevenfold." Violence begets more and more violence. The worst thing about sin is that it leads to more and worse sin.

When Adam and Eve sinned, they had to leave the garden. God drove them out the east end of the garden, but they still lived near it in the land of Eden (Gen 3:24) where they still had some sort of a relationship with God. When Cain sins, he has to go "away from the presence of the Lord" and he settles in the land of Nod "east of Eden" (Gen 4:16). Each sin takes man further away from God.

Cain commits the first sin of violence, and violence multiplies until finally Cain decides to build a city to try to keep himself and his children protected from all of the violence of which he was the cause. Cain, the first city-builder, who builds his city out of fear and distrust of God's promise to protect him, is like the last city-builders in this section that we will read about, the people of Babel, who also build their city out of fear and distrust of God.

So the whole point of Genesis 4 is to show that God's plan for the salvation of humanity had its "first try" with Adam and Eve's first two sons, Cain and Abel. God favors Abel, but Cain kills him, so Abel is no longer part of the plan. God then gives Cain every opportunity to participate in God's plan for the world (Gen 4:6–7), speaking with him and showing him mercy both before and after his sin. Cain, however, retreats from God in fear. Genesis then reports Cain's descendants, to show that God even waits to see if perhaps one of Cain's descendants will again turn to God and be righteous. Yet the sixth generation shows, in the person of Lamech, that if Cain was bad, his descendants have become even worse. That is why, just after the story of Lamech in Gen 4:24, the very next verse goes right back to Adam again—God has seen that Cain's descendants are not going to be righteous, so He is starting over again.

Adam and Eve have another son. When Eve delivers her son she names him Seth and says: *"God has given me another seed, in place of Abel whom Cain slew"* (Gen 4:25).

What is noteworthy about this is that the word "seed" (sometimes translated as "offspring" or "child") points back to the last time it was used in Genesis, which was in Gen 3:15 when God prophesied to the serpent how He would defeat his evil plan: *"I will put enmity between you and the woman, between your seed and her seed."*

Abel lives again (Gen 4:25–Gen 5:31)

We saw earlier how even though Cain killed Abel, it was still as if Abel were alive, because God still heard him. Now, it is even more so. Seth has been born and has taken the place that Abel had. Seth is a new Abel! He is "another seed" of the woman who will participate in God's plan for defeating the plan of the serpent. Seth is a son "in the likeness" and "after the image" (Gen 5:3) of his father Adam, who is in the image of God (Gen 5:1). This is Adam (=Man) as God intended him to be—in His image.

So, now that God's plan is definitely *not* taking place through Cain and his descendants, and it definitely *is* taking place through Seth's descendants, Genesis records Adam's descendants through Seth for most of the rest of chapter 5 of Genesis.

Now if you've really been paying careful attention, you will notice that some of the names on this list are similar or the same as names on the list of Cain's descendants in Gen 4:17–24.

			Genesis 5:1-29						
Adam	Seth	Enosh	Kenan	Mahalalel	Jared	Enoch	Methuselah	Lamech	Noah
			Genesis 4:17-24						
—	—	—	Cain	Enoch	Irad	Mehujael	Methusael	Lamech	—

The most important thing to notice is that after Seth and Enosh, every name on the Seth genealogy has a counterpart that sounds like it, or is even exactly like it, on the Cain genealogy—all except Noah. So, for example, Cain and Kenan, Mehujael and Mahalalel, Methusael and Methuselah, Irad and Jared. Then there are the two Enochs and the two Lamechs.

We may think that reading these genealogies is boring, but this is only because we do not know how to read them properly. It is no accident that many of the names are similar. Rather it is so that the reader will stop and say: "Hey, wait a minute, it sounds like we are starting over again!" They tell the reader that the two lists of people should be compared. The first list of people rejected their part in God's plan, the second accepted their role in God's plan.

For the first audience, these would have been some of the most exciting reading. Why? Because reading these is even better than reading the lineup for the opposing teams at a World Series baseball game (or World Cup game, if you like soccer). It's as if the six men in the Cain genealogy are the representatives of evil matched against the six men in Seth's genealogy. Who is going to win the contest? The good guys or the bad guys? But then in Seth's genealogy there is a seventh—Noah—who tips the balance to the side of good. The six in Cain's genealogy show man apart from God and they just bring more evil as the world gets worse and worse. But the seventh in Seth's genealogy brings about the defeat of evil and a reestablishment of blessing into the world through righteousness, as we will see (Gen 6:9). Cain brought sevenfold violence into the world, his descendant Lamech brought seventy-sevenfold violence into the world, but Seth's Lamech has seven hundred and seventy-seven years, not of death and violence, but of life!

Gen 4:15	Cain	7 times the violence
Gen 4:24	Cain's descendant Lamech	77 times the violence
Gen 5:31	Seth's descendant Lamech	777 years of life

Moreover, the son of the good Lamech (Noah) is going to bring "relief" from some of the suffering and evil the earth has been subjected to. The point of this is to show that God really is starting over again with Seth. It also shows that life and blessing come through friendship with God and failure to have that friendship leads to suffering and death. As the first Lamech only increased violence and the curse given to the earth that began with Adam's and Cain's sin, so the second Lamech, when he gives birth to Noah, prophesies that Noah will bring "relief from our work and from the toil of our hands from the ground which the Lord cursed." We will see later how it is that Noah brings this relief.

The sin of the "sons of God"

Some people, even some biblical scholars, read Genesis and think that the stories don't go together very well. To them it seems like a bunch of stories thrown together into one book somewhat carelessly. And sometimes it really can seem that way to us who are so far from the time and place when they were first written. But we believe that Scripture is the word of God. Because of this we know that it is packed with meaning and is never random or meaningless. If we read the Scriptures with this attitude we will constantly be amazed at the beauty, order, and meaning of the Scriptures. But we will often have to wonder and ponder and work and study before we get to that point. St. Augustine said this about it:

> The Holy Spirit has, with admirable wisdom and care for our welfare, so arranged the Holy Scriptures as by the plainer passages to satisfy your hunger, and by the more obscure to stimulate our appetite.

The story of the Nephilim is a great example of this. It seems very strange at first. Here we are, going through Seth's genealogy to Noah and his sons. Then suddenly that story gets interrupted by the very odd story about the Nephilim. And then right after this short little story, we go back to the story of Noah. What was that all about?

The order in which things are reported in Scripture is often just as important as the things themselves.

The reason the order is so important is that in literature (and often in life) when something happens right after something else, the first thing is often the cause of the second thing. *Post hoc ergo propter hoc* (= "after this, therefore, because of this") is a fallacy in logic, but in literature, it is often used to make the point that the first thing causes or is closely related in some other way to the second thing. This is a very important principle in Scriptural interpretation because it helps us to see how things that are not obviously connected to each other are actually very much connected to each other and can help explain each other. We will soon see an example of this. So get used to asking yourself two questions:

1. "What does this part of the story mean?" but also

2. "Why does Scripture report this part of the story *right here* in relation to the other parts of the story?"

You will often find that the answer to the second question helps a lot in answering the first question!

So, let's start with the second question: why does Genesis report this story right here after the genealogy going from Adam all the way down to Noah's sons?

Well, take a few minutes to read Genesis 5. Did you notice anything unusual as you were reading the genealogy there? Perhaps you noticed that these people lived for a really long time—Adam lived 930 years; Methuselah lived 969 years. Even Enoch, who was taken up to God before his life was over, was on earth for 365 years! Why did they live for so long and why does Genesis take time to tell us all of this? Why should we care how long they lived?

To answer these questions, first note that these long life-spans are reported right after the last verse of chapter 4, which says: "At that time men began to call upon the name of the Lord" (Gen 4:26). And this comes right after the report that Seth was born to Adam and Eve and that he also began to have children who were on the "good guys" list.

So, with Seth, God is starting over and a part of mankind is starting over. The branch of mankind that comes from Seth are those who begin to "call upon the name of the Lord" that is, to turn toward the true God in prayer, something that no one else was doing. And this turning to the true God is what gives them their long lifespans.

Just as we learned in Lesson 2, a right relationship with God gives life. In a fallen world it isn't immortal life, but still long enough to signify a partial defeat of death and the serpent who brought death into the world.

In other words, Genesis 5 is basically saying: "These are the good guys and their closeness to God is the source of their long life." And their long life on earth signifies the eternal life that comes from friendship with God.

With this in mind, we realize as we read the story of the Nephilim in Genesis 6 that it is not really an interruption at all. Seth and his descendants just want a right relationship with God. They don't even care about long life. But as a benefit from their friendship with God, they also find long life. In the story of the Nephilim we see what happens when people want long life, but don't care about God. They end up getting neither. So the two stories really do belong together—together they show what flows from a right relationship with God, and also what comes from a wrong relationship with God.

In Lesson 1 we studied the *Enuma Elish* and how Genesis corrects the false views about God and creation in it. Genesis does this even though it never quotes from the *Enuma Elish*. With the story of the Nephilim, Genesis goes one step further, and actually refers to a pagan myth, and then, just as in Genesis 1, shows how the pagan myth is completely wrong.

Genesis lets the myth speak for itself and then corrects it.

Here is what the myth says: "When men began to multiply on earth and daughters were born to them, the sons of the gods saw how beautiful the daughters of man were, and so they took for their wives as many of them as they chose" (Gen 6:1-2). This is what the people who did not follow the true God believed, or at least what they wanted to believe. They thought they could be "married" to one of "the sons of the gods" even though this was really impossible and even though God had made marriage for man and woman only. Here is what Genesis says in response: "Then the LORD said: 'My spirit shall not remain in man forever, since he is but flesh. His days shall comprise one hundred and twenty years'" (Gen 6:3).

In other words, the pagan myth was telling people (especially the women, perhaps) that if they practiced idolatry they could get one of the "sons of the gods"[1] to "marry" them and give them strong, powerful, and long-lived children, like the descendents of Seth who had long lives. The reason they listened to this lie was because they wanted it to be true. They wanted to have immortal life, but they did not want the relationship with God which is the only real way to eternal life. So instead they invited demons to "marry" them, thinking that maybe the "sons of the gods" could give them what God

---

[1] Most translations say either "sons of God" or "sons of Heaven." A more literal translation of the Hebrew is "sons of the gods." In either case, the myth is presenting these beings as super-human/angelic in some way. Angels are often called "sons of God" in Scripture, and "Nephilim" just means "fallen ones." So they are fallen angels—in other words, demons, or, at least, men under demonic influence.

would not. God responds by doing the opposite, limiting their lifespans to no more than 120 years. This is a merciful act, limiting the evil they can do, and showing them the truth rather than letting them continue in their ignorance or rejection of the truth. He shows them that the demons have no power apart from what God allows them to have. God is the Lord of life and death.

Then Genesis lets the myth speak for itself again: "At that time the *Nephilim* ['the fallen ones'] appeared on earth [as well as later], after the sons of the gods came into the daughters of man, who bore them sons. They were the mighty men of old, the men of renown" (Gen 6:4). And then Genesis responds to the myth: "Then the LORD saw that the wickedness of man was great in the earth, and that every imagination of the thoughts of his heart was only evil continually" (Gen 6:5). In other words, Genesis is saying that the only thing mighty about these "mighty men" was that they were mighty evildoers. The people who believed the pagan myth were so deluded that even though they didn't get their hoped-for long lifespans, they still believed that because they had "married" one of the "sons of the gods," their children were superheroes. But in fact, since their parents had given their lives to demons, Genesis shows that they were just super-evil.

In Gen 1:28 God gave Man and Woman to each other in marriage with the command to "be fruitful and multiply and fill the earth." The people who believe this myth tried to get around this command and create their own way of having children who will have long life by giving themselves to demons. They don't care about friendship with the true God; they want to control life rather than receive it as a gift from God. It is a quality of Evil that it cannot create its own good, no matter how hard it tries. The most it can do is to try to steal and twist good things to its own purposes for a while.

The flood

So bad had the great majority of humanity become by this point that it "grieved the Lord to his heart" (Gen 6:5). Because Man has failed, and has polluted to whole earth with violence and blood, God decides to wash everything clean. Why? Why not just destroy Man and leave the animals alone? Why not keep the panda bears and the blue whales so they can exist by themselves on earth without Man? Because they were not the purpose of the whole creation; Man was. They were ordered toward Man who was supposed to order himself and them back to God. Without Man, the rest of the creation doesn't have a purpose. Because Man has failed the whole thing needs to be restarted.

With the flood, there will first be an "uncreation" (= death) and then there will be a re-creation (= new life). The waters, which God had "pushed aside" to make a space for mankind, are now allowed to flow back over the whole creation, just as they were before God created. Thus, the waters, the symbol of chaos and death, are permitted to return back over the ordered world God had made. The flood is the unmaking of creation.

However, it is not a total uncreation: within this uncreation, God chooses and saves one man and his family (Noah) from the chaos-death-waters. This saving action of God will be repeated again with His people at the Red Sea in Exodus. This is an important biblical pattern that will be repeated in many ways, all of which are foretastes of Christ's death and resurrection, and our own participation in His suffering and death which leads to the everlasting new life of Heaven.

So God restarts creation by choosing the one righteous man, Noah, and his family. As we have mentioned before and as we will see again it isn't money or power or riches or great technology that brings life and blessing to the world. Rather, righteous men are the real source of life and blessing on the earth because they are friends with God and God is the real source of all life and blessedness.

Noah builds the ark and gathers together the animals as God commands. No doubt Noah's neighbors thought he was crazy, but he followed God's command nonetheless. It is better to have God's approval than your neighbor's.

At the beginning of Genesis, the whole earth was covered with water, but God made a space in it for His first couple to live. Here again, the earth is covered with water as it rains for forty days and nights, but God makes a space in it for this righteous man and his family to live.

The number forty in Scripture is often used in connection with a time of preparation for a new stage in Man's relationship with God or a time of trial (see, for example, Numbers 13:25, 33–34; 1 Kings 19:8; Luke 4:1–2, and many others). We see from this, therefore, that these forty days and nights are both a time of trial and also a preparation for a new stage in Man's relationship with God. During all this time of darkness, with the entire earth buried in the waters, Noah had to trust that God would save him and his family. Because Noah trusted, a new stage in Man's relationship with God begins.

After the flood, God sends a wind, as He did at creation, and it separates the waters, as at creation. The waters above are separated from the waters below. It is a re-creation of the world.

When they finally come out of the ark, the first thing Noah does is to sacrifice some of the most precious animals he had with him in the Ark (8:20). This shows Noah's complete reliance on God. He knows that God is the source of all life. This act of complete faith and trust is very pleasing to God. Through it, Noah earns for mankind the promise that God will *never do this again*, despite the note that the man's heart still has an enormous tendency toward sinfulness—even after the flood (Gen 8:21). Until the end of the world nature will continue in its daily, seasonal, and yearly cycles: "Seed-time and harvest, cold and heat, summer and winter, day and night, shall not cease" (Gen 8:22).

By his willingness to sacrifice these animals, Noah also earns the right to eat them, something that was not allowed prior to this. Remember from Lesson 1 that God created the world with no death in it. Death entered the world with the original sin, but even after sin animals were not eaten, at least by the righteous, like Abel, but only used for sacrifice and perhaps for their wool and milk. When God allows Noah to eat animals this fulfills the prophecy of his father. Noah brings relief from the toil of growing all food from the ground, which the Lord cursed because of Adam's sin. The ground more easily bears thorns and thistles than food for Man. It is much easier for Man to get the food he needs by raising and eating animals than by trying to get all of his food through plants.[2] So man still has to sweat for his food, but now he sweats a little less. On the other hand, eating animals also necessitates killing them first. Through this death the people are reminded that sin causes death in the world. They are also forbidden to eat the blood of the animals, which represents their life, because all life belongs to God.

Finally, God says something very important to Noah and his sons in Gen 9:8–17:

> See, I am now establishing my covenant with you and your descendants after you and with every living creature that was with you: all the birds, and the various tame and wild animals that were with you and came out of the ark. I will establish my covenant with you, that never again shall all bodily creatures be destroyed by the waters of a flood; there shall not be another flood to devastate the earth...
>
> This is the sign that I am giving for all ages to come, of the COVENANT between me and you and every living creature with you:
>
> I set my bow in the clouds to serve as a sign of the covenant between me and the earth. When I bring clouds over the earth, and the bow appears in the clouds, I will recall the covenant I have made between me and you and all living beings, so that the waters shall never again become a flood to destroy all mortal beings. As the bow appears in the clouds, I will see it and recall the everlasting covenant that I have established between God and all living beings—all mortal creatures that are on earth.

The *covenant between God and Man* is one of the most important ideas in all of Scripture.

This is the first time Scripture uses the word "covenant," but we have already seen the basic idea behind it in Genesis 1, where God creates the world in order to have an intimate and perfect bond between Himself and Man. God and Man united in love is the purpose of all of creation. The seventh day shows that God "sevens Himself" to man, that is, gives a complete promise of Himself to man. A covenant is a solemn bond between two people

---

[2] This, by the way, is the origin of the ancient practice of not eating meat during the forty days of Lent. Lent is a time in which we focus on repentance for our sinfulness. We give up meat as a reminder that it is only allowed to us as a concession to sinful humanity's needs.

or groups that makes them one family, so that they are wholly promised and devoted to each other, like in a marriage. The most important covenants in the Bible are between God and the people He chooses, and who choose Him. Just as married people give a visible sign of the covenant they make with each other (their wedding rings), so the visible sign of God's covenant with Noah and his sons is the rainbow.

The sin of Noah's son Ham

As we mentioned earlier, the flood washed away the effects of the violence of the world up to that point, but sin is still very much in the world. The flood has not stopped the evil tendencies of the human heart. Noah plants the first vineyard and makes wine. Not knowing its power, he drinks it and becomes drunk, laying naked in his tent. His son Ham (father of Canaan) "sees the nakedness" of his father. We saw at the end of Lesson 2 (Gen 2:25) that the man and woman were naked and unashamed. As God planned it, nakedness is only between a man and a woman in the innocence, purity, and reverence for each other (Gen 2:23) found in God's plan for the marriage covenant. Ham breaks this reverence for marriage and thinks of nakedness as something to ridicule. As Shem and Japheth were reverent in covering their father, so we can deduce that Ham was irreverent and ridiculed his father, making fun of him and abusing him.

This is what earns Ham the curse Noah later pronounces on him. The curse is on Ham, but Noah calls him "Canaan" because he is the ancestor of the Canaanites, who were known for their terrible immorality. In other words, Genesis is saying that the immorality of the descendants comes from the immorality of their forefather Ham.

Shem and Japheth, on the other hand, receive a blessing from Noah for their reverence and respect toward their father.

In Chapter 10 of Genesis we get another set of genealogies. This is often called "the table of nations" because it tells which nations came from each of Noah's three sons, through whom the whole earth was repopulated. Ham's genealogy, starting in Gen 10:6, is basically a list of all of the peoples who would later be Israel's enemies. Especially important are Egypt, Canaan, Babel (Babylon), Assyria, Nineveh, and the Philistines.

If you go through these genealogies carefully, you will see that there are 14 nations in Japheth's genealogy, 31 in Ham's, and 25 in Shem's. This makes for a grand total of 70 nations, which makes 70 a number for representing all the nations of the earth (see for example, Exodus 1:5).

The sixth and final sin

Now that Genesis 10 has set out the 70 nations and where they came from, ending with Shem's descendants, Genesis 11 tells us: "And the whole earth was of one language, and of one speech" (Gen 11:1). Before there were many nations with many languages, there was one human family who all came from the one family of Noah and his three sons. They are so unified that they have one language and even one dialect. They all speak one language in exactly the same way. So far so good.

But here is what they say to each other about how they want to use their God-given unity: "Come, let us build ourselves a city and a tower with its top in the sky, and so make a name for ourselves; otherwise we shall be scattered all over the earth" (Gen 11:3–4).

This doesn't sound so bad, but there is a lot going on in this brief statement. Just before this, Gen 10:32 reminded us of the flood. One of the reasons these people want to build a city with a tall tower is that they are afraid of another flood, unlike the descendants of Shem who do not inhabit the hill country (see Gen 10:30). They don't trust God's covenant with Noah, which has passed on to his son Shem. Secondly, they want to "make a name" for themselves. In Hebrew, the word "name" is *shem*. So the people here are saying "Let's make a *shem* for ourselves because we don't want to be scattered over the whole earth." But wait a minute, Shem is also a person in the story—the eldest son of Noah, whose descendants we just finished talking about! So, Shem has a double meaning in the story. It means "name" but it is also the name of a man in the story. His name is "Name."

The Old Testament Hebrew is FULL of these double-meanings with words, so much so that we can only cover some of the most important ones in these lessons, otherwise, we would never get done!

The point is that the people do not want to follow the covenant and teaching of the righteous man Shem, but rather, they want to make a *shem* for themselves—they want to make their own rules rather than follow the rule that comes to them from God through Shem. Why? Because the man Shem is following God's original command in Gen 1:28 to "fill the earth." Either they don't trust God or His covenant or His servant Shem who reveals it to them, or they don't care about any of this. So they want to make a *shem* of their own, building a city with a tower as a protection against another flood. That way they don't have to trust God or God's Shem and "be scattered over the whole earth"/"fill the earth."

"Shem" is the key then to understanding the long lifespans we spoke of earlier and the ones we see here again right after the tower of Babel story. There are only two lists of people in the Bible that mention these long life spans—the first leads from Seth to Shem (Gen 5:32), and comes right after the statement that "at that time men began to call upon the name (= *shem*) of the Lord" (Gen 4:26) and the second leads from Shem to Abram (Gen 11:10–26). Moreover, Shem is also the key to the Babel story, since the genealogies of the man whose name is "Name" surround on both sides the story of the people who wanted to make a "Name" for themselves. They lose their name, their unity, and become many names and nations. The people who call upon the *shem* of the Lord have life in abundance. The people who try to make a *shem* for themselves end up being forced to do what they would have done willingly had they accepted God's Shem (Gen 11:9).

Why did Moses choose these six sins?

The earth was "full of violence" and the thoughts of man's heart were "only evil continually," so obviously, there were plenty to choose from. Why did he choose to show us *these*? The answer is that these sins have the same order and the same content as God's first command in Genesis. They show that mankind is undoing and breaking God's first universal commandment piece-by-piece. This command, as Genesis states it, has an introduction and two parts, for a total of three parts: the first part is broken by the first three sins, the second by the next two, and the last part by the last sin, as in the following chart:

Parts	God's first command	The six sins of Mankind
PART 1	1. *So God created man in his own image,* IN THE IMAGE OF GOD *he created him,*	(1) Man and Woman (2) Cain (3) Lamech All of these sin against *the image of God*. Man and Woman spiritually deface the image of God in themselves by desiring to "be as gods" and Cain and Lamech physically destroy the image of God by murder.
PART 2	2. MALE AND FEMALE *he created them. And God blessed them and said to them, "*BE FRUITFUL AND MULTIPLY,	(4) The Nephilim (5) Ham Both of these *deface marriage* as God intended it—the "one flesh" union between man and woman for the purpose of bearing children for God and being a model of God's love for mankind.
PART 3	3. *and fill the earth...*"	(6) The people of Babel These people *refuse to fill the earth.*

If we add to these six sins of man the sin of the serpent we get seven sins—a "perfectly" sinful world. The six sins of man are brought to a "perfect evil" by the sin of the serpent. This is the opposite of Genesis 1 where the six days of creation, and the creation of man on the sixth day, are brought to their perfection of "good" (7x) by God on the seventh day. The seven sins have been attempting to undo the work of the seven days. But God is a God of Justice. These seven sins are matched by seven particular parts of the story where God Himself personally enters the story to punish and limit the effects of sin. These are:

1. The Curse on the Serpent (Gen 3:14)
2. The Punishment of the Woman (Gen 3:16)
3. The Punishment of the Man (Gen 3:17)
4. The Banishment of Cain (Gen 4:11)
5. The Reduction of Man's lifespan (Gen 6:3)
6. The Flood (6:13)
7. The Dispersion of the Nations (Gen 11:8)

Seven days, seven sins, seven punishments for sin. Mankind is dispersed to the four winds and is on a slippery slope to evil and self-destruction. But all of this is in preparation for what God is going to do next to resolve this problem. Beyond punishing sin, God is going to reestablish His original blessing of the whole world—through the man whose name shows up at the very end of the genealogy of Shem in Gen 11:26—a man whose name (for the time being) is Abram.

Summary

Genesis 4–11:26 shows clearly that something "broke" in human nature after the sin of our first parents. The downward tendency of the human heart leads to a world full of violence, such that even the flood does not completely wash it away. You have learned what the six specific sins Genesis focuses on in this section are, why there are six, and why these six are used to illustrate mankind's overall rejection of God, which is brought to a kind of "evil perfection" (7) by that of the serpent. You have also learned the importance of the order in which these six are presented and the order of things in Scripture generally. In the midst of this sin and violence, God continues to call righteous men to be His friends and to work out His plans for humanity's good through them. We saw this especially in the use Genesis makes of the genealogies and the covenants. The "perfect sin" of this section is remedied with God's perfect JUSTICE in the seven punishments for sin, culminating in the dispersal of the nations after Babel. But God is not only a God of justice. As we will see next lesson, He is so good that even His perfect justice itself can be perfected: He is now ready to show mankind His MERCY through the person of Abram, through whom all the nations of the world (who were dispersed at Babel), will find a blessing.

QUESTIONS

1. What is the significance of the number six in Scripture?
   Six signifies man and his work apart from or in opposition to the work of God.

2. Why is the order of things in Scripture important?
   The order of things in Scripture shows how one part is related to another part, even though this may not be obvious at first.

3. Does Scripture use parts of myths that come from other cultures?
   Scripture does use parts of myths from other cultures to perfect what is imperfect and to correct what is false in them.

4. What is the significance of the number forty in Scripture?
   Forty signifies a time of preparation or trial before a new stage in Man's relationship with God.

5. What is a covenant in Scripture?
   A covenant is like a marriage: a solemn bond between two people or groups, ratified by a visible sign, that makes them one new family.

6. What is a genealogy in Scripture?
   In Scripture, a genealogy lists people by generations showing God's plan for the world being carried out (or not) through those people.

Lesson 5

God Has a Big Problem

It is so big that it can rightly be called the cosmic crisis. "Cosmic" comes from a Greek word *kosmos*, which means "the world" or what we would call "the universe." God's problem is as big as the whole universe. God created a perfectly beautiful universe and gave the greatest of His earthly creatures control over that world and even offered them His own friendship. But God's friend (Man) betrayed Him, attempting to decide for himself what was good and evil. In doing so, Man showed that actually he was practically powerless against evil and almost unable to choose good anymore. He unleashed a plague of sin, violence, death, and evil on the whole world, a plague that he could not stop.

Despite all of the limits God puts on this tendency toward evil, Mankind, God's own image, is getting further and further from God. Mankind, called to be God's closest friend, and to order the world back to Him, has instead become His enemy. As a consequence, he is ruining himself and the world. God's own image, which He made, hates God and wants nothing to do with Him or His ways. If this is going to stop, *God* will have to do something because fallen Man has only made things worse.

On the other hand, God has promised that He would not destroy the earth again as He did with the flood (Gen 9:11). So He can't just scrap the project and start over. He has also promised that somehow, some way, He will bring about an even greater good from this miserable state of affairs (Gen 3:15).

So, yes, it's a big problem. How is He going to do all of this?

One person—with God—makes all the difference

From the genealogies we studied in the last lesson, we saw the amazing difference one man who chooses to follow the true God can make. The best example of this in the last reading was Noah. Because of one righteous man, the whole human (and animal!) family could begin creation anew. One man who listened to the voice of God and lived according to it, who was tough enough to ignore the taunts of his neighbors, or the hard labor involved in this process, saved the human family from complete annihilation. Not only that, but he became the father of a son like himself (Shem) who started a new branch of the family tree that went in a direction different from the rest of the human family who were not close to God. Perhaps someone reading this today will be that person in their family tree.

Let's take a look at this biblical family tree so far.

Genealogy of Abraham					
1. Adam	5. Mahalalel	9. Lamech	13. Shelah	17. Serug	
2. Seth	6. Jared	10. Noah	14. Eber	18. Nahor	
3. Enosh	7. Enoch	11. Shem	15. Peleg	19. Terah	
4. Kenan	8. Methuselah	12. Arpachshad	16. Reu	20. Abram	

From this list you can see that there are 10 generations from Adam to Noah, and another 10 from Shem to Abram, for a total of 20. The number 10 in Scripture often indicates the completion of a divine ordering of things or a divine plan or action. The most famous examples from the Pentateuch are in the book of Exodus—the 10 plagues God sends upon Egypt and the 10 commandments He gives to His People. But the basic idea is present here in Genesis as well. Adam to Noah (Creation to re-creation, the completion of God's justice) completes part one of God's plan and Shem to Abram brings to completion the second part of God's plan (the preparation for God's mercy).

The number 20 on the other hand frequently signifies expectancy. When someone has been waiting and hoping intensely for something, Scripture often shows them waiting for a period of 20—twenty years or twenty generations. See, for example, Gen 25:20, 26 (Isaac's twenty-year prayer for his barren wife) and Gen 31:38, 41 (Jacob's twenty years of labor for his wives and possessions).

With this is mind, we can see that these 20 generations have all been expecting and preparing, hoping and waiting for Abram, and that Abram is going to be, in some very powerful and special way, the man through whom God will answer the cosmic crisis. Thus, if we are reading this book the way it was read originally, we would understand now that everything up to this point was just a preparation for something great and wonderful that was coming. And that something is some*one*. And that someone is *Abram!*

Part Seven: Abraham is the divine perfection of God's plan

Part	Scripture	The one(s) who "came out" of:
1	1:1–2:3	The Creation of Heaven and Earth = Adam
2	2:4–4:26	Adam = Adam's Descendants
3	5:1–6:8	Adam's descendants = Noah
4	6:9–9:29	Noah = Noah's Sons
5	10:1–11:9	Noah's Sons = Shem
6	11:10–26	Shem = Terah
7	11:27–25:11	Terah = Abram/Abraham who by Hagar was father of Ishmael, and by Sarah was father of Isaac.
8	25:12–18	Ishmael = his twelve sons, who with Ishmael are outside the covenant relationship with God.
9	25:19–35:29	Isaac = Jacob and Esau
10	36:1–8	Esau inside of the Promised Land
11	36:9–37:1	Esau outside of the Promised Land (outside the covenant)
12	37:2–50:26	Jacob = his twelve sons, the twelve patriarchs of Israel, who are inside the covenant relationship with God.

All of this would have been enough. But then Genesis goes even further in raising our expectations about the great thing God is going to do in the person of Abram by making the *seventh* part of the book all about Abram. As you know very well by this time, seven is the biblical number of spiritual perfection.

Numerology is the study of the meaning and significance of numbers. You have already been doing a lot of biblical numerology. You have learned the biblical significance for the numbers 4, 6, 7, 10, 12, 20, 40, and 70. So the numerology of combining 10, 20, and 7 in Abram means something like this: he is the divine perfection (7) of the long-expected (20) divine plan (10).

In the first *toledoth* part we saw God at work, creating the world for man in six days. That creation was then called into the perfection of God's rest on the seventh day. Then there were a lot of sins—seven of them, as we learned last lesson. This brought us to the end of the sixth part of Genesis. In these six parts we saw God respond in justice to each of the seven sins.

If we read Genesis rightly then, we can see how it is a battle between good and evil, between God, who wants to fill the world with His own life and blessing, and His creatures who, in rejecting God, bring death and the curse into the world.

Seven Days	Seven Sins	Seven Punishments for Sins
God's perfect good	Creatures' "perfect" evil	God's perfect justice toward evil

This series of "sevens" is continued in the life of Abraham, but it is taken one step further. Genesis records seven times that God speaks to Abraham promising him that through him, blessing will be restored in place of the curse that sin brought to the world. *But then there is an eighth.* Seven is the number of completion and perfection and seven plus one more (eight) in Scripture, often indicates a superabundance, an overflowing, a new life that goes beyond all expectations. So, for example, when creation was "restarted" with the flood, there were eight people on the ark (see also 2 Peter 2:5). We will see how God's first *everlasting* covenant with Abram is given with the sign of circumcision, which happens on the eighth day after birth (Gen 17:12) and marks a new life. In the New Testament, both Jesus's Transfiguration and His Resurrection are referred to the eighth day (see Luke 9:28; 24:1). This is God's superabundant mercy, bringing even His perfect justice to a superabundant perfection beyond all expectation. The musical octave, based on mathematics and physics, fits into this pattern by indicating that the eighth note is both the end of one octave and the beginning of a new one.

In this lesson and the next one we will follow these eight promises of God to Abraham like a line of stars that run through the whole story and give it unity, order, meaning, and beauty. This lesson will cover the first five times that God speaks to Abraham, in Genesis 12–17, and the next lesson will cover the last three (Gen 18–22).

From the many nations that came to be from the dispersion of the nations from the Tower of Babel God now chooses one man, Abram, through whom He will restore the original blessings of creation.

What were the original blessings of creation? Well, there were many, but they basically come down to three.
1. Our first parents enjoyed a sacred place,
2. where they were commanded to have (good) descendants;
3. where they and their descendants were to enjoy the greatest blessing = intimacy with God.

Now if these were the three original blessings, then these three were what was lost when Man sinned. And if Abram is God's long-expected restoration of what was lost in the Fall, then these three blessings should be what are restored through Abram. Let's see if they match up.

God speaks to Abraham

The narratives about Abraham, Isaac, and Jacob, which cover the rest of Genesis, are often referred to as the Patriarchal narratives. Patriarch just means "first father" and these men were the first fathers of God's chosen people. So our job for the rest of this lesson and the next is to see how the original blessings of creation match up with the patriarchal blessings given first to Abram.

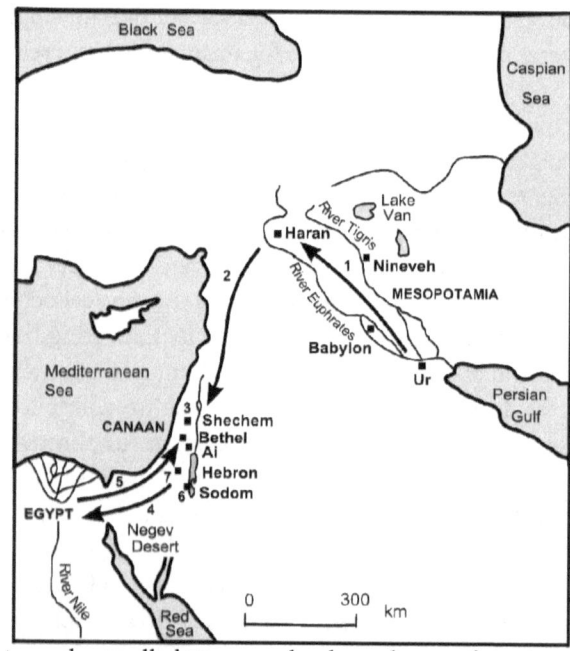

In Gen 11:27–32 we learn how Abram's father, Terah, and Abram's nephew Lot, travel with him and his wife Sarai from "Ur of the Chaldeans" to Canaan, which later becomes the Holy Land, or the Land of Israel. Ur is in the south eastern part of modern-day Iraq, about 600 miles due east of the city of Jerusalem. Terah and his family can't go straight west to Canaan because between Ur and Canaan is a big desert. So they travel northwest to a place called Haran, a land northeast of Canaan. This route keeps them and their flocks (which need to drink) in Mesopotamia, a name which means "land between the rivers" because it is between two of the rivers we heard about in Lesson 2—the Tigris and the Euphrates. Terah decides to stop in Haran and there he dies.

If you look back at Gen 11:27 you will see that Terah had three sons—Abram, Nahor, and Haran. He had originally planned to go to Canaan, but then he decided to stay instead in . . . Haran. Terah's son and the place where he stops have the same name. Why? Probably because Terah had relatives in that place, who had named the place "Haran" after some more ancient relative. This may be why he had named his son with the same name AND why he decided to stop there instead of continuing to Canaan.

This also explains why God comes into the story at this point to speak to Abram. Terah had been taking Abram to the Land God wanted him to be in (Canaan), but then decided to stop short. So now God steps in to make sure that Abram goes where He wants him to go. When God speaks, it does sound as if he is still living among relatives, even in Haran. God says:

> "Go forth out of thy country, and from thy kindred, and out of thy father's house, and come into *the land* which I shall show thee. And I will make of thee a *great nation*, and I will *bless* thee, and magnify thy name, and thou shalt *be blessed*. I will *bless* them that *bless* thee, and curse them that curse thee, and IN THEE shall all the kindred of the earth *be blessed*." (Gen 12:1–3)

Now if we read what God says here (especially the emphasized words) while remembering the three original blessings, we find that they match up perfectly with the patriarchal blessings. God gave Adam and Eve a sacred place, descendants, and the Blessing of intimacy with Himself. Now He is going to restore those blessings through Abram, to whom He promises Land, descendants, and Blessing.

It is not perfectly clear what God means by "blessing" at this point, but by the end of this lesson, it will be very clear that it means for Abram what it meant for Adam and Eve—intimacy with God Himself—a close covenantal bond with the Lord of the whole universe.

Just as God "sevens Himself" to mankind in the seven days of creation, so the first time God speaks to Abram, He makes a seven-part promise.

1. I will make of thee a great nation;
2. I will bless thee,
3. and magnify thy name;
4. thou shalt be blessed;
5. I will bless them that bless thee,
6. and curse them that curse thee;
7. IN THEE shall all the kindred of the earth be blessed.

When God tells Abram to leave his country, kindred, and father's house, He is telling him to leave everything that gave him safety and security. It also means leaving behind the false religion of that place to follow where the true God will lead him. Abram must really trust this God who speaks to him. He gets up and leaves. Right from the beginning Abram has a certain amount of faith in God. Over the course of Abram's life, we will see his faith in God grow through tests and trials.

The second statement of the promise

Abram goes southwest from Haran to Canaan and passes through the land to Shechem, a place in northern Canaan. Genesis then tells us: "At that time the Canaanites were in the land." From this we know that Abram REALLY had to trust God. What he was doing was absolutely crazy. Here he is, a foreigner, walking into a land already inhabited by other people and thinking that he and his descendants will own the place. Oh yes, and his wife is barren (Gen 11:30), so how will he have descendants? But because he trusts God, he *does* own the place, or at least his descendants will, as God reassures him at this point:

> And the Lord appeared to Abram, and said to him: To thy seed will I give this land. And he built there an altar to the Lord, who had appeared to him. (Gen 12:7)

As a way of confirming Abram's faith God not only speaks to him but appears to him. And Abram, for his part, beyond obeying the command of the Lord, worships this God who appeared to him, as the altar indicates.

Abram continues his "tour" of the land God promised him starting in the north in Shechem, stopping at Bethel, and passing south toward the "Negeb" in the South of the land of Canaan. Then there is a famine in the land and so he just continues to go south and west to Egypt.

The usual cause of famine in this part of the world is drought, lack of rain. The agriculture of Egypt, however, isn't as dependant on rain because the farmers there use the water from the great Nile river. This is why Abram (and later his grandson Jacob and his family) go to Egypt when there is a famine.

This may be a sign that Abram's faith wavered a little. He leaves the land God commanded him to occupy. Then when he gets to Egypt, he doesn't completely trust that God will take care of him and so tells his wife to tell the

Egyptians that she is his sister, which we later find out is only half true. But God is faithful nonetheless, afflicting the Egyptians with plagues until they give Abram lots of gifts and tell him to please go away. This of course is a foretaste of what will happen later, on a grand scale, with Abram's descendants in the next book of the Pentateuch—Exodus.

The third statement of the promise

So Abram returns to Canaan a very wealthy man, basically going the reverse of the way he went down to Egypt. He and his nephew Lot, who has been with him, decide to separate because there just isn't enough room for both of their enormous households and flocks of animals to live in the same location.

With the story of their parting, it helps to know that in ancient times men usually oriented themselves toward the east, because that was the most obvious and first direction, since that is where the sun rises. Our word "orient" comes from a word that just means "east." It also helps to know the Jordan river runs from the Sea of Galilee in the north of Canaan about 70 miles to the Dead Sea in the South of Canaan and that it was the natural eastern boundary of the land.

With this in mind, when Abram tells Lot to choose "the left hand or the right hand," he is telling him to choose the north or the south part of Canaan. Lot, apparently something of a sneak, instead chooses "the whole Jordan valley" instead of the northern or southern part of it. Abram stays in Canaan, but Lot leaves it. Abram may have been thinking that since he had no children Lot would be the one through whom God would give him descendants. But now Lot has gone out of the Promised Land.

If Abram was thinking something like this, it makes sense out of what God promises him next:

> And the LORD said to Abram, after Lot had separated from him, "Now lift up your eyes and look from the place where you are, northward and southward and eastward and westward; for all the land which you see, I will give it to you and to your descendants forever. And I will make your descendants as the dust of the earth; so that if anyone can number the dust of the earth, then your descendants can also be numbered. Arise, walk about the land through its length and breadth; for I will give it to you."

In other words, the land really is going to be yours and it really is going to belong to your descendants and you really are going to have lots of descendants. So don't worry about Lot!

In fact, Lot's decision was really as foolish as it was sneaky. He left Abram, whom God promised to bless. He left the promised Land God is giving to Abram. And he chooses to live in a place that looks nice (Gen 13:10) but is full of extremely wicked men (Gen 13:13).

Genesis then uses the next chapter to show what a foolish decision Lot made and how great Abram is in comparison. Lot and his entire household and goods get captured in a battle. Abram comes to his rescue, leading a small army and defeating the five kings who had captured Lot. Abram first tithes (gives a tenth) of the booty to Melchizedek, who is a priest of God and who blesses Abram. He then returns all of the goods and people and won't take anything for payment or as a reward because he doesn't want to give the bad example of getting rich through an evil man (the king of Sodom).

The fourth statement of the promise

As if to answer for all of that treasure and reward that Abram just gave up, God speaks to him (in a vision) the fourth time saying: "Do not fear Abram! I am a shield to you and your wages exceedingly great!" (Gen 15:2).

Abram had given up everything, including Lot as his heir, and any reward he might have had for rescuing him from the other kings, but in response God promises HIMSELF as Abram's "wages."

Abram then asks God frankly how He is going to fulfill His promise of descendants because Abram has none, but is planning on taking as his heir one of the slaves of his household, Eliezer.

God negates this and says:

> "No, that one shall not be your heir; rather, the one that comes from your own body—he shall be your heir." He took him outside and said: "Look up to the sky and count the stars, if you can. Just so," he added, "shall your seed be." And he believed in the Lord, and He reckoned it to him as righteousness. (Gen 15:4-6)

Abram believes but he still would like some kind of sign so that he can KNOW that he is to possess the Land. So God humors him, and tells him to take several animals and split them in half and set the halves opposite each other. Verse 11 about the birds of prey is interesting though—it shows that

Abram has been sitting there with his dead animals waiting for quite a while, just as he is going to have to wait patiently for the fulfillment of God's promises (Gen 15:8–11).

God appears as smoke and fire and passes in between the pieces of the animals. The point of this ceremony in the ancient world was this: if I break my end of the bargain, let me be like these animals (split in half and dead). This is a serious promise!

One other interesting thing about this scene is that right before it happens, Genesis tells us that the sun was going down (Gen 15:12). This tells us something fascinating about earlier when God told Abram to count stars (Gen 15:5). Now, of course, Abram can't count all the stars, because there are too many of them. But now we know that there was another reason he couldn't count them—because he couldn't even see them. It was still daylight! When God says "your descendants/seed will be like the stars," it means both that they will be extremely numerous and also that Abram can't see them now, but he can still trust that they really are there.

So in verse 18 God makes a solemn covenant with Abram that he will indeed possess the Land promised to him. He even describes the boundaries of the land for him. The borders God describes here will be the boundaries of the Land of Israel during the time of king David and his son Solomon. Notice that the boundaries will extend all the way to the Euphrates—the Land will encompass even the land that Abram gave up to come to this Land! God is exceedingly generous and gives back far more than He takes to those who sacrifice for Him. So, Abram now has not simply a promise, but a solemn covenant with God that God will in fact give him the first part of the patriarchal blessing, which is also the first part of the original blessing = Land.

The fifth statement of the promise

Now that this first part of the patriarchal blessing—land—has been taken care of in chapters 12-15, the narrative turns to the next one, descendants, in chapter 16 and 17.

Chapter 16 opens by turning right to the business of descendants—Sarai is barren; she can't have children. She does not seem to have as much faith as Abram in this regard so she begins to take matters into her own hands. She thinks something like this: "Lot didn't work as an heir to Abram, Eliezer didn't work either. Maybe what God meant when He said we'd have descendants from Abram's own body (see Gen 15:4) was that Abram needs to marry someone else, since obviously I can't have children."

Instead of simply trusting in what God said in a straightforward manner she begins to try to interpret God's promise in a way that she can understand in merely human terms—and in a way that she can control! Always beware of this kind of interpretation of the word of God!

So Abram "hearkens to the voice of his wife" (Gen 16:2). Remember the last time someone did that? (See Gen 3:17.)

Uh oh . . .

Nowhere does the Pentateuch ever explicitly forbid a man to have more than one wife. But, the evil Lamech is the first man to have two wives, and every time a man in the Bible has more than one wife lots of trouble happens. So you'd have to be a real blockhead to think that the Torah is supportive of the idea of multiple wives.

Abram's marriage to Hagar the Egyptian slave is no exception. Things are soon so bad between her and Abram's first wife Sarai that she flees and only an angel can convince her to return to bear her son Ishmael (Gen 16:11).

Thirteen years after this happens, when Abram is 99 years old and way past the age when he can beget children, God appears to him again to clarify several things, all having to do with the issue of Abram's *descendants* (Genesis 17). First of all He changes his name Abram ("exalted father") to Abraham, which means "father of a multitude." God's covenant is going to be not only with Abraham but also *with his descendants* (Gen 17:7). The sign of this covenant is circumcision, which also has to do with *descendants*. Then God clarifies that, yes, the son He is going to give Abraham will really be the son of himself and his first wife Sarai, who is also way past the age when she can bear children. God changes her name to Sarah ("Princess"—indicating the royal aspect of the descendants who will come through her) as a sign that this really is going to happen.

Then God makes the most important clarification of all. Abraham laughs at the thought of his aged wife and himself having a son and then basically says, "Ishmael is good enough, Lord! We like him—you don't need to do anything else" (Gen 17:18). Here we see even Abraham try to whittle down God's enormous, wonderful, miraculous plans to something small that he can understand (and control).

In this and many other ways, the Bible will show that the constant temptation of fallen human beings is either to think that God is bad (like in the *Enuma Elish*) or, to think that God can only be good to a certain extent or in a certain way. In fact, however, He is infinite goodness, wisdom, and power. His ways are so far beyond our own that it makes far more sense to trust in the good God whom we do not always understand than it does to trust in our own ideas, even though we can (sometimes) understand them.

This relationship is like that of a father and a little child. When the father tells his child not to play in the street, of course the child wants to know why he can't play in the street. It's fine that the child wonders why, but the fact of the matter is that even if the father explained it to the child, the child wouldn't understand it. So what's best in the meantime is that the child should obey and trust that his father is telling him this for his own good.

What the creature is called to do first and foremost is to trust God, even when he cannot understand Him perfectly. Understanding will come later. St. Anselm made up a Latin phrase that explains this all very well. He said that what we should have toward God is *fides quaerens intellectum*, that is, faith seeking understanding. This is the definition of theology.

Now back to Abram. God promises in response that Ishmael will also be a great nation, the father of twelve princes, and that he will have many descendants and he will have lots of *blessings*. But His *covenant* will be with Isaac, not with Ishmael.

> And *as for Ishmael, I have heard you; behold, I will bless him*, and will make him fruitful, and will multiply him exceedingly. He shall become the father of twelve princes, and I will make him a great nation. *But My covenant I will establish with Isaac*, whom Sarah will bear to you at this season next year." (Gen 17: 20–21)

Here God is saying that there is a difference between *blessing* and *covenant*. Every covenant is a blessing, but not every blessing is a covenant. In general, blessing just means the reception of good things from God and this is the kind of blessing that Ishmael is going to receive. But the blessing that is also a covenant is something more than this. It is a deep solemn relationship with God Himself, which is not only the greatest blessing that God can give, but is also the source of every other blessing in the whole world. Moreover, it makes one who receives it a source of blessing to others. It's the difference between having someone bring you a cup of water when you are thirsty, which is a blessing, and being yourself the owner of the spring from which the water comes. There is a huge difference, though in some respects they look the same. God's people have the source of all blessing (God) and become the source of blessing for all peoples. The rest of the peoples are receivers of this blessing from them.

This gives us a great insight into the original three patriarchal blessings: Land, descendants, and "blessing." That first time God spoke to Abraham He said that he would not only be blessed, but that he would be a blessing—that all the families of the earth would be blessed through him. He and his descendants will be a blessing to the whole world. And the blessing they will give to the world is nothing less than God Himself, the source of all blessing.

So already we can see that the three parts of the patriarchal blessing aren't just three random things. Not only do they correspond to the original blessings of creation, but they also have an order among them: the Land is given so that there can be descendants, and the descendants are given so that there can be this blessing to all of the nations. This is fulfilled in many partial ways prior to the New Testament as we will see, but it is most completely fulfilled in that the Messiah (who is God incarnate and is therefore the blessing which is the source of all blessing) will come from the Israelite people. So will His Apostles, who will carry this blessing to every nation under heaven.

Summary

In this lesson you have learned what the "cosmic problem" is and the many ways (structural, numerological, genealogical, etc.) in which Genesis shows that Abraham is going to be God's answer to that problem. Through Abraham, God is going to restore the three original blessings of creation—Land, descendants, and blessing. You have seen the Land and the descendants parts of the three-part blessing, ratified with an oath or covenant from God. In the next lesson we will see the most important part—blessing to all nations—also confirmed with an oath from God. But before that happens God is going to test Abraham with the most difficult test that any man has ever faced.

QUESTIONS

1. What is biblical numerology?

Biblical numerology is the study of the significance of numbers in Scripture.

NOTE: You should know the scriptural-numerological significance of the following numbers and be able to give an example of them from Genesis: 4, 6, 7, 8, 10, 12, 20, 40, and 70.

2. What were the three original blessings of creation?

The original blessings were
(1) a sacred land,
(2) where they could raise their descendants
(3) to enjoy the greatest blessing of friendship with God.

3. What is this blessing to all nations that will come through Abraham?

The blessing to all nations that will come through Abraham is friendship with God which comes most perfectly through God-made-man, Jesus Christ, who is Abraham's descendant.

In this beautiful icon by the Russian iconographer Andrei Rublev (c. 1360s–c. 1430), which pictures Abraham's three visitors as three angels who represent the three Persons of the Holy Trinity. The Church Fathers of East and West commonly understood the appearance of the angels as a revelation of the Trinity.

Lesson 6

Abraham Attains Perfection

This sixth lesson completes the main part of the story of Abraham. Though he will still play an important role in the next lesson (Genesis 24–26) it will be as an introduction to the life of his son Isaac. In this lesson, we will see the completion of the eight times that God speaks to Abraham and how the eighth time God gives superabundant blessing to the whole world through him and his seed. We will also see the completion of the three patriarchal blessings: Land, Descendants, and Blessing to all nations. God has already solemnly sworn to give Abraham the promised Land, and also promised descendants through Isaac (who is not born yet). Now we will also see God solemnly swear that He will bless all the nations through Abraham and his seed. As Abraham grows closer to God, he is offered and accepts the responsibilities of being a redeemer, a receiver of revelation, a teacher of righteousness, and an intercessor. At the end of this section, God offers Abraham the last and greatest of all responsibilities and the ultimate test of his life—the command to sacrifice of his son Isaac.

The sixth statement of the promise (Genesis 18)

"*The Lord appeared to Abraham again at the oaks at Mamre*" (Gen 18:1). Genesis tells us that it was the Lord, so we all know who it is, but Abraham didn't know it was the Lord. He thinks these are three men passing along on a journey. One of them is the Lord and the other two, as we will learn, are angels.

In Scripture angels often appear as men and are simply called men in the story because that's what they looked like. The word "angel" comes from a Greek word that means "messenger," which is a translation of the Hebrew word *malak*, which means the same thing. Angels don't have bodies, but if they want to be seen then they can appear in a body and often do appear as men.

Thus, angels are sometimes called "men" (as in Gen 18:16) and sometimes "angels" (because that's what they actually are, as in Gen 19:1). Sometimes they are even referred to as "God" because they are delivering His messages: if you are speaking to an angel, it's like speaking to God Himself. The change from one to the other in the story might even be to show Abraham's own understanding—first he thought they were men, then later he understood that they were angels, and later still that one of them was the Lord Himself! Whatever the case, don't get confused—the two men and the two angels accompanying the Lord on this journey are the same two beings.

Abraham shows great hospitality to these strangers, asking them to stop, have their feet washed, eat, drink, and rest. When they are finished eating, one of the strangers tells him that they will return in the spring and Sarah will have a son. Sarah, who overhears this, is now so old and so far past the age when she could have children, that even the thought of child-bearing seems totally ridiculous—so ridiculous that she can't keep from laughing out loud. It would be like hearing someone say to a crippled person who has been in a wheel chair for 50 years, "Next Spring I'll come back and you'll win a marathon!" The whole thing is just crazy—good for a laugh, but that's about it.

The Stranger however, isn't laughing. He calmly responds, "Why did Sarah laugh? Is anything too hard for God?"

This is exactly the question everyone needs to ask themselves when faced with things that seem good but impossible. Remember that the Serpent works mainly by getting people to think that God can't really be as good as people think He is. The constant temptation even for righteous people is to place limits on God's goodness, as if to say, "I know God is good, but He can't be THAT good, can He? Well, God is Lord of life and death and everything. Nothing is beyond His power, as Abraham and Sarah will soon learn. They will see their aged bodies, which seem barely able to maintain their own life, being used by God to produce the new life of their son Isaac.

Sarah, frightened that the Stranger knew her secret thoughts, tries to lie about the laugh, but of course the Stranger sees right through this and says, "No, but you did laugh." She was probably really scared then.

All of the laughing that has been going on about this child (and that will continue to go on, see Gen 21:6) is another instance of double-meanings in the Hebrew. Abraham laughed about this child back in Gen 17:17 and Sarah laughs about him in Gen 18:12. Then the Stranger asks about her laughing (Gen 18:13) and she denies laughing (Gen 18:15) and then the Stranger says that yes, she did laugh (Gen 18:15). And the boy's name will be . . . Isaac, which in Hebrew means "He laughed."

This might just seem playful, but there is something deep and wonderful about it too. All of this laughter points out that the goodness God is giving to the world through Abraham's son Isaac is going to be so good, so impossibly good, so superabundantly good, that the response everyone has is laughter. It's even God who first gave him the name (Gen 17:19).

There is a link with the laughter here and the laughter reported by one of the Psalms. These two "laughters" are connected in that they are the only two joyful laughters reported in the Bible. All other laughter is derisive laughter. So the psalm-laughter echoes the Isaac-laughter by using the same word when speaking about how overjoyed the Israelites were to finally be released from their exile and bondage in a foreign land. "When the Lord delivered Zion from bondage it seemed like a dream, then was our mouth filled with laughter, on our lips there were songs!" (Psalm 126:1–2)

Why is Isaac so great? Why is the thing that God is bringing into the world through him so amazingly good that everyone who hears it can't keep from laughing? Even though they often laugh for the wrong reason, the laughter still signifies how amazing Isaac is. By the end of this lesson we will see in detail what it is, but we can already guess that it has to do with the third part of the patriarchal blessing: through Isaac, God is going to bind Himself by the most solemn oath to His promise of blessing to all the nations of the world. Isaac is somehow the answer to the problem of the whole world.

Abraham: revealer, teacher, intercessor

The Stranger, who Abraham now knows is the Lord, sends His two angel companions down to the cities of Sodom and Gomorrah and stays behind to talk with Abraham:

> The LORD said: "Shall I hide from Abraham what I am about to do, now that he is to become a great and populous nation, and all the nations of the earth are to find blessing in him? Indeed, I have singled him out that he may direct his sons and his posterity to keep the way of the LORD by doing what is right and just, so that the LORD may carry into effect for Abraham the promises he made about him." (Gen 18:17–19)

The first thing to note here is that God reveals His secret plan to Abraham, much as He did to Noah. Think about that: *Abraham knows what is on God's mind.* That makes Abraham pretty important. He receives a revelation from God. Now that he knows the mind of God, he is also duty-bound to make it known to others—first and foremost (as with Noah) to his own family and children and descendants. Abraham's role as father of a great nation and receiver of revelation brings with it the duty to teach his children the way of righteousness.

Simply having a lot of descendants isn't all that great in God's eyes. The only way descendants will be a blessing is if they keep the way of the Lord. Otherwise they will just be more of the curse on the earth. So God's first commandment to "Be fruitful and multiply" has to be understood with this in mind. Multiply and fill the earth...*with good.*

This is the reason why this part of the story which shows Abraham as a teacher of righteousness is followed by the story of Sodom and Gomorrah (Genesis 19). Sodom and Gomorrah show what you get when descendants are not taught the way of the Lord. It's not pretty.

Sodom and Gomorrah

Speaking of Sodom and Gomorrah, this is how Abraham steps into another important job—that of intercessor. He intercedes for any righteous people who may still be living in the evil towns of Sodom and Gomorrah, asking God if He will still destroy the city if there are fifty, forty-five, forty, thirty, twenty, or *just ten* good people there. Each time God says that He won't destroy the city if that many good people are there. Abraham is, of course, thinking primarily of his nephew Lot and hoping to save him from the coming destruction. And God does end up sparing Lot, not for his own sake, but for Abraham's sake, because of his intercession (Gen 19:29). This is now the second time that Abraham has redeemed, or saved Lot from slavery or death (see also Gen 14:16).

Lot is righteous enough that he, like Abraham, welcomes the two Strangers who come to his town and shows them hospitality and tries to shield them from the evil intentions of the men of the place (Gen 19:2-4, 7). The angels however, end up rescuing Lot rather than him rescuing them (Gen 19:10-11, 15-16). Lot lingers in the doomed town. His sons-in-law won't listen to his warning (perhaps because Lot himself wasn't entirely convinced of it). When he finally is forced to leave, his wife looks back and is turned into a pillar of salt. Lot and his two daughters end up living in a cave (because now they are afraid to live in towns) and he spends his evenings being extremely drunk while his daughters break the command that "a man shall leave father and mother and cleave to his wife and the two shall become one flesh."

It's all very ugly and is intended to be so—this is what happens without the training in righteousness that God has charged Abraham to give to his children. It's not surprising that Lot's daughters give birth to the fathers of the Moabites and the Ammonites, later enemies of the Israelites.

Abraham's wife/sister ... again

Sodom and Gomorrah, as far as we can tell, were located somewhere in the southern part of what is now the Dead Sea, in the southeastern part of the Promised Land. Abraham, who was northwest of this (and higher up), gets up in the morning and looks east and sees the sun rise through the smoke that rises from the destroyed cities of the valley (Gen 19:27). Just as Lot overlooked the beautiful valley and chose it even though wicked people lived there, so Abraham looks over the same valley, now burned, and sees the effects of unrighteousness. It is as if the evil that dwelt in the valley has finally shown its true face.

Abraham moves on from the area overlooking the Dead Sea valley and heads southwest toward the Negeb again and stops in a place called Gerar. Then we get what looks like a repeat of the same strange story we had in our last lesson (Genesis 12) about Abraham saying that his wife is his sister. Certain scholars look at this and see nothing but another weird repetition of an already weird story and they conclude that the Bible is carelessly put together and contains a lot of material that is just useless.

A wise man once said: "You cannot step in the same river twice." This quotation comes from a Greek philosopher, Heraclitus, who lived about 500 years before Christ. Heraclitus used this statement as a way of illustrating how everything in the material universe always changes—like the way the water of a river is always changing. Even if you step in the same spot, it isn't exactly the same water you are stepping in. Although he wasn't speaking about the Bible when he said this, Heraclitus's words do apply to the Bible.

Repetition is a common feature of both the Old and New Testament, and, if you haven't noticed, also a common feature of your everyday life and of history generally. Repetition is one of the major ways God teaches in nature and it is also one of the major ways that Scripture teaches and makes sure that you learn what it is teaching. But it is rarely if ever merely repetition. You don't step in the same river twice. Something has changed.

Whenever you get what seems like a repetition, that's when you really need to start paying attention because something will have changed, even if it is something very small. If you are careful to focus on the differences, then you will find the key to the story and understand why the repetition was there and how it teaches something new. Believe it or not, we will actually see one more version of this story in our next lesson with Isaac and his wife Rebekah. All of these stories invite you to compare them. They are like three arrows shot from the same bow at the same target, one after the other—they trace out similar lines, but the lines are slightly different and they will hit three different spots on the target.

So if we pay attention to the similarities and differences, what do we find?

Similarities. In both of the Abraham wife-sister stories, Abraham is on a journey southwest; in both he says that his wife is his sister; in both his wife gets taken from him; in both, problems begin to afflict the household of the one who takes Abraham's wife; in both, the deceived people find out and restore Sarah to Abraham. And in both Abraham ends up a rich man because of the whole event. Those are the basic similarities; what are the differences?

Differences. The major difference in the second story is that it highlights Abraham's role as a prophet and an intercessor (Gen 20:7, 17–18), something that was completely absent from the first story. The first story emphasizes that God will protect Abraham because of His first promise to "Bless those who bless you and curse those who curse you"(Gen 12:3). But in the second story, because Abraham is now called a prophet, he knows God. Because he knows God, He has received from God Himself the right way to pray to God for others. In this way, God is already fulfilling His other promise—to bless all the nations through Abraham.

Never outdone in generosity

Already the nations that come from Lot and his daughters owe their very life to Abraham's prayers (Gen 19:29). Now Abimelech's whole household likewise owes its life to Abraham's prayers. So, there is actually a beautiful order among these stories, which at first seemed random and strange. This order, once we see it, makes the wife-sister story in chapter 20 the perfect link between chapters 18–19 and 21.

- *In chapter 18* (God's visit to Abraham at the Oaks of Mamre), God leads Abraham into the roles of teacher and intercessor.
- *In chapter 19* (Sodom and Gomorrah), Abraham actually attains, through his intercession, mercy for Lot, a member of his extended family.
- *In chapter 20* (the wife-sister story #2), Abraham does the same for Abimelech, who isn't even a member of his extended family.

It's especially noteworthy that the plague he has to ask God to lift from Abimelech's household is one that was afflicting the women—they could not have children. So, when Abraham intercedes for these people, he is asking God to help the women be able to bear children again.

Then, lo and behold, what's the very next thing we hear, right at the beginning of Chapter 21? Sarah is expecting a baby! The prayers of a holy man are powerful indeed. It's as if the grace God sends in response to his prayer for the women of Abimelech's household has spilled over onto his own wife as well. Not only are they able to have children once again, but his own wife, who has never been able to have children, and is far beyond the age when it's even possible for her to have children, is also expecting a baby.

The Blessing starts with Abraham, moves to his family, and from there even to others outside his family—only to return to his own immediate family in a superabundant and miraculous way. God will not be outdone in generosity!

God charged Abraham not only to have descendants, but also (and more importantly) to teach them the way of righteousness, which he has learned from God. Since Abraham has proved that he can do it for others, all the more is he ready now to do it for his own household. His willingness to carry out

God's command for others proves he is now ready to have that descendant that God has been promising him for so long.

As we can see a little more clearly now, these stories are all very orderly and put together artfully and purposefully, even though they may not seem that way at first.

Abraham's wife/slave

When we get into the rest of chapter 21, you should already know what to do, because now we are getting a "repeat" of another story—Sarah versus Hagar, or, as we might call it, the second "wife-slave" story. There are the two wife-sister stories (Genesis 12 and 20) and now the two wife-slave stories (Genesis 16 and 21). What do we do with this one? St. Paul will have much more to tell us about Sarah and Hagar when we get to his letter to the Galatians, but what can we see right now?

Similarities. In both stories, Hagar flees because Sarah dislikes her. In both she ends up by a spring of water. In both, an angel of God speaks to her; in both God promises that He will also make Ishmael a great nation. In both, Ishmael is described as a tough man, a hunter, who will even fight his kinsmen.

Differences. The most important difference between the two is just this: in the first one, God tells Hagar to go back and to submit to Sarah. In the second, Hagar and Ishmael do not go back. As much as it grieves Abraham (Gen 21:11), they have become officially and finally separated from him. Ishmael will become his own nation "over against his kinsmen," but he will be blessed simply because Abraham was his father. It even says that God "was with" Ishmael to keep him alive and ensure that he became a great nation (Gen 21:20-21). However, Ishmael will not be blessed in the most important way—he will not be the receiver of the covenant with God. And this covenant with God is the answer to the cosmic crisis. It is the defeat of the work of the serpent.

The seventh statement of the promise

Genesis 21:12 is the seventh time God speaks to Abraham. It is the key to understanding why God is doing what He is doing because in it God explains why He wants Hagar and Ishmael to leave. Unfortunately, some modern translations of this passage try to explain the Hebrew rather than translate it. Their explanation for what the Hebrew means ends up making it less meaningful than the Hebrew. For example, one translation says, "It is through Isaac that descendants shall bear your name" (Gen 21:12).[3]

The word "name" never occurs here in the Hebrew. The verb "bear" doesn't either. The word "descendants"(= "seed") is singular in the Hebrew, not plural, though it can refer to a collective. (A collection of a million seeds would still be called "seed" just like a pile of money would still be called "money" and not "monies.") But translating it "Seed" rather than descendants allows it to be BOTH singular and plural, to refer to BOTH the group of Abraham's descendants and also to Abraham's one descendant (Christ), who more than anyone, will defeat the seed of the Serpent. The Hebrew literally says: "For through Isaac [a] Seed will be called yours" (Gen 21:12).[4]

Well, now you can see why the translators tried to explain this passage. What in the world does it mean? It may seem like nonsense at first, but if you have been paying attention to what we have said about the word "seed" in these lessons, you should be able to figure out the answer. Take a minute or two before you continue and try think about what this might mean ...

If you guessed that it has something to do with the enmity between the Seed of the Woman and the seed of the Serpent, then you are on the right track. What God is saying here is that Hagar and Ishmael need to go, and Abraham needs to let them go because the Seed of the Woman who will defeat the seed of the Serpent is not going to come through Hagar and Ishmael. Rather, the Seed we have all been waiting for, the Seed who will defeat the seed of the Serpent, and through whom all nations of the earth will be blessed, will come through Isaac.

All of this talk about numerous descendants is actually not as important as something else—the Seed who will come from these descendants, the Seed who will defeat the seed of the Serpent. After all, Ishmael will have his own land and twelve descendants and blessing—and he is even circumcised! But he cannot claim the greatest blessing of all because it will not be through him that the Seed of the Woman comes, but rather through Isaac.

---

[3] Older translations, such as the Douay Rheims, do much better than most modern ones here. This is an example of the importance of translations. St. Augustine gives this as a rule in his book on the interpretation of Scripture (*De Doctrina Christiana*): "For the examination of a number of translations has often thrown light upon some of the more obscure passages."

[4] These words are so important that I have given my own translation of them from the Hebrew. My translations are very literal, both in terms of the words and the word order, as much as possible.

As we will soon see, Christ is the descendant, the Seed of Isaac, in more ways than one. We will also see another reason God got Ishmael and Hagar out of the way—it was to make the final testing of Abraham the ultimate grand finale of all tests. Abraham finally has the long awaited son from Sarah ... but now Isaac is all he has. Lot is not going to be his heir. Eliezer is not going to be his heir. Ishmael is gone. Hagar is gone. All hope for carrying on the covenant, the whole hope for the defeat of the serpent, the hope of the whole world, rests on Abraham and Sarah's ONE and ONLY descendant. It all rests on Isaac.

Keep that in mind.

Abimelech ... again

Next we have another visit from Abimelech. Is it just so we can learn about a dispute he had with Abraham over some wells and how it was all resolved by a gift of seven sheep? You know better than that.

The point of this little story is the same but more intense than the point of the story we just finished. Ishmael was blessed because he is Abraham's descendant; now even others who are NOT Abraham's descendants are coming to realize the power of God's blessing in Abraham.

Abimelech understands that only if he is friends with Abraham, whose God is so powerful, will he be blessed. So, he comes to Abraham begging to be friends with him. Genesis even mentions that Abimelech brought the commander of his army with him which shows the submission of human power to divine power (Gen 21:22). Even those outside of Abraham's family are coming to realize that unless they are connected to Abraham they won't be blessed. Again, the blessing starts with God, moves to Abraham, his extended family, and then outside his family with Abimelech.

So, the focus of this whole chapter has been on how God is blessing two other nations through Abraham, one related to him, and one not. These two represent all nations, all the nations who await a blessing through Abraham and through the Seed who will come through his only son Isaac.

The sacrifice of Isaac

Now, just when we see this all perfectly ordered and set up; just when we finally have had it pounded into us through various repetitions; just when we understand that all the nations are dying to receive the blessing that can come to them only through Abraham—more precisely, only through Abraham's son Isaac, and through the Seed who will come through Isaac—just when we understand that the fate of the whole fallen world hangs on a thread, and that Isaac is that thread, then, at that very moment, God commands Abraham . . .

> Take your son, your only one, the one you love, Isaac, and go to the land of Moriah. There you shall offer him up as a burnt offering on a height that I will point out to you. (Gen 22:2)

The way the words are ordered in the Hebrew made one ancient Jewish biblical scholar imagine this as a dialogue between God and Abraham that went like this:

> GOD: Take your son . . .
> ABRAHAM: Lord, I have two sons!
> GOD: Your only son . . .
> ABRAHAM: Lord, Ishmael is my only son by Hagar and Isaac is my only son by Sarah.
> GOD: The one you love . . .
> ABRAHAM: Lord, I love both of my sons!
> GOD: Isaac.   *(End of discussion)*

What is God doing? Well, as the first verse of this chapter says, He is testing Abraham. Abraham has grown in faith and trust, but this is the ultimate test of his obedience and faith. He knows that this is God speaking—the same God who has done so much good for him; the same God who promised him descendants through Isaac. And yet now this same God is telling him to sacrifice Isaac—to take Isaac and kill him and burn him as an offering to God on an altar on Mount Moriah.

Why this? Is this just the most horrible thing God could think of to test Abraham? Why not have him walk through fire or throw himself off a cliff? Abraham's temptation up to this point, and it is the same temptation we have seen in mankind at large, has been to seize God's blessings by his own efforts. Note the Ishmael affair. God proposes what appears to be an impossible scenario and asks Abraham to trust: just wait and trust me, without taking things into your own hands. This test strikes at the very heart of Abraham's trust in God.

We can only imagine what went through Abraham's mind at this point. God seems to be doing two very strange things: Commanding him to do something that is morally horrible. Going against His promise to raise up "seed" through Isaac. But Abraham obeys anyway.

Abraham undoing Adam

The first test in Genesis is in the garden of Eden where the man and the woman fail to follow the Lord's command. The two temptations the Serpent gives to the woman are:
1. You can't trust God to give you what is good, you have to make it happen for yourself.
2. Doing this will make you "god-like." You will get to decide for yourself what is good and what is evil (Gen 3:4–5).

The message of the Serpent is clear: take it all for yourself and make yourself a god. God's testing of Abraham in Genesis 22 goes against these two prime temptations. Abraham must
3. Sacrifice (literally) any hope he had of making the promises happen for himself.
4. NOT decide for himself what is good and evil, but rather trust in God's decision.

The command to sacrifice his son makes Abraham's obedience to God total—he cannot even attempt to decide for himself what is good and what is evil in this case. He must simply trust and obey the God whom he knows is good. God's message is equally clear: Give it all to me and let me be God.

Meanwhile, what was *Isaac* thinking? Well, we don't know exactly, but Genesis gives us another repetition that may help us to see that Isaac, although he doesn't really understand what God is about to do any more than Abraham does, still is ready to obey his father, as his father is obeying God.

Abraham goes with Isaac to the place God pointed out to him, lays the wood (literally "the trees") upon Isaac, takes the knife and fire for the sacrifice and, they set out, two of them together. As they are walking Isaac wants to know: "Where is the lamb for a burnt offering?"(Gen 22:7) His question here shows that he is accustomed to performing animal sacrifices, as was Abel. Abraham responds: "God will provide for Himself the lamb for the sacrifice, my son" (Gen 22:8). Then once again it says: "They set out, the two of them together."

These two phrases are identical in the Hebrew and the word translated "together" is the same basic word as the word for "one": "And they set out, the two of them as one." So the first time Isaac agrees with Abraham about going to do a sacrifice. In the second he agrees to completely trust in God to provide the lamb for the sacrifice, even if that lamb, as Abraham says, might be "my son" (Gen 22:8).

This story of the father freely sacrificing his only beloved Son for the blessing of the world, with the son willingly carrying the wood (= "trees") to sacrifice himself, led many a Church Father to see in this story a foretaste, a type, of the sacrifice of God's only beloved Son, Jesus, who also carried the tree of the cross up the mountain to sacrifice Himself on it for the blessing of the whole world. Abraham is like God the Father and Isaac is like God the Son. If you take a minute to go back to your table of contents and look up the page number for 23:1, you will find another interesting connection. Mt. Moriah is where the temple was built later in Israel's history. The place where Abraham offered Isaac, his beloved son, as a sacrifice is related to the place where the temple sacrifices will be and where Jesus, God's beloved son, will also be sacrificed!

So Abraham's sacrifice of Isaac and Isaac's participation are together a partial defeat of the Serpent, since they choose God over self. At the same time as it looks back to the defeat Man had in Eden (maybe Eden's "trees" are why the wood here is called "trees" as well!) it also looks forward to the total defeat of the works of the Serpent—death and sin—on the tree/altar of the cross.

The eighth statement of the promise

Abraham obeys God and is about to slay his only beloved son as a sacrifice, when the Lord stops him and speaks the eighth and final statement of the promises to Abraham:

> "By myself I have sworn [sevened!], declares the LORD, that because you did this thing and did not withhold your only son:
> 1. Blessing I will bless you
> 2. And increasing I will increase *your Seed*
> 3. Like the stars of the heavens
> 4. And like the sand which is on the shore of the sea.
> 5. *Your Seed* will possess the gate of His enemies
> 6. And all nations of the earth shall bless themselves by *Your Seed*—
> 7. Because you listened to my voice." (Gen 22:16-18)

Remember God's last promise to Abraham? *"Through Isaac a Seed will be called yours."*

Now that Seed, through Isaac, has been called *his*—three times. This Seed will increase superabundantly, will possess the gates of his enemies, and will be the one by whom the nations of the earth bless themselves. In the first promise, God said that Abraham would be a blessing; in this last promise, Abraham's Seed is also the superabundant blessing to the whole world. And in this last blessing God swears the most solemn and binding oath possible: "By myself I have sworn."

To possess the gates of one's enemies is to have utterly defeated them. If you control the gate of the city, you control everything. So the Seed will conquer all of His enemies. But how? With military might like Abimelech coming out to meet Abraham with the commander of his army? No. Because the enemies are none other than the people mentioned next—the nations who will bless themselves by the Seed. In other words the nations are going to be overjoyed to have been "conquered" by Abraham's Seed, just as Abimelech begged to be Abraham's friend, even though Abimelech was the one with the big army. The Seed's other enemy, of course, is the Serpent and his seed. With this in mind, you should skip ahead for a minute to Matthew's Gospel and read Matt 16:18!

God, through Abraham's Seed, is going to turn the whole earth, and heaven, and hell, inside out and upside down for the blessing of the whole world—all because Abraham believed, trusted, taught, and obeyed what God told him.

In this eighth promise, this superabundant blessing of the whole world through Abraham's Seed, Abraham sacrifices his son but receives his son Isaac back alive again through the gift of God. The eighth time God speaks to Abraham brings new life and superabundant blessing for the whole world. Wow. Thank God for Abraham!

The rest of this part of Scripture about Abraham tells us a few important things to get us ready for the next part—the (new) life of his son Isaac. First, and foremost, it introduces Rebekah into the story (Gen 22:23). She will be the wife of Isaac and the mother of Jacob and Esau. Also, it tells us that Abraham's wife Sarah died and that Abraham asked the Hittites in the land of Canaan to sell him a piece of land in which he could bury his wife. As a result, Abraham is no longer simply a "sojourner" in the Land—he actually owns a small piece of it. The experience of his only son's symbolic death and resurrection, followed by his wife's death, has made Abraham look forward, beyond death, to the hope of resurrection. He buys the property in the Promised Land for his wife and for himself, and for his son and grandson and their wives so they can be buried there. He wants to be in the Promised Land with his family when God restores them to New Life.

Summary

In this lesson, you have completed the eight times that God speaks His promises to Abraham, as it comes to its climax in God's oath to bless all the nations through Abraham's Seed. You have also learned some things about the importance of translations, and about biblical repetition, how it is a teaching tool, and how to learn from it. You have seen Abraham's progress in his relationship with God as he has become a redeemer, revealer, teacher, and intercessor. You have seen how his willingness to sacrifice his only beloved son "undid" the first sin of Man, and how it is a foreshadowing image (or "type" in the older language) of God the Father's willingness to sacrifice His only beloved son to save the world from sin and death. Abraham is the model for his descendants, the Israelites, who will come through his son Isaac. In our next lesson, we will learn more about this man Isaac, whose entry into the world caused everyone to laugh for joy.

QUESTIONS

1. What is the purpose of biblical repetition?

By repetition the Bible teaches—drawing attention by the similarities and showing something new by the differences.

2. What are the major features of Genesis thus far?

Thus far, there have been four major features of Genesis:
1. *The 7 Days of Creation (God's Perfect Good)*
2. *The 7 Sins of Creatures (= Creatures' "Perfect" Evil)*
3. *The 7 Punishments for Sin (= God's Perfect Justice)*
4. *The 7 + 1 Promises to Abraham (= God's Superabundant Mercy, Blessing, and New Life)*

Lesson 7

The Story of Isaac

This seventh lesson covers the main part of the life of Abraham's son Isaac. You will learn how the covenant God made with Abraham is carried on in Isaac's own relationship with God. In this part we are also introduced to Isaac's sons, Jacob and Esau, and how Jacob is chosen by God to be the next heir of the promises made to Abraham.

Abraham has a problem

In our last lesson, we saw Abraham purchasing the cave and the field at Macphelah as a burial place for himself and his wife. His son Isaac and grandson Jacob and their wives will also be buried there. Now that Abraham has settled affairs for the dead, he has one last thing to take care of for the living (Isaac). And it is a bit of a problem. He knows that the covenant, which includes descendants, is going to pass on through Isaac, but Isaac is unmarried.

- He wants to find a virtuous wife for his son Isaac, but the only young women around him are the "daughters of the Canaanites" and Abraham doesn't trust them as wives for his son. The only people he trusts are the people he originally came from in Mesopotamia, in the city of Nahor, Abraham's brother.

- But, he does NOT want his son going back to Mesopotamia because the Lord has sworn to give him THIS land, the land of Canaan, where he is living. Remember, it's not a short journey and all they have to go on are camels. If he lets his son go back to Mesopotamia he might never come back. Or it might be twenty years before he comes back (—that's what happens to Isaac's son Jacob, but more on him next lesson!).

- In the meantime, Abraham is getting very old and might die at any time.

The solution to all of these problems is that Abraham commands his head servant (probably Eliezer, see Gen 15:2) to go back to Abraham's people to find a wife for Isaac. And he makes Eliezer swear that he will NOT take Isaac back there and that he will NOT take a Canaanite wife for him no matter what happens. Why does Abraham make such a big deal about all of this?

Although it is wrapped up in very human stories, we know that these stories of real people point to something beyond themselves because whatever Scripture is talking about, it is ultimately talking about God. The very human details of finding a wife from a certain place, travels with camels, etc., all reveal the working out of God's secret plan for the world. In this case, Abraham's concern for a particular kind of wife from a particular kind of place, and his desire that Isaac not go there, but rather stay here, all come down to one thing: Abraham is doing his utmost to safeguard the promises God has given to him.

You should remember from past lessons what the three main patriarchal blessings are and the purpose and order of each. They are:

- A holy land for the sake of
- Holy descendants through whom there can be
- A blessing to all nations, to make all nations holy.

It is God's work to bring about the final blessing of all nations, but it is Abraham's to do what he can to make sure that his son is at least in a position to carry on the hope of universal blessing by keeping him in the Land and finding a good wife so there can be descendants. Thus Abraham's job as his life nears its end is to secure the right place and the right people for his son Isaac to be the father of.

A lot depends on Isaac. He has to get both the right place and the right people or all will be lost.

- If Isaac goes back to Mesopotamia he may never come back and then he will not be different than his other family members living there. He will have the people right, but not the place.
- If he becomes one with the Canaanites by marrying one of them he will not be different from the Canaanites. He will have the place right, but not the people.
- In either case, Isaac will end up being no different than those around him.

But Isaac is supposed to be different!

Everyone who chooses to follow God is choosing to be different in the most important way. The constant temptation of God's people even today is to forget this and to begin to desire to be like the people around them who have not chosen to follow God. But God wants a people who are set apart for Him. The whole purpose of God choosing Abraham, remember, is so that through one man and the one holy nation that comes from him, God might save all nations. If some people are drowning because they cannot swim, another man can only help them if he is different from them in two important ways: 1. He does know how to swim and 2. He is willing to help the drowning people. So, God is going to form one nation that can "swim" and that will be willing to help all the rest of the nations who are drowning. This is how they must be set apart.

In fact, the word "holy" in Hebrew can also be translated as—"set apart." Hence, the Sabbath day was called "holy" or "sanctified" because it was a day "set apart" from all the other days. It was a day set apart for God. And now God is forming a people to be "set apart" from all other peoples of the earth, a people through whom and in whom the whole creation can enter into God's Sabbath rest, which is Heaven.

So, yes, a lot depends on Isaac and his being set apart. And Abraham, as a good father, is careful to ensure his chosen son's spiritual future by finding him a virtuous wife and keeping him in the land God promised him. After his spiritual future is secure, we will also see Abraham taking care of Isaac's material needs for the future (Gen 25:5–6).

Search for the perfect bride . . . for the perfect bridegroom (Genesis 24)

So Abraham entrusts this mission to Eliezer, and Eliezer entrusts it to "the Lord, God of my master Abraham." He sets out for the city of Nahor in Mesopotamia with a caravan of ten camels, laden with choice gifts. When he reaches it, he asks the God of his master for some help finding the right girl:

> LORD, God of my master Abraham, let it turn out favorably for me today and thus deal graciously with my master Abraham. While I stand here at the spring and the daughters of the townsmen are coming out to draw water, if I say to a girl, "Please lower your jug, that I may drink," and she answers, "Take a drink, and let me give water to your camels, too," let her be the one whom you have decided upon for your servant Isaac. In this way I shall know that you have dealt graciously with my master. (Gen 24:12–14)

This might seem like a strange way to ask, but it is actually very clever. If it works out as Eliezer asks, he will not only know that "this is the girl for Isaac" but he will know several important things about her: she is generous, hospitable, caring, and polite. Perhaps most importantly, he will see that she is good to strangers, which is a good thing, considering she is going be marrying someone she has never met.

The young Rebekah, who is extremely beautiful, comes to the well and does just what Eliezer had asked for from God. This is no small task—watering ten thirsty camels with only a water jug and a well to draw water from. On top of all her other perfections, she is a hard worker, too!

Eliezer ends up staying at the house of Rebekah's father Bethuel where he and his party are treated hospitably and offered food to eat. Eliezer won't take anything, however, till he delivers his message. He tells the whole amazing story again. The end of it all is that Rebekah's father and brother see God's hand in all of this and allow Rebekah to go with Eliezer to become Isaac's wife.

After a feast and a night's rest, Eliezer wants to get going. Rebekah's mother and brother, Laban, ask him to let Rebekah stay a while longer (watch out for Laban—he's sneaky and we will meet him again later in the story of Jacob). But Eliezer wants to go and so they ask Rebekah if she will go. She says simply, "I will go." This is quite a young woman here. Now she adds to her other perfections that she is courageous and believes in God. She is about to leave her family and homeland and go to a land she has never seen, to marry a man she has never met—all because she was convinced by what Eliezer had said—this is God's will!

The crown of all Rebekah's virtues comes last of all—when, after the long trek back to Canaan, she sees Isaac out "meditating" in the field (Gen 24:63). Your translation might say that Isaac was "walking" in the field—or it might not. The Hebrew verb that reports Isaac's action in Gen 24:63 occurs only here in the entire Bible and no one is certain what it means. Some of the earliest attempts to translate it seem to favor a meaning like "to meditate." The Greek translation of the Hebrew, the Septuagint, translates it as a word which can mean to converse, to reason. When Rebekah sees Isaac out "meditating" in the field, "she took her veil and covered herself" adding modesty to her already impressive list of virtues.

Biblical typology

The two are married and for the first time in the Bible, it says explicitly that a man loved a woman (Gen 24:67). There is something very special about Isaac and Rebekah. Because Isaac is a type of Christ, as we already saw in the story of Abraham's offering of his beloved son in sacrifice, many Church Fathers saw in Isaac and Rebekah a type of the marriage between Christ and His perfect bride, the Church.

We have used the word "type" a couple of times in this lesson and the lesson before. What do we mean by it? When we say that a person or thing is a "type" of something else, we mean that that person or thing anticipates and participates in the reality of what they are a type of. That sounds confusing, but it isn't really. "Type" comes from a Greek word that just means "a stamp" or a mold. So, if you've ever seen how a rubber stamp works, you will understand the basic meaning of "type." If I make a rubber stamp of my signature and use that on my papers instead of signing all of them by hand, I can say that the stamp is a "type" of my signature—it participates in and looks toward ("anticipates") my real signature. So Isaac "looks like" and "looks forward to" Jesus Christ. Rebekah "looks like" and "looks forward to" the bride of Christ, the Church. This does not mean that Isaac and Rebekah weren't real people, rather it means that the real events of their life were already participating in and looking forward to an even more perfect reality in Jesus Christ and His Bride the Church. Typology, the study of types, is one of the most important tools for understanding how the classical tradition, especially the

Church Fathers, read and understood Scripture. Without typology, most of the Christian (and much of the Jewish) tradition of reading Scripture, especially the Old Testament, disappears.

At the beginning of this chapter, Abraham set out to procure two things for his son: 1. that he stay in the Land; 2. that he find a good wife. It is noteworthy then that Isaac is the only one of the three patriarchs—Abraham, Isaac, and Jacob—to have ONE land (Isaac never leaves the promised land) and ONE wife (he never marries anyone else). On top of these perfections Isaac also has this: that of all the patriarchs, he alone has only ONE name throughout his life, the name given him by God Himself.

These three unique qualities about Isaac line up with the three patriarchal blessings:

One Land	The Promised Land (in which Abraham and God command him to stay)
One Wife	The Promised Descendants (who come through his one wife)
One Name	The Blessing to all nations (Isaac = "laughter." Review Psalm 126:1–2 and lesson 6 if you don't understand)

Two more *toledoth*-refrains (Genesis 25)

Chapter 25 has two main parts. They are both related to the purpose of the *toledoth* refrains, which, as you remember, is to trace out the fulfillment of God's plan for the world through those righteous people who choose Him and whom He chooses. The first part of Genesis 25 is all about the sons of Abraham who did NOT receive the covenant. The second part is all about the son who DID receive the covenant = Isaac.

You have seen the table below a few times now, but let's review where we are in it. The first seven parts lead from Adam to Abraham. The eighth part is about Ishmael, who did not receive the covenant. The ninth part, which also begins here in chapter 25 and continues all the way to the end of chapter 35, introduces the story of "the descendants of Isaac" who are Jacob and Esau.

#	Ch./Verse	The one(s) who "came out" of
1	1:1–2:3	The Creation of Heaven and earth = Adam
2	2:4–4:26	Adam = Adam's descendants
3	5:1–6:8	Adam's descendants = Noah
4	6:9–9:29	Noah = Noah's sons
5	10:1–11:9	Noah's sons = Shem
6	11:10–26	Shem = Terah
7	11:27–25:11	Terah = Abram/Abraham who by Hagar was father of Ishmael, and by Sarah was father of Isaac.
8	25:12–18	Ishmael = his twelve sons, who with Ishmael are outside the covenant relationship with God.
9	25:19–35:29	Isaac = Jacob and Esau
10	36:1–8	Esau inside of the Promised Land
11	36:9–37:1	Esau outside of the Promised Land (outside the covenant)
12	37:2–50:26	Jacob = his twelve sons, the twelve patriarchs of Israel, who are inside the covenant relationship with God.

The Bible and chronology

It may seem strange that in Genesis 24 Abraham seemed like he was near death and then Genesis 25 tells us that he married again and had six more children with his new wife, Keturah. This must have taken a decade or two at least. Shouldn't Abraham be dead by now? Strictly speaking, Abraham was 140 years old when Isaac married Rebekah (see Gen 21:5; 25:20) and he didn't die until 35 years later (see Gen 25:7), so maybe this 35 years is the time in which he married Keturah and raised and sent away six sons. Whatever the case may have been, what you should note at this point as a general principle of reading the Bible is that the order of presentation is not always strictly chronological. In other words, just because chapter 25 comes *after* chapter 24 on the paper, it does *not* necessarily mean that the events described in 25 came after the events described in chapter 24 in history. The events described in chapter 25 are organized together not because they all came immediately after the events in 24, but because they all fit together under the same topic or subject.

The important topic is this: which of Abraham's sons has (and which do not have) the covenant that God gave to Abraham? The whole point of telling us about Abraham's other wife and their children is just so that we know that there are a total of 8 sons that Abraham has. The seven who do not carry on the covenant are followed in this chapter by the eighth who does. And of course, you remember God spoke to Abraham eight times and that Isaac WAS the sacrifice that called down the superabundant eighth promise from God to Abraham. So here he is shown to be the special "eighth" son, the one in whom the covenant finds new life in the world and through whom the world will find new life in the covenant.

So again, the order in which events are presented in the Bible is chronological overall, starting at the beginning of time in Genesis 1:1 and going up to (and a little beyond) the end of time in the last book of the Bible—Revelation. However, in particular places it departs from strict chronology in order to make some other point. It will sometimes look ahead to the future, and then back up to the past, and then return to the present story. We do this all the time in our own speech when we talk about things, so it shouldn't surprise us that the Bible does it too. In the Bible, the Word of God becomes like human words in every way but error, just as Christ became completely human in every way but sin.

Some people get upset by this because they think that it means that the Bible is unhistorical, but this really isn't the case. The Bible is telling a history overall, but telling the history is not its ultimate purpose. In fact, in the middle of one of the books that seems *most* like a history book in the Bible (the books of Kings), the author even tells the reader that if what they are looking for is mere history, then they should go look at some other book! (1 Kings 14:19, 29, and many others). The ultimate purpose of the Bible, as you already know, is to reveal God. So, if the presentation of the history needs to be rearranged in order to better accomplish the revelation of God, then that's what happens. In the Bible, history serves theology (the knowledge of God), and theology serves liturgy (the worship of God).

This principle is true within one book of the Bible, such as Genesis, and is even true of whole books. Amos comes after Joel in your table of contents, but this does NOT mean necessarily that Amos came after Joel in history (he actually came before). We will clarify these things in detail as we get further into the Bible, but for now just remember the basic principle: in the Bible the order of presentation is not always strictly chronological.

We will see one more example of this in this lesson when we look at Genesis 26, which records the testing of Isaac. There we have another account of the wife-sister story, only this time with Isaac and Rebekah, where he is able to pass off his wife as if she were his sister and as if they were not married. This would have been impossible if they had already had children. But their children are born in Genesis 25 and then in Genesis 26 they don't have children yet. Why? You know the answer: in the Bible, the order of presentation is not always strictly chronological.

A man of patient prayer

In Gen 25:21, we are told that Isaac prays. In biblical stories, the first thing mentioned about a person often has a special importance. We have already seen Isaac out "meditating" in the field and now, before we are even told WHY Isaac is praying here after the *toledoth* that introduces his story, we are simply told THAT he prayed to the Lord. We then find out that he prayed for Rebekah, because she couldn't have children. From there the story goes on very quickly to other things, but we should notice one more thing about Isaac's prayer that isn't so obvious. Skip ahead a few verses to Gen 25:26. There it says "Isaac was sixty years old" when Rebekah gave birth to the children that he had prayed for. So what? Well, how old was he when he married Rebekah? He was forty years old (see Gen 25:20). That means that he didn't just say a prayer one day for Rebekah and the next day she conceived. It means that *he prayed and prayed and waited and waited patiently for twenty years!* This is an example of how seemingly insignificant details, such as Isaac's age when he married Rebekah, or his age when the children were born, are put into the story with a purpose.

Isaac and Rebekah have twin boys

God hears his prayer and Rebekah conceives twins. In Hebrew the first word of the story that talks about the boys who will be Jacob and Esau is a verb that means "and they struggled." The twins wrestle back and forth around inside of her so much that she doesn't understand why this is happening to her. So she goes to ask the Lord for an answer. He answers:

> Two nations in your womb,
> And two peoples, from your body, shall be divided
> But one people shall be stronger than the other people,
> And the elder shall serve the younger. (Gen 25:22–23)

As we will see a little in this lesson, and a *lot* in the next two lessons, struggle and strife will be the main theme of Jacob's life—not only his struggle with his "older" brother, but with just about everyone else in the story, including God. This contrasts strongly with his father Isaac, who relies more on prayer, and who refuses to strive and contend with people, even when they deserve it.

Nevertheless, Jacob is the one chosen by God, before he is even born, to be the bearer of the covenant made with Abraham. In the stories thus far, we have been mainly concerned with righteous people who choose God, such as Noah, Abraham, and now Isaac. There is however, another side to how God works with people. Sometimes there are people who, at first, are not that interested in God or in being chosen by Him—but God chooses them anyway. In a special way these people reveal the goodness and patience and power of God. We will see what happens with them in the story of Jacob, but also with Moses, and again with Jonah the prophet and others. So, although it is true that to be righteous one must make a deliberate choice to follow God, it is also true that even this deliberate choice is a gift that comes from God, who chose us first (see, for example, John 15:16).

This does not mean that if we don't feel like choosing God or find it too hard to be good then we can just excuse ourselves from the effort while we ignore God and ignore being good and wait around for Him to "choose us" and make us righteous. That's called laziness and God hates it. (For a view of what God does with lazy people, take a look at Matthew 25:26-30). What it means is that sometimes, as with many of the saints, God has to work on them for a while before they choose Him.

"Hairy" and "heel-grabber"

When the boys are born, the first one comes out all reddish looking and hairy. Then your text will say, "So they named him Esau." And your response should be "I don't get it." But now you will—once you learn a few things about Hebrew names.

1. In biblical stories, children are often named from something that happens on or around their birth.

2. A person's name often shows their character, who they are, what they are like, or what they will be in the future.

3. Hebrew often plays with the spellings or the sounds of words when they are similar or the same, connecting two or more words in this way to make a point. The same is true of Hebrew names.

4. Sometimes the Bible will even change the obvious normal meaning of a word or name in order to surprise the reader and make him pay attention to the new meaning being given to the word or name in the story.

This may sound a little confusing, but it's not really that hard once you know the Hebrew words. As a play on words, it is actually kind of fun, and teaches something important at the same time.

In the case of Esau, there is a similarity between the way his name sounds and is spelled in Hebrew and the Hebrew word for "hairy." Gen 25:25 would sound something like this in Hebrew (use classical pronunciation for words in caps):

> The first came forth all reddish,
> all of him like a cloak of SE-AR,
> so they named him ES-AU.

So, even though the first three letter-sounds are not in the same order, they are close enough that the connection is made between SE-AR (hair) and ES-AU (Esau).

After Esau, it is Jacob's turn. He comes out of the womb, grasping his older brother by the heel (*aqev*), so they give him the Hebrew name YA' AQOV, which means "he grabs by the heel" or "heel-grabber."

It might seem laughable to name your children "Hairy" and "Heel-grabber" and there certainly is an element of humor here, but the ultimate purpose is something much more serious. God said to Rebekah that the younger, or second-born, would be the chosen one, but here young Jacob has been wrestling with his brother in the womb in order to come out first. Despite his efforts, he comes out second, but grabbing his brother by the heel. The last time Genesis used the word "heel" was in Genesis 3:15 and it was used to describe the action of the Serpent: "You will strike at his heel." So it is a little scary and surprising that the younger, the one God has chosen, Jacob, not only grabs his brother by the heel, but is even named "heel-grabber." How is God going to take "heel-grabber" and make him into the one takes hold of the covenant instead of people's heels? Well, you will see much more of Jacob, and God, in the next two lessons. Jacob may be a "heel-grabber" even toward God, but God, as Jacob will find out, is much tougher to handle than Esau.

Selling of the birthright

The next scene is from the early life of the two boys, who are already complete opposites. Esau is an outdoorsman (like Ishmael) while Jacob is "indoors" in the tents, helping his mother cook. Isaac loves Esau because of the good meat that he brings in from hunting, but Rebekah loves Jacob and we aren't told why—perhaps because of what the Lord had told her earlier about the younger of the two.

One day Jacob is fixing some stew when Esau (who didn't catch anything while out hunting) comes in hungry. He is so hungry and the reddish stew that Jacob is fixing smells so good, that Esau can't even manage to speak correctly to ask for it. A very literal translation of the Hebrew sounds like this:

> And Esau said to Jacob, "O please! Let me feed from the red—that red! (*ha-adom ha-adom*), for I am famished!" Thus he was called Edom.

Jacob is very quick with his answer: "First sell your birthright to me."

What is a birthright?

If you are asking that question, you are asking exactly the question that the author of this story wants you to ask at this point. The birthright is one of the great keys that unlock much of the mystery in Scripture. Some of what follows you can already see from the firstborn/second-born stories of Cain and Abel, Shem and Ham, Ishmael and Isaac. The rest of it will become clearer in the life of Jacob and his sons and the people who come from them.

A birthright is also called the "right of the firstborn." In Hebrew, the word is spelled only slightly different than the word for "blessing." Birthright = *bekor* and "Blessing" = *barak*. When it was originally written Hebrew didn't use vowels, which makes the two words even more similar—*bkr* and *brk*. We will see that the two ideas are connected.

The birthright is that which gives the one who has it the special blessings and responsibilities of the firstborn.

The blessings are: a double portion of the inheritance, material and spiritual (Deut 21:15-17). The responsibilities are: leadership and management of the household, material and spiritual. The firstborn because he is the first and best, belongs to God in a special way (Exodus 22:28-29). He is the representative of the father of the household and when the father dies, he becomes the new head of the household. He is a kind of priest in the family who goes between God and the other family members (see Numbers 3:11–13). As such he is a redeemer and intercessor for those of his household who are imprisoned, enslaved, or in trouble. And he is a revealer of God's will. These qualities should remind you of virtues we have already seen Abraham. If not, go back and review lesson 6.

There are two main reasons that the *bekor* frequently ends up being a matter of contention and fighting. The first is that the son who has the right of the firstborn gets a double portion of everything that his father owns. The second is that he will be his father's heir, having charge of the household. So, if Dad has 33 sheep and a household, the *bekor* will get 22 of the sheep, plus take over the management of the household. The other son would get 11 sheep and that's it. We have already seen some of this contention in the story of Isaac and Ishmael, who were *both* firstborns, in a way. This is why Sarah did not want Ishmael around.

But there is *much* more to being a firstborn than simply being in charge of everyone in the household and getting a double share of the goods. Problems happen when those who are the firstborn do not have a complete understanding of what it really means. They think mainly of the goods and the power, and fail to think about the responsibilities, or think about them imperfectly. The firstborn is supposed to be the leader, the ruler among his brothers, but also their servant and helper. He is exalted, but in order to serve others humbly. He has special rights and material goods but they are not for himself, but rather for the sake of fulfilling his special responsibilities, especially his spiritual ones, toward the members of the household. Most importantly, *all* of his other duties are for the sake of his main duty of being the one who stands between God and the other members of the household.

Ultimately God doesn't care who happened to be born first, but is rather looking for someone who will act like a good firstborn even if he isn't strictly speaking the firstborn. We saw this already in that God favored the offering of Abel, who was actually second-born, but acted like a firstborn should act. And He favored Isaac, who was Abraham's second son.

In brief: the birthright or right of the firstborn gives the bearer a special relationship with God and a special place of self-sacrificial servant-leadership in his household. His most important roles are the roles of leader, priest, redeemer, intercessor, and revealer.

With all of this in mind, two things should come clearly into focus for you as you read the rest of the story of Jacob's buying of the birthright.

1. As the narrator of the story says, "Esau despised the birthright." He didn't care about all of that responsibility or even the blessings. He wanted to satisfy his hunger now and didn't care about the future or responsibility: what good is a birthright?

2. Jacob certainly thinks more highly of the birthright than Esau, but does not really seem to want it for the best of reasons at this point in his life. Esau despises the birthright for a pot of stew, but Jacob is the one who buys it for the same price. As mentioned above, it often happens that someone wants to be the firstborn, but for imperfect reasons. Jacob, even though he is the chosen one, has a long way to go at this point before he is seeing things as a true firstborn does.

The testing of Isaac (Genesis 26)

All of the patriarch are tested by God. Isaac, we could say, already was tested in that he WAS the sacrifice Abraham (almost) offered. But now he is tested not in obedience to his father, but directly in obedience to God. Genesis 26 shows us Isaac's test. There is another famine in the land, like there was in Abraham's time. So Isaac begins to do as Abraham did—travel southwest, through Gerar, to Egypt. Egypt, you will remember is less prone to famine because its agriculture is based on the Nile river, not rain. But when Isaac gets to Gerar, God appears to him and commands him *not* to go down to Egypt, but to stay in the Promised Land.

This may not seem as drastic as Abraham's test, but in reality it is every bit as intense and in some ways more difficult. Isaac, a sojourner in this land, must stay in a land that is in the midst of a severe famine and simply trust that God is going to take care of him and his household. At this point, we have gone back to a time before Isaac even had children, so Isaac also has to wonder how he will ever have descendants if he dies in this land of famine—or (as we will see soon) if he loses his wife. His test is not a quick sacrifice of an individual, but rather the slow, long, enduring offering of himself, his wife, and his servants in a time of famine and strife.

God then gives Isaac a seven-part blessing. Each of the patriarchs, the first time God speaks to them, receive a seven-part blessing. You have already studied Abraham's. Isaac's goes like this (Gen 26:3-4):

- I will be with you
  - And I will bless you
    - For to you and to your descendants I will give all these lands
      - And I will fulfill the oath which I swore to Abraham your father
        - I will multiply your descendants as the stars of heaven
          - And will give to your descendants all these lands
            - And by your descendants (Seed) all nations of the earth shall bless themselves because Abraham obeyed my voice...

This seven-part promise is a basic outline of Isaac's life as related in Genesis 26, as God fulfills, either in fact or in promise, each of the seven promises He made. The first three focus on Isaac, the fourth and centerpiece focuses on Abraham, the last three focus on Isaac's descendants.

Promise	Fulfillment
1. *I will be with you*	Gen 26:6–11 God protects Isaac and Rebekah among the pagan foreigners.
2. *And **I will bless you***	Gen 26:12 "**The Lord blessed him** and the man became rich . . ."
3. *For to you and to your descendants I will give all **these lands***	Gen 26:22 "For now the Lord has made room for us and we shall be fruitful **in the land**."
4. *And I will fulfill the oath which I swore to **Abraham your father***	Gen 26:24a "I am the God of **Abraham your father**; fear not for I am with you and will bless you..."
5. *I will **multiply your descendants** as the stars of heaven*	Gen 26:24b ...and **multiply your descendants** for my servant Abraham's sake."
6. *And will give to your descendants all these lands*	Gen 26:26–28 "Let there be an oath between us and let us make a covenant with you..." (This meeting between Isaac and Abimelech shows that Isaac is so great that his descendants will also possess this land even as the current inhabitants have agreed to leave Isaac "in peace" in the land.)
7. *And by your descendants **all nations of the earth shall bless themselves** because Abraham obeyed my voice*	Gen 26:29 "You are now the **blessed** of the Lord." (Abimelech representing all nations, recognizes God's blessing of Isaac, also in Gen 26:28.)

Promise #1: I will be with you

We then get yet another version of the wife-sister story that we saw twice in Abraham's life. The first wife-sister story happened the first time Abraham left the land and went down to Egypt because of a famine (Genesis 12). The second one happened in Gerar (Genesis 21). This one also happens in Gerar again. We tend to gloss over the story and fail to appreciate the serious danger Isaac and Rebekah were in, living among foreigners. Nevertheless, God is "with him" as He promised, to protect him.

Promise #2: I will bless you

Because God is with him, this wife-sister story ends with similar results—the Lord blesses Isaac and he becomes very wealthy. The Philistines, among whom Isaac is living, become jealous of his wealth. Apparently they had also envied Abraham, because as it mentions here, they had filled up with dirt all of the wells which Abraham had dug.

Promise #3: I will give you the land

Isaac sets out and re-digs them. Three of them are mentioned here. Isaac's servants dig a well, the people of the place quarrel with him over it, so he goes somewhere else and digs again. Then they quarrel with him again and he moves again and digs again. The wells are all named, like children, for something that happened around each one. Finally they find water and the people don't quarrel with him and so he says: *"Now the Lord has made room for us and we shall be fruitful in the land"* (Gen 26:22).

God has fulfilled His promise again.

Here we see that Isaac's concerns are the same as Abraham's—the land and the descendants. We also see his generosity versus the envy and selfishness of the Philistines. It is not surprising that a famine caused by drought leads to fighting over water. What is surprising is that Isaac refuses to fight, even though the Philistines themselves admit and see plainly that "you are much mightier than we are" (Gen 26:16). He is generous with the water as with everything. His generosity leads to even greater wealth and blessing to himself and others.

Promises #4 and #5: Because of Abraham, I will multiply your descendents

The Lord appears to him just after this, encouraging him in his perseverance and generosity. Here God promises again—because of Abraham—the things He promised to Isaac at the beginning of chapter 26—I will bless you and multiply you, because you are the heir of the covenant I made to Abraham. Isaac responds by building an altar and calling upon the name of the Lord, a formal act of worship.

Promises #6 and #7: Your descendents shall possess the land and all nations will bless themselves by your descendents

It is just after this second encounter with God that Isaac's servants dig another well, the fourth mentioned. The same well is mentioned in Gen 26:25 and again in Gen 26:32-33. Sandwiched in between these two mentions of the fourth well is another story about Abimelech and Phicol coming to make peace with Isaac (Review Gen 21:22-32). Just as they had with Abraham, these powerful pagans still recognize that Isaac is "the blessed of the Lord" (Gen 26:29) and that their own happiness and well-being depends on being friends with him.

Just as the river split and became four at the Garden of Eden to symbolize intimacy with God as the source of life for the whole world, so these four wells dug by Isaac do the same. As Isaac re-digs the wells, he is reopening the blessing given to Abraham, the blessing that most importantly includes the blessing of all nations, who are represented by Abimelech and Phicol. Ultimately, all earthly power is subject to divine power, whose earthly representative is Isaac at this point. Even the pagan State finds its own blessedness in a covenant relationship with the man of God, Isaac, the leader of God's people on earth (Gen 26:28-31).

Conclusion of chapter 26

It would have been *much* easier for Isaac to go down to Egypt and wait for the famine to end before returning to Canaan. But in obedience to the desires of his father and the command of God, he remains. This was his test. If he had not remained, he would have suffered less, but the Philistines, despite their envy and ingratitude, would have had even less water. Isaac's willingness to obey God and suffer turns out to be for his own blessedness and the blessing of those around him. Abraham offered Isaac; Isaac offered himself and his wife and his future. Because Isaac believed in the (seven) promises of God, he becomes a source of promise and blessing to the world.

This chapter finishes with a brief mention of Esau's behavior. Just before chapter 26 we hear that "Esau despised the birthright." Just after it, we see Esau again showing that he is unworthy to be the bearer of the covenant. He is doing exactly what Abraham forbade Isaac to do—marry a Canaanite. Except that Esau is marrying not one, but two Canaanites. This is the second strike against Esau. Next lesson we will see the third and final strike. And then he is out.

Summary

In this lesson you have learned how the human details of the life of Isaac are all ordered toward revealing how God is carrying out His plan for the world, now through Isaac. Just as Abraham had his test, so now Isaac has his. He, like Abraham, obeys, and thus becomes a source of blessing for the world. You also learned that Jacob will carry on this hope for the world after Isaac, but that he has a long way to go before he has the complete understanding of what it means to be a firstborn. You have learned that the "birthright" or "right of the firstborn" gives the bearer a special relationship with God and a special place of self-sacrificial servant-leadership in his household. His most important roles are the roles of leader, priest, redeemer, intercessor, and revealer. You have learned some basic principles for better understanding (1) the relationship between the Bible's order of presentation and chronology and (2) Hebrew names of people and places as they occur in the Bible.

In our next lesson, you will see the life of the man named "Heel-Grabber" and how God works to change him into someone ready to bear the name of God's "firstborn son" who is Israel. (If you want a sneak preview, see Gen 35:10 and Exodus 4:22!)

Questions

1. What is biblical typology?
   Biblical typology is the study of how the things of the Old Covenant participate in and anticipate the greater things of the New Covenant.

2. What is the typology of Isaac and Rebekah?
   Isaac, the beloved son offered by his father for the blessing of the world, is a type Christ. Rebekah is a type of the bride of Christ, the Church.

3. Are the books of the Bible in chronological order?
   The books of the Bible, and even parts of books, are not in strict chronological order, though overall they do follow chronological order.

4. What are the major features of Genesis thus far?
   Thus far, there have been five major features of Genesis:
   1. The 7 days of creation (= God's perfect good)
   2. The 7 sins of creatures (= creatures' "perfect" evil)
   3. The 7 punishments for sin (= God's perfect justice)
   4. The 7 + 1 times God speaks to Abraham (= God's superabundant mercy, blessing, and new life)
   5. The 7 promises to Isaac (God's redemption)

Lesson 8

The Story of Jacob

This eighth lesson covers the main part of the life of Isaac's son Jacob. Last lesson we saw how God has to work in order to mold Jacob into a good "firstborn son" who will carry on the Abrahamic covenant. In this lesson we will see the continuation and completion of the drama whereby Jacob is changed into a more perfect receiver of the covenant and how he becomes the father of God's chosen people, the Israelites. God elects Abraham, redeems Isaac, and now we will see how He sanctifies Jacob.

The story of Jacob is a masterpiece of biblical literature and the spiritual life. It records the drama by which Jacob at first resists, but eventually comes to accept, the God of his fathers as his own God.

Jacob comes to the covenant because his father Isaac did, just as many of us are a part of the Catholic Church simply because our parents are. This may be fine for the beginning stage, but there comes a time when each of us must get serious about what we believe and make a decision of our own—are we with God or against Him? Are we just interested in God because we want Him to do things for us, or are we really on God's side, and interested in doing God's work in the world? If you haven't thought about these questions or made that decision yet, I hope the story of Jacob will move you to do so.

Chiasm and the life of Jacob

Jacob's story is beautifully organized in a structure called a "chiasm." You have already learned the importance of structures in general with the *toledoth* refrains. We talked about how knowing these structures is like having a map of the Bible or the particular story you are reading. Knowing the structure allows you to see the whole all at once and to see how the parts fit together into a beautiful whole. A chiasm is one of those structures. It occurs frequently throughout the Bible and is actually one of the ways the entire Bible and even the whole history of Salvation is organized (more on this later).

Chiasm (sometimes called *chiasmus*) is a name that comes from the Greek letter *chi* which looks like the English letter X and is pronounced like "kie" (rhymes with "pie"). Because the two bars of the X cross each other, "chiasm" means "a crossing" and refers to how different parts of a story or poem "cross" each other. The basic idea behind a chiasm is symmetry: one part of the story "matches" another part of the story, as your left hand matches your right hand, your left foot your right foot, and so on. They are not the same, but they are similar. In a story this means that the first part is like the last part, the second part is like the second-to-last part, the third part is like the third-to-last part, and so on, until you reach the center part. For example, the parts of a story could be shown as in the box to the right.

A		
	B	
		C
	B'	
A'		

As you might expect, the pairs made by this structure are supposed to be compared to one another. Part A will help you understand part A' and vice versa. B will help with B' and so on. The center part, then, is the event on which the whole story turns, like a wheel on its axle. Thus, a chiasm does two things: it organizes the story and it helps to interpret the story, by comparing one part of the story to its counterpart and showing us the important turning point or center of the story. A chiasm is also a natural pattern in nature and life—sunrise is like sunset, going out is like coming back, and so on.

You have already encountered more than one of these structures in your reading. As we read further, you will begin to see even more. The following is an example of a chiasm from the story of Noah. Take a few minutes with your Bible open to Genesis 6–9 and find and compare these passages.

Chiasm of the Noah Story (Gen 6:9–9:29)

A. Noah is righteous; he has three sons 6:9-10
  B. The command to make the ark 6:11-16
    C. I will bring a flood of waters. 6:17
      D. I will establish my covenant with you; take two of every animal 6:18-20
        E. Command to store up food 6:21-22
          F. Go into the ark; take 7 pairs of every clean animal 7:1-3
            G. In 7 days I will send rain 7:4-5
              H. Noah and sons enter the ark and after 7 days, 7:6-10
                I. Record of the day they and all the animals entered; 7:11-16
                  J. The Lord shut the ark 7:16

     K. The flood continued 40 days 7:17
      L. Waters increased, covered the mountains 7:17–18
       M. All flesh died; waters prevailed 150 days 7:21–24
        N. But God remembered Noah 8:1
       M'. God blows a wind over; waters abated 8:1–3
      L'. Waters abated until mountain tops are seen 8:4–5
     K'. After 40 days 8:6
    J'. Noah opened the window 8:6
   I'. Noah sent birds out of the ark 8:7–9
  H'. He waited 7 days, and sent birds out of the ark 8:10–11
 G'. He waited 7 days, and sent the bird; she didn't return. 8:12–14
F'. Go forth from the ark; Noah sacrificed from clean animals 8:15–22
E'. God gave Noah all the animals as food 9:1–7
D'. Behold, I establish my covenant with you and every creature 9:8–10
C'. Never again will I flood the whole earth 9:11–17
B'. The sons of Noah went forth from the ark 9:18
A'. Noah curses one son, and Blesses the other two 9:20–29

So, you can see how the parts match up and make the whole symmetrical. You can also see how the center of the story is the important turning point—the fact that God remembered Noah. Now let's look at the chiasm of the Jacob story.

Chiasm of the Jacob Story (Gen 25–36)

Genealogy of the Unchosen Son (Ishmael) (25:12–18)
 A. Beginnings. Birth, God's promises, Jacob and Esau divided (25:19–34)
  B. Isaac relates to the people in the land of Canaan in peace (Gen 26)
   C. Jacob obtains the blessing—"He took away (*laqah*)" (Gen 27:1–40)
    D. Jacob flees from Esau into EXILE in Haran (Gen 27:41–28:9)
     E. Jacob meets God's angels when leaving the Land (Gen 28:10–22)
      F. Jacob arrives in Haran: Rachel, Laban (and Leah) (29:1–30)
       G. Children: Jacob acquires a family (30:1–24)
        H. Jacob attempts to RETURN when Joseph is born
       G'. Flocks: Jacob acquires wealth (30:25–43)
      F'. Jacob departs from Haran: Rachel, Laban (31:1–55)
     E'. Jacob encounters God's angels when returning to the Land (32:1–2)
    D'. Jacob approaches Esau (32:3–32)
   C'. Jacob returns the stolen blessing to Esau "Take back (*laqah*)" (33:1–20)
  B'. Jacob relates to the people of Canaan in violence (chapter 34)
 A'. Endings. Death, fulfillment of promises, Jacob and Esau together (35)
Genealogy of the Unchosen Son (Esau) (36)

Notice that the whole story of Jacob in this intricate pattern has a kind of "picture frame" around it. On one side of it is the genealogy of Ishmael, who has a blessing, but not the covenant, and on the other side are two genealogies of Esau who also (by that point) has a blessing, but not the covenant. These three are the last *toledoth* refrains in the book of Genesis. All that's left after these final refrains is the last "verse" of Genesis, which is the story of the last part of Jacob's life, which is mostly about Jacob's son Joseph and his brothers. (We're almost done with Genesis!) Thus, the *toledoth* refrains divide Genesis up into two basic parts. Part 1 is *toledoths* 1–7. They cover what "came out" of creation and the fall, which is, most importantly, Abraham. Part 2 is *toledoths* 8–11. They cover what "came out" of Abraham. Part of the ones who came out of Abraham have the covenant (Isaac and Jacob and Jacob's twelve sons), and part of them do not (Ishmael and Esau).

#	Ch./Verse	The one(s) who "came out" of
1	1:1–2:3	The Creation of Heaven and earth = Adam
2	2:4–4:26	Adam = Adam's descendants
3	5:1–6:8	Adam's descendants = Noah
4	6:9–9:29	Noah = Noah's sons
5	10:1–11:9	Noah's sons = Shem
6	11:10–26	Shem = Terah
7	11:27–25:11	Terah = Abram/Abraham who by Hagar was father of Ishmael, and by Sarah was father of Isaac.
8	25:12–18	Ishmael = his twelve sons, who with Ishmael are outside the covenant relationship with God.
9	25:19–35:29	Isaac = Jacob and Esau
10	36:1–8	Esau inside of the Promised Land
11	36:9–37:1	Esau outside of the Promised Land (outside the covenant)
12	37:2–50:26	Jacob = his twelve sons, the twelve patriarchs of Israel, who are inside the covenant relationship with God.

So, inside the *toledoth* refrains that record the *unchosen* sons (Ishmael and Esau) we have the story of the son who IS chosen—Jacob. Jacob is chosen for the covenant, but is more interested in the blessing. As we have already seen, Jacob is chosen by the God of his fathers before he is even born, but it will be a LONG time before Jacob returns the love that God has for him by choosing the God of his fathers to be his own God. The story you are about to read is the story of how God works patiently to change Jacob so that he will freely choose the God of his fathers as his own God. So, in the midst of the many human and even humorous details of the story, do not lose sight of the whole point of the story, which is to reveal God's grace, patience, and goodness toward Jacob and Jacob's growth toward God—mainly through suffering.

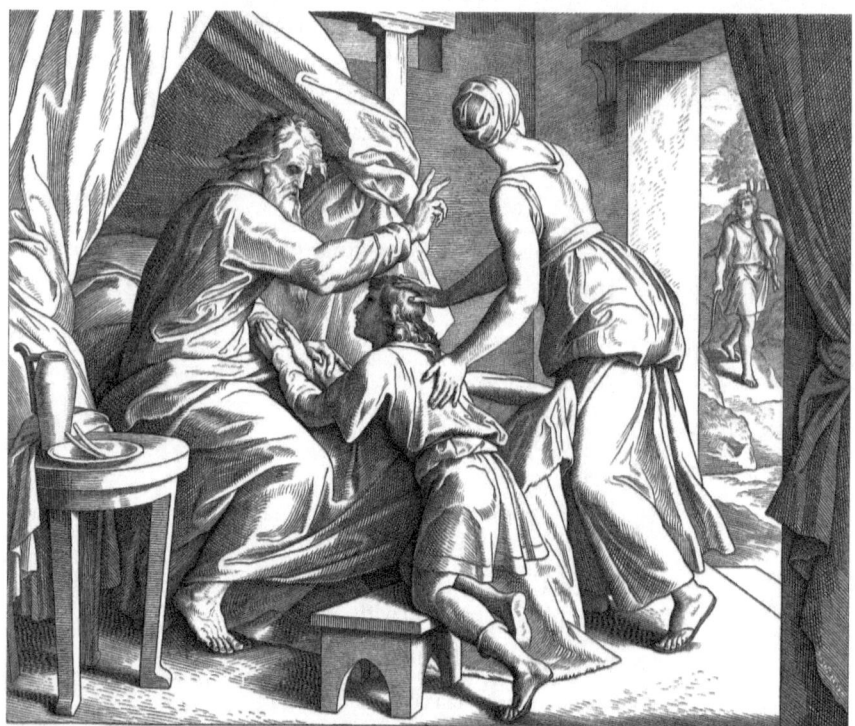

The theft of the father's blessing

We have already covered parts A and B of the chiasm in your last lesson so we will begin this lesson with part C, the theft of the blessing: Jacob obtains the blessing by guile—"He took away (*laqah*) my *beraka*" (Gen 27:1–40).

This passage of Scripture has scandalized many people over the millennia since it was written. Why? Because in it, Jacob, who is the hero of the story and the father of the Israelite people—God's chosen people—lies, cheats, and steals! This is not the kind of behavior we would expect from God's chosen one. But that is the whole point of this story—to show that Jacob is this way at the beginning simply because he does not know and love God as he ought. God has chosen him, but he has not yet chosen God.

At the encouragement of his mother (who, remember, is the only one who knows what God said about Jacob before he was born—Gen 25:23), Jacob dresses up as his brother Esau in order to deceive his blind father who wants to "bless" Esau before he dies.

Now you already know very well that there is a big difference between "blessing" and "covenant" from what we learned in Genesis 17:20-21. If you don't remember, take a minute now and go read that passage again. Anything good that comes from God can be called a blessing. Even a covenant can be called a Blessing and in the Bible it often is. In this lesson we will use a capital B for the Blessing that means a covenant, and a small b for a blessing that does not mean a covenant with God. A covenant with God has this difference—it is the highest and best of all Blessings. It makes the one who has it a source of Blessing for others rather than just a receiver of blessings from God. It's the difference between a man who owns a cup of water and one who owns a whole river and the spring that feeds the river. Do both people have water? Yes. Are both things good? Yes, both are good, but the second one is incomparably greater and better than the first. It's the difference between possessing the gifts of God and possessing God Himself, between possessing creatures and possessing the Creator (see for example, Psalm 16:5 or 73:26).

Why do we keep talking about this distinction? Because it is both difficult and extremely important to make this distinction. In fact, failing to make this distinction is exactly what Adam and Eve did when they sinned. They chose a blessing of good things rather than the best thing—a covenant friendship with God. A blessing is just good things for yourself. A covenant is friendship with God Himself. Any other blessing gives you creatures, but a covenant gives you the Creator. This does not mean that blessings are bad; it just means that a covenant is infinitely better and that other blessings are only good insofar as they come from and lead back to God. All good things will ultimately come to nothing unless they are ordered toward God, who alone endures. The covenant is better not because it gives more, but because it gives something entirely different and better. Which is better—to own a thing or to be friends with the Maker of all things?

It is difficult to know for certain what the different people in this story are thinking and exactly why they act as they do. Does Rebekah think that this blessing IS the covenant, and is that why she wants to make sure Jacob gets it? And why does Jacob want it? Is he doing this just for his own benefit? And why does Isaac, who is so close to God, want to bless Esau, who "despised the birthright"? Is Isaac spiritually blind as well as physically blind?

The best answer seems to be that Isaac never intended to give the covenant to Esau, since, indeed, only God can really give the covenant, though humans may pray for it, as we will soon see Isaac doing. But Isaac did intend to give Esau the blessing that would confer material wealth and power on him, because he saw that the more precious, but less obvious gift of the covenant was going to be for Jacob. Jacob's mother however, either misunderstands what Isaac was doing, or, she disagrees with it and wants to make sure that Jacob gets the blessing AND the covenant too!

So Jacob dresses up in his brother's clothes, puts extra hair on his neck and arms, and lies to his blind father in order to get this blessing. Just like at birth, Jacob is again trying to BE the older brother, even though God favored the younger. God doesn't care about who came out first; He wants someone who acts like a true firstborn should.

When we look at the words of the blessing that Isaac gives to Jacob-disguised-as-Esau, we can see more clearly that this blessing is *not* the covenant, but simply a blessing:

> May God give you of the dew of heaven and of the fatness of the earth and plenty of grain and wine. Let peoples serve you and nations bow down to you. Be lord over your brothers and may your mother's sons bow down to you. Cursed be everyone who curses you and blessed be everyone who blesses you! (Gen 27:28-29)

Now, this may sound alright, and it is alright as far as it goes. But what is missing? What is missing is Abraham and the key patriarchal blessings of land, descendants, and blessing to all nations! We know that this isn't the covenant because the covenant comes through Abraham and this blessing doesn't even mention him, as God did when He gave the covenant to Isaac (Gen 26:3). We know that it isn't the covenant because it doesn't promise the Land, the descendants, or the blessing to all nations. This blessing grants the receiver lots of material wealth, power, and a kind of divine guarantee of these blessings, but that's it.

From studying the chiasm above you can gain one final sign that this is not the covenant, but only a blessing. How? Well, if you compare C with C' what do you see? In C, Esau says that Jacob "took my blessing" (Gen 27:36) but then in C' we will see Jacob asking Esau, using the very same Hebrew words, to please "take back my blessing." Jacob, after he grows closer to God through suffering, gives the blessing back to Esau! So you can see how chiasms help us to interpret the story and also how this blessing cannot be the covenant given to Abraham, Isaac, and Jacob.

The covenant comes only later, when Isaac *again* blesses Jacob. But this time there is no disguise so he *knows* it is Jacob. In this different situation he says the following prayer-blessing, asking that Jacob may be the one whom God favors with the covenant:

> God almighty bless you and make you fruitful and multiply you, that you may become a company of peoples. May he give the blessing of Abraham to you and to your descendants with you, that you may take possession of the land of your sojournings which God gave to Abraham! (Gen 28:3–4)

Here we see Isaac clearly praying that the covenant (= "the Blessing of Abraham"), as distinct from the mere blessing, may be conferred on Jacob, even though Jacob has also received the blessing. It's all there—land, descendants, and the Blessing of Abraham.

All of this talk about blessing and covenants, what each is, who gave which one to whom and when, may seem confusing, so let's take a minute to summarize and clarify. There are only two things that exist, as Genesis 1 shows us. They are (1) God and (2) Creatures. Now if we ask which of these are good, the obvious answer is that BOTH are good. But, as all of the "goods" in Genesis 1 show so clearly, every good that is in a creature comes ultimately from the good that is God.

Blessing and covenant are the same in that both confer something good, but they differ as to what that good is. In the case of a mere blessing, its ultimate meaning is a good creature of some sort or another. In the case of covenant, its ultimate meaning is not a good creature, but rather the good God who made all creatures. Obviously the covenant includes creatures—the land and the descendants—but it doesn't stop there. As we have already seen, the land is for the sake of the descendants and the descendants are for the sake of the blessing to all nations. And that Blessing is nothing less than God

Himself. If someone has the covenant, he has both God and everything else. But in order to test the purity of the intentions of those who choose Him, God often makes the possession of creatures less obvious so that the person will really be choosing God for His own sake, as Abraham did, and not God for the sake of the created goods that God can give him, as Jacob is still doing. If he has a mere blessing, he may have everything else for a time, but he doesn't have God and so will ultimately lose everything.

This may seem difficult to understand, but it isn't really. We all have to make the same choice every day: do we primarily love God or do we primarily love His gifts? Adam and Eve chose themselves and other creatures over God. What will we choose? Will we choose creation or the Creator? Will we choose the gifts of God or God Himself? That is, will we choose the blessing or the covenant? This is the meaning of Jesus's words in Matthew's Gospel "Seek first the kingdom of God and His righteousness [choose the covenant] and all these other things [creaturely blessings] will be added to you besides" (Matt 6:33).

Blessing = covenant = God
blessing = good things = creatures

D. Jacob flees from Esau into *exile* in Haran (Gen 27:41–28:9)

Esau is so angry that he did not get the blessing that he plans to kill Jacob. Rebekah hears about this and so sends Jacob away to her brother's house in Haran. Isaac takes the opportunity to do for Jacob what his father did for him. He forbids him to marry a Canaanite woman and tells him to go to Haran to find a wife, blessing him with the prayer that God may give to him the "blessing of Abraham" (= the covenant). Jacob leaves, both in obedience to the command to get a wife from Haran and also to avoid Esau's wrath. In the meantime, Esau goes even further toward showing his unworthiness to be the bearer of the covenant by doing what Abraham forbade Isaac to do, and what Isaac just forbade Jacob to do. You recall from last lesson how Esau had already married two Canaanite women (Gen 26:34), now he marries one of Ishmael's daughters. This marriage signifies that Esau has allied himself with Ishmael, the one who gets the blessing, but not the covenant (Gen 17:20–21).

Esau has definitively put himself outside the covenant and Jacob is all set to be the one who receives it. But as we mentioned before, it's going to be a bit more complicated than that. God is all ready to give it to him, but Jacob is not ready to receive it.

E. Jacob meets God's angels when leaving the Land (Gen 28:10–22)

As Jacob travels and comes near to leaving the promised Land, he falls asleep in a "place" and has a dream-vision in which he sees a stairway going from earth to heaven. There are angels going up and coming down the stairway, and God Himself at the top of the stairway. The appearance of angels is to show Jacob that God is protecting him on his journey. The appearance of God is to show that God is and will be with him. The stairway is to show what God is calling Jacob to be: he and the people who will come from him are to be a stairway between earth and Heaven. The people, Israel, are the ones called to bring Heaven down to earth and to raise earth up to heaven. This is the blessing to all nations that God speaks about when He talks to Jacob.

Because the people, Israel, are called to this role of being mediators between earth and heaven, between God and humanity, and because this was most perfectly accomplished in the person of the Blessed Virgin Mary, who most literally brought God down to earth and humanity, ancient icons of Mary often show her with a ladder somewhere in the picture and the Church Fathers frequently saw in Jacob's "ladder" (or stairway) a type of the Virgin Mary.

This is the first time God speaks to Jacob, and, as with his father and grandfather, the first time God speaks, He speaks a seven-part promise:

1. The Land on which you lie I will give to you and to your descendants,
2. And your descendants shall be like the dust of the earth,
3. And you shall spread abroad to the west and to the east and to the north and to the south;
4. And by you and your descendants shall all the families of the earth bless themselves.
5. Behold I am with you and will keep you wherever you go,
6. And will bring you back to this land,
7. For I will not leave you until I have done what I have spoken to you.
(Gen 28:12–15)

First of all, notice that these seven promises divide up into two groups. 1–4 are all about the standard patriarchal blessings: Land, descendants and blessing to all nations, that is, they are about the accomplishment of God's plan for the world. Parts 5–7 are for Jacob personally.

When Jacob wakes up in the morning, he responds to God in a rather surprising way. He makes a vow and says,

1. If God will be with me,
2. And will keep me in this way that I go,
3. And will give me bread to eat and clothing to wear,
4. so that I come again to my father's house in peace,
5. then the Lord shall be my God.
6. And this stone which I have set up for a pillar shall be God's house,
7. And of all that thou givest me, I will give the tenth to thee. (Gen 28:20-22)

This might sound fine at first, but let's look at this closely. Jacob gives no attention to parts 1–4 of what God offered him—the patriarchal Blessings of Land, descendants, and blessing to all nations. Rather, he pays all his attention to parts 5–7, the personal promises God made to him. God has already promised Jacob *everything* that he bargains for in this vow, but Jacob turns the promises into something they were never intended to be. God's promise was an unconditional "I will be with you and I will do all of this for you" but Jacob's vow is a conditional "If you do all of this for me, then you can be my God." He will accept the God of his fathers as his own God only "if" he first sees God do a few things for him. Moreover, Jacob has switched things around in his seven-part response by making parts 1–4 all about himself and 5–7 all about what Jacob will do for God in return for what God will give him. The covenant offered to him out of love has been changed by Jacob into a business contract of sorts: "You do x, y, and z for me and I'll do a, b, and c for you." Jacob is still more interested in the gifts of God than he is in God Himself.

We have already seen that Jacob is something of a shrewd dealer with his brother Esau but now he tries the same sort of thing with God! While this shows Jacob's potential for a certain kind of boldness which is not entirely bad, it also shows a certain confusion on his part between blessing and covenant. God comes offering him the covenant and friendship—"I will be with you"—in answer to the prayers of his father Isaac (Gen 28:3-4) but Jacob turns it into an opportunity for himself to get ahead in the world. This is not to say that Jacob is evil, but it is to say that Jacob's understanding and devotion to God need purification and growth. (OUR understanding and devotion also need purification and growth!)

There is an old Latin phrase which St. Thomas Aquinas used from the philosophers that went like this: *quidquid recipitur ad modum recipientis recipitur.* "Whatever is received is received according to the mode of the receiver." Let's take an example. Imagine an empty cup sitting on the floor. If I pour water into the cup it receives the water in one way, making it "stand up" in the shape of the inside of the cup. If I pour the water on the floor it receives it in a different way, making it lie flat, because the floor is flat. So depending on what the receiver is (a cup or a floor), the thing (water) is received differently. Another example would be fire. If fire is received by wet wood it produces only a little heat and a lot of smoke. If fire is received by dry wood it produces great heat and glowing light!

This principle helps us to better understand what is going on between God and Jacob. The covenant is like fire when it comes from God, but Jacob is more like the wet wood at this point and the fire produces a lot of smoke. God comes to Jacob offering the greatest gift possible—Himself—to Jacob. Plus He offers this gift to the whole world through Jacob. This is the unconditional, seven-part promise He makes to Jacob. But Jacob is only ready to receive that promise in a certain way. In God the covenant is unconditional and universal (for the whole world). After passing through Jacob (a different receiver), the seven part unconditional covenant that Blesses the whole world is turned into a conditional seven-part bargain that blesses Jacob. So, as we mentioned before, God has work to do to change Jacob, His chosen receiver, into someone who can be the true bearer of so great a gift that will give warmth and light to the whole world.

Jacob renames the place "Beth-el" which means "house of God." But as God made clear in His promises—what He really wants to be His "house" is not a place or a pillar of stone, but rather a person. God wants Jacob himself, and the people who will come from him, to be His "house" on earth.

F. Jacob arrives in Haran: Rachel, Laban (and Leah) (29:1–30)

Jacob continues to Haran and meets Rachel, the daughter of his mother's brother Laban, at a well, perhaps the same well at which Eliezer had found Rebekah so many years earlier. Laban, after perceiving that Jacob is in love with his extremely beautiful daughter Rachel, offers him a job tending his herds of sheep. He can work for seven years and at the end of them he can have Rachel for his wife—or so Laban says. What actually happens is that after the seven years of work he gives Jacob his elder daughter Leah, disguised as Rachel. So Jacob marries Leah, thinking it is Rachel. When he finds out that it isn't Rachel, he is angry, but agrees to work another seven years so he can marry Rachel too.

From ancient times scholars have understood that the trick that Laban plays on Jacob here is the tool of divine justice whereby Jacob gets what he gave. He (the younger) disguised himself as the elder in order to deceive his father. Now Laban disguises his elder daughter as the younger in order to deceive Jacob. Although God isn't speaking in this part of the story, He is still active. This is all part of God teaching and changing Jacob so that he can be a better receiver of the covenant God offered him.

The two sisters, in fact, show forth the characteristics of the two kinds of blessings we have been talking about, or, the blessing versus the covenant. Jacob desires the blessing, even when God offers him the covenant. Jacob is always working and scheming to get the blessing, but the covenant comes to him as a free gift. Likewise, Jacob desires Rachel, who is more beautiful, but he is freely and unexpectedly given Leah, who is more fruitful.

G. Children: Jacob acquires a family (29:31–30:24)

It sometimes surprises people when God takes sides with Laban and Leah by favoring Leah with many children: "When the Lord saw that Leah was hated, he opened her womb, but Rachel was barren" (Gen 29:31); "and God hearkened to Leah, and she conceived and bore Jacob a fifth son" (Gen 30:17). But once we understand that the two wives, in all of their historical realism, are also theological types of the two kinds of blessings (covenant versus blessing), it makes perfect sense. In Jacob's life, God always favors the covenant over the blessing by putting it first.

The covenant also bears more abundant fruit than just a blessing. Leah bears SEVEN children.

Leah = Reuben, Simeon, Levi, Judah, Issachar, Zebulun; and one daughter: Dinah

Rachel and the two slave-girls Jacob marries (Bilhah = Rachel's maid; Zilpah = Leah's maid) all together have SIX children, each giving birth to two sons each.

Bilhah = Dan and Naphtali
Zilpah = Gad and Asher
Rachel = Joseph (and later in Genesis) Benjamin

You should be able to figure out the numerological significance of six and seven here. You should also note that all together there are TWELVE sons of Jacob, who will become the twelve tribes of the people Israel. (Do you remember the biblical numerology of twelve?)

In comparing the two sisters, one ancient scholar even saw that Rachel was called the "little" sister because she was "little" in the blessings that she brought to the people Israel. Her son Joseph ruled over the people for a time (as we will read in the next two lessons) and her son Benjamin, through his descendent Saul, also ruled the people for a time (1 Sam 9:1-2). But Leah was called the "big" sister because the Blessings she brought were "big." Through her son Judah (who is ancestor of David, king of all Israel and the ancestor of Jesus, king of all creation forever) there came an everlasting kingship. Through her son Levi there came the Levitical priesthood.

Again, this does not mean that Rachel (or the blessing) is bad, but it does mean that Leah (and the covenant) is better and that she comes first, both in time and in importance. "Seek FIRST the kingdom of God and His righteousness, THEN all these other things will be added to you besides." If part G of the chiasm shows God putting the covenant first (even if Jacob hasn't done so yet), we will see in G' that "all these other things" are added to Jacob too.

Now we can add to our earlier equations:

Blessing = covenant = God = universal = eternal

blessing = good things = creatures = personal = temporary

H. Jacob attempts to *return* as soon as Joseph, the firstborn son of his favorite wife Rachel, is born (Gen 30:25-26)

This brief notice of Joseph's birth and Jacob's attempt to return home is the center of the chiasm. We can see its importance now that we are familiar with the typology. He won't think of leaving for the promised Land until Rachel has given birth. Jacob's favoritism toward Rachel indicates that he still favors the blessing over the covenant, or that he still confuses the covenant for a mere blessing, and expects the blessing to "bear fruit" before he will return home to take the God of his fathers as his own God.

G'. Flocks: Jacob acquires wealth (30:27-43)

Because Jacob still favors the blessing over the covenant, Laban is able to talk Jacob into staying in exile and working for another SIX years, thus delaying his vow to return to God at Bethel and take the God of his fathers as his own God for another six years also. During the next six years he gains much wealth in livestock through the bargain he strikes with Laban (whose name means "white" and who gets to keep the white animals) and gets to keep all of the stronger (and speckled) animals. As we mentioned in G above, now "all these things" have been added to Jacob because God put the covenant (Leah) first, even against Jacob's desires. It is unlikely that Jacob understands this at this point.

F'. Jacob departs from Haran: Rachel, Laban (31:1-55)

Laban's sons and Laban himself get angry at Jacob because of his success in the bargain, so Jacob calls a secret meeting with his wives, who, for once, agree on something—it's time to go. So they make a secret escape with all of their belongings. Laban hears about it and chases after them. He finally overtakes them, accusing Jacob of stealing his household gods (idols). Rachel had taken the gods and is sitting on them when her father comes to look for them, so he doesn't find them. Jacob and Laban make an agreement that neither one will pass beyond this point to hurt the other. They part with an agreement, but not as friends really. Laban even says that he would have forced Jacob to come back and work for him again except that God appeared to him in a dream and told him to let Jacob go home (Gen 31:24, 29). Jacob, for his part, begins to recognize that the most important thing—more important than his possessions and even than his family—is having the God of his fathers on his side:

> If the God of my father, the God of Abraham and the Fear of Isaac had not been on my side, surely now you would have sent me away empty-handed. God saw my affliction and the labor of my hands, and rebuked you last night. (Gen 31:42)

E'. Jacob encounters God's angels when returning to the Land (32:1-2)

The angels Jacob sees here are again, as they are in part E, a message of protection for Jacob. Once again, however, it is doubtful whether Jacob understands them that way, as his fears in the next part reveal.

D'. Jacob approaches and fears Esau (32:3-32)

Jacob's fear as Esau approaches, does have one good effect: it causes him to pray to the God of his fathers for the first time (Gen 32:9-12). Though he has still not taken this God to be his own God, he has come to recognize Him and, now, to pray to Him. This is the first time Jacob prays. His father prayed for twenty years before Jacob was born; Jacob prays only after the twenty years in Haran are over!

Later that night (Gen 32:24–31), the strife Jacob has had with Esau since before he was born shows up in an even bigger strife—he wrestles with God! The person Jacob wrestles with is called both "a man" and also "God," which led the prophet Hosea to say that Jacob was wrestling with an angel (Hos 12:3-4) as a representative of God. Jacob, as always, is wrestling for a "blessing" (I will not let you go until you bless me!) but this blessing is ultimately just another wound, because what Jacob really needs is the covenant, not a blessing.

In this strange part of the story, Jacob is renamed as "Israel." In Hebrew, the word *el* is short for *Elohim*, which means "God." Many Hebrew names are composed of two parts: a verb and the word *el*, which is the subject of the verb. So all of these types of names mean "God is or has done x."

Nathanael = God has given
Raphael = God has healed

Daniel = God has judged
Gabriel = God is strong
and ... Israel = ?

Well, you would think that it means "God has wrestled/fought/contended/striven" but instead the angel says to Jacob that his name will be "Israel"...

"Because YOU have striven WITH GOD"

This is another case where a Hebrew name or word is "played with" a little bit in order to change its meaning and surprise the one reading it. Anyone who knows Hebrew and who was reading this or hearing it would expect the meaning of "Israel" to be "God strives" that is, God strives/fights for His people. But in the case of Jacob, God's people are fighting God! As long as Jacob is striving always to get the blessing, then he will be wrestling with God. Later, we will see that he gives up the blessing and any hope of the blessing, and places all his hope rather in the covenant, in his friendship with God. When he does this, he stops being "Israel" = "he fights with God" and starts being "Israel" = "God fights for him!"

C'. Jacob returns the stolen blessing to Esau—"Accept (*laqah*) my *beraka*" (33:1–20)

As we mentioned earlier in part C above, the final proof that the blessing Jacob stole from his brother in part C (Genesis 27) is NOT the covenant comes here in C'. Isaac had said in the blessing "may your mother's sons bow down to you" but here in C' it is Jacob and all his household who bow down to Esau, seven times (Gen 33:3, 6–7). So this blessing is more proper to Esau. Jacob is called to a higher Blessing, namely, the covenant. Here Jacob even gives back that earlier blessing in a way. In Gen 33:10 when Jacob is urging Esau to accept something, most modern translations have Jacob saying "accept my gift/present" but the older translations, which come from people trained in the classical tradition, more correctly show Jacob saying just what the Hebrew says, which is, "take my blessing"—the very same Hebrew words Esau used in part C when he said that Jacob "took my blessing." So at this moment Jacob symbolically gives back the blessing he stole twenty years earlier in part C. Because of this he is getting closer and closer to being ready to be a more perfect receiver of the covenant, but ... he's not there yet.

He is still afraid of Esau. He lies to Esau, saying that he will follow along after Esau and go to Esau's land of Seir (Gen 33:14). Seir is also called Edom and is located South east of the promised land. At this point we need to stop for a minute and get clear on a number of geographical points. If we don't, we will miss all the excitement of the climax of Jacob's story.

When Jacob left home, he was living in Beersheba. Beersheba is in the south western part of the Promised land. He was heading toward Haran which is northeast of the Promised Land. Directly in between these two points is Bethel, where Jacob had the dream-vision. He also promised God that he would return THERE and take the Lord as his God.

At the end of his time in Haran, God commanded Jacob to return "to the land of your birth" (Gen 31:13), which is basically sending him back along the route that he came. That route would take him right through Bethel, where Jacob would fulfill his vow of taking the Lord as his God, which is what God really wants Jacob to do.

Jacob obeys God and starts out in Gen 33:18 to return to "to his father Isaac" that is, to go back to Beersheba, and, God hopes, to stop on the way at Bethel and fulfill his vow.

All goes well until he meets Esau. Then, instead of going south west to Bethel and Beer Sheba, he lies and says that he will go SOUTHEAST to Seir. As soon as Esau is gone, Jacob turns around and goes NORTHWEST to a place called "Succoth." But wait a minute, God told Jacob to go SOUTHWEST! When he chooses to go in the opposite direction from Esau, he also goes away from Bethel and Beersheba. He eventually goes even a little further north to a place called Shechem. If we are not aware of these details we will miss the important fact that Jacob is disobeying God's command at this point. He is moving away from where God told him to go. He is moving away from Bethel where God wants him to go to fulfill his vow and take Him as his God!

Jacob seems to be aware of this problem, since he builds an altar to God in Shechem, but, as we will learn later, obedience is better than sacrifice (1 Sam 15:22). Shechem can't be a replacement for Bethel, even though Jacob seems to think it can be.

B'. Jacob relates to the people of Canaan in violence (Genesis 34)

All seems to be going well at first in Shechem, but pretty soon things go very badly. Dinah gets taken advantage of by one of the men of the town. Her brothers, Simeon and Levi, trick the men into getting circumcised, and, while they are still in pain, take their swords and go into the town and capture or kill *everything* and *everyone* (Gen 34:27-28). Jacob is extremely angry at Simeon and Levi for doing this and says to them:

> You have made me odious to the inhabitants of the Land, the Canaanites and the Perizzites; my numbers are few, and if they gather themselves against me and attack me, I shall be destroyed, both I and my household. (Gen 34:30)

This reveals that Jacob is now almost totally surrounded by enemies.

To the NORTHEAST there is uncle Laban, to the SOUTHEAST there is Esau, to the SOUTHWEST there are the Perizzites and to the WEST are the Canaanites. He is temporarily safe in Shechem, which has been completely destroyed, but everywhere else he looks, he sees enemies. In fact, the very center of all of these enemies is not the place where he IS, but rather the place where he was supposed to have gone ... BETHEL.

This contrasts sharply with how peacefully Jacob's father was able to deal with the other people round about him, who recognized him as "the blessed of the Lord" because he was obedient in going and staying where God told him to (Genesis 26).

- As soon as we see all of this violence and death and sorrow,
- As soon as we see that it was caused by Jacob's disobedience,
- As soon as we see that his disobedience was his NOT returning to BETHEL to take the Lord as his God,
- As soon as we see that BETHEL is now surrounded by Jacob's enemies
- And as soon as we see that BETHEL is the center of a circle of certain death for him,
- As soon as we see with Jacob that BETHEL = DEATH for him and all his household ...

What is the very next thing that happens?

A'. Endings. Death of Isaac, fulfillment of promises, Jacob and Esau together (Genesis 35)

The very next thing that happens is this: "God said to Jacob, Arise! Go up to BETHEL!" (Gen 35:1)

This is the testing of Jacob. As Abraham had to trust God with his beloved son, as Isaac had to entrust the life of his family to God's care, so now

Jacob must place himself, all of his family, his whole household and all of his wealth on the "altar" of Bethel and simply trust in God—he must give up his choice for the blessing and make a definitive choice for the covenant.

He really is in danger of death from the people of the Land. They want to kill him. The threat is real.

"A terror from God fell upon the cities that were round about them, so that they did not pursue the sons of Jacob." (Gen 35:5)

We know that God is protecting Jacob from death because we are reading it, but Jacob himself simply has to place everything in trust in God's hands, just as his fathers did. This final trial is the one that changes Jacob into the kind of man who can be a good receiver of the covenant. All it takes is a man who puts his trust in God, but he must put ALL of his trust in God.

Jacob arrives safely in Bethel and builds an altar to God (Gen 35:7). The stone that Jacob had set up in Bethel twenty years earlier was a witness to the vow that he took. The altar that he sets up now is a witness to his worship of God, a witness to the fact that he has fulfilled his vow and has (finally!) taken the God of his fathers to be his own God.

Jacob is again renamed Israel (Gen 35:10), but this time it means what it is SUPPOSED to mean = "God fights/strives." God fights for Jacob and against the people of the Land. God's protection of Jacob in this time of grave danger when Jacob trusted in Him is now enshrined forever in Jacob-Israel's new name.

When Jacob chooses the blessing he is "Jacob" the heel-grabber and "Israel" the God-grabber/wrestler. When Jacob chooses the covenant he becomes what "Israel" is supposed to be = "God wrestles/fights" for him. If we resist God, nothing we do will be any good! If we surrender to God, He will do everything for us.

At long last, Jacob finds a time of peace in his father's house as he and Esau come together to bury Isaac when he dies (Gen 35:29). The two even dwell "together" or, more literally "as one" (Gen 36:7) before they part ways forever.

Chapter 36 begins with a *toledoth* of Esau IN the land of Canaan and ends with a *toledoth* of Esau OUTSIDE of the land of Canaan. This is significant in that it shows the two sides of Esau that will become important much later in the Bible.

Esau is a type of the gentiles, that is, of the people who are NOT God's specially chosen people, that is, the people who do not have the covenant. But, as we have seen, the whole point of God's choosing one special people is so that through them He may bless the whole world, and bring the whole world into a covenant relationship with Him. The first *toledoth* of Esau inside the land, signifies the time when he will be inside the covenant (this won't happen till after Christ), the second *toledoth* outside the land signifies the time between his time and Christ when the gentiles will be outside of the covenant. (If you just can't handle the suspense, you can have a sneak preview of how "Esau" comes into the covenant by reading Romans 9:13-26.)

God speaks to Jacob seven times in his life

(1) Gen 28:13-15, (2) Gen 31:3, (3) Gen 31:13, (4) Gen 32:26-38, (5) Gen 35:1, (6) Gen 35:10-12, (7) Gen 46:2-4. The first time, Jacob's response totally lacks faith—he responds by calling God's words into question. He responds with an "If." The last time God speaks to Jacob (Gen 46:2), Jacob responds the way the prophets do, the way Abraham did. He says "Here I am!" (or, as some translations have it, "Ready!"). Jacob has gone from not being at all sure about serving God to being "ready" to serve Him. Or, as we have also learned, he has gone

from desiring to be the firstborn for the wrong reasons to being a true firstborn for the right reasons. God has shown His generosity in choosing Abraham, His power in redeeming Isaac, and now His holiness in sanctifying Jacob.

Summary

In this lesson you have learned how the often messy details of Jacob's life reveal how God patiently works to change Jacob. His goal is to make Jacob into a better receiver of the covenant so he can carry on God's plan of covenant-blessing for the world. You have also learned the importance of the distinction between the covenant and the blessing. Before he can be a good bearer of the covenant, Jacob must learn to choose the covenant, choose God, for His own sake, not for the sake of blessing. we also covered the typology of Jacob's wives as it relates to the covenant and the blessing. You learned how the choice between covenant and blessing is the ultimate choice that everyone must make— we must choose God or ourselves. Just as Abraham and Isaac had their tests, so now Jacob has had his, where he must place all of his trust in God, choosing to believe, obey, and hope in God despite everything else and instead of everything else. In doing so, he gains everything. You have also learned what a chiasm is, why it is called that, and what purposes it serves in the story of Jacob and elsewhere in the Bible. Although Jacob has taken the God of his fathers to be his own God, and has found the peace to which this leads, he still has many things to suffer as his twelve sons begin their own drama of sin and repentance and drawing closer to God, so that the covenant, and the life and light that comes from God through it, may continue to be brought to the whole world.

QUESTIONS

1. What does the name Israel mean?
   "Israel" has two meanings in the Bible, "He strives with God" or, more correctly, "God strives (for him)."

2. Why does "Israel" have two meanings?
   Israel has two meanings to signify the two ways a man can respond to God.

3. What are the two ways a man can respond to God as it relates to "Israel"?
   If a man chooses God then "God strives" for him; if he chooses anything else, then "he strives against God."

4. What is a chiasm?
   A chiasm is a symmetrical structure in which the first part is like the last part, the second is like the second to last, and so on, until the center which is the turning point.

5. Why are chiasms important in the Bible?
   Chiasms are important in the Bible because they help to order and interpret the story.

6. Why is it called a chiasm?
   It is called a chiasm from the Greek letter "Chi" = X and refers to how the matching parts of the story "cross" each other, as do the bars of the X.

7. What are the main features of Genesis thus far?
   There are six main features of Genesis thus far. They are:
   1. The 7 days of creation (= God's perfect good).
   2. The 7 sins of creatures (= creatures' "perfect" evil).
   3. The 7 punishments for sin (= God's perfect justice toward creation).
   4. The 7 + 1 times God speaks to Abraham (= God's superabundant mercy, Blessing, and new life for creation).
   5. The 7 promises to Isaac (God's redemption of his people).
   6. The 7 times God speaks to Jacob (= God's sanctification of his people).

LESSON 9

Jacob's Sons

This ninth and final lesson in Genesis covers the life of Jacob's twelve sons. It focuses especially on Joseph and Judah, and their respective growth toward complete acceptance of their role as firstborn.

Where is God?

We know that all of Scripture reveals God, and yet God speaks just once, briefly, toward the end of this last major part of Genesis, telling Jacob not to be afraid to go down to Egypt (Gen 46:2–4). So, just as we have seen before in the lives of the patriarchs, we need to be prepared to see in the very human details of the very human story of Joseph and his brothers, God's continuing revelation of Himself and the fulfillment of His plan for the world. The story of Joseph is a very dramatic and important "grand finale" that completes the message of the first book of the Bible and prepares for the second book—the book of Exodus. In all of the human details, God is secretly working out His plan for the restoration of the world and the redemption of the human race from sin and death.

You have now seen the chart on the next page so many times that perhaps you have stopped looking at it. Well, look at it one last time before we finish Genesis. The parts that are *not* shaded in signify those parts of Genesis which are primarily telling the story of those who are being prepared for or are receiving and living the covenant with God. That means, primarily (and in this order) Adam, Seth, Noah, Shem, Abraham, Isaac, Jacob and Jacob's twelve sons. Seven individuals, plus one group of the twelve sons who will come to constitute the community of the twelve tribes of Israel. (You should know the numerology of 7+1 by now. If not, go back and reread the lessons on Abraham. You should also know the numerology of twelve.)

The parts that are now *shaded* signify those parts of Genesis which give a brief notice of those who were from Abraham (and Isaac) but who did not enter into the covenant relationship with God—Ishmael and Esau. We already learned in the last lesson how the two genealogies of Esau signify the two typologies of Esau as a type of the gentiles—one where he is inside and one where he is outside of the promised Land and the covenant. Ishmael, on the other hand, has blessing from God but not the covenant with God (Gen 17:21). He has his own twelve sons (Gen 17:20) and so becomes a kind of opposite to Jacob who, with his twelve sons, is inside the covenant with God. Jacob sometimes "fights God" but eventually comes to embrace Him; Ishmael, on the other hand, is shown as one who "fights his brothers," (Gen 16:12; 25:18).

We will be seeing some of the sons of Ishmael soon in the story of Joseph.

#	Ch./Verse	The one(s) who "came out" of
1	1:1–2:3	The Creation of Heaven and earth = Adam
2	2:4–4:26	Adam = Adam's descendants
3	5:1–6:8	Adam's descendants = Noah
4	6:9–9:29	Noah = Noah's sons
5	10:1–11:9	Noah's sons = Shem
6	11:10–26	Shem = Terah
7	11:27–25:11	Terah = Abram/Abraham who by Hagar was father of Ishmael, and by Sarah was father of Isaac.
8	25:12–18	Ishmael = his twelve sons, who with Ishmael are outside the covenant relationship with God.
9	25:19–35:29	Isaac = Jacob and Esau
10	36:1–8	Esau inside of the Promised Land
11	36:9–37:1	Esau outside of the Promised Land (outside the covenant)
12	37:2–50:26	Jacob = his twelve sons, the twelve patriarchs of Israel, who are inside the covenant relationship with God.

Joseph or Judah?

We have already seen in the lives of Ishmael and Isaac, Esau and Jacob, how the most important thing in the whole world is being in a covenant relationship with God. Compared to this, nothing else matters very much. This is why, as in the chart above, you can see that most of the time and space in Genesis is devoted to talking about those who DO end up in the covenant and almost no time is spent dealing with those who do not. The Bible is not concerned with every detail of history, but only with those that reveal the "secret" history of the world—the history of how God is patiently working out

His plan to save the creature created in His image. Since the Fall of Man, we have been carefully tracing out the fragile and faint line by which God preserved the Hope of the world, one slender branch of the human family tree which will culminate in Jesus Christ, the son of God and the son of Mary.

In these stories, there is always some question as to who will be the one who receives the covenant. Now the people who first heard these stories were all Israelites, so they would have already known that Abraham, Isaac, Jacob and Jacob's twelve sons were the chosen ones. But this is precisely what would have made these stories so amazing to them. They *know* that Isaac is the chosen one—but for a while in the story it *looks* like Lot or Eliezer or Ishmael will be. Even when Isaac is chosen, it *looks* like he is going to be killed in sacrifice! They *know* that Jacob is the chosen one, but for a while it *looks* like Esau might get the Blessing. Even when Jacob does get the blessing, it *looks* like he might never choose to take the God of his fathers as his own God! Now, here again, these original Israelites would have known that Judah has a special role of leadership among the sons of Jacob because he is the ancestor of king David (and also of Jesus!). But this story is all about Joseph. Judah, when he does appear in the story, often acts like a complete scoundrel!

Rachel & Leah / Joseph & Judah

The rivalry between Jacob's wives continues in the lives of their respective children—especially Joseph and Judah. (It even continues into the history of Israel's kings and kingdoms!) Joseph is the first born of Jacob and Rachel and is clearly Jacob's favorite son, just as Rachel was his favorite wife. The sons of Jacob and Leah, on the other hand, start with Reuben, Simeon, Levi, and Judah. Reuben broke the sixth commandment with one of his father's wives, and his father heard about it (Gen 35:22). This effectively takes him out of the office of firstborn. Simeon and Levi did the evil in Shechem which Jacob saw (Gen 34:30), so likewise this takes them out of the office of firstborn. This leaves us with Judah as the next son of Jacob and Leah in line for the office of firstborn. Judah does more than enough rotten things in the beginning of this part of the story to remove himself from the office of firstborn as well. The only difference is that Jacob doesn't find out about those things. So there is some question throughout this story: Will Jacob find out about Judah's evil deeds? Will he eliminate Judah from the office of firstborn? How will Judah, who we all know becomes the leader of all the tribes and the ancestor of David, become what he is supposed to be—a good firstborn? We shall see . . .

The seven "sevens" of Genesis

One of your memory questions for the past several lessons has asked, "What are the main features of Genesis so far?" If you don't remember that one, go back and study it now. You should remember that thus far there have been six "sevens" that show the main features and the main message of the book of Genesis. With the Joseph Story, we get the seventh set of seven.

1. The 7 days of creation (= God's perfect good).
2. The 7 sins of creatures (= creatures' "perfect" evil).
3. The 7 punishments for sin (= God's perfect justice toward creation).
4. The 7+1 times God speaks to Abraham (= God's superabundant mercy, Blessing, and new life for creation).
5. The 7 promises to Isaac (God's redemption of his people).
6. The 7 times God speaks to Jacob (= God's sanctification of his people).
7. **The 7 times Joseph speaks about God (= God's reunion of His people with Himself).**

Although God never speaks to Joseph or his brothers directly in the story, Joseph does speak to his brothers seven times about God and what God has revealed to him.

1. Gen 37:5–7	Joseph's **first dream**	Joseph reveals what God is going to do, though **he does not understand.**
2. Gen 37:9	Joseph's **second dream**	Joseph reveals the timing of what God is going to do with him and his brothers; **no one understands**
3. Gen 42:7–20	Joseph's **first meeting** with (ten of) his brothers in Egypt	Joseph, having drawn closer to God through suffering, **now understands** the meaning of his earlier dreams and begins by revealing to his brothers that **God is Just.**
4. Gen 43:23–29	Joseph's **second meeting** with (all eleven of) his brothers in Egypt	Joseph continues by revealing to his brothers that **the God of their fathers is gracious and merciful.**
5. Gen 44:15–45:8	Joseph's **third meeting** with his brothers in Egypt (Joseph reveals his true identity).	Joseph continues by revealing to his brothers that **God is all powerful** and that His power is ordered toward life: "God sent me before you to preserve for you a remnant . . . It was not you who sent me here, but God."

6. Gen 50:19–21	Joseph's **fourth meeting** with his brothers in Egypt (after Jacob's death)	Joseph continues by revealing that **God is so completely good and powerful** that He even brings greater good out of the freely-willed evil actions of His creatures. "You meant it for evil, but God meant it for good . . . that many people should be kept alive."
7. Gen 50:24–25	Joseph's **fifth and final meeting** with his brothers (before he dies)	Joseph finishes by revealing to His brothers that **God will visit them and will keep His promise to reunite them to Himself** in the Land promised to Abraham, Isaac, and Jacob.

We will use these seven times that Joseph speaks to his brothers about God as our guide through this remarkable story.

1. Joseph's first dream (Gen 37:1–8)

Genesis 37:2 is the eleventh and final *toledoth* refrain in Genesis, letting us know that we are entering the twelfth and final "verse" of the "song" of Genesis. As we will see, this *twelfth* verse ends with not one, but *all twelve* of Jacob's son's entering into the covenant.

We learn in this part that Joseph is Jacob's favorite son. Because of Jacob's favoritism, Joseph's brothers hate him. Their relationship becomes strained when Joseph brings a bad report of his brothers' behavior to their father. To make matters worse, Jacob gives Joseph a special robe, probably a priestly garment, which makes his brothers jealous because this is yet another sign that Joseph is going to be the one who gets to take the office of firstborn. To make matters even worse, Joseph has a dream from God indicating that his brothers will one day bow down before him. To make matters worse still, he *tells* his brothers about this dream: "We were all binding wheat sheaves together and your sheaves all bowed down to mine." To make matters about as bad as they can be, Joseph gives the dream to them *without any interpretation*.

Revelation, even though it comes from God, still needs to be interpreted correctly. Joseph is not wise enough to interpret dreams at this point, so his brothers interpret it for themselves. Of course, they get it all wrong. Like the serpent, they can think of power only in terms of selfishness—Joseph is putting himself above everyone else so he can enslave everyone else—depriving them of life and freedom. While true that Joseph's brothers will bow down to him, it will ultimately be so that Joseph can save them from starvation and give them life!

2. Joseph's second dream (Gen 37:8–42:6)

As if things weren't bad enough already, Joseph has a second dream and tells his brother and his father the dream: *"The sun and the moon and eleven stars were bowing down to me!"*

This time Jacob tries to interpret the dream. He also gets the dream wrong, but at least is wise enough to know that there is probably more to it than what he thinks, since he keeps on thinking about it (see Gen 37:11). Jacob thinks the sun and the moon stand for himself (the sun) and his wife (the moon), and the eleven stars stand for his eleven sons. However, we will never see Jacob or his wife bow down before Joseph.

Really you should already know what the sun, moon, and stars stand for from the first chapter of Genesis. The sun, moon, and stars are for marking the passing of time (Gen 1:14). The sun and moon are two (2) and the stars are eleven (11). Well, 2 and 11 make 13 years, while 2 × 11 = 22 years. As we (and Joseph) will learn, it will be exactly 13 years before he becomes the manager of all Egypt and exactly 22 years will pass before the first dream will come true when his brothers bow down to him. Moreover, the 22 years are broken into two sets of 11 in the story—11 years before Joseph is able to interpret dreams and 11 years when he does interpret dreams.

> **Why dreams?**
> In the Bible, why does God communicate to people in dreams? The main reason this is fitting is to show the super-natural nature of what God is telling them. We dream when we are asleep. When we are asleep, our reason is also "asleep." The kind of dream that this *usually* leads to is one governed by a power that is *lower* than reason—our imagination. Most dreams are just a mix of things from our imagination. But in these cases God uses the same state of "asleep-reason" to show that a power *higher* than reason is now at work—supernatural revelation. So although in most cases dreams are subrational, God can use the same state to communicate something that is *superrational*. The "deep sleep" of Adam is the prototype of this reality in the Bible.

When Joseph tells this second dream to his brothers, it leads to a chain of events that fill up the rest of this part. It begins with Joseph at his lowest point—literally—at the bottom of a well and sold into slavery by his brothers. But these events end with Joseph at his highest point—he is put in command over all of the land of Egypt...13 years later. Though it must have looked like he had been totally forsaken by God, Joseph continues to draw closer to God through all of these sufferings, and God raises him up to a position of glory—as prophesied in his dreams.

Joseph sold into slavery

Joseph's brothers are angry, resentful, and jealous. When Joseph comes to check on them while they are away from home watching their flocks, his brothers conspire to kill him and then lie to their father, saying that Jacob got eaten by wild beasts. Reuben, to his credit, begins to act like a first born should, attempting to deliver Joseph. He convinces them to put Joseph down into the pit and plans to rescue Joseph later on and restore him to Jacob.

Judah, however, NOT acting like a firstborn should, convinces his brothers to sell Joseph to some Ishmaelites (descendants of Ishmael). Then they have the triple advantage of not having the guilt of killing him AND they get paid for it AND they can get rid of their annoying younger brother!

They dip Joseph's priestly cloak in animal blood and show it to their father, asking if he can identify it so that they can also avoid lying to him, as if this somehow makes them less guilty. As we already learned, sin is stupid.

Many a Church Father saw in Joseph a type of Christ, who was also the beloved Son of His Father, and also sold by one of His "brothers" for thirty pieces of silver. The one who sold Jesus even had the same name as the one who sold Joseph ("Judas" is just the Greek version of "Judah"; see Matthew 27:3,9).

Chapter 38 continues showing us more about Judah not acting like a firstborn ought to, and God teaching Judah through suffering. Judah and his sons do not keep the law with regard to Tamar who was married first to Judah's son Er, and, when Er died, Onan. Both of these men displease God and die as a result. This is divine justice: as a result of depriving his father Jacob of his son Joseph, God deprives Judah of two of his sons. Tamar, seeing that Judah will not give her his third son, Shelah, for a husband, takes matters into her own hands, disguising herself and becoming pregnant by Judah himself who thus fulfills the law for his sons, despite his own wishes! The twin sons born to Tamar and Judah "replace" the two sons he lost. One of them (Perez) becomes an ancestor of king David and Jesus (see Matt 1:3).

Joseph in charge of Potiphar's house

Joseph is sold to the captain of the guard of Pharaoh, king of Egypt. Then we are reminded (as Joseph no doubt had to remind himself frequently during all of this) that "The Lord was with Joseph." Because of this, Potiphar puts Joseph in charge of his whole household. Potiphar's wife wants Joseph to sin with her but he refuses. Just as his brothers used his garment to "prove" that he was dead, so she uses his garment to "prove" that he had tried to sin against her.

Joseph in charge of the prison

So Joseph is thrown into prison. But again we are reminded (as Joseph no doubt had to remind himself . . .) that "The Lord was with Joseph." As a result, Joseph is put in charge of the entire prison! While in prison, two men have dreams which foretell their future. As earlier with Joseph's dreams, they need an interpretation.

All that he has suffered has made Joseph draw closer to God than he was before. This is the mystery of suffering—since the Fall, the path to reunion with God is a path of suffering. Suffering undergone for God's sake draws one closer to God. The sign that this is the case is that now Joseph is able to interpret the dreams. As he says to these men, "Do not interpretations belong to God? Tell the dreams to me" (Gen 40:8). So, interpretations belong to God, but Joseph also belongs to God. As a result, he can interpret the dreams.

He interprets both of the dreams correctly. Pharaoh's cup-bearer is restored to his former life and position; the baker is hanged, all just as Joseph said.

Joseph in charge of all Egypt

Two years later (11+2!), Pharaoh himself has two dreams. No one can interpret these strange dreams. Joseph is still in prison. Suddenly, the Cup-bearer remembers that he had promised to tell pharaoh about Joseph . . . two years ago. Oh well, better late than never, right? So they call Joseph in and he correctly interprets the dreams. Just as in the cup-bearer's and baker's dream, and in Joseph's own second dream, the things in the dream indicate periods of time. Pharaoh's dreams indicate that there will be seven years of very good harvests, with lots of food, followed by seven years of famine, when there will be hardly any food at all. Joseph advises that they store up food during the plentiful years so that they can live on that during the famine years. Pharaoh recognizes that the "spirit of God" is with Joseph and so puts him in charge of the whole of Egypt!

We also learn that Joseph was thirty years old when he took over the management of Egypt (Gen 41:46). We also know that he was seventeen years old when he started having his dreams (Gen 37:2). So, it has been thirteen years since then (11 years, plus the two spent in prison during which the cup bearer forgot him, see Gen 41:1). Then Joseph is in Egypt for the seven years of plenty (Gen 41:47–48). So, Joseph has been away from home for twenty years when the famine begins. And two years later we have . . .

3. Joseph meets his brothers (Gen 42:1–43:22)

The land of Canaan, where Joseph's father and brothers are living, also suffers from the famine. Two years into the famine (see Gen 45:11) they are running out of food. Jacob sends all of his sons except Benjamin (Joseph's full brother) down to Egypt to buy grain to eat. When they arrive, Joseph recognizes them, but of course, they don't recognize him. The ten brothers bow down before Jacob in partial fulfillment of his first dream. As we know, Joseph is now able to interpret the dreams. It says that when Joseph saw his brothers he "remembered his dreams which he had dreamed about them."

Because he knows what the dreams signify now, he begins to work toward making the dreams a reality. His brothers have already bowed down to him, but not ALL of his brothers, as in the first dream. And the brother he most longs to see is the one who is not there—his full brother Benjamin.

So Joseph accuses them all of being spies and throws them in prison. This gets their attention and they begin to realize that they are getting divine justice for what they did all those years ago to Joseph (Gen 42:22). Joseph begins revealing God's justice to them in this way and then tells them that he won't keep them in prison—"for I fear God" which means, he is a man who acts with justice, like God does. In order to ensure that ALL of the brothers (including Benjamin) come back, he keeps Simeon in prison. He also secretly places the money they had spent on grain back in their sacks as a way of testing them to see if they will be honest and just and return it. All English translations say Joseph put their "money" back in their bags, but the Hebrew word is the word for "silver." This is a reminder to each brother of the "silver" for which they sold Joseph into slavery!

The brothers return and tell Jacob all that happened. Jacob does NOT want his other beloved son going down to Egypt—he's already lost two sons—Joseph and Simeon. But, starvation is a powerful motivator. So they return with Benjamin after Judah, who is beginning to act more like a firstborn should, promises to make sure that Benjamin returns safely.

4. Joseph meets his brothers #2 (Gen 43:23–44:14)

Joseph greets the brothers, all eleven of them bow down, and the dreams are fulfilled. Last time Joseph showed them God's justice, this time he shows them His mercy and graciousness: "Is this your youngest brother of whom you spoke to me? God be gracious to you my son!" (Gen 43:29). This time instead of throwing them in prison, he throws his brothers a feast and sends them on their way . . .with one final test . . .

The test is to see if Judah, who sold Joseph into slavery will redeem himself by his willingness to redeem his half-brother Benjamin, Joseph's full brother.

5. Joseph meets his brothers #3 (Gen 44:15–50:18)

Joseph hides his own silver drinking cup in Benjamin's sack of grain. When this apparent theft is discovered, Joseph orders that Benjamin be kept back as a slave in Egypt. But Judah intervenes. He offers to stay as a slave in Egypt in place of Benjamin, so that Benjamin can return home to their father.

Judah is now acting as a true firstborn son. He is being true to his promise to his father and he is offering his own life as a sacrifice for his younger brother.

This act of redemption is what leads Joseph to finally reveal his true identity to his brothers:

> I am your brother Joseph, whom you sold into Egypt. And now do not be distressed or angry with yourselves, because you sold me here; for God sent me before you to preserve life . . . And God sent me before you to preserve for you a remnant on earth, and to keep alive for you many survivors. So it was not you who sent me here, but God; and He has made me a father to Pharaoh, and lord of all his house and ruler over all the land of Egypt. (Gen 45:7–8)

Joseph now reveals to his brothers that God is all-powerful. He is in charge of the whole world and all that is in it, just as Joseph is in charge of all of Egypt and ordering all of its people and affairs for the sake of life. The brothers all weep for sadness at their former deeds and joy at this unexpected happiness that they have found. Joseph has come back from the dead and their sin is forgiven! (No wonder the Church Fathers saw in Joseph a type of Christ!)

Joseph sends them on their way so that they can go home, retrieve their families and possessions, and return to Egypt to wait out the famine. Jacob is assured by God (the only time God speaks in this story) that he should not be afraid to go down to Egypt because God will go with him and will bring him up again (Gen 46:3-4). So they all come to Egypt and see Joseph again. After Jacob has seen Joseph alive again, he feels that his life is complete and he is ready to die. But before he dies he does three important things:

1. *He makes Joseph promise to bury him* in the cave at Macphelah, where Abraham and Isaac are buried in the Promised Land.

2. *He blesses the sons of Joseph.* Joseph was married to Asenath, daughter of the priest of On, an Egyptian. Their two sons were Ephraim and Manasseh. In some of the lists of the twelve tribes that come later in the Bible, they are named instead of Joseph. Ephraim receives the blessing of the firstborn when Jacob crosses his hands to put his right hand on Ephraim's head. Ephraim will later be one of the names for the entire northern kingdom of Israel.

3. *He blesses ALL 12 of his sons.* All of these blessings are in chapter 49. They are in highly poetic language and are sometimes difficult to translate, let alone understand. Some of them sound more like curses than blessings, but the main point of all of them is to show that here, in the twelfth and last *toledoth*-part of Genesis ALL TWELVE of Jacob's sons are received into the covenant.

Note that Reuben, Simeon, and Levi seemed to be "scolded" more than blessed, but even in the case of Simeon and Levi, it is clear that they are still "in Israel" (Gen 49:7), which means in the covenant.

It should not surprise you too much at this point to learn that the greatest and longest blessings are given to Judah and Joseph. Judah is given a blessing primarily of kingship, ruling, leadership and Joseph primarily a blessing of fruitfulness and fertility. We will learn more about this later in the Bible, but for now you already know that Judah is the tribe from which Jesus will come and that Joseph = Ephraim. We will see later on, especially in the Prophets, how Ephraim is a type of the gentiles, from whom most of the "fruit" that is harvested for God in His Church will come. The relationship between Judah and Joseph is similar to that between St. Peter and St. John. Peter is chosen as the leader, but is far from perfect, while John is the chosen "beloved disciple."

6. Joseph meets his brothers #4 (Gen 50:19–21)

After Jacob dies and is buried, Joseph's brothers are again afraid of him. Why? Because they think that maybe the only reason Joseph was being so good to them was so that their father wouldn't be upset. But now Jacob is gone. So, Joseph reassures them all and adds to this the most important message of this story:

> As for you, you meant evil against me; but God meant it for good, to bring it about that many people should be kept alive, as they are today. (Gen 50:20)

Here, Joseph has become so close to God and so wise about God that he is able to reveal the very mind and will of God to others. Joseph knows the two great secrets of the universe and tells them both to his brothers:

1. You do have free will and the power to do evil;
2. But God has an infinitely free will and an infinite power for Good, so no evil of yours will defeat God's plans for Good.

God is SO GOOD and SO POWERFUL that He has already brought greater Good even out of evil. This leads up to the final time that Joseph speaks to his brothers, when he reveals something about what the "greater good" will be in the future.

7. Joseph meets his brothers #5 (Gen 50:22–end)

Before he dies, Joseph speaks one last (seventh) time to his brothers and their children. He speaks here to encourage and remind all of them that even though they are living and thriving in Egypt, Egypt is *NOT* the promised Land.

> God will surely visit you, and bring you up out of this land to the land which he swore to Abraham, to Isaac, and to Jacob. . . . God will surely visit you, and you shall carry up my bones from here.

So Joseph's messages to his brothers begin with prophecies about what will happen during the life of his brothers and himself and end with a prophecy about what will happen after their life is over. Here he reveals to them what God also revealed to Jacob—that God will be with them in Egypt but will deliver them from Egypt into the Promised Land.

The Church Fathers thus saw Egypt as a type of this world and our current state of separation from God. The Promised Land is a type of Heaven and of reunion with God.

The "greater good" that comes out of the evil of separation from God is repeated twice in what Joseph says: "God will surely visit you." The phrase "will surely visit" is actually the same word "visit" repeated in two different forms. Literally it would say something like "*visiting* He will *visit* you." Thus that word appears four times in Joseph's short sayings and is the major focus of what he is talking about.

The "greater good" that will come from this time of separation from the Promised Land is that God is going to "visit" His people in order to deliver them from Egypt. He is going to come to them with great signs and wonders to rescue them from Egypt and bring them to the Promised Land. The rest of the Pentateuch (and of this course) recounts how God "visits" His people in Egypt and brings them to the Promised Land.

Summary

In this lesson you have completed the story of Joseph—and the book of Genesis. You have learned how there are seven main features of the book of Genesis, each of which has seven parts. You have learned what these are and how they show the main message of the book of Genesis. God created everything perfectly good. Creatures, by turning away from God, brought evil into the world. The evil was so great that the world was filled with it. God in His justice punishes the evil but at the same time begins to work on His own plan for the defeat of evil and the victory of good, especially in the lives of Abraham, Isaac, and Jacob. Joseph, both by his life and his words, proclaims the good news that God is SO perfectly good and powerful that He brings greater good even out of evil. The greatest of all of these goods is that He is going to "visit" His people to redeem them from sin and sanctify them, and bring them back to Himself. In our next lesson we will begin the book of Exodus, in which God begins to "visit" His people to redeem them, sanctify them, and reunite them to Himself.

QUESTIONS

1. What is the purpose of the story of Joseph?
   The purpose of the story of Joseph is to reveal that God is infinitely Good.

2. How does the story of Joseph reveal that God is infinitely Good?
   The story of Joseph reveals that God is infinitely Good by showing how God brings good even out of evil.

3. What is the typology of Joseph?
   1. *Joseph is a type of Christ who*
   2. *was His Father's beloved son,*
   3. *was betrayed by Juda(s),*
   4. *was miraculously restored to life,*
   5. *was given power over all,*
   6. *who used his power to save the lives of many*
   7. *and who used his wisdom to reveal God's will to his brothers.*

4. What are the seven main features of the book of Genesis?
   The seven main features of Genesis are:
   1. *The 7 days of creation (God's perfect good).*
   2. *The 7 sins of creatures (creatures' "perfect" evil).*
   3. *The 7 punishments for sin (God's perfect justice toward creation).*
   4. *The 7+1 times God speaks to Abraham (God's superabundant mercy, Blessing, and new life for creation).*
   5. *The 7 promises to Isaac (God's redemption of His people).*
   6. *The 7 times God speaks to Jacob (God's sanctification of His people).*
   7. *The 7 times Joseph speaks about God (God's reunion of His people with Himself).*

Note: Since you have now finished the book of Genesis, the examination for Lesson 9 may include many questions and topics from earlier examinations as a way to review Genesis before we begin Exodus.

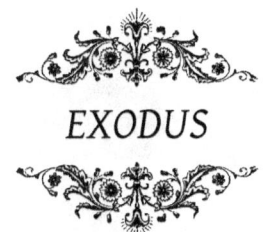

EXODUS

LESSON 10

Israel in Egypt

This lesson covers the details of how the Israelites fared in Egypt in the generations after the death of Joseph and prepares for the story of the call of Moses (next lesson) by telling of his birth and early life.

Review

In our last lesson, we completed the Book of Genesis, the first book of the Pentateuch and the Bible. It told the story of God's plan for the world by means of seven groups of seven, each of which had a major theme or point. They were: the goodness of God's creation, creatures bringing evil into God's good creation, God justly punishing evil, God having mercy, redeeming His people, sanctifying them, and reuniting them with Himself. That story takes us from Adam and Eve up through Jacob and his twelve sons and their families moving down into Egypt to be reunited with Joseph. That's the story of Genesis and also the whole of salvation history up to this point.

Exodus

The first five books of the Bible are called the Pentateuch (*penta* means five in Greek). In Hebrew these first five books are called the Torah, a word which means "law." Although Genesis does reveal God giving law and order to the universe, the next book in the Torah shows God revealing Himself and His laws to His People in a new way. The second book of the Pentateuch is the Book of Exodus. *Exodus* is a Greek word that means "to go out." The book is named this in Greek because it recounts the history of how God's chosen people, the descendants of Jacob's twelve sons, "went out" from the land of Egypt after being there for four hundred years. It records the important events of the people's relationship with God from their time in Egypt until their time at Mount Sinai in the desert, on their way back to the Promised Land. In Hebrew the book is named from the first line: "these are the names" = *shemot*. *Shemot* is a fitting title not only because we learn the names of the descendants of Jacob who were in Egypt, but more importantly because this is the book where God reveals His Holy Name to Moses.

Seventy persons, seventy nations (Exodus 1:1–8)

Back in Genesis 46:8–27 we learned that all the offspring of Jacob who came down into Egypt with him were seventy people in number. Here at the beginning of Exodus, we get a reminder of the same fact: "All the offspring of Jacob were seventy persons" (Exod 1:5). Why is this important? You already learned in Genesis 10 the numerology of seventy—in the Bible it is often symbolic of all the nations of the world. Thus, even though Israel is God's specially chosen nation, when they go down to Egypt as a group of seventy they are also a symbol of all nations, all humanity. The Israelites, in their own history, are going to repeat in miniature the history of humanity. In this story, therefore, Egypt also becomes a type of the whole world under the dominion of the devil. It oppresses God's chosen ones until He hears their prayers and sets them free with great signs and wonders.

The king who did not know Joseph (Exodus 1:9–22)

When it says next that there arose a king who did not know Joseph, it doesn't mean that this king was ignorant of his Egyptian history. It simply means that he did not acknowledge all that Joseph had done. He knew what Joseph had done—giving the people of Israel the best land in Egypt. He just didn't like it. When the Israelites followed God's first command (to be fruitful and multiply—Gen 1:28) he liked it even less. He was afraid the Israelites were going to take over his kingdom. So his first act regarding them is to make them slaves, oppressing them with hard labor building cities in the hopes of slowing them down and keeping them from rebelling and reproducing.

It doesn't work. The more they are oppressed, the more they multiply. In the early Church, the same thing happened—the Romans and others tortured and killed the Christians and what happened? The Church spread like wildfire! You can't defeat God's will and any attempt to do so only makes His will happen better. If I were the devil, this would convince me to give up. But he doesn't give up fighting against God's plan because, as we already learned, sin makes you stupid.

So, this king of Egypt tries another plan—if enslaving them won't slow them down, killing them definitely will. So, he commands the Hebrew women who help at the birth of children (midwives) to kill any sons who are born. Why not the daughters too? Because the males inherit land and they also determine the character of the family. If an Israelite woman marries an Egyptian man, she and her children will be Egyptians, not Israelites. In this way, the Egyptians could slowly but surely regain control of the land and the population, which were becoming increasingly Hebrew ("Hebrew" comes from *Eber* of Gen 11:14).

This doesn't work either, because the Hebrew midwives have the courage to obey God rather than men. God rewards them for their courage by giving each of them their own "houses" which means households or families (Exod 1:21). Pharaoh's scheme to lessen the number of Israelites has completely backfired—now there are more than ever.

Since that scheme doesn't work, Pharaoh commands all of his people to throw the sons of the Hebrews into the Nile River. Now let's see ... where have we heard of this set of events before—a bad ruler, who makes his subjects slaves, and is extremely upset when they increase in population? This is the same as in the Babylonian creation myth you read about in your first lesson—the *Enuma Elish*. In the Bible God commands the first couple to be fruitful, multiply, and fill the earth; the gods of the *Enuma Elish* hate human fertility. One thing you didn't learn in lesson 1 was that when the god in the *Enuma Elish* decides he doesn't like all the noise from the numerous humans slaves, he decides to kill them—by means of water. This is exactly what Pharaoh decides to do when he commands his people to throw the sons of the Hebrews into the waters of the Nile river. Pharaoh is acting just like the gods in the *Enuma Elish* and the Israelites are being treated just like humanity in the *Enuma Elish*.

What is going on?

What's going on is just the next step in what we already learned about the numerology of 70. The view of God and the world manifested in the *Enuma Elish* is not just in Babylon. Rather, it is the view practically all of humanity had because they were either worshipping devils directly, or their view of the true God was distorted by sin. The nations of the world, as exemplified in the *Enuma Elish*, think that the gods created them to be slaves, that the gods basically hate humanity, and that whenever they feel like doing so, they will kill humanity. So Israel, being seventy in number, is a symbol for all of humanity in this situation. They are a miniature version of humanity. Over them are the Egyptians, who are miniatures of their own gods (= devils)—enslaving and killing the Israelites. Above all of these, however, is the One God, "God Most High, Maker of Heaven and Earth" (Gen 14:19). As we will see, the fight between the Israelites and the Egyptians is a small version of the fight between God and the gods of Egypt, who will all, one-by-one, be utterly defeated by the One true God of Israel. As always, the Bible makes use of pagan myths only for the sake of correcting and completing them. So Egypt is a type of this world as it is ruled by the demons (see Ephesians 6:12); the Israelites in slavery are a type of all of humanity enslaved to sin, which makes us slaves of the devil, crying out to God to be set free.

The birth of Moses

During the period of time in which Pharaoh had commanded all the Israelite boys to be thrown into the Nile, a man and a woman from the tribe of Levi get married. She bears a son and keeps him a secret as long as she can. When she can no longer hide the baby's existence, she does what Pharaoh commanded the Egyptians to do—she puts him in the Nile! Of course, she doesn't drown him there, but rather makes him a little basket in which he can stay afloat. One interesting thing about this "basket" is that in Hebrew it is exactly the same word as "ark" in the story of Noah. Just as Noah's family in their ark kept the hope of God's plan for the world's salvation alive, so the ark that carries this boy carries the same hope. The boy's sister hides in the distance so she can watch what happens to her little brother.

Pharaoh's daughter comes to bathe in the Nile and finds the boy in his little "ark." When it is clear that Pharaoh's daughter wants to keep the child as her own, the boy's sister offers to find a woman to nurse the child for her. Of course, she just goes back and gets her mother, who is commanded by the Pharaoh's daughter to do just what she wanted—take care of the boy. Now, however, she gets paid for it, plus one more Hebrew child has slipped through Pharaoh's fingers! When the child is grown up enough, he legally becomes the son of Pharaoh's daughter. She names him "Moses" which means "drawn out" because she drew him out of the water. This is a prophetic name because through this "Moses," God will also "draw out" His own people from the powers of Egypt and the waters that would have destroyed them. Moses is thus a type of the people Israel, who will also be saved through being drawn out from the waters. Since Israel is here a type of all humanity enslaved to sin, Moses is a type of Israel, called to "draw out" all humanity from slavery to sin.

Moses's flight from Egypt

So Moses is raised and educated as an Egyptian (see Acts of the Apostles 7:22). At a certain point, however, he becomes aware that he is not an Egyptian, but rather is one of the Hebrews—the slave people. Then he sees an Egyptian beating a Hebrew. Angered by this injustice, he takes matters into his own hands, killing the Egyptian and burying him in the sand. The next day he goes out and this time two Hebrews are fighting each other. So he asked the one who was causing the trouble, "Why do you strike your fellow Hebrew?" Instead of answering Moses's question, the man says, "Who put you in charge? What are you going to do—kill me like you killed the Egyptian?" In this way Moses's learns that his deed of yesterday has been discovered. Now he is in big trouble. When Pharaoh finds out about it, he is in even bigger trouble—Pharaoh seeks to kill him. When Moses attempts to lead his people based on his own wisdom and effort, he fails. He will later receive the same mission from God and will not fail, despite the continuing stubbornness of his people. In the meantime, he will have much to suffer.

So he runs away the to northeast, to a land called Midian, modern day Saudi Arabia. There he stops to rest at a well. Just as Isaac and Jacob's future wives were met at wells, so here Moses meets the seven daughters of Jethro, the priest of Midian. The girls were all there to water their father's flocks of sheep and goats. Apparently, they were frequently oppressed by some other local shepherds (men) who wouldn't let them water their father's flocks until they had all watered theirs. Moses fares better here as a leader and deliverer. He stands up to these shepherds, driving them away and watering the flocks of Jethro himself. This deed earns him a place in Jethro's household, where he marries Jethro's daughter Zipporah who gives birth to their firstborn son, Gershom. The Hebrew word "ger" means "sojourner" or "wanderer." From this point forward in his life, Moses is going to be a sojourner—wandering back down to Egypt and wandering back again with God's people.

God remembers

Right after we learn this, this section of the story ends with:

> And the people of Israel groaned ender their bondage, and cried out for help, and their cry under bondage came up to God. And God heard their groaning, and God remembered his covenant with Abraham, with Isaac, and with Jacob. And God saw the people of Israel and God knew their condition.

That God "remembered" doesn't mean that He was so busy running the universe that He forgot about His people. It is a human way of speaking, often used in the Scriptures, where, for those of us in time it seems that God forgets about us and doesn't help us in our troubles, but rather lets us suffer. But this is not the case, of course. Rather, God knows everything. He knows what we need before we ask and He knows what we need better than we do ourselves. God frequently allows His people to undergo suffering, because only suffering causes them to turn away from selfishness and to turn toward Him. Only suffering makes them realize that without God their work is meaningless. As we saw in the story of Jacob, God has to reshape His vessel Israel so that they will be able to receive all of the great and glorious things He is about to give to them—most especially, Himself.

When God "remembers" it means that God chose to act in history (remember that the centerpoint of the chiasm of the story of Noah is: "And God remembered Noah," after which the flood recedes). Just as this part of Exodus begins with pharaoh "forgetting" Joseph, so it ends with God "remembering" the people Joseph had brought to Egypt, the Israelites.

God is about to act in history in wonderful and powerful ways that will leave the whole world amazed. But before He does we need to know two things. The first is that God's powerful action in history depends on our willingness to suffer for Him and pray to Him. If we don't see God acting in our lives, perhaps it is because we have not opened ourselves up to all that He wants of us in terms of suffering, hard work, and prayer. The second is that it is God who acts to bring these things about. Without God, we can do nothing. So our primary "work" should be to make sure we are right with God, calling out to Him in our utter need for Him, and making sure that we are doing His will.

Summary

In this lesson you have reviewed what "Pentateuch" and "Torah" mean, and have begun the second book of the Torah/Pentateuch, the Book of Exodus, by learning what the name of the book means in Greek and in Hebrew.

You have also learned more about the numerology of 70 as it applies to the typology of Israel and Egypt. You have learned some more about the *Enuma Elish* and how its view of the gods appears in the book of Exodus and is corrected by it. You have learned about Moses's early life, what his name means, and how it applies to the whole story of the Exodus. After his education as an Egyptian, Moses flees Egypt because he killed an Egyptian who was beating a Hebrew. He marries Zipporah, daughter of the Priest of Midian, and has by her a son named Gershom. You have learned the importance of the meaning of his name for Moses's life. For, as we will see in the next lesson, it is while Moses is keeping the flocks of his father-in-law that he receives his first call from the God he does not yet know—the God of his forefathers, Abraham, Isaac, and Jacob, Who will call him to begin the greatest "wandering" the world has yet known.

Questions

1. What is Exodus?
    Exodus is the Greek name of the second book of the Pentateuch.

2. What does Exodus mean?
    Exodus means "a going out."

3. Why is this the title of this book?
    This is a fitting title of this book because it records the "going out" of the Israelites from Egypt.

4. Who is Moses?
    Moses is the son of Levites, raised as an Egyptian, whom God calls to lead His people out of Egypt.

5. What does "Moses" signify?
    "Moses" means "drawn out" because he was "drawn out" of the water as a child and he will be the one through whom God will "draw out" His people from the power of Egypt through the waters of the Red Sea.

6. What is the typology of Israel and Moses in Egypt?
    Israel in Egypt is a type of mankind in slavery to sin; Egypt is a type of the world under the power of the devil; Moses is a type of Israel, called to lead all humanity into freedom from sin and life with God.

LESSON 11

Who Will Deliver Israel?

This lesson covers the increased persecution of the Israelites in the years after Moses's birth. God calls Moses to set His people free and Moses goes through a series of seven objections to God's call, but begins to deliver God's message to the Israelites and to Pharaoh.

Review

God created the world full of goodness. Mankind sinned and turned away from God and toward his own destruction. To save the creature created in His own Image, God began forming one people, Israel, through whom He would bless the whole world and offer salvation to people of every nation. That one nation, Israel, was enslaved in Egypt. Their slavery is a sign of the universal slavery to sin that all mankind is suffering. Just as God raises up one nation to save all nations, so within that one nation, God raises up one man, Moses, to save the one nation from slavery. In our last lesson, we covered the persecution of the Israelites in Egypt, the birth of Moses, how he was raised as an Egyptian, how he fled to Midian and married Zipporah, daughter of Jethro the priest of Midian. By her he had a son, Gershom. Meanwhile, the Israelites continue to cry out to God, and God hears their prayer by calling Moses and sending him to bring them forth from slavery in Egypt.

The burning bush: the call of Moses

As Moses is shepherding near Mount Horeb (also called Mt. Sinai), east of the Red Sea, he sees a bush that burns but is not consumed by the fire. He goes to see it and God speaks to him from the midst of the bush:

> Moses! Moses! . . . I am the God of your father, the God of Abraham, the God of Isaac, and the God of Jacob . . . I have seen the affliction of my people who are in Egypt, and have heard their cry because of their taskmasters; I know their sufferings, and I have come down to deliver them out of the hand of the Egyptians and to bring them up out of that land to a good and spacious land, a land flowing with milk and honey . . . Come, I

will send you to Pharaoh, that you may bring forth my people, the sons of Israel, out of Egypt. (Exod 3:7-10)

In the Bible (and in life) it is almost always the case that the person who receives God's call has some question, hesitation, or objection to what God asks of them. God doesn't come to us just to talk about the weather—He challenges us to do great things for Him and in the process often frightens us out of our ignorance and laziness. Between here and the genealogy of Moses in Exod 6:14, Moses, not to his credit, has SEVEN objections to God's call. These objections are typical excuses people have for not following God wholeheartedly. God responds to all of them, still calling Moses to perfection. Following each of these objections will take us to the end of this lesson.

Objection 1: Doubting himself (Exod 3:11)

Moses's first objection is to doubt himself—who am I to go and do all of this? God's response is as simple as it is direct: I will be with you, as if to say: "It doesn't matter who you are. What matters is that God has chosen you. What more could you possibly want? An all-powerful God is on your side!" He then offers Moses a sign that it really is God who has sent him to do this: when you have brought forth the people out of Egypt, you shall serve God upon this Mountain. Of course, to make this sign "work," Moses will first have to act in faith and actually go and try it.

Objection 2: Doubting God (Exod 3:13)

Moses began by doubting himself and continues by wondering about God: Who am I supposed to say sent me? I don't even know who you are! God proceeds to tell him who He is:

I AM WHO AM ...
THE LORD.

As we have seen in other biblical stories, someone's name does more than just stick a nametag or label on them. Their name says something about who and what that person is or will be. You have learned, just to name a few, the meaning of the names of Adam, Eve, Shem, Noah, Abraham, Sarah, Isaac, Jacob, and Moses, and how these names "fit" the person to whom they were given. When God reveals His own Holy Name, He is revealing something of His essence. This is a big moment!

So what does this name reveal about God? It reveals that God is simply the ONE WHO IS. His existence is not dependent on anything else. He just IS. You have already learned that, in Scripture, the order of events is often as important as the events themselves. So why is this a good time for God to be revealing His name to Moses? He reveals Himself at this time as "HE WHO IS" so that Moses and the Israelites can know that God and His promises do not depend on anything else, but rather everything in the world depends on Him. "HE WHO IS" means that He is LORD of everything. God is totally trustworthy! In fact He is ultimately the ONLY ONE who is totally trustworthy. Anything else can change or pass away, but God simply IS. The manner in which God chose to reveal Himself visibly to Moses also supports this. God is alive (burning) but does not derive His life from anything (the bush). He always was, and always is, and always will be. And therefore He always was and always is and always will be faithful to His promises.

> **The Name of God**
>
> When English translations say "THE LORD" usually what is behind it is the four letter Hebrew name of God. In English these letters would look like this: YHWH (in Hebrew, which goes from right to left, they look like this: יהוה). When Biblical Hebrew was written down the scribes did not use vowels, but only consonants. They simply remembered the consonants from the spoken language. If you think this sounds impossible, modern Hebrew-speakers still write this way! Because it is God's name this name is holy and mysterious. As a sign of reverence for the Holy Name of God, it became traditional to say "the Lord" or "the Name" rather than actually pronouncing His Name. When the Bible was translated into Greek about 300 years before Christ, the translators used the Greek word *Kyrie* in place of YHWH, a tradition which was carried over into the New Testament. *Kyrie* means "Lord." (You may have heard "*Kyrie eleison*" at Mass, which means "Lord, have mercy.") YHWH has a few possible interpretations, but the best one is simply "He who is." So be aware that where most English translations say "THE LORD" it is actually the Holy Name of God revealed to Moses at the burning bush.

Objection 3: Doubting the people (Exod 4:1)

Since he can no longer doubt who God is or that God has chosen Him, Moses begins to doubt the people to whom God sends him. Moses answered, "But behold, they will not believe me or listen to my voice, for they will say, 'The Lord did not appear to you.'" God responds by giving Moses three signs that he can show to convince the people that God has sent him. First, He has Moses cast his staff on the ground where it turns into a serpent. Moses sees the serpent and runs away. God then shows him how to turn the serpent back into his staff by taking it back in his hand. For the second sign, He has Moses put his hand into his garments. When he does so, God turns his hand leprous. Leprosy is a terrible disease that causes the skin and other body parts to rot, die, and fall off. God makes his hand healthy and whole again by telling Moses to remove it from his garment. The third sign God gives is just in case the first two don't work to convince the people. God tells Moses that if he takes some water from the Nile, and pours it out on the ground, it will turn into blood.

Why *these* signs?

Now why did God choose to give these signs to Moses to show to the people? Why not something more spectacular and beautiful than snakes and leprosy and blood? Just as the burning bush itself helped to reveal God as HE-WHO-IS, so these signs help to reveal what God wants to show the Israelites—that He has appeared to Moses and given him the mission to set them free from Egypt. All of the signs are rather fearful and as such are meant to move the people to fear and obey the Lord. But we can get more particular than that as the following chart shows:

Moses	Staff	Serpent	Leprosy
God	Israel	Devil	Sin

Moses is like God to the people. The staff is like the people Israel themselves. The staff is that by which Moses guards and guides his sheep. Likewise it will be that by which he guards and guides the people of Israel. And the people Israel are supposed to be that by which God leads ALL nations. When they are separate from God—cast out from God's hand—they come under the power of the serpent (the devil). Currently, they are under the power of the serpent in Egypt, but God, by taking them up again, can change them from serpent to staff again. Likewise with the leprosy—God can take that which has become diseased and dead and bring it back to life. Throughout the Scriptures, leprosy is a symbol for the soul that is separated from God by sin. As leprosy is to the body, so sin is to the soul. So both the serpent and the leprosy symbolize what the people Israel are in danger of becoming if they do not listen to Moses and God, while the staff and the healthy hand signify what they can become if they do listen to Moses and to God.

The final sign is different than the first two. It is the last of these signs and is only to be used if the other two do not convince. Moses is to take water from the Nile and pour it upon the ground, and it will turn into blood. The Nile was the life of all Egypt. Its waters, overflowing their banks and depositing the fertile silt on the ground, made the land of Egypt fruitful and prosperous. Without it, Egypt would just be a vast desert. Water upon dry ground means life for the plants, animals, and man. But if that water turned to blood it would mean death for all. This last sign warns that the destruction of Egypt is imminent and is meant to convince the Israelites that they will be doomed along with Egypt unless they leave with Moses. As we will see next lesson, the changing of the Nile into blood will be the first of the ten plagues that will destroy Egypt. Thus, these signs ensure that the people listen to Moses and give some idea of what God is going to accomplish through him.

Objection 4: Doubting his ability (Exod 4:10)

By doubting himself, then God, then the people, Moses has exhausted his possibilities . . . or so one would think. But now he returns to himself by doubting his own abilities. He tells God that he has never been a good public speaker—as if God's complete control over EVERYTHING in nature hadn't already been revealed in the three signs God just showed him! God, asks him the obvious question: Who has made man's mouth? Who makes him dumb, or deaf, or seeing, or blind? Is it not I, the Lord? Now therefore go, and I will be with your mouth and teach you what you shall speak (Exod 4:11). Just as God promised to be with him when Moses raised a doubt about himself, so now God promises to be with Moses's mouth, when he has a doubt about it!

Objection 5: Unwillingness (Exod 4:13)

Moses finally comes to the point of all his earlier objections. The *real* objection behind all of the other objections is simply this: I do not want to go. Send someone else, please. This is not really an objection based on a bad reason but rather a rejection based on a bad will. Moses is unwilling. He probably felt altogether unworthy and unable to be doing this *supernatural* work. But the point is not whether or not Moses is worthy or able. The point is that God is the one calling and therefore He will MAKE Moses worthy and able to do it all. Although this is the fifth objection, it is the first time Scripture says that God gets angry with Moses (Exod 4:14). As a result of Moses's unwillingness to speak for God, God appoints Moses's brother Aaron to be the spokesman. Moses will be like God to Aaron and to Pharaoh (Exod 4:16; 7:1, also see the chart above).

God's firstborn son

A few verses later God says one of the most important things that we have heard about Israel. God speaks once more to Moses telling him to say to Pharaoh:

> Thus says the Lord, Israel is my firstborn son and I say to you, Let my son go that he may serve Me; if you refuse to let him go, behold, I will slay your firstborn son. (Exod 4:22)

Up to this point, we have been reading in Genesis about the formation of God's people Israel. We studied how Genesis is in many ways a "manual" for how to be a good firstborn son. Through God's grace and guidance in their lives, Abraham, Isaac, Jacob, Judah, and Joseph have all had to learn what a good firstborn son should be: someone who redeems his brothers and reveals God's will to them, so that they may worship and follow the true God who sets them free. The words "redeem," "redemption," and "redeemer" come from Latin *redimere* which means "to take/buy back." So, that's what we mean when we say Abraham redeemed Lot, Judah redeemed Benjamin, Joseph redeemed his family from death, etc.

With the sin of Adam (= "humanity"), all of humanity "sold itself" or gave itself into the ownership of sin, death, and the devil. This passage in Exodus shows that Israel, as the firstborn, has the vocation of being a redeemer to all nations who can then reveal to them the will of God. As we learned last lesson, Pharaoh is acting toward Israel as his gods act toward all of humanity. If he won't listen to God and let God's "son" (= Israel) go so that His son may worship Him (the true God), then God will destroy Pharaoh's firstborn son (= Egypt = the world under the dominion of the devil).

What about Jesus?

Perhaps you have an objection of your own at this point: "I thought Jesus was God's firstborn son, so why does God say to Moses that Israel is His firstborn son?" Israel, the people, is God's "firstborn son" by a special gift of God's grace and favor. He brought them into His covenant through a special grace or favor, adopting them into His family, as it were. Jesus, the second person of the Trinity, is the firstborn son of God *by nature*. He is already in "the family," in virtue of who and what He is. You can already see that there is a very close relationship between Israel and their mission and purpose in the world and Jesus and His mission and purpose in the world. For this reason, Israel itself is a type of Christ. Jesus, in His own person, brings to perfection and completion all that Israel was called by God to be and to do.

God tries to kill Moses's firstborn son

Once all of these things about firstborn sons have been revealed, something that seems very strange happens.

> On the way at a lodging place the Lord met him and sought to kill him. Then Zipporah took a flint and cut the foreskin of her son and she cast it at his feet and she said, "For a bridegroom of blood you are to me!" And so he left from him at the time she said, "a bridegroom of blood" because of the circumcision. (Exod 4:24–26)

This passage is very difficult to translate and has many possible interpretations because it is all pronouns. Do "him" and "his" refer to Moses or Gershom or the Lord? But if we read it along with the passage that immediately precedes it the main point seems to be that Moses's firstborn son has not been circumcised. Circumcision is the Old Testament equivalent of baptism—it is that by which an Israelite enters into God's service. Therefore, Gershom has not been "set free" to serve God. Moses has kept his own firstborn son in "bondage" by not bringing him into the covenant by circumcision. God is going to kill Pharaoh's firstborn son if he doesn't set God's firstborn son free. God puts Moses in the place of Pharaoh—he too is going to lose his firstborn son if he doesn't release him for the service of God.

In this way, God warns Moses of the deadly seriousness of all of this. This is very much a life and death affair. Either you are with God or you are against Him (see Matt 12:30). Moses needs to see the seriousness of this because he is the chosen instrument by which God is going to bring HIS firstborn son (Israel) into covenant with Him. Being in the covenant is life; not being in it is death. Moses now understands this because he has seen it in his own house! Zipporah saves her son's life by her willingness to sacrifice her son and let him go into God's service. She also seems to be the instrument by which God chides Moses for failing to circumcise their son ("you are a bridegroom of blood!"). We will see in the future how the firstborn sons of ALL the Israelites are likewise saved from death by blood (Exod 12:13).

Objection 6: Bad results (Exod 5:22)

Moses meets with Aaron, and together they do the signs and deliver the message to the Israelites in Egypt, who at first respond very favorably, by believing and bowing their heads in worship of God (Exod 4:31). Hurrah! All is going well! But then they take their message to Pharaoh, who, not surprisingly, completely rejects their message. Even worse, Pharaoh now makes the slavery of the Israelites harder—telling them that they have the same number of bricks to make but no longer supplying them with the materials to make them. The people are in a panic—how are they to make bricks with no materials? They can't keep up! The foremen of the Israelite laborers even get beaten by the Egyptians for not making the same number of bricks (Exod 5:14). The foremen turn on Moses and get angry with him and Aaron for bringing this added oppression and persecution into their lives (Exod 5:21). Moses follows suit by turning on God and complaining to Him:

> O Lord, why hast though done evil to this people? Why didst thou ever send me? For since I came to Pharaoh to speak in thy name, he has done evil to this people, and thou hast not delivered thy people at all!

Moses is upset because he has seen nothing but bad results from obeying God. Why bother if this is all that is going to happen? In response, God gives Moses a message filled with great hope and promise to give to the Israelites:

> I am the Lord and I will bring you out from under the burdens of the Egyptians, and I will deliver you from their bondage, and I will redeem you with an outstretched arm and with great acts of judgment and I will take you for my people, and I will be your God; and you shall know that I am the Lord your God, who has brought you out from under the burdens of the Egyptians and I will bring you into the land which I swore to give to Abraham, Isaac, and Jacob; I will give it to you for a possession. I AM THE LORD! (Exod 6: 6-8)

Moses is obedient and tells this to the people, but now they won't listen to him "because of their broken spirit and their cruel bondage" (Exod 6:9). All of this talk about a God who cares for them and a happy life seem like a lot of nonsense. What seems "real" to them is their slavery and suffering. God's promises do not seem real at all. St. Paul once had to encourage the early Christians in Rome who were undergoing persecution with these words: "The sufferings of the present life are as nothing compared to the glory to be revealed in us" (Romans 8:18). Suffering is real and it really hurts, but compared to the glory that God has in store for those who choose to be His friends all suffering is "as nothing." God, with the victory of His friends firmly in mind, commands Moses to go in and speak to Pharaoh again, demanding that he let the Israelites go.

Objection 7: This is all pointless (Exod 5:12)

Moses offers one final objection: Lord, I have listened to you and obeyed you and delivered your messages. Your own people have turned against me and have not listened. Pharaoh is even less likely to listen. And to top it off, I am a bad messenger. In Hebrew, Moses literally says that cannot go to speak to Pharaoh because he (Moses) is a man of "foreskinned lips" or "uncircumcised lips." What does this mean?

On the physical level it may point to some speech impediment Moses may have had, which may have been the point of Objection #4. On another level, circumcision is that by which an Israelite becomes consecrated to God. A "circumcised" mouth would be a mouth consecrated to God's purposes; in like manner, later on Moses will tell the people that they need to "circumcise" their hearts, that is, consecrate them totally to God's service (see Deut 10:16). Moses may be saying that his lack of success thus far proves that he is an unfit instrument of God's word. God reassures Moses by charging him and Aaron again to speak to the people of Israel and to Pharaoh (Exod 6: 13). This whole section then ends with a genealogy of Moses and Aaron (Exod 6:14–25), which divides this section off from the next, in which God will begin to deliver His people.

The image of Moses here is not what we might expect. It is not the image of the great leader, revealer, and friend of God that he will become as he grows closer and more obedient to God. When first confronted with God's will, Moses obeys somewhat, but mostly has objections. Many of the religions of the world have founders who were exceptional human beings—people with great personal charisma and even virtue. It's not a surprise that these exceptional people were able to gain followers for their religion because there was something exceptional about them personally. In contrast, it is a sign of the true religion that it often shows candidly the flaws and foibles of its human founders and followers; in this way it makes clear that this religion is not man-made but must come from God. Even the Apostles who lived with God Himself for three years were weak and unsure at the start. Through their obedience and faith in the true God, they come, despite human weakness, to the perfection to which God calls everyone. God loves His people despite their imperfections, but this doesn't mean that He doesn't care about imperfections. He wants His people to be perfect, as He is perfect (Matt 5:48).

Summary

In this lesson we have seen the increased suffering of the people Israel and how this prepares for the call of Moses. You have learned about God's Holy Name that He revealed to Moses, its spelling, meaning, and translation into Greek. You have learned how the burning bush and the three signs that God gave Moses to show the people are more than mere attention grabbers, but are signs of what God is accomplishing and revealing through Moses. They are also warnings of what will happen if they do not listen. You have learned how Moses has seven objections to God's call, and how God deals with each one, calling Moses to obedience to His plan for the deliverance of His people from slavery. As we have seen many times already, the main way in which God purifies and perfects those He chooses is through suffering (see Hebrews 12:7–8). The people's increased suffering after Moses arrives is a sign that their deliverance from Egypt is near at hand as God prepares to reveal His strength and power to them and the Egyptians with great signs and wonders.

QUESTIONS

1. What is God's Name as He reveals it to Moses in the Burning Bush?
    The Name of God as He reveals it to Moses in the Burning Bush is YHWH.

2. What does YHWH mean?
    YHWH means "HE WHO IS."

3. Why doesn't YHWH have any vowels?
YHWH doesn't have any vowels because Hebrew scribes did not write down the vowels, but simply remembered them.

4. How was YHWH translated in the Greek Old Testament and in the New Testament?
In the Greek Old Testament and the New Testament, YHWH was translated as Kyrie, which means "Lord."

5. Why is this a fitting name for God?
This is a fitting name for God because God does not derive His existence from anything. He always was, and always is, and always will be, which shows that He is Lord of everything.

6. What are the seven objections Moses has to God's call?
Moses objects to God's call based on
1) himself,
2) God,
3) the people,
4) his abilities,
5) his unwillingness,
6) bad results, and
7) the apparent pointlessness of all that he is doing.

7. What is God's response to Moses's objections?
God's responds to Moses's objections by continuing to reveal Himself to Moses and continuing to command him and help him to obey His call.

Lesson 12

"The Egyptians shall know that I am the Lord"

Having answered all of Moses's objections, God is now ready to set His people free with great signs and wonders. Many of us have heard about the ten plagues that God sent upon the Egyptians through Moses, or perhaps seen them in a movie. The purpose of these plagues was twofold. First, and most obviously, they are a series of punishments that fulfill God's justice for all of the crimes the Egyptians had committed against the Israelites. They are also ordered toward getting Pharaoh to release the Israelites from bondage and let them go to serve the Lord.

But there is a more important reason for all of them: so that "the Egyptians shall know that I am the Lord." As we learned last lesson, "the Lord" is a translation of the Holy Name of God: "He Who Is." So the Egyptians are to know that this God of the Israelites is "He Who Is"—that He is the one who is not dependent on anything, but rather, the one upon whom everything in the universe depends. In the plagues that are coming, God will show His complete mastery over everything in nature. To the Egyptians, however, this would mean more than that, because in their false religion, practically every aspect of nature—the rivers, the earth, the sun, the animals, Pharaoh, etc.—were believed to be the manifestations of gods whom the Egyptians worshipped. They worshipped these false deities out of a desire to control the world for personal benefit. This is the original sin of mankind—to want to control everything. God's control over these "gods" will show the Egyptians that the God of the Hebrews is God of everything and every place. He cannot be controlled or appeased for selfish and false reasons. He is not some local god, having power over some little part of the earth or over some aspect of the natural world. Rather, He is the One who is Creator and Lord of everything.

One last chance before the plagues

Before the plagues begin, God gives Pharaoh a last chance to change his mind and obey. Moses and Aaron go to Pharaoh where Aaron casts down his staff and it changes into a serpent. Pharaoh calls his "wise men" in to see if they can do the same sort of "trick." They are able to do so—changing all of their staffs into serpents. But then the serpent that came from the staff of Moses's wise man (Aaron) eats all the serpents that came from the staffs of the Egyptian wise men. Aaron is the servant of God's servant and his serpent eats the serpents of Pharaoh's servants men. This shows that the wisdom of the servant of the servant of God is wiser than the wisdom of men! As we will see, just as it meant death for these serpents, so this greater wisdom of God will mean death to all those who do not follow it. Jesus will one day say "be as wise as serpents" (Matt 10:16), and this is the kind of "serpent" he is talking about—the one that outsmarts and defeats all the enemies of God simply by obeying God's will in everything!

Pharaoh is unimpressed. His "heart was hardened" means that he stubbornly set his will against God's will, refusing to do what God wanted. Because of this hardness of heart, God is going to visit Pharaoh and Egypt with a judgment of ten plagues. This will be both a just punishment toward the Egyptians for all of the injustice they had done to the Israelites and the means by which God will make Himself known to the Egyptians—and to the Israelites.

The pattern of the plagues

We will spend the rest of this lesson looking at the ten plagues. They follow a basic pattern and are divided into three groups of three and then one more at the end. The pattern of threes is set up by the location and time of the warning given to Pharaoh: 1. In the first one, the warning is always given *by the water, in the morning*; 2. the second warning is always *in the palace, with time unspecified*; 3. for the third, no warning is given.

Again, this pattern occurs three times, making for three sets of three separated off from the final plague, the tenth. While each of the plagues is directed toward a certain part of Egypt, it is more properly directed toward the gods of Egypt, each of which was thought to control some part of Egypt. The plagues show that the Lord, not the false gods of Egypt, is in control of everything.

The chart shows that the plagues are set in groups of three, with a final one by itself. It also shows that they intensify as they go on.

PLAGUE	WARNING	GODS OF EGYPT JUDGED
1. Nile to blood	By the water, in the morning	Hapi, god of the Nile
2. Frogs	In the palace, no time given	Heka, toad goddess
3. Gnats	No warning	Geb, god of earth/dust
4. Flies	By the water, in the morning	Khepfi, god of insects
5. Pestilence	In the palace, no time given	Apis the bull god, Hathor, cow goddess
6. Boils	No warning	Imhotep and Thoth, gods of magic and healing
7. Hail	By the water, in the morning	Nut, sky goddess
8. Locusts	In the palace, no time given	Anubis and Isis, protectors against locusts
9. Darkness	No warning	Amon-Ra, sun god
10. Death of Firstborn	No warning	Pharaoh and his son, considered to be gods

The first three plagues: blood, frogs, gnats

First Moses is sent to warn Pharaoh to let the people of Israel go. He doesn't listen and so Moses strikes the water of the Nile and it turns to blood in the sight of all Egypt. The fish die and the people can't drink the water of the Nile. This was bad news, of course, but the crops had already been planted for the year, so the Nile wasn't as necessary as at the time before planting. Plus, the people dug wells next to the Nile which didn't have the polluted water in them and they can drink from them. Moreover, Pharaoh's magicians manage to change some water to make it look like blood and this is enough for Pharaoh to think that it is all some cheap magic trick of Moses, and therefore doesn't come from God.

Then Moses and Aaron take another warning to Pharaoh—the Nile is going to swarm with frogs which will invade your houses and the whole land! This is a sort of double miracle—the blood had just killed everything in the Nile, but now here it is swarming with life again! Frogs were sacred to the Egyptians, and now there are so many of them that they cannot help stepping on them and killing them, thereby dishonoring their god. The magicians manage to do a trick that looks the same on a small scale and so, once again, Pharaoh won't listen. The dumb thing about this is that the blood and the frogs are destroying Egypt . . . and then the magicians say: "Look! We can destroy Egypt, too!" The fact that his own magicians can destroy Egypt just as well as Moses convinces Pharaoh to reject Moses's message. As we have learned before, sin is irrational and makes you stupid.

At the prayer of Moses and Aaron, the frogs die just when Pharaoh was told they would. Pharaoh still doesn't listen, and so, without a warning, the gnats come out of the dust of the earth when Aaron strikes it and they afflict man and beast alike. The magicians try to produce gnats, too, but they cannot do it. The magicians, at least, learn their lesson. They say, "This is the finger of God." Thus ends the first series of three plagues. Up to this point, Aaron has had an active part in the plagues. Now Moses begins to take a more active role, becoming more courageous as his trust in the Lord grows.

The second three plagues: flies, pestilence, boils

The first three plagues affected the whole land of Egypt. Now, however, God begins to make a distinction between the land of Goshen (where the Israelites are) and the rest of Egypt (8:23). When the warning about the flies comes in, Pharaoh is in a mood to compromise: Go sacrifice to your God within the land (8:26). Moses replies that the people must go a three day's journey into the wilderness to do so as God commanded. Pharaoh says that they can go—"only don't go too far." Moses prays that the flies will leave, and of course they do. But, of course, Pharaoh doesn't keep his promise to let the people go.

The Lord sends Moses with the message of another plague: pestilence will strike the livestock of the Egyptians, but not the livestock of the Israelites. As it begins to happen, Pharaoh sends to find out if it is really true that the pestilence has struck all of Egypt but not Goshen, the part of the Egypt that houses the Israelites. Not a single one of their cattle is dead. Pharaoh hardens his heart all the more and does not let the people go.

Next God tells Moses and Aaron to take handfuls of ashes and throw them in the air. They fill the air and cause boils on the skin of all the people and animals in Egypt. Now it says that the magicians "could not stand before Moses because of the boils."

The first three ended with the magicians being unable to replicate the plague that came from the dust; now they cannot even stand before Moses because of the plague that came from the ashes.

The third three plagues: hail, locusts, darkness

God has Moses arise early in the morning for the warning of the seventh plague and reminds Moses and Pharaoh of the real purpose of all of this:

> For this time I will send all my plagues upon your heart and upon your servants and your people that you may know that there is none like me in all the earth. For by now I could have put forth my hand and struck you and your people with pestilence, and you would have been cut off from the earth; but for this purpose have I let you live, to show you my power, so that my name may be declared throughout all the earth. You are still exalting yourself against my people, and will not let them go. (Exod 9:14-16)

These plagues are for the purpose of making the true God known to the whole world. Thus, even though God is doing this to rescue His people from Egypt, He is also doing it that ALL nations may know the true God. This, of course, has been God's plan from the beginning—to create so that other creatures might know and enjoy the goodness and beauty of God. Why doesn't God just show good and beautiful things to the Egyptians then? You know the answer: *quidquid recipitur ad modum recipientis recipitur*. Whatever is received is received according to the mode of the receiver. Those who have made themselves God's enemies by exalting and preferring themselves to God have made themselves "receivers" such that they can receive even the goodness of God only as punishment. It is something like a stubborn child who will not obey his loving parents. Eventually, the only good thing that the child is able to receive is punishment. It is the very goodness of the parents that moves them to punish, though for the child, obviously, it means suffering. At the very least, the stubborn child and the stubborn Egyptians will be changed in that they will come to know that the Lord is the true God—even if they don't like it.

The next plague is a huge hail storm. Moses warns Pharaoh that the people and animals should get under cover so that they do not get killed by the enormous hail. This time, some of the Egyptians wisely begin to listen to Moses. Those who don't are killed. Hail fell and shattered everything that was growing in the fields and orchards and killed all the animals and people that had not taken cover. But none fell in the land of Goshen because God was protecting them.

After this, Pharaoh says that he and his people have sinned. He promises to let the people go if only Moses will stop the hail and thunder and lightning. Moses promises to stop the storm as soon as he leaves the city, "that you may know that the earth is the Lord's" (9:29). He also tells Pharaoh that he isn't fooled by Pharaoh's phony change of heart: "I know that you do not yet fear the Lord God." They were still banking on the later crops that had not flowered yet and so were not destroyed by the hail. They really aren't convinced yet that the Lord is an all-powerful God but are placing their hope in their possessions.

Moses is right. As soon as the hail stops, Pharaoh sins again and won't let the people go. Since Pharaoh was hanging his hopes on the wheat harvest which was still coming up, God next warns Pharaoh that a plague of locusts is on the way. When locusts swarm and descend on a place, they eat EVERYTHING. After Moses gives the warning and leaves, the servants of Pharaoh try to convince him to at least let the Hebrew MEN go: How long shall this man be a snare to us? Let the men go that they may serve the Lord their God; do you not yet understand that Egypt is ruined? So Pharaoh tries to make a bargain—how about just you men go and the women and little ones stay behind? He wants to make sure that the men come back to be his slaves. He's going to need a lot of slave labor to rebuild after all of the destruction that has fallen upon his land. Moses tells him that they ALL need to go to hold a feast for the Lord.

Pharaoh refuses, and God sends the locusts as His response. They eat everything that hadn't been destroyed by the other plagues. The land is COVERED in them. Pharaoh has another fake repentance. Moses asks God to remove the locusts; God removes all the locusts; and Pharaoh ... hardens his heart again.

Then without warning, God sends three days of darkness over Egypt. It was so thick that it could be *felt*! So Pharaoh agrees to let ALL the Israelites go, but he demands that they leave behind all their livestock so that if the Israelites don't return, at least he and his servants will have herds from which to eat. Moses says that the herds must come with them. Pharaoh is so angry that he tells Moses not to come again or he will kill him. Moses replies "As you say! I will not see your face again," and he goes out from Pharaoh "in hot anger" (11:8), after warning him of the final plague that is to come because of Pharaoh's stubbornness.

The final plague: passover and the death of the firstborn

Here the story pauses for a moment while the Lord goes into a lengthy explanation about the Passover. This pause in the story to explain the origin and purpose of the Passover means that it is extremely important. God is about to send the angel of death to pass though the land of Egypt and kill all of the firstborn of the Egyptians, of man and beast alike, but He will "pass over" the homes of the Israelites who have followed His commands. Here are those commands:

- This month shall be the first of months
- each household shall procure a lamb
- the lamb must be a male without blemish
- the lamb must be slaughtered
- its blood must be put on the lintels and doorposts of the house with a branch of hyssop
- the people shall remain inside and eat its roasted flesh
- they shall be dressed and ready to go out of Egypt as they eat the meal
- they shall eat unleavened bread (flat bread with no yeast in it, as a sign that they had not time to let it rise)
- they shall observe this rite as an ordinance forever (12:24).

Let's see: a meal that is also a sacrifice, and the sacrifice saves people from death, by the blood of the lamb; a sacrificial meal in which the flesh of the one who died to save the people is eaten, and in which unleavened bread is also eaten; where the meal is eaten as a preparation for the journey away from the land of slavery and sin to the land of the promise. Does this remind you of anything? It should remind you of the Mass. Jesus instituted the Mass within the Passover meal that He ate with His Apostles. He is the Lamb of God whose flesh we eat in the Eucharist and whose blood saves us from sin and the death of separation from God, all of which strengthens us on our journey from this world to Heaven! Thus, once again, Egypt is a type of this world, under the power of sin, and the Passover sacrificial meal is a type of the Eucharistic sacrificial meal.

Then the last plague strikes. At midnight all the firstborn of the Egyptians are killed—of both man and beast, but God "passes over" the Israelites whose houses are marked with the blood of the lamb. Pharaoh is defeated and he knows it. He calls Moses and Aaron and tells them to take all the people and all the flocks and to go away and serve the Lord as they had said (Exod 12:31-32)—he even asks for their blessing! After this, the Egyptians are so anxious to get rid of the Israelites that they offer them gold, jewelry, and cloth to get them going! As we will see later in Exodus, the Israelites will use these "spoils of the Egyptians" to build the holy Ark of the covenant and the Tabernacle or Tent of Meeting, wherein the ark and the presence of God dwells. The Church Fathers saw in this action a very profound truth: God's people should take whatever is good and true even from pagan philosophies and religions that exist, and they should put them into the service of the true God. As St. Augustine said, "Wherever there is truth, it belongs to the Lord!"

Summary

The plagues have defeated the pride of Pharaoh and the Egyptians. God has been faithful to His promises. You have learned in this lesson about the ten plagues by which God defeats Egypt and sets His people free. You have learned the pattern that they follow in the scriptural text, how they reveal the defeat of Egyptian gods and goddesses and the triumph of the true God, and how this reveals the almighty power of the Lord, the only true God. You have learned that God is revealing His almighty power not only to the Israelites, but also to the Egyptians and to all nations. This is part of God's original plan in creation—to reveal His goodness and power to creatures who could share friendship with Him. God had promised that if Pharaoh did not let His firstborn son (Israel) go, then He would kill Pharaoh's firstborn son (Exod 4:22). God allowed His own firstborn son to go away from the promised land, into Egypt, but now He has defeated Egypt and is going to bring His firstborn son forth from the land of slavery and death and into the freedom and life that befits the firstborn son of God.

QUESTIONS

1. What are the ten plagues of Egypt?

The ten plagues of Egypt are, in order, the plagues of blood, frogs, gnats, flies, pestilence, boils, hail, locusts, darkness, and death of the firstborn, each of which corresponds to one of the false gods of the Egyptians.

2. What is the purpose of the ten plagues God sends against Egypt?

The purpose of the ten plagues against Egypt is to reveal to all people the power of the true God over all the false gods.

3. What do the false gods represent?

The false gods of the nations represent the desire for selfish control of everything, the worship of created goods, and the worship of self.

4. What is the Passover?

The Passover is when God destroyed the firstborn of the Egyptians but "passed over" the homes of the Israelites that were marked with the blood of the sacrificial lamb.

5. Of what is Passover a type?

The Passover—a sacrificial meal that delivers God's people from death and prepares them for leaving Egypt (the life of sin)—is a type of the Eucharist.

6. Why do the Israelites despoil the Egyptians?

God commanded the Israelites to despoil the Egyptians in order to show that all that is good belongs to God and should be put into His service.

Lesson 13

Consecrate to Me All the Firstborn

Having defeated the pride of Pharaoh by the ten plagues, God now leads His people forth from Egypt. As the people begin to travel from the Egyptian cities of Rameses to Succoth (Exod 12:37), God reminds Moses that no foreigner shall eat the Passover in days to come. If foreigners wish to eat it, they must first be circumcised. As circumcision is required before eating the Passover, so baptism is required before eating the Eucharist. He also says of the sacrificial lamb, "You shall not break a bone of it," just as Jesus's bones were not broken when He was sacrificed (John 19:36).

The Lord goes on to say, "Consecrate to me all the firstborn; whatever is the first to open the womb among the people of Israel, both of man and of beast, is mine." Why does God say this? He has just saved all of the firstborn of the Israelites from the destruction of the last plague; and because He saved the firstborn from death, they belong to Him in a special way. All of the firstborn of their animals they are to sacrifice to the Lord as a reminder that He saved them. The firstborn were seen as the best, and therefore they belong to God because God deserves the best. Their firstborn sons they also have to redeem or "buy back" from the Lord, so that every Israelite father has to undergo, in some way, what Abraham did (Exod 13:11–16). They redeem their firstborn sons by sacrificing an animal which takes the place of the son—just as the ram took the place of Abraham's firstborn son Isaac. All of this is to remind them that ALL of Israel is God's "firstborn son," that they belong to God in a special and irrevocable way. In a household, the firstborn son was his father's replacement when he died and his representative while alive. That is what Israel is called to be—God's representative on earth—the visible image of the invisible God (see Colossians 1:15).

Why didn't they go straight to Canaan?

Although Israel is called to be God's representative on earth, they are still in need of much formation for this exalted vocation. God therefore does not lead them straight from Egypt to Canaan along the south eastern coast of the Mediterranean Sea. As you can see in the map and picture below, this would have brought them into the land of the Philistines. Spend a little time with the map and the satellite photo. It will help to have an image of these in your mind as you continue.

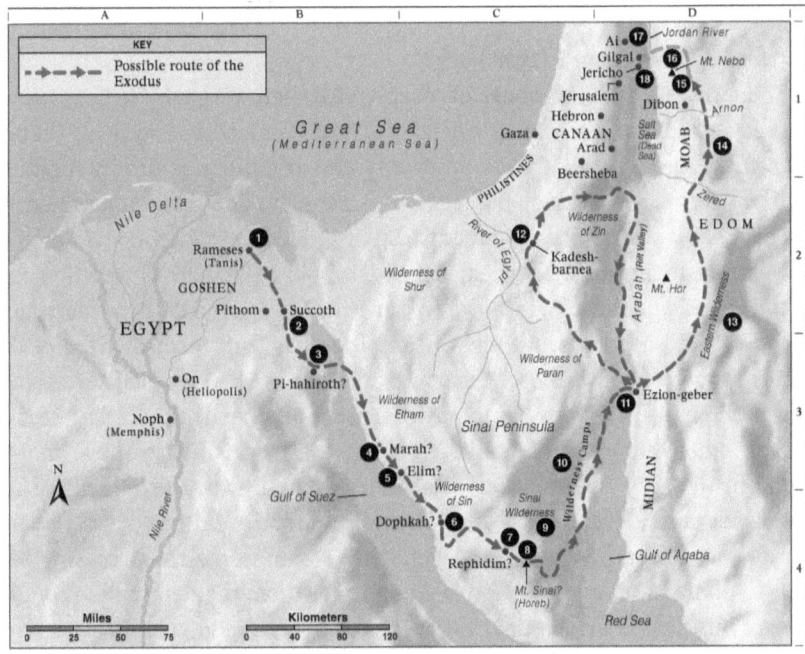

God knows that the people would have lost heart at having to fight the Philistines (Exod 13:17–18). Instead, God wishes to lead them into the wilderness of the Sinai peninsula. The map shows that the northern end of the Red sea divides into two fingers, one that goes northwest and the other northeast. The land between the two fingers of the Red Sea is the Sinai Peninsula. This will be the place where God and Israel can be alone with one another, where He can speak to the Israelites and teach them. So instead of going east and north, He takes them east and south, toward the Red Sea.

There is an important spiritual truth in all of this. After God has chosen someone, He first leads him away from a life of sin (Egypt), shielding him from difficulties that might cause him to relapse (the Philistines), as He leads him toward Himself.

Why does God tell them to turn back?

The people take the bones of Joseph with them on their journey, as his prophecy of so many centuries earlier has now come true. God leads them—appearing as a great pillar of cloud by day and as a pillar of fire by night, so that they can travel even at night. Then, strangely, God commands them to turn back a little. They had camped at Etham (Exod 13:20), which is north of the western finger of the Red Sea, and so it would have put the Israelites in a position to escape directly into the wilderness. Now God has them turn back, going west and a little south and encamping near the western shore of the western finger of the Red Sea (Pi-hahiroth). So now the Egyptians are to the west of them and the Red Sea is to the East. God does this as a last test of Pharaoh, and Pharaoh falls for it. Thinking that the Israelites have moved around in this way because they are confused and lost in the wilderness, he and his servants decide to go after them and force them back into slavery. Pharaoh hasn't learned his lesson yet. The Israelites see them coming and begin to panic, thinking that God is going to let them die. Pharaoh is coming with six hundred chariots. Chariots were the ancient equivalent to modern-day tanks. Six hundred of them coming after you would be very frightful: "It would have been better for us to serve the Egyptians than to die in the wilderness!" (Exod 14:12). It is as much a test for the people as it is for Pharaoh. The perennial problem of the Israelites in their relationship with God is one of MEMORY. Failing to keep in mind all the good that God has already done, failing to remember that God is good and that He is all-powerful, and that He has His people's best good in mind. Failing to make this knowledge the wellspring of all actions is the cause of all unhappiness.

The crossing of the Red Sea (Exod 14:13–31)

Moses answers the people's lack of faith with his own statement of faith, encouraging them to trust God:

> Fear not, stand firm, and see the salvation of the Lord, which he will work for you today; for the Egyptians whom you see today, you shall never see again. The Lord will fight for you, and you have only to be still!

Remember how in the story of Jacob-Israel, his name, Israel can mean either "he fights God" or "God fights for him"? We will see here what happens when Israel is what they should be—allowing God to fight for them, instead of fighting against God. God tells Moses to lift up his staff over the Red Sea to divide it, so that the people of Israel can pass through on dry ground. Meanwhile, the pillar of cloud moves to the back of the Israelites and comes between them and the Egyptians. That night, God causes a strong wind to blow over the waters and make the dry land appear. Sounds like creation again, right? Right. It's supposed to, so that we realize that this is a new creation. This is God re-creating and remaking His people. Just as He parted the waters of creation to make space for His creation and the first couple, and as He sent the wind over the waters of the flood to make dry land appear for Noah and his family, so now He makes the wind part the Red Sea so that this huge host of people may pass through on dry ground, with the water for a wall to their right side and their left side.

Pharaoh is so obstinate that he sends his army of chariots into the midst of the Sea after the Israelites, but God clogs the wheels of their chariots and they are slow to catch up. Finally even the Egyptians see that they can't win because "the Lord fights for them" (Exod 14:25). After the last Israelite has passed through onto the dry ground on the other side of the Sea, the waters close back upon the Egyptians, destroying them all.

From ancient times, this event in the history of God's people has been seen as a type of baptism, wherein the person baptized goes down into the water and dies to his old life of sin, just as the Egyptians die, and comes out again a new man, ready to live for God. The people of Israel have been created as a new people for God and begin a new life with Him. The goal of this life is the perfect joy to be found in the worship of the true God, which we see as Moses and Miriam lead the people in song at this point.

The song of Moses & Miriam

Moses leads the men in a song of glory in God's triumph over His enemies. Moses is so happy to have been saved from death and slavery, he is so overjoyed that there is a good God who has chosen this people, to love them and draw them to Himself, that he cannot keep from singing! He recounts the acts of God that saved them all from death, thanking God for His steadfast love in redeeming His people (Exod 15:13), and places his faith in God's promises that He will bring His people into His sanctuary, where He will reign forever and ever (Exod 15:17-18)! Then Miriam leads the women in a similar song, dancing and playing the tambourine. This is a joyful occasion! The Exodus from Egypt through the waters of the Red Sea followed by the song of praise is a type of leaving sin behind and beginning a new life—a life with God as its source and its goal. This glorious freedom found by the redeemed is a type of Heaven, where we will leave this world behind and enter into the JOY of God's reign forever. In the last book of the Bible, St. John has a vision of Heaven. He sees those who have come through the battle of this life victorious over sin. They too are singing a song, a song that St. John calls "the song of Moses" (Rev 15:3).

Divine view versus human view

You have already learned the principle that Scripture frequently changes from a divine to a human perspective and back again. After this very exalted and divine view of the situation of the Israelites, we are taken into a very human view of the situation. The people can't find water. When they do find some it is bitter, undrinkable water. So they murmur against Moses, naming the place *Marah*, which in Hebrew means "bitterness" (Exod 15:23). Switching to a divine view, God shows Moses a tree which, if thrown in the water, makes it drinkable. God promises them also that if they are diligent in following Him, He will keep them free from all the diseases of the Egyptians, but that He will heal them so that they are no longer afflicted by the physical and spiritual diseases of the Egyptians. After saying this, He brings them to Elim, a place with 12 springs of water (one for each tribe) and 70 palm trees (the number of all nations), showing that the nations will all be "watered" and brought to life by the twelve tribes. If they follow God's commands, the twelve tribes will be able to bring the true life to all the nations of the earth.

Later, we switch back to a human view. The people run out of food and begin to doubt Moses and God and to complain.

> Would that we had died by the hand of the Lord in the land of Egypt, when we sat by the fleshpots and ate our fill of bread; for you have brought us out into this wilderness to kill this whole assembly with hunger. (Exod 16:3)

Again, the people have forgotten everything they learned about God in Egypt—that He is good, all-powerful, and on their side. God proposes something new: He will give them "bread from heaven" each morning. Every morning the people can go out and gather what they need of this bread. The day before the

Sabbath they can gather twice as much, so they can keep the Sabbath day holy. This will be a test for the people as well as a teaching. They will once again learn that God provides all that they need and they will be tested to see if they will trust the Lord and not try to hoard extra for themselves. Moses tries to raise the very human view of the people up to the divine view of things: "Your murmurings are not against us but against the Lord" (Exod 16:8).

Manna: bread from heaven

God sends a flock of quail in the evening so that the people can have meat to eat. Then in the morning He sends a strange gift—something that looks like flakes of frost on the ground. The people see it and, pointing, say, "What's that?" In Hebrew this is *man-hu?*, which is what they name the bread: *manna*. This bread from heaven, that comes each day, that feeds them on their journey through the wilderness, to the Promised land, is a type of the Eucharist. Jesus will one day call Himself the true bread from Heaven, the food that feeds for eternal life (see John 6:30-51). Jesus also refers to this when He teaches His disciples to pray: "Give us this day our daily bread" (Matt 6:11). Some of the people fail to have the divine view and to obey God. They try to gather more than they need, or they keep some back to hoard it for the next day, or they go out and gather it on the Sabbath. Of course none of this works—the extra that they kept over turns all wormy, and when they go out on the Sabbath there isn't any to gather. Israel is not supposed to worry itself about food and drink, but about following the commands of God and being His firstborn son in the world. They will eat this bread for the whole 40 years that they are in the wilderness (Exod 16:35).

The wilderness of "Sin"

In Chapter 17 of Exodus it says that the people of Israel moved on from "the wilderness of Sin." The word *Sin* here is not the English word "sin," so don't get the words confused. It is just the way the Hebrew name for this place sounds. It is what we call a *homophone*—two different words that have the same sound. So it is not named "the wilderness of Sin" because the people sinned there, even though, in fact, the people do sin there.

They sin, as always, by failing to trust and believe that God will provide for them. As a result they grumble and complain: "Why did you bring us up out of Egypt to kill us and our children and our cattle with thirst?" (Exod 17:3). For the first time, God has Moses bring forth water from the rock to water the Israelites and their flocks. Moses names the place *Meribah* and *Massah*, which in Hebrew mean "Contention and Testing," because the people contended with Moses and put God to the test. They ask: "Is the Lord with us, or not?" As we have seen before, the first way the devil works is to get people to question that which is absolutely clear—that God is good and on our side.

Battle with the Amalekites

As a means of showing them they need Him, and that He is on their side, and that they should revere Moses as God's prophet, God allows the Amalekites (descendants of Amalek, see Gen 36:12) to attack the people as they travel down the western side of the Sinai peninsula. As Joshua leads the people in battle, Moses goes above the battle on a hill, holding the staff of God up in his hand. As long as his hands are raised, the Israelites have the better of the fight. When his arms get tired, Israel loses and Amalek wins. So Aaron and Hur hold up Moses's arms and let him sit down so that the Israelites win the battle. After the victory, God tells Moses: "Write this as a memorial in a book and recite it in the ears of Joshua..." This is the first (though not the last!) place where the Bible mentions that Moses is the human author of the Pentateuch. These passages, as well as other reasons, led many ancient Jews and Christians to hold that Moses is the author of the Torah. Because of this, the five books of the Pentateuch are sometimes referred to as "The Books of Moses."

Moses's meeting with Jethro

After this decisive victory, Moses is met and congratulated by his father-in-law Jethro. Jethro, a foreign priest, rejoices to hear of their release from bondage.

> Blessed be the Lord who has delivered you out of the hands of the Egyptians and out of the hand of Pharaoh. Now I know that the Lord is greater than all gods, because he delivered the people from under the hand of the Egyptians when they dealt arrogantly with them. (Exod 18:10–11)

He offers a burnt sacrifice to God. Jethro has come to worship the true God because of all that God has done for Israel! The purpose of the plagues is beginning to come true—the nations are coming to recognize the Lord, the God of Israel, as the true and only God.

After Jethro has become a worshipper of the true God, he then gives Moses some sage advice. Moses used to sit all day long with the people, seeking God's help for them, teaching them what God wants them to do, and judging between people who had disputes. This was all fine except, as Jethro points out, Moses can't really handle this much work—the people are 600,000 men and Moses is just one man. So he tells Moses to keep doing the things that only he can do—representing the people before God and teaching them what God says. Other men, who are noble and have good sense can take over the job of deciding smaller questions and disputes. If they can't settle it, they can appeal to Moses. This is an example of what we learned in your last lesson about the spoils of the Egyptians. St. Augustine's rule "wherever there is truth, it is the Lord's" applies here as well. God has prompted a foreign priest to propose the very structure and ordering of His people Israel.

Summary

In this lesson you have learned how God set His people free from Egypt and how he parted the Red Sea so that they could pass through on dry land. You have learned how this event in the history of salvation is a type of Baptism, which is both death to sin and life for God. The Song of Moses that follows this is the goal of all that God is doing in creation—that His creatures may be filled with joy to be His friends—at all that He has done for them. You have learned about manna, what its Hebrew name means, and how, as the miraculous food from Heaven that feeds the Israelites on their trek through the wilderness, it is a type of the Eucharist. Aside from the divine perspective on what Israel is, you have also seen the human view of Israel—grumbling and complaining in their failure to remember God's goodness and to trust in Him. God still works (through the Amalekites and Jethro) to show them how He is entirely worthy of their trust and how they should obey Him. In your next lesson, you will see how God is going to call His people even deeper into the wilderness and even deeper into relationship with Himself as He meets with them to make a new covenant at the mountain of God: Sinai.

Questions

1. Why do all of the firstborn of the Israelites belong to God?
    The firstborn of the Israelites belong to God because they are the best and God deserves the best. In a special way they belong to God because God saved them from the angel of death.

2. How do the Israelites show that their firstborn belong to God?
    The Israelites show that their firstborn belong to God by sacrificing their firstborn animals to Him and by redeeming their firstborn sons with an animal sacrifice.

3. What does "redeem" mean?
    "Redeem" means to "buy back."

4. What do we mean when we say that God "redeems" His people?
    When we say that God redeems His people we mean that humanity had "sold itself" into the slavery of sin, death, and the devil, but God has "bought back" humanity for holiness, life, and freedom with Him.

5. How did God set His people free from Egypt?
    God set His people free from the Egyptians by leading them through the Red Sea and causing the Sea to fall back on the Egyptians.

6. What is the typology of the crossing of the Red Sea?
    The crossing of the Red Sea is a type of Baptism, by which humanity goes down into the water, dies to sin (Egyptians) and comes out again alive for God—filled with joy to worship the true God (The Song of Moses).

7. Why doesn't God lead the Israelites directly to the Promised Land?
    God does not lead the Israelites directly to the Promised Land because they are in need of a time of formation and perfection in order to fulfill their vocation as God's firstborn son.

8. How does God feed the Israelites in the desert?
    God feeds the Israelites with manna, a miraculous bread from heaven, which comes to them daily and feeds them on their journey to the Promised Land.

9. What is the typology of manna?
    Manna is a type of the Eucharist, which nourishes and strengthens the baptized on their journey toward Heaven.

LESSON 14

Up and Down the Mountain

In this lesson God brings His people to Mount Sinai where He begins to teach them through Moses, so that through following the commandments of the covenant they may be holy—a nation of priests to the other nations of the world. Israel promises to obey the commandments and God and Israel make a covenant with one another.

Having led His people forth from slavery to the Egyptians and brought them into new life through the waters of the Red Sea, and strengthened them on their journey with Manna, the bread from Heaven, God calls them deeper into the wilderness, to the Mountain of Sinai, where He will reveal Himself to them to teach them.

At Mount Sinai

We will be at Mount Sinai with the people Israel for the rest of the Book of Exodus and all of the Book of Leviticus. They do not begin to move from Sinai until the Book of Numbers. This is the time of God's teaching of His people, the time when He gave them the Torah, the law, the rule by which they should live as His people. Sometimes modern readers are bored by all of this talk about laws and rules, but that is because they do not understand them in terms of the love between God and His People. Really all of these laws and rules are just pointing out two very simple things—1. how the people are to act toward God now that they are in this covenant relationship with Him and 2. how the people are to act toward other people, so as to reveal the goodness of the God they love. That's it. This time of teaching and formation, with God and Israel alone in the wilderness is a holy and intimate time. The prophet Hosea even described this period of time in the wilderness as a honeymoon (Hos 2:14-15)—as if God and Israel were like a young man and a young woman in love and just married, who need this time alone to come to know each other, learning to live with each other in intimacy and harmony before entering into their relationships with the rest of the world. Even God Himself leaves everything to cleave to His "wife" (Gen 2:24)!

Seven ups and seven downs

Thus, this part of the Pentateuch is all about Israel coming to know God. To show this, the rest of the book of Exodus from this point on is marked by the seven times Moses goes up the mountain to meet with God and the seven times he comes down the mountain to speak with the people. He is the "perfect" mediator between God and the people, so the people can come to know God. In this way, Moses is a type of Christ, who is the ultimate mediator between God and humanity. "*Mediator*" is a Latin word that means "one who is between." Moses "goes between" God and the people. These seven mediations of Moses "undo" the seven objections he had to God's call at the beginning of Exodus. His lack of faith there is replaced by perfect faith, obedience, and love here. We will see how Moses grows closer to God, knowing Him, loving Him, making Him known to others, and even, eventually, imitating Him as a redeemer of Israel! In this lesson, we will cover the first four times Moses goes up and down the mountain between God and the people. In the next lesson, we will cover the last three.

Up & Down #1: God offers Israel a covenant (Ex 19:1–8a)

In the chapter and verse citation above, you will notice something you haven't seen before. It says Exod 19:1–8, which you know means "Exodus chapter nineteen, verses one through eight. But then after the 8 there is a small letter "a." Sometimes, when a Scripture scholar wishes to divide a verse into even smaller parts, he can do so by using the lowercase letters. If he wishes to draw attention to the first half of a verse, he uses the letter "a." For the second half, he would use "b." If he wishes to divide it into three parts, he could use "c," and then "d" for four parts, and so on. Usually we don't need to get that specific, but sometimes it is very helpful. We are dividing it this way because in 8a Moses is down talking with the people and in 8b he goes up a second time to speak with God. (Remember, there is nothing divine or inspired about the chapter and verse divisions of the text of Scripture. They were just added later by scholars as a useful tool.)

Chapter 19 begins by telling us that it has been about three months since the Israelites left Egypt. From there they traveled across the northern tip of the western finger of the Red Sea and then south along the western side of the Sinai peninsula. They are now entering the wilderness of Sinai, which surrounds Mt. Sinai. Mt. Sinai is at the southern tip of the Sinai peninsula. There Israel encamps before the Lord.

Moses then goes up the mountain, while the people wait below (Exod 19:3). God has done as He promised Moses back in Exod 3:12—He has brought out the people from Egypt and brought them here to Himself at the Mountain. Now that they are here, and they can see for themselves that this God who calls them is all-powerful, faithful, and true, they should be ready to hear what it is that God is asking of them. If the people will keep the covenant God makes with them here, then they will be His special possession among all the peoples. The world and all its peoples belong to God, but Israel will be especially God's. They will be His firstborn son, called to be a priestly and holy people who will minister to God's "younger" sons, the other nations of the world. All the earth is supposed to come to God, but Israel will have a priestly role in this. In some way, not yet known perfectly, Israel will bring the gifts of God to men and the prayers of men to God, standing as a mediator before God on behalf of the nations, just like Moses is for the people.

As you studied in your first lesson, in the beginning, God gave man dominion over the world to make him a "cosmic priest." He was to order the world back to God by worship. This is the purpose of Man in creation. He is like a train engineer, driving creation back to God. When Man sinned and sought himself rather than God, this got the train off the tracks and into an awful wreck (Genesis 4–11). Everything since the call of Abraham (Genesis 12) has been to fix the derailment and put the train back on the tracks and going the right direction. Now we see the plan in more detail: Israel is to be a kind of new Adam, with a religious authority to bring all the world back to God. The land they will be given will not be just any land, but holy land, a place of intimacy with God, like Eden. Remember, God created the man OUTSIDE of the Garden and later brought him in. So now, Israel is being created outside of the promised land and the covenant, but God is preparing to bring them into the covenant, and then into the Land. God made creation outside of Himself, outside of Heaven, but He never ceases to draw all things to Himself (see John 12:32).

Up & Down #2: Preparations for the Covenant (Exod 19:8b–19)

Moses goes back up the mountain to report the words of the people to God (Exod 19:8b). Since the people have expressed their readiness to enter into this covenant with God, God tells Moses how to prepare the people for His coming. They are to "consecrate themselves" and wash their garments. God is so holy and so extra-ordinary that He has them set boundaries around the mountain. To teach them the seriousness of God's presence, anyone who touches the mountain will die. Moses tells the men "do not go near a woman" because He wants them to give their full attention to God. The whole mountain is wrapped in smoke and in fire as thunder and loud blasts of a trumpet announce that the Lord of the cosmos is coming to Sinai mountain!

Up & Down #3: The laws of the covenant (Exod 19:20–20:20)

The Lord calls Moses up to the top of the mountain and Moses goes back up a third time, God tells him to go back down and warn the people not to break through the boundary, but to bring Aaron and the priests back up with him. While he is down, Moses reports to the people that "God spoke all these words." Then he proceeds to tell them the ten commandments.

1. I am the Lord your God . . . You shall have no other gods before me . . .
2. You shall not take the name of the Lord your God in vain . . .
3. Remember the Sabbath Day, to keep it holy . . .
4. Honor your Father and your Mother.

5. You shall not kill.
6. You shall not commit adultery.
7. You shall not steal.
8. You shall not bear false witness.
9. You shall not covet your neighbor's wife.
10. You shall not covet your neighbor's goods.

These are the basic conditions of the covenant God is making with His people here at Sinai. Following these commands will prepare the people for their vocation as God's priestly nation, the firstborn of the nations. The people, however, are afraid. Moses commands them NOT to be afraid—this is all just part of the training that God is putting them through so that they can turn away from sin and begin to fulfill their exalted vocation as God's firstborn son to the nations.

Note that the commandments are not just ten random commandments. They are a list of things that cause a man to have happiness and the fullness of life (see John 10:10). As with everything that comes from God, they have division and order. They are divided into two groups: three that deal with a man's relationship with God and seven that deal with his relationship to his fellow man. So the two groups are: 1. commandments relating to God; 2. commandments relating to other people.

First let's look at the three that deal with God.

1. No other God;
2. Revere God's Name;
3. Keep holy the Sabbath.

Happiness comes from (1) recognizing, then (2) revering, then (3) worshipping the Lord as the true and only God.

Now let's look at the rest of the commandments, which deal with a man's relation with his fellow man. Among these there is an order as well.

4. Father and Mother. Happiness depends on existence. Your existence depends first upon God and a right relationship to Him (commandments 1–3). Next it depends upon your parents. Your parents are like God in this way. Therefore, you must honor, respect, and obey them. Compared to you they are like God. You owe them a debt (existence) which you can never repay. Just as father and mother are the gateway through which a man has life and therefore a relationship with God and other men, so this commandment stands as the gateway between the commands about God and the commands about other men.

5. Murder. After the causes of your existence (God and parents), the most important thing is your existence itself—your life.

6. Adultery. The next most important thing for happiness and life in a society is the protection of the marriage covenant, which is the source of life and the foundation of the family and society.

7. Stealing. Next comes material possessions, which support life.

8. Lying. Next comes a man's good name in relation to other people in society, which is harmed by lying or "bearing false witness" against him.

9. Covet wife. Next comes a man's knowledge that not only are others not speaking evil against him (#8), but they are not even desiring evil against him regarding #6.

10. Covet goods. Next comes a man's knowledge that others are not even desiring evil against him as regards #7.

In summary: life comes to us first and foremost from God—from recognizing, honoring, and worshipping the true God. Next it comes to us from our parents. Next it comes from the fact that we have our own life, next it comes from the integrity of marriage and the family, next from external goods, next from the good name we enjoy in society, next from a correct ordering of our desires with respect to other's people and other's things.

Thus, as Jesus will say, the heart of the Scriptures is the Torah, and the heart of the Torah is the commandments, and the heart of the commandments is love of God and love of neighbor (see Matt 5:17-18; Mark 12:28-33).

Up & Down #4: Sealing the covenant (Exod 20:21–24:8)

The people are afraid and stand afar off, but Moses again goes up into the thick cloud and darkness where God is (Exod 20:21).

God first gives the general covenant rules about their relationship to God and to their fellow man in the ten commandments. Now, God goes on to give more specific instructions about the correct relationship to God and the correct relationship to their fellow men. The laws of the covenant need to be clear before they can finally seal the covenant with the sign of blood.

The long list of laws that follows all relate to God or neighbor. They all follow the basic form of "When you go to worship God, you shall (or shall not) do a, b, and c." For neighbors, they follow the basic form of "When such and such happens between neighbors, then x is the right thing to do." All of the laws help to illustrate the underlying commandment of loving God and loving neighbor. God, through Moses, is teaching His people by giving many particular examples of the general rules given in the ten commandments.

Rather than going through all of these laws one-by-one, which would make for a very long lesson, it would be a good exercise for you while reading this part to think which of the ten commandments is being talked about in the case of each law. Have your parents or siblings read one of the laws from this section, and you answer them by telling them which of the 10 commandments it is talking about. Sometimes a particular law will deal with more than one commandment.

A strange law

Together, we will cover just one of these laws that is perhaps the most difficult to understand: "You shall not boil a kid in its mother's milk" (Exod 23:19b). We will see this law again in Exod 34:26 and Deut 14:21. Next to this command, the rest should seem pretty easy to understand! Why would God take the time to give such a strange law, when it seems to have more to do with goats than with God or neighbor?

Every time it is mentioned, it is part of a list of laws about what the people should or should not do to worship the Lord. Hence, we can be sure that this is NOT one of the ways God wanted to be honored and sacrificed to by the people. Obedience is better than sacrifice. This implies that this practice WAS done for worship, but for idolatrous worship. It was a practice of the idolatrous peoples in Canaan and elsewhere—something that they would do in order to try to magically increase the fertility of their land. According to their way of thinking, nothing says "LIFE!" like a young kid nursing the milk that its mother gives to it. Put the two together by boiling the one in the other and you get a magic life-potion to make land and flocks fertile. This rule ensures that the Israelites remain separate from the idolatry and false beliefs of the other peoples.

Which of the Ten Commandments?

This rule relates to the first commandment—the recognition that there is only one God who has power over all. He cannot be manipulated like pagan gods by idolatrous practices. The way we worship God must come to us from God Himself. It isn't something we can just make up as we go along. On the other hand, the pagans were right insofar as they saw the kid and its mother's milk as signs of fertility and life. We have seen already with the unleavened bread that God uses what and how people ate as a symbol of something else (the haste of the exodus, etc.). A kid and its mother's milk as food meant something. But the pagans would take the milk, which can only mean life, and then use life to cause death! As we know from the story of creation, life is upheld in the world through upholding the divisions and order that God set up in the beginning. The mixing and twisting of the signs of life and death in this practice breaks God's division and order and hence destroys life. We will learn more about this in the next book of Moses, Leviticus.

Sealing the covenant

Since the text has been discussing various laws for a long time, Exod 24:1-2 begins by reminding you of what's going on—Moses is still up talking to God, receiving all of these laws. If you remember your numerology and typology, then the seventy elders who come part of the way up with Moses should remind you that following these laws concerning God and neighbor is the way that Israel (Moses) will bring all nations (70 elders) "up the mountain" to God.

Moses then comes down in Exod 24:3 to tell all of these laws to the people, and the people again promise their obedience. As a sign of the permanence of the covenant which relies on these laws, Moses writes down all of the words of the Lord. The time has now come for the final ratification and sealing of the covenant. This means that now that both parties of the covenant (God and the People) have agreed to the terms of the Covenant, they are now going to make the Covenant real and binding, as in a marriage. God, for His part, is promising to take this people as His own specially chosen people. The people, for their part, are to take the Lord as their one and only God, revering Him and obeying His laws.

Moses sets up an altar and animals are sacrificed upon it. Half of the blood from the animals is sprinkled on the altar, which represents God, and the other half is sprinkled on the people. God and the people are both sealed with the blood. Since the blood of an animal is its life while it is in the animal, and death if it all comes out of the animal (see Gen 9:4), this blood signifies that Israelites are "dead" to their old way of living but are now alive to the new life that they are beginning together with God in this covenant. Unlike milk, which can only mean life, the blood of an animal can symbolize both life and death. Hence, the idolaters (like the devil) take life and used it for death, but God (as only God can do) does the reverse—He takes death and uses it for new life!

Summary

In this lesson we have seen how Moses has brought the people to Mt. Sinai. There God comes to them and they learn, through Moses, what is expected of them in the covenant. You have learned the purpose and order of the ten commandments and their relationship to all of the particular laws that follow. You have learned that this section of Exodus is marked by the seven times Moses goes up the mountain to speak with God and the seven times he comes down to speak God's word to the people, acting as a mediator. Each of these seven has to do with the covenant that God is making with the Israelites. They also "undo" the seven objections Moses had to God's call at the beginning of Exodus and indicate how Moses is coming closer to God.

After a man and a woman get married, they build a house and live together. Now that the covenant has been ratified and the new shared life of God and the People has begun, we will see in the next lesson how God begins to reveal to them the plans for His House—God's dwelling place on earth!

QUESTIONS

1. What are the laws of the covenant God makes with the people at Sinai?

The laws of the covenant that God makes with the people at Sinai are the ten commandments.

2. What are the ten commandments?

The ten commandments are
1. I am the Lord your God...You shall have no other gods before me...
2. You shall not take the name of the Lord your God in vain...
3. Remember the Sabbath Day, to keep it holy...
4. Honor your Father and your Mother.
5. You shall not kill.
6. You shall not commit adultery.
7. You shall not steal.
8. You shall not bear false witness.
9. You shall not covet your neighbor's wife.
10. You shall not covet your neighbor's goods.

3. What is the division of the ten commandments?
   The first three commandments are about Man's relation to God; the rest are about Man's relation to his neighbor.

4. What is the order of the Commandments relating to God?
   The order of the commandments relating to God shows that to be happy and fully alive a man must first:
   1. Recognize,
   2. then Revere,
   3. then Worship the True God.

5. What is the order of the commandments relating to neighbor?
   The order of the commandments relating to neighbor show that a man's life and happiness depend first on
   4. respect for the causes of one's existence (parents), then
   5. respect for one's individual existence (human life), then
   6. respect for marriage (the foundation of society), then
   7. respect for property (material support of individuals and society), then
   8. respect for his good name (legal support of individuals in society), then
   9. correct ordering of desires regarding people (the safeguarding of #6), then
   10. correct ordering of desires regarding things (the safeguarding of #7).

LESSON 15

From Riches to Ruin

In this lesson, after God gives Moses the directions for building the tabernacle, the people break the covenant at Sinai by worshipping the golden calf. Through the intercession of Moses, God renews the covenant with those who are faithful.

God has formed His people by giving them His law and the people have pledged their obedience. This covenant has been sealed by blood and now God prepares to make His dwelling among the people by giving them directions for the building of the tabernacle.

Up & Down #5–#7

In the last lesson, you learned how this part of Exodus emphasizes the role of Mediator in Moses, who seven times goes up to learn from God and then comes down to the people to teach what he has received from God. Each of these seven times is about the covenant.

Last lesson we covered #1–4, which were:
- Up and Down #1 = Offer of a Covenant (Exod 19:1–8a)
- Up and Down #2 = Preparations for the Laws of the Covenant (Exod 19:8b–19)
- Up and Down #3 = Receiving and Agreeing to the Laws (Exod 19:20–20:20)
- Up and Down #4 = Solemnly sealing the Covenant with Blood (Exod 20:21–24:8)

The final three, which we will cover in this lesson, will be:
- Up and Down #5 = Preparations for Covenant Fulfillment—the Sanctuary / Covenant broken
- Up and Down #6 = Moses Intercedes for a Renewed Covenant
- Up and Down #7 = Covenant renewed

As you have learned, the covenantal bond is most clearly seen in the way that Scripture itself often describes it: in terms of a family that begins as a marriage. God, like a great warrior, has rescued the lady in distress (Israel) from the mouth of the dragon (Egypt). (1) He offers to marry her and she agrees. (2) Bride and bridegroom make preparations for living with one another, (3) clearly setting down the "law" of their life together. (4) They solemnly seal the marriage by promises and ceremonies, and (5) now are ready to fulfill and consummate the marriage, so they begin plans for building a home and life together.

Up & Down #5: Covenant fulfillment and breaking (Exod 24:9–32:29)

With the covenant sealed, God is now making preparations for coming to live among the people Israel. Think of that—God wanting to make a home with you! Moses reascends to the top of the mountain, leaving the elders and Aaron half-way up the mountain, and the people at the bottom (Exod 24:14). Moses is in the cloud at the top of the mountain for forty days and forty nights. Do you remember the numerology of forty? How does it fit here?

While Moses is there with God in the clouds at the top of the mountain, God gives very detailed instructions for building a sanctuary. "Let them make me a sanctuary that I may dwell in their midst" (Exod 25: 8). All that is most precious and beautiful the Israelites are to freely offer so that it can be used in the construction and decoration of the ark of the covenant, the Tent of Meeting (tabernacle), the various tools needed for sacrifice, and the priestly garments. It is as if Moses, in ascending the mountain, has looked into Heaven and seen God's home. Then, from God, he receives instructions for how to make an earthly "copy" of God's heavenly home. That is why the instructions are so specific, and why Moses must be so careful to follow them. Again, we do not make up how we are to live with and worship God, rather, we receive it from God Himself (see Hebrews 8:4–5).

The Epistle to the Hebrews in the New Testament describes how everything in the tent (and later the temple) were shadows and copies of the true spiritual realities that exist in Heaven. It also has a helpful summary of the arrangement and contents of the Tent of Meeting. Here is what it says:

Now even the first covenant had regulations for worship and an earthly sanctuary. For a tent was prepared, the outer one, in which were the lampstand and the table and the bread of the Presence; it is called the Holy Place. Beyond the second curtain stood a tent called the Holy of Holies, having the golden altar of incense and the ark of the covenant covered on all sides with gold, which contained the golden urn holding the manna, and Aaron's rod that budded, and the tables of the covenant; above it were the cherubim of glory overshadowing the mercy seat. (Heb 9:1–5)

It can be hard to imagine what this all looks like when reading the long descriptions in this section, so some diagrams and pictures will help you. Compare the diagram and the artist's rendering to get an idea of how the sanctuary might have looked inside and outside.

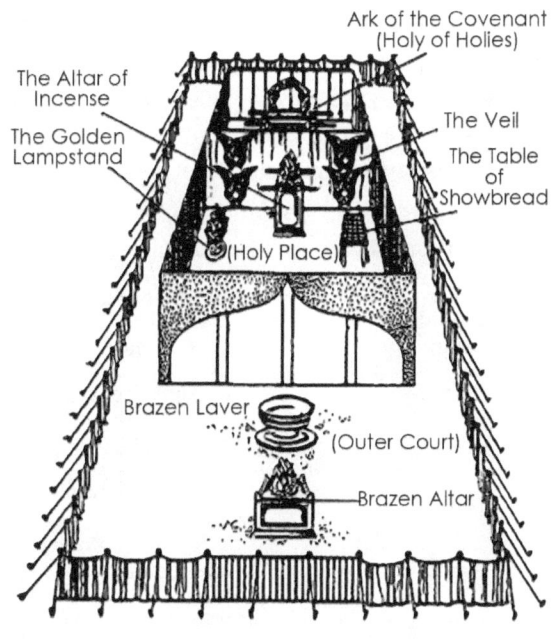

The whole sanctuary has two main parts: 1. the outer court, which surrounds 2. the tent of meeting. The tent of meeting also has two parts—1. the holy place and 2. the most holy place. The outer court is the largest part, a solid fence that is open to the sky and surrounds the tent of meeting. In it are the altar of sacrifice and the laver of water. Inside this court is the Tent of Meeting, also called the Tabernacle or in Hebrew "dwelling place." The Tent is divided into two parts by a veil—the holy place and the holiest place, sometimes called "the holy of holies." In the holy place stands the altar of incense, the table with the bread of the presence, and the golden candle-stand. In the holy of holies stands the ark of the covenant. Only the priests may enter the tent of meeting, and only the high priest, once a year, may enter into the holy of holies. This is the same basic set up we will see later in the temple. Now let's take a closer look at the six main articles of furniture of the Tabernacle.

Note that something like all of these things can still be found in Catholic Churches today. The ark of the covenant and the bread of the presence is like our tabernacles, which hold the presence of God in the Eucharist and like the lectern which holds the Word of God, as the ark held the stone tablets with the law written on them. The laver is like the holy water or baptismal fonts with which we bless ourselves before entering the sanctuary. The altar of incense is like the censer used in the liturgy, and the lamp-stand is like the candles used on or around the altar of sacrifice. The perfection of the revelation that Jesus brought from God also brought with it a perfection of everything in the sacrificial system that was established here in Exodus.

The meaning of all of this is that God is seeking to reestablish in Israel the original order of creation, wherein man offers all of creation back to God in love and adoration. The courtyard and tabernacle are a miniature cosmos with God's presence in the Holy of Holies. The major components of creation as seen in Genesis 1 are earth, water, light, plants, animals, and man. We know that there are also angels, and, outside of creation, the creator, God Himself.

Earth and sky	The altar and outer courtyard
Water	The bronze basin of water
Light	The lampstand
Plants	Bread (and other vegetable sacrifices)
Animals	Animal sacrifices
Man	The priests and people of Israel who offer things to God
Angels	The Cherubim over the Ark
God	His presence over the Ark

In short, we have a representation of the whole material creation, the whole spiritual creation (angels), and the Creator. All of this is like a sweet smelling aroma, like the incense, which rise with man's prayers, up to God (see Revelation 8:4). Other things that are meant to represent the original order of creation are the jewels in the priest's breastplate (Exod 28:9), which were mentioned also in Gen 2:11–12, and the many flowers, trees, and gold used to decorate everything. Be sure to pay attention to these as you read.

In Chapter 31, God tells Moses that He is going to call a man named Bezalel from the tribe of Judah. He is going to bless Bezalel with His Spirit, so that he will be wise and intelligent in every craft needed to build all of these things. Chapter 31 ends with God giving a final reminder to the people of Israel through Moses to keep the third commandment—the Sabbath. Now why does God remind them of this commandment and not of the others? And why does He remind them right here? He reminds them of this commandment here because the Sabbath is the best and most perfect of all the commandments. As you learned in your first lesson, the Sabbath is about worship, about God and creation resting in one another. This Sabbath rest, the goal of all of creation, is exactly what God is attempting to reestablish right here, by doing all that He is doing with the people Israel.

Covenant broken

So ends the divine view of things. We have been up on the mountain with Moses and God, getting to look at all that God is doing to restore, in Israel, His original blessing of the world. Now, at chapter 32, the story turns to a (fallen) human view of things. The people have been down at the bottom of the mountain waiting for forty days for Moses to come back and tell them what God said. They grow impatient and say to Aaron "Get up! Make us gods, who shall go before us, as for this Moses . . . we do not know what has become of him!" (Exod 32:1). Remember the principle that the way we know and worship God has to come to us from God Himself, otherwise we are just making things up. This is exactly what is going on here. The Israelites, tired of waiting for the true God, decide to take matters into their own hands, and make their own gods.

So they get their gold, taken from the Egyptians and intended for the service of the true God, and give it to Aaron, who fashions it into a golden calf. The golden calf was a very popular god of the time which symbolized power and fertility and pleasure. Aaron presents them with the bull, builds an altar for it, and says to the people: "Tomorrow shall be a feast to the Lord" (Exod 32:5). Now, why did he say that it was a feast to "the Lord" (which, we know, is the name of the true God), when really they were worshipping a golden calf? It is the same thing we just talked about: the correct way to worship God can only come from God Himself. But the people, tired of waiting for Moses, decide that they are going to make up their own way to worship the true God. That is why

Aaron says this is still a feast to "the Lord." He tries to make it seem all right because it's the true God, but as should be clear by now, worshipping the true God according to our own ideas and whims is really just idolatry.

So the people "sat down to eat and rose up to play" (Exod 32:6). This does not mean the people were playing some nice games of hopscotch and ring-around-the-rosy. It is a subtle way of saying that the people were involved in a drunken and riotous party. The word "to play" is from the same Hebrew word that went into making Isaac's name. Here, the joyful laughter of the redeemed who rejoice in the victory of God has become the riotous "play" of those who reject God and rejoice in their own victory over Him. Israel in the desert has become like Sodom and Gomorrah.

Meanwhile, back up on the mountain, God and Moses are engaged in their own "game" in which Israel is like the hot potato being thrown back and forth from one to another. God doesn't seem to want the people any more and Moses is trying to convince God to keep them.

> And the Lord said to Moses, "Go down, for *your* people, whom *you* brought up out of the land of Egypt, have corrupted themselves . . . Now therefore, let me alone that my wrath may burn hot against them and I may consume them, but of you I will make a great nation."

Let's stop for a minute and think about this: God has just offered Moses an unbelievable opportunity: HE could become a new Abraham, the one from whom a new nation will come who will REALLY serve the Lord as they should. This seems so much better. It seems like all these people have done since they left Egypt is whine and complain and drag their feet and prove unfaithful. So why keep them? That is how a normal man might think. But it is not how God has trained Moses to think.

> But Moses said to the Lord "O Lord, why does your wrath burn hot against *your* people who *you* brought forth out of the land of Egypt? . . . Why should the Egyptians say, 'With evil intent did He bring them forth, to slay them in the mountains, and to consume them from the face of the earth.' Turn from thy fierce wrath, and repent of this evil against thy people. Remember Abraham, Isaac, and Israel, thy servants to whom you did swear by thine own self..."

Moses beautifully passes the test that God has set for him. He is acting like a true firstborn—a revealer and redeemer. He shows that he truly understands the mind and heart of God. He knows that the ultimate plan of God is to reveal the true God to ALL nations. If Israel is destroyed it will send the wrong message to the nations about the God of Israel. They will think of Him as an evil god, with evil intentions for mankind. Through Moses's intercession, God "repents" and decides that He will save the people for the sake of His own reputation among the nations.

When it says that God "repents" we shouldn't think that God actually changes His mind. This is a human way of speaking about God. Frequently the Scriptures will use human attributes when speaking about God because those are the ones we understand best. When it says God "repents" it doesn't mean that God has changed, because He is unchanging. Rather, it shows that something in the human and historical situation changed. Because Moses, who is the preeminent member of Israel, changed and acted as a mediator, intercessor, revealer, and redeemer, Israel is able to continue as God's people. If Moses had not done so, God would no longer have been able to use Israel as His special people. They would have been totally and completely unfit as receivers of what God was giving, like pouring water into a bucket with holes in the bottom. Because of the faithfulness of one man, the whole people benefits. Don't underestimate the worth of one person's faithfulness to God.

Moses descends with the two tablets on which God had written the law. As he and Joshua approach the camp, they see the golden calf and the big crazy party celebrating the false god. Moses is so angry that he throws down the two tablets of stone with the law on them and they break into pieces. This is a symbolic action, indicating two things: 1. The people in their idolatry and the party that followed, have broken every one of the commandments. 2. The covenant, of which the tablets were the enduring sign, is now broken. Before they have even had a chance to build a home together, God and Israel have become separated. Israel has separated herself from the God who rescued her from slavery and freely offered Himself as her Lord.

Moses grinds the golden calf to powder, sprinkling it on the water and making the people drink it. They have exchanged the glorious communion that was coming to them in the covenant with the true God for this false and pathetic "anti-communion" with the golden calf. The book of Numbers (5:11–31) prescribes a similar drink of "bitter waters" for a wife who has been unfaithful to her husband by going with another man. Israel, as God's beloved, has been unfaithful, leaving the Lord of all for a false god in the image of a golden calf.

Then there is a riot and rebellion in the camp and war breaks out against Moses. Moses says: "Who is on the Lord's side? Come to me!" All of the men from his own tribe, the tribe of Levi, join him and go through the camp killing those who refused to repent and who were instead making war against Moses and God. Three thousand are dead after the battle and Moses says to the Levites: "Today you have ordained yourselves for the service of the Lord, each one at the cost of his son and of his brother, that he may bestow a blessing upon you this day." Originally, all of the firstborn sons of all of the tribes were called to be priestly, part of the nation of priests. Now, because of their sin, there is more distance between the people and God, with the Levites standing in between. The violence of Levi back in Genesis 34, which made Jacob so angry, here has a better counterpart in the Levites willingness to fight against evil among the people Israel.

As we mentioned earlier, Israel is a microcosm (a miniature) of mankind. They were created out of the water, they were brought into covenant with God, and now they have fallen, just like Adam in the garden. From the many nations God chose one to be His priest. From the many tribes of Israel, God has now chosen one tribe to be His priests.

Up & Down #6: Moses intercedes (Exod 32:30–33:23)

As the number six should lead you to expect, there are some negative things about this time Moses goes up and down. The first is that this is the only time he goes up and comes down with a broken covenant. Moreover, at the end of this, we find out that there already was a small version of the Tent of meeting inside the camp, but now that the covenant has been broken, Moses—and God with him—reside outside the camp (Exod 33:7).

Nevertheless, God is forming Moses more and more to be an intercessor and mediator of God's grace and forgiveness to Israel, just as Israel is called to be these things to all nations. Moses returns to the top of the mountain (Exod 32:31) and begs forgiveness for the people. He even asks God to not forgive him (Moses) if He won't also forgive and accept the people Israel.

God responds by pushing Moses a little further and deeper into a fuller understanding of God's plan for the world. This is one of the most important parts of the book of Exodus, so pay attention! God is about to help Moses to understand and to reveal the deepest secret of the universe—the whole reason for all of creation.

God says to Moses, testing him:

> Depart, go up hence, you and the people who you have brought up out of the land of Egypt, to the land of which I swore to Abraham, Isaac, and Jacob . . . And I will send an angel before you and I will drive out the Canaanites . . . Go up to a land flowing with milk and honey. . . (Exod 33:1–3a)

So far this sounds wonderful—God is going to send them up to the promised Land, flowing with milk and honey, and He will even send an angel to drive out the Canaanites before them. Wow! Great! We're all set to go! But then God says something shocking. He says,

> Go up to a land flowing with milk and honey . . . but I will not go up among you . . . for you are a stiff-necked people. (Exod 33:3b)

This is like taking the jewel out of the wedding ring. The threat is that, just as Adam and Eve lost the garden, so the people will lose intimacy with

God. The holy land will not be the new Eden. It will just be another place without God. Moses does not respond immediately, but goes down to the people to tell them what the Lord had said (Exod 33:4). They are grief-stricken. The people enter into a period of mourning and lament. They take off all of their finery from that point onward. Moses, as a sign that God has rejected this people who have rejected Him, moves the small tent of meeting outside the camp. This is to give the people time to realize what they have lost. They all stand at the doors of their tent and look with longing as Moses goes outside the camp (Exod 33:10), away from them, and speaks with God "face to face, as a man speaks to his friend" (Exod 33:11).

Then we get to listen in on one of these face-to-face conversations that God has with Moses. Here is how it goes:

> Moses said to the Lord, "See, thou sayest to me, 'Bring up this people,' but thou has not let me know whom thou wilt send with me. Yet thou hast said 'I know you by name and you have also found favor in my sight.' Now therefore I pray thee, if I have found favor in thy sigh, show me now thy ways, that I may know thee and find favor in thy sight. Consider too that this nation is THY people.
>
> And He said: "My presence will go with you and I will give you rest."
>
> And Moses said to him: "If thy presence will not go with me, do not carry us up from here. For how shall it be known that I have found favor in thy sight, I and thy people? Is it not in YOUR going with us, so that we are distinct, I and thy people, from all other people that are upon the face of the earth?" (Exod 33:12–16)

Here Moses shows that he has truly understood the deepest secret of everything that God is doing. He knows that this isn't just about a great land, or many descendants, or even about a blessing to all nations. He know that this is all about WHAT, or rather WHO, that blessing is. Here he shows that he knows WHO that blessing is. The Blessing is nothing other than God Himself. *The presence of God in their midst is the only thing that really separates the Israelites from other nations.* Without God, they are just another people and the world is just as lost as it ever was. If God is not present with the people, then Moses doesn't even care about the Land. He'd rather stay with God in the desert than go into the land of milk and honey without God. This is the kind of heart that God wants everyone to have—a heart wise enough to know that God alone suffices. God wants a heart that loves Him more than and above everything, a heart that sees everything else as worthless if it is not of God.

Because Moses has come to have such a heart, God is glad to dwell with the people, for Moses's sake. "This very thing that you have spoken I will do; for you have found favor in my sight, and I know you by name" (Exod 33:17).

Impelled by his great love and desire for God and by God's favor to Him, Moses makes a very daring request: "I pray thee—show me thy glory!"

God tells Moses that no one can see His face. We already encountered the idea of seeing God's "face" in the story of Jacob (Gen 32:30). The "face" is meant to indicate something about the true identity, the unutterable beauty of the essence of God, which a man, unassisted, cannot behold; it would be too much for him. But God will allow Moses to see His "back" as He passes by in a great theophany (in Greek, *theos* = God and *phanos* = appearance). The fact that even Moses, the man closer to God than anyone else, cannot see God's "face," but only His "back" signifies the incompleteness of the revelation received in the Law. God is spirit (John 4:24), but Scripture frequently uses the language of the body as a symbol. The Old Testament reveals God's "back" as it were, while the New Testament will begin to reveal God's "face" (see 1 John 1:1). The New Testament will be like seeing someone's face, but only through the use of a "glass" or mirror (see 1 Corinthians 13:12a). Even the New Testament revelation will be surpassed when we actually know God's essence in Heaven without the aid of the "mirror." Then we will know God as fully and completely as God knows us! (see 1 Cor 13:12b).

Up & Down #7: The Covenant Renewed

This intimacy of one man with God is enough to renew the covenant for the whole people! Those who rouse themselves to be close to God are the source of God's presence and blessing in the world. Moses's example should lead all of us to rouse ourselves in this way.

God tells Moses to cut out two new stone tablets on which He can rewrite the covenantal laws. God reveals Himself to Moses as the God of perfect Mercy and Justice: "The Lord! The Lord!, a God merciful and gracious, slow to anger and abounding in steadfast love and faithfulness . . . but who will by no means clear the guilty! Moses worshiped the Lord, begging Him: "Go in the midst of us, even though it is a stiff-necked people; and pardon our iniquity and our sin, and take us for thy inheritance" (Exod 34:6–9).

God then reviews the laws of the covenant. Since the Israelites have just shown their unfaithfulness to God, He adds a special emphasis on making sure that the people do NOT participate in the idolatry of the peoples of the land of Canaan. They are to destroy any trace of idolatry from the land (Exod 34:11-17).

Moses has grown so close to God that the glory this has put into his soul spills over even into his body. He has been up on the mountain with God for another forty days. When he comes down from the mountain for the seventh time, with the tablets of the renewed covenant in his hand, the skin of his face is shining, almost as if the garment of light lost by Adam and Eve has been restored for him! Moses did not know that this was happening, and all the people are afraid to come near him (as they were afraid to come near to God). As Moses cannot look at God's face, so the people cannot look at Moses's face. But Moses calls to them and they come back, listening to all of the commandments of the renewed covenant. After this, Moses puts a veil over his face and only unveils himself when he enters the tent and goes into the intimacy of the holiest place, to be face-to-face with his Lord, the God of Israel.

Moses transformed

The Moses we see here at the end of Exodus is VERY different than the Moses we saw in the beginning. Moses's behavior throughout the "Fall" of Israel contrasts strongly with the Moses we saw back in Exodus 4. Back then, God wanted to send him to the people and Moses had seven objections. Here we see the reverse: God says He will destroy this people, and Moses leaps into the breech voluntarily to save them, going between God and the people seven times. Moses even says to God, "If you reject this nation, then blot me out of your book" (Exod 33:31-32). Moses, the one who used to argue with God that he should *not* be Israel's savior, now says, I don't want your blessings if you will not bless the nation as well (Exod 32:32). At the burning bush Moses fell on his face because he was afraid to see God. Here he asks God: "Show me your glory" (Exod 33:18). Moses has undergone a complete transformation: he now puts his life on the line for the people, he is intimate with God, and he wants to lead the people to be intimate with God.

Summary

In this lesson, you have learned how God finished giving instructions for making His dwelling with the people of Israel. You have learned the three-part structure of the courtyard and tabernacle and the placement and purpose of the six items of furniture for the courtyard of the tent and the tent of meeting. You have learned how each of these things relates to the creation and to the heavenly liturgy. Though God gives these instructions in preparation for moving in with His covenant people, the people have already broken the covenant before God comes to dwell with them. Through this "original sin" of Israel, God leads Moses further into the role of redeemer and intercessor as he saves the people from wrath of God. He comes to understand that without God, Israel is nothing. He leads the people into a new covenant with the Lord. Moses's great love for God leads him to draw so close to God that he is transfigured, his face glowing with the glory of God as he continues to speak on Israel's behalf, face-to-face with God. In our next lesson, the hope of the covenant will finally become a reality as God comes to dwell with His people.

QUESTIONS

1. What are the two main parts of the whole Sanctuary?

The two main parts of the whole sanctuary are the outer court and the Tent of meeting.

2. What are the two main parts of the Tent of Meeting?

The two main parts of the Tent of Meeting are the holy place and the most holy place.

3. What it is in the outer court of the sanctuary?

The outer court of the sanctuary holds the altar for burnt sacrifices and the bronze laver of water for washing.

4. What is in the holy place?

The holy place holds the table with the bread of the presence, the candle-stand, and the altar of incense.

5. What is in the holy of holies?

The holy of holies holds the ark of the covenant, over which God's presence will rest.

6. What is the typology of the sanctuary and all that is in it?

The sanctuary and what is in it are types of the creation as it is ordered toward the worship of God in the eternal liturgy of heaven.

LESSON 16

Covenant Consummation

In this lesson, we will complete the book of Exodus. Though the covenant was broken by the people, Moses's intercession for them and their own repentance returned them to God's favor. The people now begin building the Tabernacle where the Lord will dwell. The book ends with God coming and dwelling among His people.

The secret hope of the world since its creation has been the Sabbath—God and creation resting in one another in love. Humanity damaged this original plan through sin, turning away from God and toward self. What God created man degraded. Because of this, the world is full of violence, death, and evil. From the many nations, God chose one man, Abraham, through whom He reestablished His original blessing of the world. From Abraham came Isaac, from Isaac, Jacob-Israel, and from Jacob, the twelve tribes of Israel. Through Moses, God rescued the people of Israel from slavery in Egypt, led them through the Red Sea, and brought them to His mountain in the wilderness, offering them a covenant with Himself. The people at first accepted, but then rejected God by worshipping the golden calf. Through the intercession of Moses, the people repented and God received them back as His own, promising to be their God and to dwell in their midst. Now the people are ready, once again, to be and to build God's dwelling place on earth.

Eight steps to covenant consummation

We learned in the story of Abraham that the number eight is often used in Scripture to signify God's superabundant and overwhelming mercy and goodness to mankind. Thus, for example, the day of circumcision, transfiguration, and resurrection are all referred to the eighth day. The greatest of all of the promises made to Abraham was also the eighth in number. This last section of the book of Exodus, which leads to God's dwelling among His people, is likewise marked by the number eight:

1. A Reminder of the Sabbath (Exod 35:1–3)
2. Moses calls for an Offering From the People (Exod 35:4–19)

3. The People Offer Everything for the Construction of the Tabernacle (Exod 35:20-36:7)
4. Construction of Everything for the Sanctuary (Exod 36:8-38:23)
5. The Precious Metals Used in the Construction (Exod 38:24-31)
6. Garments for the Priests (Exod 39:1-31)
7. Work Completed (Exod 39:32-43).
8. God Comes to His People (Exod 40:1-38)

Going through each of these eight will take us to the end of this lesson and the end of Exodus.

1. A reminder of the Sabbath (Exod 35:1-3)

In Exod 35:1 Moses assembles the whole congregation of the people of Israel. He is about to get them all very busy—offering things for the construction of the Tabernacle and all that is used for its service, making them, and bringing these things together. Before that happens, he reminds them of the third commandment—keep the Sabbath. With all the gold and other rich materials that are going to be brought together, one might have thought Moses should have reminded them of the seventh commandment—don't steal. But he chooses to remind them of the Sabbath. Why? Well, this should all sound familiar. Remember that this is now the SECOND time that everything has been all set up to build the tabernacle. The first time was back in Exodus 31:13. God finished giving the instructions for it and then He . . . reminded them to keep the Sabbath (Exod 31:13). Then the golden calf happened and derailed everything, but now, through Moses's intercession, things are back on track. So again Moses reminds the people to keep the Sabbath. This is to remind them that all of their work is for the sake of the Sabbath and what it signifies. A good beginning means having the correct end in mind. The end or goal of all the work the people are about to undertake is the goal of all of creation—God and His people resting in one another.

2. Moses calls for an offering (Exod 35:4-19)

Moses then asks all the people to make an offering to the Lord for all the things that will be necessary for making the tabernacle. The offering is to be given only by those who give freely: whoever has a generous heart. Moses lists the things that they will need for the construction of the tabernacle and everything in it: 1. gold, 2. silver, 3. bronze, 4. different colored cloths, 5. fine linen, 6. goats hair, 7. tanned rams' skins, 8. goatskins, 9. acacia wood, 10. oil,

11. spices, 12. onyx and other precious stones. Notice that there are TWELVE items that Moses mentions, inviting all of the tribes to participate in this great work which is the central work of worship, ordering all other works of this community (Remember the numerology of twelve?).

Moses also calls for every able man among the people to come and help in the work of transforming these raw materials into the tabernacle of God and all that is needed for its service.

3. The people offer everything (Exod 35:20-36:7)

And so all the people come: everyone whose heart stirred him and everyone whose spirit moved him. Both men and women partake in the work of offering their goods and services to make everything for the tabernacle. This wasn't like nowadays when we build a church—all most people are asked to give is money and then stand back and watch someone else do the work. Here the women are busy spinning and weaving cloth, the men are bringing in goods and offering their work, and the leaders of the people bring in the precious stones that will be used in the priest's breastplate. Moses assembles all the men who are skilled workers under the headship of Bezalel and Oholiab so that they can teach all of them what needs to be done and how it is to be done.

4. Construction of everything (Exod 36:8-38:23)

Thus, all of the necessary materials and skills have been assembled. Following this is a lengthy account of the actual construction of everything for the Sanctuary. What is interesting about this is that we are now half way through our list of eight and what we will see here is a detailed description of the housing and furniture of the tabernacle, which together make . . . eight items being built! They are, in order, (1) the tabernacle, (2) the Ark, (3) the table for the show-bread, (4) the lamp-stand, (5) the altar of incense, (6) the altar of burnt offering, (7) the laver of bronze, and (8) the wall for the court. All are constructed with great care and completed with great beauty. To emphasize the numbering on them and to make sure we know how many items there were, we read "This is the *sum* of the things for the tabernacle, the tabernacle of the testimony, as they were *counted* at the commandment of Moses..." (Exod 38:21—the two italicized words are the same in Hebrew).

5. Precious metals used in construction (Exod 38:24-31)

Now that the construction of everything for the tabernacle is complete, there is a pause. Here near the center of this section we pause and read how much gold, silver, and bronze were used in the construction of the various parts of the Tabernacle. Why this? Why here? The "talent" mentioned here is a measure of weight, as are the shekels. If you do the arithmetic problem offered here in verses 25–26 you'll learn that 1 talent = 3000 shekels. One talent is equal to about 75 pounds, so 29 talents of gold, 100 talents of silver, and 70 of bronze is over 15,000 pounds of valuable metals! The main point of this is to show that the people were very generous in giving of their treasure which they took from the Egyptians. Earlier they had given their gold to build the golden calf, but now they have given gold, silver, and bronze in abundance to build the sanctuary of God Most High. They are beginning to fulfill their vocation as firstborn of the nations—bringing what is good from all the nations into the service of the true God.

6. Garments for the priest (Exod 39:1-31)

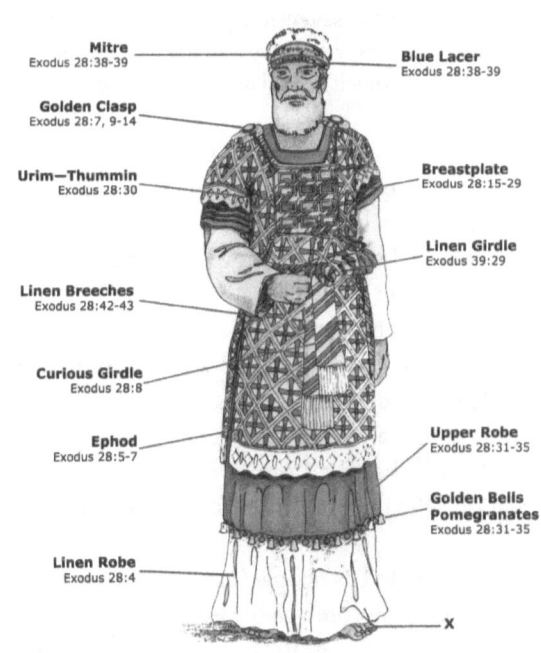

Six is the number of man. This sixth part of preparation for God's coming is all about preparing the things necessary for the men (priests) who will serve God at the Tabernacle. But they are serving God, so there are seven things mentioned for the preparation. "And they made" is repeated seven times in this section. Seven, remember, is the number of spiritual perfection. Hence we read about all of the skill and beauty that goes into making seven main items:
1. the garments, 2. ephod, 3. breast-piece, 4. robe, 5. bells, 6. coats, and 7. the plate of the holy crown. As you read this section take a look at the picture. You should be able to recognize the ephod, breast-piece, robe, bells, and the plate of the holy crown.

7. Work completed (Exod 39:32-43).

Now in this seventh part of this section of Exodus we hear,

> Thus all the work of the tabernacle of the tent of meeting was finished; and the people of Israel had done according to all that the Lord had commanded Moses . . . according to all that the Lord had commanded Moses so the people of Israel had done all the work. And Moses saw all the work, and behold, they had done it; as the Lord had commanded so had they done it. And Moses blessed them. (Exod 39:32-43)

Does this sound a little familiar to you? It should.

> And God saw everything that He had made and behold it was very good . . . Thus the heavens and the earth were finished and all the host of them. And on the seventh day God finished his work which he had done and he rested on the seventh day from all his work which he had done. So God blessed the seventh day and hallowed it because on it God rested from all his work which he had done in creation. (Gen 1:31-2:3)

God saw—Moses saw; God made—the people made; God finished His work—the people finished their work; God had done—they had done; God blessed—Moses blessed, etc. The point is just what you have learned before: the Tabernacle is a miniature creation, and Israel is a new Adam. Only now, this new Adam is being called to an even greater level of participation in reestablishing the original blessing of the world—he actually helps to build it. But note that he can only do so because he is doing "as the Lord had commanded." Obedience to God is the key to paradise, not any sort of human ingenuity. Only a willing and generous spirit in doing the work of God, and inspired with the Spirit of God as Bezalel was, can restore the original joy of creation—the intimate friendship between God and Man.

8. God comes to His people (Exod 40:1-38)

And so we come to the eighth part. We have already learned how eight in Scripture often signifies superabundance and new life. If the Sabbath is the seventh day, then the day after it is both the first day of a new week and also the eighth day. It is everything that the seventh day was, plus more! Here is what St. Augustine said about it, when speaking of the eight days (octave) of Easter:

This is the octave day of your new birth. Today is fulfilled in you the sign of faith that was prefigured in the Old Testament by the circumcision of the flesh on the eighth day after birth. When the Lord rose from the dead, he put off the mortality of the flesh; his risen body was still the same body, but it was no longer subject to death. By his resurrection he consecrated Sunday, or the Lord's day. Though the third after his passion, this day is the eighth after the Sabbath, and thus also the first day of the week.

Thus this eighth part is everything promised by the preparation of the seven parts, plus more. It makes sense then that it begins thus: The Lord said to Moses, "On the first day of the first month you shall erect the tabernacle of the tent of meeting" (Exod 40:1). The first day of the first month is the absolutely first day—it is like creation starting over again. The eighth day is the beginning of a new week, a new creation. As Moses sets up the tabernacle in this eighth part, we are again reminded—eight times!—that this was all done "As the Lord had commanded Moses" (see Exod 40:16, 19, 21, 23, 25, 27, 29, 32). This phrase is repeated before each time that Moses sets up one of the eight items of the Sanctuary, which are set up in the order in which they were made (as you read in #4 above).

Now, at long last, the moment the people have been waiting for comes.

Then the cloud covered the tent of meeting and the glory of the Lord filled the tabernacle. (Exod 40:34)

The Hebrew word translated as "tabernacle" is *mishkan* and it literally means "dwelling place." The glory of the Lord has entered His dwelling place among men! Thus, Exodus ends with a great deal of hope. Despite all obstacles, the Lord has rescued His people and come to dwell with them. When His visible presence disappears, they move on—as if in search of Him again. When He is visibly present, they stay still, enjoying His presence undisturbed (Exod 40:36–37).

The structure of the Book of Exodus

Now that we have finished the book of Exodus, it is a good idea to look back over it and see its structure, so that we can have a "map" of it to remember, as we did for Genesis. Exodus also divides into seven main parts, on each of which you spent one lesson.

1. A   God hears Israel and remembers His covenant
2.   B   God calls Moses, Moses objects 7 times
3.   C   God sends 10 plagues on Egypt
4.   D   God leads the people out of Egypt, through the Red Sea
5.   C' God gives 10 commandments to Israel
6.   B' God calls Israel, they reject Him with the golden calf
7. A' God forgives Israel and consummates His covenant

You will notice that it is in the structure of a chiasm, which should help you to understand it better and be able to remember it.

A–A' The beginning of God's action for His people in Exodus is when He "hears" Israel and "remembers" His covenant with Abraham, Isaac, and Jacob. (Exod 2:24) The end of His action in Exodus is when He forgives them their sin and consummates His covenant with His people, the children of Jacob.

B–B' In the second part, God calls Moses, but he objects to it seven times. In the second to last part, God has called Israel, but they reject His call with the golden calf.

C–C' In the third part, God saves Israel from Egypt by the 10 plagues, which separates them from the gods of Egypt. In the Third to last part God joins Israel to Himself by the 10 commandments.

D The centerpiece of Exodus, the all-important axle on which the whole book turns, is the exodus itself—leaving behind the slavery, sin, and death of Egypt and receiving new life as God's people through the waters of the Red Sea.

Summary

In this lesson, you have finished the book of Exodus. You have seen how God has done everything in order to reestablish in the people Israel the original blessing of creation. He has rescued them from Egypt, drawing them out of the waters of the Red Sea and feeding them with bread from Heaven. He has brought them to Mount Sinai and given them His law, the way to live. Despite their infidelity, He has forgiven them because of the faithfulness and intercession of Moses. Now they have built His dwelling place among them as He directed. You have seen the eight steps taken for the fulfillment of the covenant with the fulfillment itself as the final step—The Lord has come to dwell with His people. Now that the dwelling place of God has been set up and God dwells with His people, we will see in your next lessons on the book of Leviticus how Moses receives more revelation concerning how the priests should lead the people deeper into holiness and the worship of God.

QUESTIONS

1. What are the main features of the Book of Exodus?
   There are seven main features of the Book of Exodus, which form a chiasm. They are:
   1. A God Hears Israel and Remembers His Covenant with Abraham
   2. B God Calls Moses, Moses Objects 7 times
   3. C God sends 10 Plagues on Egypt
   4.   D God leads the people out of Egypt and through the Red Sea
   5. C' God gives 10 commandments to Israel
   6. B' God Calls Israel, they reject Him with the golden calf
   7. A' God Forgives Israel and Consummates His Covenant with Israel

2. What is the covenant made to Abraham?
   The covenant made to Abraham is God's promise of land, descendants, and blessing to all nations.

3. What is the consummation of the covenant made to Abraham?
   The consummation of the covenant made to Abraham is God dwelling with His people.

4. Why is this a consummation of the covenant made with Abraham?
   This is a consummation of the covenant made with Abraham because the land is for the sake of the descendants, the descendants are for the sake of blessing to all nations, and the blessing to all nations is God Himself.

5. If this is a consummation of God's covenant, why doesn't the Bible stop here?
   The Bible does not stop here because the revelation and presence with God is still imperfect and incomplete.

6. Why is the revelation and presence of God still imperfect in Exodus?
   The revelation and presence of God is still imperfect in Exodus because it still awaits the perfect revelation and presence of God in His firstborn son by nature, Jesus Christ.

LEVITICUS

LESSON 17

Making Sense of the Central Book

In this lesson, you will be introduced to the book of Leviticus. Although it is sometimes more difficult than other books of the Bible, in many ways this book is the most important one of the Pentateuch—because it is all ordered directly toward the actions of divine worship.

Review/preview

You should remember that Exodus ended with a lengthy description of how the Tabernacle and its tools were to be constructed. There you learned in detail what the Tabernacle and all of the priestly garb, lamp-stands, basins, etc look like. Now, Leviticus will give us a description of what was to *happen* in the tabernacle; how all of this elaborate material described at the end of Exodus would be used and how it would function in the life of God's people Israel.

Leviticus is difficult

For modern readers, much of the book of Leviticus will be difficult to read. After the livelier narratives of Genesis and Exodus, Leviticus seems very dry and technical—like reading a manual on how to do a lot of hard-to-understand animal sacrifices and priestly rituals that no one does anymore and that don't really seem to help us know or love God better. Some Bible studies even discourage their readers from studying this book of the Bible because it is so different and difficult!

We know, however, that ALL of Scripture is God's word and therefore ALL of it reveals God and is useful for teaching and encouragement in living our lives as God wills—even Leviticus (see 2 Tim 3:16). In fact, this book is so important in Jewish tradition, that little Jewish boys, perhaps Jesus among them, were taught this book FIRST. So, you don't need to skip Leviticus. All you need to do is to learn some basic principles for understanding Leviticus, by which you can come to see the beauty of this book of the Bible and the beauty of the holiness that it calls us to in divine worship as it looks forward to the fulfillment of all sacrifices in one eternal sacrifice of Christ.

Leviticus is central because worship is central

Why is Leviticus so important? First of all, although Leviticus is the shortest book of the Pentateuch, we can tell how important it is simply by how it is placed in the Torah. The five books of Moses are arranged in a chiasm, which we will study in more detail when we get through Deuteronomy. But right now, we can see that Leviticus is the *central book* of the five books that make up the Pentateuch. Two books come before it and two come after it. Thus, the centerpiece of God's revelation in the Torah is a book about divine worship—about the sacrifice, purity, and holiness necessary to worship God rightly. This means that sacrifice, purity, and holiness are at the very heart of what God wants from His people and how His people are to relate to Him.

The theme of Leviticus

The theme of this book of the Torah is holiness—God is holy and His people are likewise called to be holy. To be holy means to be different and set apart. Just as God is set apart from all creatures because He is the Creator and yet He is the source of blessings to all, so God's people are called to be set apart from others and a source of blessing to all others. God's people should be different from those in the world around them. As St. Paul said, "Do not be conformed to this age, but be transformed by the renewal of your mind" (see Romans 12:2). As we will see, this difference will affect *everything* in the lives of the Israelites—what and how they eat, how they dress, how they act. Even the ordinary things that God's people do will be different from other people. You should already know that the ultimate goal of everything that God is doing in creation and in revelation is the final consummation of the covenant—God and Man dwelling together (see Rev 21:3). The way that this greatest of all blessings will come to the world is through God's people—if they are holy as God is holy (Lev 19:2).

The name of this book

The name of the book, *Leviticus,* is the Latin form of the Greek word *Leviticon* which signified "priestly." The Levitical priests, remember, come from the tribe of Jacob's son Levi. The Hebrew name of the book is from the first Hebrew word *vayyiqra* which means "And He [the Lord] called." This is important in this book too because it contains the idea that God must call us to Him. As we saw so clearly in the story of the golden calf, we must *receive* how to worship *from God Himself* (see also Romans 8:26). In this book on how to do divine worship, nothing is left open for the imagination and interpretation of men. God gives very minute details about everything: THIS is the way to worship God. As we read earlier from the Epistle to the Hebrews, it all *has* to be this way to actually be a pattern of the true heavenly liturgy of which it is a shadow and participation.

Many sacrifices, one ultimate purpose

The first thing anyone reading Leviticus will notice is that there are a LOT of talk about sacrifices. The sacrifices had one ultimate purpose—the worship of the true God. The sacrifices were meant to accomplish this ultimate goal in two ways—first, the sacrifices directed the mind of the one offering toward the true God. Second, the sacrifices directed the mind of the offerer away from false gods.

1. *To direct the mind of the offerer toward the true God.* The Israelites needed to recognize and act out, so to speak, the truth that all of their blessings came to them from God the creator and should be directed to God as their final end. To do this, they would take a representative possession, such as an animal, destroy it, and place its blood on the altar. The gods of the *Enuma Elish* decided to spare mankind after the flood because they were hungry and needed the sacrifices men offer them. Unlike these gods, the Lord created absolutely everything that exists, and therefore has no need of gifts from His creatures (see Psalm 50:12). God does not need our gifts. However, man does have a need to give gifts to God. By destroying his possession, a man takes it away from himself. Because he takes it away from himself in honor of the Lord, it is counted as being given to the Lord. We have also seen in the story of Abraham and Isaac, the Israelites and the Passover, how animals are sacrificed as a way of showing how the humans, for whom they are sacrificed, really do belong totally to God.

2. *To direct the mind of the offerer away from false gods.* Leviticus, with all of its sacrificial laws, is partially God's response to the golden calf incident in Exodus. The offering of the Levitical sacrifices will keep the Israelites involved in serving the true God and so make it less likely that they will start serving other gods. Also, some of the animals offered to the Lord were those considered sacred by the Egyptians. Instead of worshipping a golden bull-calf, for example, the Israelites will now be sacrificing real bulls to God (see Exod 8:26, "we shall sacrifice to the LORD our God offerings abominable to the Egyptians.") Israel is out of Egypt, but there is still a lot of "Egypt" and its bad

beliefs and practices in Israel. Sacrifice is one important way of weeding out the remnants of idolatry in the people.

The setting of Leviticus

In the midst of these many laws and regulations, you might forget the larger story of which this book is a part. So where are we in the larger story? Leviticus takes place while the people of Israel are still encamped at the foot of Mount Sinai. This is just after God led them forth out of Egypt and across the Red Sea to Mount Sinai. They have just set up and hallowed the tabernacle when God comes to dwell visibly among them (Exod 40:34). Getting prepared for God coming to dwell with them required a lot of change on the part of the people. Now that God has actually come to them, they are being called into an even deeper change of life to "keep" God with them, and themselves with God. So, the larger story doesn't "move forward" in the sense that the people don't physically move from one place to another in Leviticus, but there is a great deepening of the story of the love between God and His people, as the people are being called to live in a more divine manner, now that God is with them.

The three basic kinds of sacrifice

We will be reading in Leviticus about many sacrifices and the rituals that go along with them. Because man is a bodily creature, the Israelites needed exterior ritual to direct and express their interior thoughts. This is still true in the New Testament where Christ gave the sacraments and sacramentals to the Church for a similar purpose. It is very important to recognize that ALL of the sacrifices are sacrifices of food—the thing that most tangibly and directly relates to our own life. The people and priests offered to God a portion of the animals and plants that were their food and therefore their life, as a sign that THEY and THEIR WHOLE LIFE belong to God. There are three basic kinds of sacrifice you will read about in Leviticus. These three correspond to the three parts of Man's relationship to God. The three parts of this relationship are:

1. *God in Himself*
2. *Man in himself*
3. *Man in relation to God*

These three correspond to the four kinds of prayer: adoration, contrition, petition, and thanksgiving.

1. When we consider *God in Himself*, we see that He is ALL in ALL—He is deserving of all honor, glory, and worship. As we have studied already in the meaning of the firstborn sons—God deserves our very life simply because of what He is. The *holocaust or burnt offering*, in which the victim was entirely burnt by fire and none of it left for man's use, acknowledged in a special way God's sovereign majesty—the fact that He deserves ALL. This offering is "consumed" only by God. This corresponds to *adoration*.

2. When we consider *Man in himself*, we see that we have nothing of ourselves except sin. Sin is the one and only thing that man can claim as his very own. It is the one thing he does all by himself and the only thing he does when he acts on his own apart from God. The best response to this fact is contrition. The *sin offering* and the *guilt offering* directed the mind of the offerer to repentance, reparation, and reconciliation with God. This offering could only be eaten by the priests, who are to make reparation for the sins of the people. It also seems a noteworthy "teaching moment" for the Israelites in that they see, every time they sin, that something must bleed and die to atone for this sin (see Heb 9:22). This looks forward to Christ on the cross and corresponds to *contrition*.

3. When we consider *Man in relation to God*, we see that He is our creator, the source of all of our blessings. Therefore, we petition or ask Him for all our needs and thank Him for all He gives us. We see that all that we have is from Him, and the appropriate response is thanksgiving. The *peace offering* expressed this above all—gratitude for benefits received. This offering could be consumed by all the people. The Passover sacrifice was a form of peace offering. This corresponds to *petition and thanksgiving*.

As you can see now, the animal sacrifices therefore directed the mind of the offerer into the four most basic kinds of prayer, which are the four proper attitudes of creatures towards God: adoration, contrition, petition, and thanksgiving. The one eternal sacrifice of Christ is the fulfillment of all of the sacrifices shown in Leviticus, as it accomplishes most completely all that they did partially.

Sacrifice	God / Man	Consumed by	Expresses
Holocaust	God in Himself	God	Adoration
Sin/guilt offering	Man in himself	Priests	Contrition
Peace offering	Man in relation to God	All the people	Petition & Thanksgiving

The structure of Leviticus

You have already learned how Genesis and Exodus each have seven main parts or features. Leviticus also has seven major parts, arranged in a chiasm. One fascinating thing about this chiasm is that, when looked at correctly, the pairs of the chiasm can be seen to correspond to the parts of the sanctuary—the outer court, the holy place, the holy of holies, and the Ark of the Covenant. This makes it so that reading through Leviticus is like starting in the outer court, entering the holy place, then the most holy place, and finally touching the presence of God above the Ark of the Covenant before turning around in the Holy of Holies, going into the holy place, and finally going back out into the open space of the outer courtyard. Since we will be using this structure as the basis for our lessons on Leviticus, we will spend some time getting familiar with it now and will review it in the following lessons.

1. Leviticus 1–7	A Code of Sacrifice	Outer Court
2. Leviticus 8–10	B Code of Priests	Holy Place
3. Leviticus 11–15	C Code of Cleanness	Holy of Holies
4. Leviticus 16	D The Day of Atonement	The Ark of the Covenant
5. Leviticus 17–23	C' Code of Holiness	Holy of Holies
6. Leviticus 24	B' Code of Reverence	Holy Place
7. Leviticus 25–27	A' Code of Redemption of the Land	Outer Court

Parts A and A' correspond to the outer court of the sanctuary because the first of these parts deals mainly with sacrifices. As you remember, the place where animals are sacrificed is in the outer courtyard. The animal and grain offerings that are to take place here represent the fruits of the land that God is going to give the people. The outer court is open to the sky and represents the Land itself, which in turn represents the earth, from which the body of Man was made. Part A' of Leviticus is all about how the Israelites are to treat the Land that God is giving them, so that they remember that the Land is for them so that they can be for God.

Parts B and B' correspond to the holy place, the first part of the Tent of Meeting where the bread of the presence, the lampstand, and the altar of incense were. Only the priests could enter here. Part B begins with the ordination of Aaron and his sons as priests and ends with two of Aaron's sons offering unholy incense in the holy place. They are consumed by fire and Aaron and his remaining sons must remain inside the tent of meeting in the holy place during this time. Part B' begins with commands about the lampstand and the bread of the presence, and goes on to record another incident of a man who dies for failure to reverence God.

Parts C and C' correspond to the Holy of Holies. Both parts have to do with the perfect holiness necessary to enter into the Holy of Holies—the very presence of the most Holy God. Part C is a long list of commands that are ordered toward separating the people from all *things* in the material creation that reveal the fallenness of the world and likewise keeping all of these things separate from the presence of God. Part C' is also a long list of commands that are ordered toward keeping the people separated from all *actions* that reveal the fallenness of the world. God's people must be perfectly Holy to enter the presence of God—cleansed of all things and actions that are effects of the Fall.

Part D, the centerpiece, is all about the Day of Atonement. It corresponds to the Ark of the Covenant, the Holiest object in the sanctuary because it was the immediate dwelling place of God. The Day of Atonement was the only day that the high priest entered the holy of holies with blood to make atonement for the sins of the people.

Summary

In this lesson, you have been introduced to the book of Leviticus. You have learned its Hebrew and Greek names and their significance, as well as the significance of the central placement of Leviticus in the Pentateuch. You have learned that holiness is the major theme of Leviticus and how the three kinds of sacrifice correspond to the four kinds of prayer. You have also learned the seven-part structure of Leviticus and the correspondence of these parts to the parts of the sanctuary—the outer court, holy place, most holy place, and the Ark of the covenant. In your next lesson we will begin to enter into the outer court of the sanctuary by studying the code of sacrifice.

QUESTIONS

1. What is the significance of the placement of Leviticus in the Pentateuch?
    The significance of the placement of Leviticus in the Pentateuch is that it is the central book, thereby showing that sacrifice, holiness, and divine worship are the central reality of all that God is accomplishing in and through His people.

2. What is the purpose of the sacrifices mentioned in Leviticus?
    The purpose of the sacrifices mentioned in Leviticus is divine worship—to direct the mind of the offerer away from idols and toward the true God.

3. What are the three basic kinds of sacrifice?
    The three basic kinds of sacrifice are the holocaust, sin offering, and peace offering.

4. How do these three kinds of sacrifice correspond to the four types of prayer?
    These three kinds of sacrifice correspond to the four types of prayer as follows:
    1. Holocaust = adoration;
    2. Sin offering = contrition;
    3. Peace offering = petition and thanksgiving.

LESSON 18

Entering the Outer Court of the Sanctuary

We will read in this section about many different kinds of sacrifices. You have learned the purpose and main types of these sacrifices in your last lesson. What all of the sacrifices in this section have in common is that they are offered on the altar of burnt offering—outside in the outer courtyard of the sanctuary. The way the parts of Leviticus are arranged makes it so that anyone reading it becomes like the high priest—beginning in the courtyard, then entering the holy place of the Tent of meeting, then, passing through the veil, entering the Holy of Holies, and standing alone before the presence of God with the Ark of the Covenant. Then this action is reversed as the High Priest turns in the holy of holies, goes back through the holy place, and finally ends outside in the outer court again. So for this first part of Leviticus (chapters 1–7), it helps to imagine yourself entering into the outer court of the sanctuary where the altar of burnt offering is present.

The mind of a priest

If you are finding Leviticus tedious to read it is because you haven't put on the right mindset. The way Leviticus is written forces the reader to think like a priest of the Sinai Covenant would think. He must put on a mind that cares about God and being in a right relationship with Him more than anything else. This priest meditates on God's law, His Torah, day and night (Psalm 1:2) seeking to please the Lord in every detail of what he does. Moreover, he must have a generous heart—seeking to know and do these difficult things rightly so that he can bring *others* into a right relationship with God. The priest is the one called to keep God and the people together in a right relationship—and the people of Israel are called to keep God and the whole world in a right relationship. Therefore, it is not exaggerating to say that the fate of the whole world depends upon the priest!

Without Leviticus, much that is essential to God's words and works would remain inexplicable. This is most true when applied to the most important event of all time—the sacrificial death of Jesus Christ on the cross. Leviticus teaches that it is only through perfect sacrifice that a person is able to even begin to enter into the presence of God. Thus, the performance of these rituals year after year is meant to teach God's people the most important things: God is worthy of all worship from His people, sin separates them from the all-Holy God, sacrifice is necessary to restore sinful humanity to a right relationship with God, and God, through sacrifice, is calling His people to be holy, as God Himself is holy. As Jesus will say: "Whoever would follow me must deny himself, take up his cross and follow me" (Mark 8:34).

Some people mistakenly think that spending time growing in wisdom and learning is a waste of time, but they are wrong—especially when it comes to the knowledge and wisdom of God and the things of God. Devoting one's time to learning well the things of God so as to follow them yourself and teach them to others is, in fact, one of the greatest acts of love. The spiritual works of mercy—to instruct the ignorant, counsel the doubtful, depend on having wisdom. You cannot give what you do not have, and it is more blessed to give than to receive (Acts 20:35). With these thoughts to urge us on, let's begin to read Leviticus.

The code of sacrifice

When we call this part of Leviticus the "code" of sacrifice, we are not talking about spies and secret messages. We are referring to an older use of the word "code." Code comes from Latin *codex* which means a book—in particular a book of laws. So the code of sacrifice is like a small book within the book of Leviticus that is devoted especially to laws concerning the sacrifices. These are the laws governing what the sacrifices are, why and how they must be offered, and by whom.

As you can see in the three charts below, the code of sacrifice is divided into three groups, which are:

GROUP I: Leviticus 1–3: Sacrifices from a Free Will
GROUP II: Leviticus 4–5: Sacrifices from a Will Wounded by Sin
GROUP III: Leviticus 6–7: Priestly Portions of Sacrifices

Each of these groups also has three classes. For example, Group I, Class 1 is devoted to burnt offerings, Class 2 to cereal offerings, and Class 3 to peace offerings. Each of the three classes is also divided into three smaller parts. For example, Group I, Class 1, has parts devoted to sacrifices from herd, flock, and fowl.

Take a few minutes now and look at each chart until you understand the basic structure and division. The rest of this lesson will be devoted to explaining and understanding these sacrifices and their relationship to one another and to God better.

GROUP I
Leviticus 1–3: Sacrifices from a Free Will

Class 1 For God The holocaust	1:1–9 Herd	1:10–13 Flock	1:14–17 Fowl
Class 2 For the Priests The cereal offering	2:1–3 Flour	2:4–13 Bread	2:14–16 First Fruits
Class 3 For the People The peace offering	3:1–5 Herd	3:6–11 Lambs	3:12–17 Goats

Group I, Class 1

Beginning then, with Group I, which covers chapters 1–3, the first thing to note about all of the sacrifices here is that they are what can be called "free will" offerings. These are sacrifices that people make not because they have sinned or are guilty, or because they are obliged to, but simply because they wish to honor or thank God. Throughout this section and this book, you will read that the sacrifices must be "without blemish." Only a perfect animal could be sacrificed to God. Because God made everything God deserves everything. Therefore, only what is best and perfect can enter the presence of God. All of these sacrifices in a way *are* the people offering *themselves* to God. This is sometimes shown by the man who is offering placing his hands on the head of the animal to be sacrificed. The people aren't perfect and could not offer themselves, so they offer a perfect animal in place of themselves, which looks forward to Christ who was THE perfect and innocent sacrificial victim offered in worship of God (holocaust) in reparation for sin (sin and guilt offerings) to reestablish fellowship and communion between God and Man (the peace offering). His sacrifice is the fulfillment of all sacrifices.

"The Herd" in this case means cattle—cows, and is the largest gift of all. "The flock" refers to sheep or goats and is a smaller gift. The smallest gift is the gift of fowl—birds. So this first Class of group I goes from largest to smallest in terms of the sacrifices offered to thank and honor God.

Group I, Class 2

As Class 1 dealt with animal holocausts, which were totally burnt on the altar and thereby given totally to God, so Class 2 deals with cereal offerings. Usually, part of it is burnt and part is given to the priests for their food. No honey or yeast is allowed to be mixed with these offerings because honey and yeast are leavening agents—they make bread rise and become fluffy. Leavened bread is much more prone to mold and rot than unleavened bread. The laws against leavening in anything having to do with God is also in part a remembrance of Passover, when they ate in haste and had no time to let bread rise. It also signifies that God prefers simplicity to finery. Salt on the other hand, is to be added, because it keeps things from rotting. So, what should and should not be added to cereal offerings is really just the same thought as what we read in the animal sacrifices: it must be without blemish. In order to ensure that bread is without blemish you do two things—don't add what is likely to cause blemish (honey and yeast) and do add what will keep blemish away (salt). This is yet another area where the commands in the Bible may seem totally random at first, but, when we learn a little more, they make sense.

Group I, Class 3

The Peace offering is in a special way the offering of thanksgiving and fellowship with God—as if God and the offerer were eating a meal together. This is why directions are given here for which parts of the animal belong ONLY to God. The prohibition against eating the fat and blood of sacrificial animals is again based on the idea that God deserves the whole of everything. The part of a thing that best represents that thing is the best part. The best part of an animal is its life. Its life is symbolized by its blood. Hence the blood belongs to God. The fat on an animal also is the best in that it indicates a certain superabundance and health in the animal, since animals put on fat when they have had plenty to eat and are healthy. Therefore the fat belongs to God also.

GROUP II
Leviticus 4–5: Sacrifices from a Will Wounded by Sin

Class 1 Sin sacrifices classified by **who sins**	4:1–21 Priests	4:22–26 Rulers	4:27–35 People
Class 2 Sin sacrifices classified by **what is offered** in expiation for the sin	5:1–6 Female Lamb or Goat	5:7–10 Two Turtle-doves or Two Young Pigeons	5:11–13 Tenth of an Ephah of Flour
Class 3 Sin sacrifices classified by specific **kinds of sins** against God and neighbor	5:14–16 Sins of Omission Against God	5:17–19 Sins of Commission Against God	5:20–26 (6:1–7 in some versions) Sins of Commission and Omission Against Neighbor

Group II, Class 1

Moving now into Group II—sacrifices for sins—you should note that these sacrifices all have to do with repairing or making reparation for sins against God and neighbor. Mankind is either in a state of fellowship and right relationship with God or he is not. There is no middle ground. Group I is all about Man in a right relationship with God. Group II is all about Man not in a right relationship with God, that is, Man in sin. Class 1 is a division of the sacrifices according to who committed the sin. Again we move from "biggest" that is, most important, to smallest. The Latin saying *corruptio optimi pessima*—the corruption of the best is the worst—applies here. Sin is bad no matter who commits it, but among those who are supposed to be closest to God and holiest, sin is far worse and does far more harm. That is why priests come first, rulers next, and the people last. This is also why the devil attacks leaders of people more than others, and why we should pray for them.

Group II, Class 2

Now that class 1 has defined the groups of sinners, class 2 is ordered according to what is offered for sin. Again it goes from greatest to least, starting with sheep and goats for those who can afford them, then on to birds for those who cannot afford something from the flocks, and finally talking about an offering for people who are too poor to afford to sacrifice a sheep or bird. They are required to offer just a tenth of an ephah of flour. An ephah is about 35 liters, so that would be about 3.5 liters of flour.

Group II, Class 3

Last of all in this group come a class that classifies sins according to what kind of sin they are. Once again they go from greatest to least. Starting with those that concern "the holy things" we read about someone who failed to take proper care with the things of God. Sins against the best things are the worst. The holy things are the best things therefore the sin against them is the greatest, therefore it comes first. This is a sin of omission—a sin of *not doing* something good—something God said to do as regards the holy things. Next comes the sins of commission—sins of *doing* something that God said not to do. Lastly come sins of omission and commission against another man.[5]

You may be surprised here to read that the guilt and sin talked about here happen even if the sinner sins "unknowingly." How can you sin if you didn't know it was a sin? Well, part of the answer is that the sin may be due to carelessness—carelessness in learning what God wanted done or not done, or carelessness in keeping it in mind. Another part of it is that sin is not just a result of God making up random laws for us to follow, as if He could have made up any set of rules like "thou shalt not wear green on Thursdays" or "whenever you see a butterfly, you must sing a song." No, the laws God makes He makes because they reflect reality—even though we may not always see it. So, for example, suppose a mother tells her young daughter that she must always look both ways before crossing the street to go play with her friends on the other side. To the little girl, who doesn't understand how fast cars can go, this might seem like a strange rule. It might *seem* as random as "don't wear green on Thursdays." But really it reflects the reality that she is in danger of getting hit by a car if she doesn't look both ways before crossing. Furthermore, let's suppose that the girl was by herself and honestly just forgot to look both ways before crossing. She didn't mean to sin, she sinned "unknowingly," but she still REALLY put herself in grave danger because the cars aren't going to stop just because she forgot about the rule. Just so, if the laws of God are not followed—even when people are unaware of them—it still puts them into a wrong relationship with God and harms them. These sacrifices were instituted to repair this type of wrong relationship with God and the harm that follows from it.

---

[5] The verses for this last part differ, but not the content. Lev 5:20 in the New American Bible = Lev 6:1 in the Douay Rheims Bible. The confusion only lasts till the end of chapter 6.

GROUP III
Leviticus 6–7: Priestly Portions of Sacrifices

Class 1 Priestly Offerings	6:1–6 (or 8–13) Burnt Offering	6:7–11 (or 14–18) Cereal Offering	6:12–16 (or 19–23) Offering for Priestly Anointing
Class 2 Expiation Offerings	6:17–23 (or 24–30) Sin Offering	7:1–6 Guilt Offering	7:7–10 Priestly Portions of These Sacrifices
Class 3 Peace Offerings	7:11–21 Peace Offering	7:22–27 Fat and Blood are God's	7:28–38 Priestly Portions of All Sacrifices

Group III, Class 1

Group I represents Man in a right relationship with God. Group II represents Man in a broken relationship with God. In both of these groups, the priest has the role of mediator between God and Man/creation. So Group III is devoted to the priests and to the portion of these sacrifices that belong to them. Class 1 gives very specific instructions for how the different offerings are to be made and about other priestly duties in the sanctuary.

Group III, Class 2

Class 2 is devoted to further instructions regarding sin and guilt offerings and the priestly portion of these sacrifices. Here we receive further instructions on what it means when something is holy. If anything touches these sacrifices, those things become "holy." This doesn't mean that a pot or a piece of clothing has become "pious" or prays a lot, but rather that it is now totally dedicated to God's purposes and no longer fit for common use.

Group III, Class 3

Class 3 is devoted to further instructions for the priests regarding the peace offering, ending with a summary of all of the sacrifices and the priestly portions of all of them, as well as those portions (fat and blood) which belong to God alone.

Summary

In this lesson you have learned the structure and content of the first of the seven parts of Leviticus—the code of sacrifice. You have learned what "code" means in this case and why it is called a code. You have learned the different divisions of the code of sacrifice, how they are ordered, and how all of this is ordered toward putting the people in a right relationship with God and teaching them of the unutterable and perfect holiness of God. You have learned how this part of Leviticus takes place in the outer court of the sanctuary, where the altar of burnt offering is. The way to God for fallen humanity demands sacrifice. Humanity is fallen precisely because of a turn away from God and toward self. Sacrifice begins to reverse this motion, repairing the damage done by sin and turning man away from his fallen self and toward the all-holy God. The code of sacrifice ended with the section about the priests, their responsibilities and their rights. In our next lesson, Leviticus takes us into that part of the sanctuary where *only the priests* could enter—the outer room of the Tent of Meeting.

QUESTIONS

1. What is the first major part of Leviticus?
   The first major part of Leviticus is the code of sacrifice, Leviticus 1–7.

2. What is the code of sacrifice?
   The code of sacrifice is a book of laws governing sacrifices.

3. Why is this the first major part of Leviticus?
   This is the first major part of Leviticus to signify that sacrifice is the first step by which fallen humanity returns to God.

4. Why is sacrifice that by which fallen humanity returns to God?
   Sacrifice is that by which fallen humanity draws near to God because humanity fell by turning away from God and toward self; sacrifice reverses this by turning the offerer away from self and toward God, making satisfaction for God's justice, appealing for God's mercy, and entering into fellowship with God.

LESSON 19

The Code of the Priests

Up to this point in your lessons, we have been taking our time and moving at a slow pace through this part of Scripture. There are three main reasons for this.

1. *These first parts of the Bible, especially Genesis and Exodus, are extremely important to do well.* A small mistake or omission in the beginning leads to big problems in the end. The Pentateuch is the foundation. It isn't the most important part of Scripture, but it is the most important part of the Old Testament. Without doing it well, the rest of the "house" on top of it will not stand up.

2. *We have not only been reading the Scriptures, but learning about HOW to read them.* This is why you've learned all kinds of rules for the correct reading of Scripture. For example, numerology, the importance of the order of events, the divine and human views of Scripture, the beauty and helpfulness of structures in Scripture, and most importantly, typology, by which we can see that the mysteries of the Old Testament look forward to their fulfillment in Jesus Christ in the New Testament.

3. *You are acquiring a new habit.* Through the slow and careful learning you have been doing, you have been getting more and more accustomed to studying the Scriptures the way the Church Fathers did. Learning how to read God's Words well is similar to learning how to read any words: at first it is difficult, you have to learn the alphabet and rules of pronunciation, you have to go slowly and it may seem like you'll never get there. But along the way there are little joys of discovery and you keep going and eventually, not only can you read, but you actually LIKE reading. It's easy and even pleasant. Well, you've made it this far in the course and now you are getting close to that point in reading the Scriptures. You know that even if a part of Scripture at first seems dry or dull or strange, you can look at it with confidence that it is the word of God and has something good, beautiful, and true to teach you.

But Now...

All of these things will continue to be true in future lessons: You will still be required to read the texts carefully. You will still be learning new rules for how to read the Scriptures, You will still be deepening your habit of reading Scripture well. BUT, you already have enough of the habit at this point to make it possible for us to move a little more quickly through the rest of the Pentateuch. You know that it is beautifully organized and structured without me stopping to explain every little thing about the structure of each little part. You know that Scripture is always revealing God and His goodness without having to stop and have it explained to you how each part does so. You know the significance of numerology and typology without having to stop and have every single instance of it explained. So, from here on out, your lessons will sometimes be much shorter than they have been, focusing our attention on the most important points and leaving you to do some of the deeper reading on your own. We have been crawling. Now we are beginning to walk. As you grow stronger, we will even begin to run!

The Code of the Priests

From our previous lessons on Leviticus, you remember that Leviticus, which is all about Worship, is structured like the place where worship took place. The first part (the code of sacrifice) is like the outer court of the sanctuary, where the sacrifices took place. The second part is like the Holy Place, where the lamp and "bread of the presence" are, and where only the priests can go. Chapters 8-10 of Leviticus is this second part—the code of the priests—which describes four things:

1. The ordination of the priests;
2. The consecration of the priests and people;
3. The revelation of the glory of God;
4. A lesson about the life-and-death importance of obeying God's laws regarding divine worship.

The rest of this lesson will deal with each of these parts.

1. Ordination of the priests

All of this ceremony is completed by sacrificial offerings of a bullock and a ram, the blood of which is put on the altar and on the priests. What is the point of all of this? The point is that all of these things accomplish and teach, not only for the people, but also for the priests themselves, that they have been set apart totally for God's service. They are leaving behind an "ordinary" life in which they would have owned land, raised crops, or been craftsmen. Their "craft" instead is to be priests—to be the ones who maintain the community's relationship with God, the ones who teach the Israelites the law of God, and help them to fulfill that law. So just as the whole people of Israel are to be set apart from all the nations for God's purposes, so within Israel, the priests are set apart for God's purposes. This is made very real at the end of the ordination ceremony when Aaron and his sons must stay inside the holy place for seven whole days and nights (8:33)! They are literally "set apart" with God! You should know the significance of seven in this case.

2. Consecration of the priests and people (Lev 9:1-21)

After this ordination, on the eighth day, they offer further sacrifices, first for the priests, and then for the people. When these special sacrifices are completed, on the eighth day, what happens? First Aaron blesses the people, then Aaron and Moses together bless the people again. This should help to remind you of the significance of eight.

3. The revelation of the glory of God (Lev 9:23)

Then, for the grand finale, the glory of the Lord was revealed to "ALL THE PEOPLE" (Lev 9:23) and fire comes forth from the Lord's presence and burns the remnants of the sacrifices on the altar. This is indeed the eighth day: superabundant blessings and new life for the people. Seeing this glorious miracle, the people fall on their faces before the Lord and worship Him. It is worth noting that most of the time when your English Bible has the word "presence" as in "fire came forth from the Lord's *presence*" (or "from *before* the Lord") or "the bread of the *presence*," the word literally means "face." So literally Lev 9:23-24 is saying that fire came forth from the Lord's face and the people fell down in worship on their faces. While the "bread of the face of God" is a wonderful type of the Holy Eucharist, there is also a more general but deep spiritual truth in this: when we meet with the beauty, power, and grace of God's "face," we wish to hide our own, to lose ourselves (Matt 16:25) so that He may be All in All, as St. Paul says (1 Cor 15:28). In divine worship we "lose" our own life in order to take on the very life of God in us.

4. A lesson about the life-and-death importance of obeying God's laws regarding divine worship (Lev 10:1-20).

As often happens in Scripture (because it happens in life) just after things have been perfectly set up by God, man begins to mess it up. Nadab and Abihu, Aaron's sons, offer incense that was not what God had instructed, treating as trivial or unimportant the messages of God. This is similar to the golden calf incident, in which the people decided how they would worship God, rather than receiving it from God Himself. So just a few verses earlier, fire came forth from the face of the Lord and consumed the sacrifices, giving the people divine life in the true worship of the true God, so now, fire comes forth from the face of the Lord and consumes these priests who had not followed God's commands about worship, bringing death to them and sorrow to the community. Obedience is better than sacrifice of any sort! (1 Sam 15:22). Moses steps into this situation, cleaning up the mess and exhorting the remaining priests: your conduct means life or death—not only to you but to the whole community of God's people! Don't do anything that would cause you to be unable to remember your duties and carry them out properly! The grief and sorrow that is upon Aaron at the loss of his sons is made even larger by the fact that he cannot mourn for them, because his priestly duties call him to do otherwise. This is a wonderful example of what it means to be a priest—to set oneself aside, to hide one's own face, so to speak, so that God's face may shine forth for the life of the world. And all Christians have a priestly duty toward the world—not just ordained priests, as the following quote from the *Catechism of the Catholic Church* shows:

> Christ, high priest and unique mediator, has made of the Church "a kingdom, priests for his God and Father."[20] The whole community of believers is, as such, priestly. The faithful exercise their baptismal priesthood through their participation, each according to his own vocation, in Christ's mission as priest, prophet, and king. Through the sacraments of Baptism and Confirmation the faithful are "consecrated to be . . . a holy priesthood." (#1546)

As we go about our daily duties, we should bear in mind that our first duty is to God. All Christians have a priestly duty to perform: the duty of worship, sacrifice, and teaching, so that the world may find true life in God.

Summary

In this lesson you have studied the code of the priests in Leviticus and what this reveals about the importance and dignity of priesthood. We have entered the Tent of Meeting, so to speak. In your next lesson you will enter more deeply into the Tabernacle, as we study the code of cleanliness, looking at the spiritual truth that the Tabernacle is a picture of Heaven and earth and nothing unclean can enter Heaven.

Questions

1. What is the second major part of Leviticus?

The second major part of Leviticus is the code of priests, governing the ordination and behavior of the priests.

2. What is a priest?

A priest is one who is set apart to offer sacrifice as a mediator between God and His people.

LESSON 20

Entering the Holy of Holies

In our last lesson, we studied that part of Leviticus that corresponds to the holy place of the Tabernacle—the place where only the priests can go, where the bread of the presence, the lamp stand, and the altar of incense are.

The next step, which we will take in this lesson, corresponds to entering the Holy of Holies, where the Ark of the Covenant resides. The emphasis of this whole part of Leviticus is on cleanliness or purity. The long lists of laws governing physical cleanliness and complete separation from anything "unclean" are all meant to point to spiritual purity. Jesus made clear in the New Covenant that the laws about external bodily cleanliness were meant to train and teach the people for interior spiritual purity (Luke 11:39).

So, as you read these laws of Leviticus, don't forget their ultimate purpose. They are pointing to the necessity of having a pure heart. Moses had already indicated this in Lev 10:10–11. As these laws trained the Israelites to associate purity with going to "see God" in the Holy of Holies, so we should think of the words of Jesus: "Blessed are the pure of heart, for they shall see God." Only the High Priest could enter the Holy of Holies, but Israel the people IS the High Priest, the Firstborn Son, to the Nations. So they must be pure. As St. John the Apostle said about Heaven, the true dwelling place of God, of which the Holy of Holies was a copy: "Nothing unclean can enter there" (Rev 21:27). He isn't talking about mud, he's talking about sin. And sin is simply the failure of creatures to love God.

Separation from the effects of the Fall

How do all these laws train the people for purity of heart? From our reading of Genesis, we know that the Fall had many negative consequences for the human race and all of creation. The laws given here are given with a view to separating the people of Israel from the effects of the Fall. All of the sicknesses and bodily bleeding and other problems discussed here are not just a bunch of medical-hygiene rules and regulations about how to clean up after yourself and other people. They are much more than that. They are saying something about the state of affairs in the world because of the Fall and

Israel's special call to holiness within the world. Without the Fall, none of these things would have been an issue. There was no death, and no tending toward death (= diseases and disorders).

Holiness, as you should know by now, means to be set apart, but this has two aspects. The positive one means to be set apart *for* God and His purposes. But for fallen humanity, there is also a negative side to being set apart: it means to be set apart *from* everything that is *not* of God. We must love God *and* hate sin. In these regulations, God is separating His people from the natural consequences of the Fall. Is bleeding a sin? No. Is getting leprosy a sin? No. But both things are consequences of the Fall. They manifest in a potent way what St. Paul says in Rom 8:22 "The whole created order groans as it awaits the freedom of the sons of God." The fallenness of the world is manifested everywhere in the world, but nowhere so forcefully as in the diseases and disorders of our own bodies and souls. This is why even Jesus, when He came to save humanity from sin (spiritual sickness), He began by healing people's bodies (physical sickness).

So, when you read "such and such shall make that person unclean" this does not mean that it makes them sinful, but rather that the sinful fallenness of the world is being manifested in that person's sufferings. These things do not reveal whether that individual person sinned, but they do manifest the general effect of sin in the world. Because it is showing the fallenness of the world, Israel must be separated from it. Separation from the EFFECTS of the Fall (diseases, etc.) trains the Israelites to separate themselves from the CAUSES of the Fall (sin). Thus, the rites of purity are put in place to teach. The physical things that manifest the fallenness of the world and so prevent access to God *point* toward the spiritual things that really prevent access to God. Physical diseases and disorders are a material picture of spiritual diseases and disorders. The purpose of separation FROM these things is so that the People can then be separated FOR all that is God's.

Two basic kinds of laws; one ultimate law

There are two basic kinds of laws given in this section—those that refer to People (12–15) and those that refer to animals as food for people (11).

Most of the ones that refer to people and their discharges, diseases, and death make some sense to us. It's gross or it's physically dirty or contagious in some way; so it makes sense to keep separate from it. But remember, if that's all we get out of it, we're missing its ultimate purpose, which you now know (if not, go back and read the paragraphs above again!).

The laws that refer to animals, however, often seem random. But really there is one ultimate law governing both of these. The one ultimate law governing these is this: *Keep separate from anything that is a sign of the Fall.*

First we should note that no plant or fruit is forbidden. This is because plants and fruit were supposed to be food for humanity (and animals) from the beginning, before the Fall. This, you will remember, was because there is no death involved in this kind of eating. Man was allowed to eat animals only as a concession after God's covenant with Noah. In that covenant, because it was general and with all of humanity, God did not place any limits on which animals could be eaten. But with Israel, because of their special role as priest to the nations, there are limits that God will place on the animals that they can eat. And these limits are to train them in their role as priest.

There is something in the very nature of these forbidden animals that manifests the fallenness of the world. How so? Looking at the following questions and answers as one example will help us get to the bottom of why this is so.

Q: Why can the Israelites eat cows but not pigs?

A: Because pigs have a cloven hoof but don't chew the cud.

Q: But why is it such a big deal that the pig doesn't chew the cud? Why does that make the pig "unclean"?

A: Because in so doing the pig manifests the fallenness of the world.

Q: Why does this make the pig a sign of the fallenness of the world?

A: For two reasons.

Q: Which two reasons?

A: First, because to "chew the cud" means to be a plant-eater. Second, because the animals that are rejected as food for the Israelites are animals that do not fit into the order given for animals set up in Genesis 1.

Q: As for the first reason—why does not being a plant eater make an animal "unclean"?

A: Because ANY animal that doesn't eat just plants, is either totally or partly a predator of other animals. This manifests the fallenness of the world because in the original plan of creation there were no predators because there was no death (see Gen 1:30). God gave the animals only plants for food. Pigs are not pure plant eaters, even though their cloven hoof makes them look like other land animals that are pure plant eaters (such as cows, sheep, and goats).

Q: Okay, but what about the second reason—how is it that some animals do not fit into the original order of creation?

A: In Genesis 1 God made animals in perfect order: land animals for the ground, birds for the air, and fish for the water (go back and read again if you need to). If there are animals that don't "fit" neatly into their element, then they are forbidden. Hence, the list of forbidden sea-creatures includes those that have no fins or scales. This lack of fins and scales indicates to the Israelites that these "water" creatures can do what water creatures are not supposed to do—walk, or slither around, on the bottom of the pond in the mud instead of the water. Likewise, the list of forbidden birds includes birds that don't do what birds are supposed to do—fly in the air. They "transgress" (literally means "to go across") the order given in the original creation. They look like a fish, but don't have fins and scales like fish do. They look like a bird but they don't fly. This fact of their nature is used to indicate a certain disharmony with the order set up in Genesis, so they are not eaten. These "disharmonious" animals were seen in some way as a result of the Fall.

Q: But how could these animals exist unless God created them?

A: Of course God created them, but all of creation fell when Man fell and was affected by that Fall. These creatures were used by God in a special way to manifest the Fall, but they are still God's creatures and as such are good. They were used as part of the teaching and training that God was accomplishing in Israel. Once the training was complete and Jesus, through His resurrection, defeated death and cleansed all things (Acts 10:15), these laws regarding bodily things were no longer binding, but only the spiritual things toward which the bodily laws had always being pointing.

And yet, it is also true that every part of creation still awaits a further deliverance from the power of death (Rom 8:22). This deliverance began with Jesus, continues in those who believe in Him, and will be completed at His Second Coming, the Resurrection of the Dead, and the Life of Heaven (Rev 21:4).

You should be able to see now that Israel's outlook on food was not random at all but rather very profound. Food isn't merely for nourishment. It was also a chance to reflect on and participate in God's good order in creation. The food laws make it clear that the worship of God and the following of His way is not merely something that happens in the temple/tabernacle, but something that affects the intimate aspects of everyday life for the people who are to be the High Priest to the Nations.

Summary

In this lesson, you have learned that the ultimate purpose of the purity laws was spiritual teaching and training in the purity that is necessary to "see God." You have learned that the forbidden foods were forbidden with a clear purpose, and not randomly. You have learned what that purpose is and how it relates to the original order of creation and to God's purposes with Israel, His "firstborn son" who is also priest to the nations. You should remember that the book of Leviticus is the "centerpiece" of the Pentateuch. In our next lesson, we will study the centerpiece of the centerpiece. Now that Israel has been purified to enter the Holy of Holies, the high priest will even touch the Presence of God above the Ark of the Covenant on the holy Day of Atonement.

Questions

1. What does "unclean" mean in the code of cleanliness?

The meaning of "unclean" is that the thing called unclean manifests, or has come into contact with something that manifests, the fallen state of the world after sin.

2. Why were the Israelites forbidden to eat unclean animals?

The Israelites were forbidden to eat certain animals because those animals manifested the fallen state of the world.

3. How did these animals manifest the fallen state of the world?

These animals manifested the fallen state of the world either by being predators or by "going across" the original order set up in creation of Land, Water, and Air animals.

4. Does this mean that these animals were evil?

No, God created these animals and so they are good, but they were used by Him to teach and train the Israelites in holiness.

5. Are these animals still "unclean"?

No, these animals are no longer unclean because Christ defeated sin and death (Acts 10:15) and has begun to renew all of creation, though it is still true that all creation still awaits the perfection of this redemption, when there will be no more death of any kind (Rom 8:22 and Rev 21:4).

LESSON 21

The Center of the Center

From your earlier Lessons, you should remember the following chart of the chiasm of the book of Leviticus. You have studied the codes of sacrifice, priests, and cleanness which correspond to beginning in the outer court of the sanctuary, then entering the Holy Place, and then entering into the Holy of Holies. In this lesson we will be studying the central object—the Ark of the covenant, in the central part the sanctuary, in the central part of the chiasm, which is the central part of Leviticus, which is the central part of the Pentateuch, which is the foundational revelation of the Old Testament. This must be important!

1. Leviticus 1–7	A Code of Sacrifice	Outer Court
2. Leviticus 8–10	B Code of Priests	Holy Place
3. Leviticus 11–15	C Code of Cleanness	Holy of Holies
4. Leviticus 16	D The Day of Atonement	The Ark of the Covenant
5. Leviticus 17–23	C' Code of Holiness	Holy of Holies
6. Leviticus 24	B' Code of Reverence	Holy Place
7. Leviticus 25–27	A' Code of Redemption of the Land	Outer Court

The Day of Atonement

This part of Leviticus reports the "Day of Atonement." You may have heard of the Jewish Holy Day called "Yom Kippur," which Jews still celebrate. The Hebrew word *Yom* = day and *Kippur* = atonement (literally "to cover"). On this day the people were to "afflict themselves" that is, to fast, do penance, confess sins, and seek reconciliation and forgiveness as a means of expressing sorrow and making atonement for all sin and rebellion against God. Sin separates them from God; atonement, in English, literally means at-one-ment, that is, "to be made at one." Through this atonement, God and His people are reunited. The idea of "covering" in the Hebrew comes both from the idea that the sins of the people were "covered over" on this day, but most especially from the idea that God's presence and glory "covered over" the mercy seat or propitiatory of the ark of covenant.

The mercy seat

The "mercy seat" or "propitiatory" was the place above the ark between the outstretched wings of the Seraphim where God "sat" when He came to dwell among the people (see the replica above). Other pagan religions round about Israel would put a bodily image of their god on top of their own "arks" but the ark of Israel was very unique. The God of Israel remained for the most part invisible, overshadowing or "covering" the ark only in a cloud of light and glory. The Hebrew word for "mercy seat" or "propitiatory" is spelled and sounds very similar to the other word you just learned, *kippur*, and has a similar meaning. This "mercy seat" was where the Israelites, on the Day of Atonement, could find reunion with God who dwelt among them. (This was a type of the Virgin Mary, who was "overshadowed" by the Holy Spirit and who carried within her the Word of God made flesh, as the Ark contained the words of God made "flesh" by being written down by Moses.)

For the sins of ALL the people

Up to this point we have read about all sorts of sacrifices made for individuals and their sins. But here at the day of Atonement, expiation is to be made for the sins of the *whole people*. Only on this great day did the high priest (and only the high priest) enter into the Holy of Holies with the blood of a bull and a goat to sprinkle it upon the mercy seat of the ark of the covenant as a sign of expiation of the sins of the people. The solemnity and singularity of this day looked forward to the once-for-all nature of the atoning sacrifice of Jesus and the sprinkling of His blood upon the cross. You might be wondering, how does blood purify people? The blood of animals is a symbol of their life. Indeed, when God spoke to Noah, allowing him to eat animals, he said that he could NOT eat animals' blood because the blood is the life of the animal and the life belongs to God.

The reason, then, that blood purifies is that it symbolizes the giving of everything (= life) back over to God. Sin and all the disorders of fallen angels and fallen humanity come from one and only one source. And that is . . . NOT giving one's life totally to God out of love. We tend to think that as long as we aren't sinning, we are doing "alright." But that's not really true. Only in total giving of ourselves to God in adoration and service are we doing what is truly right and just. Thus, in this sacrifice, in symbolically giving life back over to God, the correct order of things is partially restored. It will be totally restored when the one who IS the way and the truth and the LIFE gives His BLOOD over to the Father in atonement for the sins of the whole world.

The Apostle says in Hebrews 10:4 that "it is impossible that the blood of bulls and goats should ever take away sin," and that's true. But because this blood was a sign of the blood of Christ and because the people undertook this day in obedience to God's command to do penance, it did purify them, making the people of Israel ever more ready to be the ones who will receive from God the gift of giving the world its Redeemer in the person of Christ. Jesus is the one High Priest who will enter once for all into THE Holy of Holies—into Heaven—not with the blood of bulls and goats, but with His own blood, and who will not sprinkle His blood on the ark of the covenant, but will offer His whole life totally and directly to God the Father.

The scapegoat

This is the essence of this chapter of Leviticus. But there is one other important part of the ritual of the Day of Atonement that we need to study because it might be confusing and is very important. In Lev 16:5, Moses writes:

> From the Israelite community he shall receive two male goats for a sin offering and one ram for a holocaust....Taking the two male goats and

setting them before the LORD at the entrance of the meeting tent, he shall cast lots to determine which one is for the LORD and which for Azazel. The goat that is determined by lot for the LORD, Aaron shall bring in and offer up as a sin offering. But the goat determined by lot for Azazel he shall set alive before the LORD, so that with it he may make atonement by sending it off to Azazel in the desert . . .When he has completed the atonement rite for the sanctuary, the meeting tent and the altar, Aaron shall bring forward the live goat. Laying both hands on its head, he shall confess over it all the sinful faults and transgressions of the Israelites, and so put them on the goat's head. He shall then have it led into the desert by an attendant. Since the goat is to carry off their iniquities to an isolated region, it must be sent away into the desert. *(NAB translation)*

Azazel?

One goat was "for the Lord" and one was "for Azazel." Some translations do not have "Azazel" here, but rather "emissary goat" or "scapegoat." What's does this mean? *Azazel* is just the word in Hebrew. Some translations take it as the name of a demon and hence leave it just as a name, while some take it as a form of the word which means "to remove or send." No, this does NOT mean that the Lord was telling the Israelites to offer a goat up to a demon. That's foolish. The best answer to the question comes from understanding what the two goats were for. We already know that the goat "for the Lord" was offered as a sin offering for the people. So far so good. We've seen sin offerings before.

But what about the other? The other goat was taken into the presence of the Lord, Aaron laid his hands on the goat's head and, while doing so, confessed all of the sins of the people aloud, symbolically placing all of the sins of the people onto the goat. Then this goat, with all the sins of the people on him, was sent out into the wilderness, far away from the camp—symbolically taking the sins of the people far away from them. So much is pretty clear from what you just read. What isn't as clear, but which is really the most important part is that this goat was also killed. For a domesticated goat to be sent out into the wilderness alone was a death sentence. He would be torn to pieces and eaten by the wild animals before the night was over.

Again, the point for the Israelites is that sin = death, and also that only through a sacrificial death can we be saved from sin and the death that it brings. Understanding the typology of this passage may help us even to understand its literal sense better. The two goats are types of the two natures, human and divine, of Christ. His divine nature is offered directly to the Lord, like the first goat. His human nature, while also being an offering to God, was, like the scapegoat, given over to the ravages of the devil and sinful men = the wild beasts in the wilderness (see Mk 1:13). Jesus said as His crucifixion was approaching: "This is your hour, when darkness reigns" (Lk 22:53). Christ took upon Himself the punishment that was justly ours. The punishment our sins deserved *was Hell*—to be given up to the ravages of the devil. But upon Christ's human nature God placed all of the punishment for the sins of ALL people for ALL time, so that Christ could make reparation for the sins of men. As the Apostle also notes in the letter to the Hebrews, Jesus, like the scapegoat, was killed "outside the camp" (Hebrews 13:12-13).

Repairing the relationship with God and the damage done by sin

Thus these two goats make sense even on the literal level of the text. Why did there have to be two? Because, repairing the damage done by sin has two aspects: 1. Reestablishing the relationship with God (= the goat "for the Lord") and 2. Repairing the damage in ourselves and in the world caused by our sin (= the scapegoat).

Thus at the "center of the center" is the Day of Atonement, which looks forward to the day of the Crucifixion, when sacrifice is offered for the sin of all the people, repairing their relationship with God and damage done by sin.

Summary

In this lesson you have learned about the Day of Atonement, the importance of it's placement in the Pentateuch, the goal of this day, the way in which this goal was accomplished, and the meaning of its various rituals, and their fulfillment in Christ. Now that the whole people has been "made at one" with God, we will see in our next lesson, how they are to live out their life with God in holiness, with the commandment that is *the* essential command of Leviticus "Be Holy, For I the Lord your God am Holy" (Lev 19:2).

Questions

1. What is the central part of Leviticus?
The central part of Leviticus is devoted to explaining the Day of Atonement.

2. What is the Day of Atonement?
On this solemn great day the high priest entered the Holy of Holies with the blood of a bull and a goat to sprinkle it upon the mercy seat of the ark of the covenant as a sign of expiation of the sins of the people.

3. Of what is the Day of Atonement a type?
The day of Atonement looked forward to the once-for-all atoning sacrifice of Jesus and the "sprinkling" of His blood upon the cross.

4. What is the scapegoat?
The scapegoat was a goat which was taken by the high priest into the presence of the Lord on the Day of Atonement. The sins of the people were confessed over the goat. Then this goat, symbolically burdened with the sins of the people, would be sent away into the wilderness to be killed by wild beasts.

5. Of what is the scapegoat a type?
The scapegoat is a type of Christ's human nature, burdened with the sins of man, given up to the ravages of the devil, and sent "outside the camp" (Jerusalem) to die in reparation for sin.

Lesson 22

The Code of Holiness

From your first lesson on Leviticus, you should recall the structure of the book and how its parts are arranged in a chiasm and correspond to the parts of the Tabernacle. Since we are now past the central part of the chiasm, we will begin to see how the parts on the one side of the center match up with the parts on the other side. Let's review parts C and C' from the chart below, since that is what we will be studying now.

1. Leviticus 1–7	A Code of Sacrifice	Outer Court
2. Leviticus 8–10	B Code of Priests	Holy Place
3. Leviticus 11–15	C Code of Cleanness	Holy of Holies
4. Leviticus 16	D The Day of Atonement	The Ark of the Covenant
5. Leviticus 17–23	C' Code of Holiness	Holy of Holies
6. Leviticus 24	B' Code of Reverence	Holy Place
7. Leviticus 25–27	A' Code of Redemption of the Land	Outer Court

Parts C and C' correspond to the Holy of Holies. Both parts have to do with the perfect holiness necessary to enter into the Holy of Holies—the place of the presence of the most Holy God. Part C, which you have already studied, is a long list of commands that are ordered toward separating the people from all *things* in the material creation that reveal the fallenness of the world and likewise keeping all of these things separate from the presence of God. Part C', which we are studying in this lesson, is also a long list of commands. These commands are ordered toward keeping the people separated from all *actions* that reveal the fallenness of the world and moving them to act in a way that more perfectly reflects the all-perfect God whom they serve. God's people must be perfectly Holy to enter the presence of God—cleansed of all things and actions that are effects of the Fall, and full of the goodness that comes from being and acting like God.

Chiasm within a chiasm

It is often the case that each of the parts of a chiasm in scripture can be broken down into further parts. Sometimes these further parts are themselves a little chiasm-within-a-chiasm. There is so much beauty and order within the Scriptures that it will take the rest of Time to discover them all—and even then we may only have scratched the surface. The Scriptures may not look all that orderly at first, and our lives, like the Scriptures, can sometimes seem to be rather disorderly and merely thrown together. But God orders all things in our lives as He does all things in Scripture. If we become images of His Word, then our lives too will come to reveal the beauty and goodness of God, as the words of Scripture do.

The part of Leviticus we are studying in this lesson is an example of this. Reading it at first, it may just seem like another jumble of laws and sacrifices, etc. But if we study it more carefully, it reveals a beautiful order. Take a look at the following chart.

A	Lev 17	Priests and the Every Day Sacrifices of the people for God	God
B	Lev 18	Laws regarding the right use of marriage/family for the people	Family/spouse
C	Lev 19	Laws regarding the right treatment of neighbor	Neighbor/society
B'	Lev 20–21	Laws regarding the right use of marriage/family for people and for priests	Family/spouse
A'	Lev 22–23	Priests and the Weekly and Yearly Festivals for God	God

The order that this chart of Leviticus 17–23 reveals is

1. God
2. Family/spouse
3. Neighbor

This should remind you of something: It follows the same order as the Ten commandments, (which are revisited in the central part of this portion of Leviticus). God comes first (commandments 1–3), family (commandment #4) and spouse (commandment #5) come next, and finally, neighbor (commandments 6–10) come last. The treatment of neighbor is placed in the center of this chiasm because these laws are the most universal. They apply to everyone whereas the others apply more specifically to God or family members. Our most important relationship is our relationship with God, next with our family or spouse, and lastly with everyone else, but all of these relationships are important and affect one another. The way we treat our neighbors and family shows how we treat God. As St. John said: "How can you love the God whom you cannot see, if you do not love your brother whom you can see?" We will deal with each of the pairs in the chiasm and then deal with the center.

A and A' = God (Leviticus 17 and 22–23)

Chapters 17 and 22–23 have to do directly with the people's service of God. In chapter 17 we find numerous commandments about how the people are to bring to the priests, at the tabernacle, any animal that they kill for eating *so that it can be offered to God* as a peace offering. Otherwise, the temptation will be to offer the animal in the wilderness to false gods (demons, see Lev 17:7). These would be sacrifices that would happen at any time during the year. The people are reminded by this that the life of the animal is symbolized by its blood and that all life, especially their own, belongs to God.

In chapter 22 the priests are commanded regarding correct behavior toward the "holy things." These "holy things" are the sacrificial food offerings dedicated to God. You should remember from your first lesson on Leviticus that these were the food for the priests and their family members. This part of Leviticus is simply making clear that a priest who has any "uncleanness" or personal deformity cannot partake of these things dedicated to God, for the reasons you have already studied.

Finally, in chapter 23, we have a chapter devoted entirely to spelling out the date and duration and correct celebration of all of the festivals in which the whole people honor the Lord together. Aside from the weekly celebration of the Sabbath, there are seven yearly feasts:

1. Passover	1 day	14th day of 1st month (Lev 23:5)
2. Unleavened Bread	7 days	15th day of 1st month (Lev 23:6)
3. First Fruits	1 day	The day after the Sabbath during Passover (23:15a)
4. Pentecost ("Weeks")	1 day	Seven weeks (50th day) after first fruits (23:15b)
5. Feast of Trumpets	1 day	1st day of 7th month (23:23–25)
6. Day of Atonement	1 day	10th day of 7th month (23:26)
7. Booths or Tabernacles	7 days	15th day of 7th month (23:34)

The calendar that these feasts were based on was a lunar calendar—based on the movements of the moon and also the agricultural year. Thus, the first feast of the year is in the first month of the year, which fell in early springtime—March or April—just as the early barley crop was ripening. In the middle was the feast of Pentecost—just as the wheat harvest was ripe. And the last of the feasts was at the culmination of the final harvest of the year, the fruit harvest, in the fall. Later in Israel's history, these three feasts—First fruits, Pentecost, and Tabernacles, were when all adult Israelite men would travel to Jerusalem to celebrate them.

The feasts divide naturally into two groups. The first four are all connected since the 4th depends on the 3rd, which depends on the 2nd which depends on the 1st (as to the date of celebration). They are also connected in that they were all in the early part of the year. After Pentecost (in the third month), there was a long period, during which the people would be working hard on their farms during the long hot days of summer.

After this long period of labor, the last three feasts came in close succession—on days 1, 10, and 15-21 of the seventh month. Because it is the seventh, it is the month of perfection and completion—of bringing to completion the work begun in month one. These feasts served to bring the people together to honor the Lord and praise Him for all that He had done for them.

These feasts also look forward to their fulfillment in Christ and His Church.

1. Christ's last supper was a *Passover* meal. His blood saves us from spiritual death just as the blood of the Passover lamb saved the Israelites from physical death.

2. At the last supper, Jesus instituted the Eucharist, which St. Paul calls "the *unleavened bread* of sincerity and truth" (1 Cor 5:8). Leaven is most often used in Scripture as sign of sin. Once we have been rescued from sin, we need to feed ourselves on the bread of sincerity and truth, the Eucharistic "bread" which is Christ Himself.

3. Jesus's resurrection from the dead occurred on the day after the Sabbath during Passover, that is, on the feast of first fruits. St. Paul calls Christ the *"first-fruits"* of fallen humanity (see 1 Cor 15:20). He is the first good fruit that the earth has produced since Adam ate the forbidden fruit.

4. The Fiftieth day after Christ's resurrection was *Pentecost,* which is when the Holy Spirit came upon the disciples. This feast was the only time leavened bread was offered to God. The only time in Scripture when leaven is

used as a symbol for something other than sin is when Christ used it as a symbol for the kingdom of God, the Church (see Mat 13:33). The coming of the Holy Spirit on Pentecost is celebrated as the birthday of the Church—when the great, long, arduous work of the Church began. This is the period of the Church in which we are now—working hard to bring about the "leavening" of the world.

5. The work of the Church is the work of calling all men to Christ. The feast of *Trumpets* indicates this, since the trumpets (ram's horns) were blown for three main reasons—1. to warn of danger, 2. to announce important news, and 3. to announce the coming of the king. The Church's work is the same. She warns men of the dangers of sin, and of the coming judgment. She announces the good news of salvation, and She announces the coming of Christ as King.

6. The Church gives these messages to lead men to repentance (*Day of Atonement*)

7. Repentance leads men to life, to their everlasting dwelling with God in perfect rest (the feast of *Tabernacles*).

B and B' = Family and Spouse (Leviticus 18 and 20)

Moving from the most intimate sphere of our relationship with God ("God is closer to us than we are to ourselves," says St. Augustine), we now move into the next most intimate sphere of our relationship with family or spouse. Chapter 18 begins with the Lord forbidding His people to do as other people do. He says that they should act neither like the Egyptians (from whom they are coming) nor like the Canaanites (to whom they are still journeying). So that they know what He means, God goes on to give a number of details about how NOT to act, having especially to do with marriage and family, which is the basis every person's existence and the basis of society. Ultimately all of these commands are just spelling out the original command of God for marriage and family. The command to "be fruitful and multiply and fill the earth" (Gen 1:28) is accomplished when a man "leaves his father and his mother and cleaves to his wife" (Gen 2:24). If a man marries a person too closely related to him, he is not really leaving his father and mother.

St. John Chrysostom said of these chapters that God, through these laws, was seeking to extend the affectionate bonds of marriage to ever more and more people, so that love might increase, since love is the life of Heaven. Since bonds of affection already naturally exist between a man and his mother, daughter, sisters, aunts, etc., he should seek outside of these relationships for marriage, otherwise he would "narrow the breadth of love."

C = The Center: Neighbor and Society (Leviticus 19)

The opening command of this central chapter is the heart and soul of the message of the book of Leviticus:

> "Be holy for I the Lord your God am holy." (Lev 19:2)

The list of commands that follows this seems like another jumble of random commands, but you know better than that. Everything here is just making clear what this command to "Be Holy" means for the people. It is teaching them to act like God does—to act in a divine manner.

In this chapter we get what Jesus says was the fulfillment of the Law, that is, the command to "Love your neighbor as yourself" (Lev 19:18). That's right, the Gospels weren't the first to record that; Leviticus was. Study these commands carefully, asking yourself how each of them reveals how to act like God does, loving others as you love yourself. Even the commands in this section that are about God (19:4 for example) are placed in the context of how our attitude and actions toward God affect our neighbor. If your neighbor sees you acting irreverently toward God, he may be led astray by your bad example. There is no such thing as a private sin, nor is religion a matter of private opinion.

Summary

In this lesson you have studied the fifth part of the book of Leviticus and its correspondence to the third part of Leviticus, with their respective focus on keeping the people of Israel free from all things and actions that reveal the fallenness of the world. The theme of the book of Leviticus is found in this portion: "Be holy, for I the Lord your God am holy." You have learned the seven major feasts of the Israelite liturgical year, their connection to the agricultural cycle of the year, and their fulfillment in the life and work of Christ and His Church. Here the focus is actions—God is preparing a people who act like Him so that they can dwell with Him and He with them. In your next lesson, we will see what happens to a person who does not care about dwelling with God and so does not act reverently toward God.

QUESTIONS

1. What are the seven festivals of the Old Law given in the code of Holiness in Leviticus?

> The seven festivals of the Old Law given in the code of holiness are, in order:
> 1. Passover (spring, late March/early April)
> 2. Unleavened Bread (just after Passover)
> 3. First Fruits (first barley harvest, on the Sunday after Passover)
> 4. Pentecost (50 days after first fruits, first wheat harvest, late May/early June)
> 5. Trumpets (day 1 of seventh month) (September/October)
> 6. Atonement (day 10 of seventh month)
> 7. Tabernacles (days 15-21 of seventh month, final fruit harvest)

2. How are each of the festivals of the Old Law fulfilled in the New?

> 1. Passover - The Last supper, the sacrifice of the Mass.
> 2. Unleavened Bread - The Eucharist.
> 3. First fruits - The day of Christ's Resurrection.
> 4. Pentecost - The coming of the Holy Spirit.
> 5. Trumpets - The work of the church calling all men to Christ before Christ returns.
> 6. Atonement—The message of repentance.
> 7. Tabernacles—Loving God and neighbor and living with them forever in Heaven.

3. What is the essential command of Leviticus?

> The essential command of Leviticus, found in the fourth part, the code of holiness, is "Be holy, for I the Lord your God am holy" (Lev 19:2).

LESSON 23

The Code of Reverence

You remember from your last lesson that since we are beyond the central part of the chiasm of Leviticus, we are now comparing the parts that "match up" on either side of the center. In this lesson we will be studying part B' which is Leviticus 24. Let's review how it fits together with part B (Leviticus 8–10, the code of priests) and with the structure of the Tabernacle.

1. Leviticus 1–7	A Code of Sacrifice	Outer Court
2. Leviticus 8–10	B Code of Priests	Holy Place
3. Leviticus 11–15	C Code of Cleanness	Holy of Holies
4. Leviticus 16	D The Day of Atonement	The Ark of the Covenant
5. Leviticus 17–23	C' Code of Holiness	Holy of Holies
6. Leviticus 24	B' Code of Reverence	Holy Place
7. Leviticus 25–27	A' Code of Redemption of the Land	Outer Court

Parts B and B' correspond to *the holy place,* the first part of the Tent of Meeting where the bread of the presence, the lamp-stand, and the altar of incense were. Only the priests could enter here. Part B begins with the ordination of Aaron and his sons as priests and ends with two of Aaron's sons *dying* because they offered unholy incense *in the holy place.* They are consumed by fire and Aaron and his remaining sons must remain inside the tent of meeting *in the holy place* during that time. Part B' begins with commands for Aaron and his sons about the lamp-stand and the bread of the presence, which were *in the holy place,* and goes on to record another incident of a man who *dies* for failure to reverence God.

Things and actions

You should remember from last lesson how part C focused on *things* while C' focused on *actions.* In parts B and B' it is the same: Aaron's sons died from offering an unholy *thing,* so in B' a man whose father was Egyptian but whose mother was an Israelite of the tribe of Dan, dies from an unholy *action*—blaspheming God's name. The same will hold true, as we will see in the next lesson, for parts A–A'. In the first half of Leviticus the people are coming to know God—coming closer and closer to Him. Coming physically nearer to Him in the Tent of Meeting symbolizes coming near to Him through knowledge. In the second half of Leviticus we are symbolically moving further away from the Holy of Holies. This doesn't represent getting less knowledge of God, but rather the Israelites being called to *act* like what they have come to know: God. This corresponds to Gen 1:28 where the first commandment is to go out and fill the earth with the image of God. It also corresponds to the Mass wherein we are first called deeper and deeper into the mystery of God, especially in the Eucharist, but then are sent forth to live it.

Light and bread in the Holy Place (Lev 24:1–9)

In the first part of this chapter, the Lord describes to Moses what Aaron and his sons should care for in the Holy place. There are two main items, the lamp-stand and the twelve loaves of the memorial bread.

Light. The outer courtyard, being open to the sky, is illuminated by the sun—the light that is common to all men. This symbolizes the light of reason. But the light of the lamp-stand is of a different sort. It is not available to everyone, but only to those who come into the Holy place. It is the sacred light of revelation, in which the deeper mysteries of God, not accessible to human reason, can come to be known. Since we are now on the "way out" of the Tabernacle, the reminder of this light here is so that this light be "kept burning continually" (Lev 24:2), even as we go forth out of the holy place and into the common light of day. Even the common life of God's people is to be illuminated continually by the sacred light of the truths God has revealed.

Bread. The next part of Leviticus describes the memorial bread or more literally "bread for remembrance" (Lev 24:8). In other places this bread is called the "show bread" or the "bread of the presence" (literally, *bread of the face*). This type of the Eucharist (remember Jesus said: "Do this in *memory* of me...") is meant to show that, this divine knowledge and life received in the presence of God needs to be kept alive and strong, now that we are leaving the presence of God to go out into the world. Bread is for strength (see Psalm 104:15), but this bread is also "for remembrance." The primary way the divine life is kept alive and strong is by remembering it. It can only get into your heart if it is first on your mind. This doesn't just mean to remember the things of God as one group of things among many things on a list that you have to remember. It means to hold them as most precious—loving them and living them with your whole heart. So remember!

What is the greatest danger to the practice of your faith?
"And the son of the Israelite woman blasphemed the Name and he cursed" (Lev 24:11).

The story that comes next may seem random. Here we were talking about the Holy Place and what is in it, and then suddenly we are back out in the camp talking about a half-Israelite man who "blasphemed" and "cursed" God. Why?

The connection between these two things is not as apparent in English translations as it is in Hebrew. First of all, remember that in the second half of Leviticus the focus has been on action—on living and acting according to the truth about God learned in the first half.

This story about the man who "cursed" is a way of warning against that action which is the greatest danger to the divine truths we have learned.

The word translated as "blasphemed" literally means "pierced," while the word translated as "curse" literally means "to make light of" or "to hold of little account" or "to be trifling." The point here is that to treat God as "trifling" is ultimately to "pierce" Him. To fail to revere God is to kill Him. To be given the things of God, and then to fail to hold them as the most precious of all things—to fail to hold them continually in remembrance as your most precious possession—is the gravest danger to your faith.

This man is half-Egyptian. Egypt, you remember, is the type of this world under the dominion of sin. So this man who is still "half" under the dominion of sin treats the things of God as if they were trifling and not that important. People, even people who bear the name of Christian, say and do stupid and bad things that reveal a lack of reverence for God and the truths of the faith all the time, and justify it by thinking "it's no big deal" or "we were just having fun," or maybe they don't think about it at all. They treat it lightly, as if God and fulfilling the commands of God were not the most important thing. The end result of this is to kill the reverence that others have for God, which is ultimately to seek a life without God, to kill the life of God in the soul. This is serious.

Why is this law of strict justice given here?

Following this incident, a number of laws illustrating a strict justice are given: Whatever evil you do, it will be done back to you. Why are these here? What is the connection between these and the story of the half-Egyptian man who cursed God? This connection is made more explicit by the laws which follow. To fail to reverence God is to "kill" Him, which is ultimately to kill yourself. To fail to reverence God in your neighbor is also to kill yourself. These laws of Justice also are indicating here that in blaspheming God the man deserves death because he has, insofar as he was able, killed God. He killed God so he gets killed. He killed the life of God in him, so He deserves to lose his life.

You should love your neighbor as yourself, and guess who your closest neighbor is? God is your closest of neighbors—the guest of our own soul!

These laws show the intimate connection between God and the one made in God's image—between a person and his neighbor. You are to love your neighbor as yourself. So if you hate your neighbor, and do something evil to him, the law states that you should have the same thing done to you. Why? Because you should be so convinced that loving your neighbor *is* loving yourself that if you break that rule and hate your neighbor, then it is like hating yourself—something bad will happen to you. Hating your neighbor is as stupid as hating yourself. These laws help to make this truth more obvious. If you do something bad to someone else, the same thing happens to you.

It's almost as if a man hit some one on the head but immediately felt the pain in his own head. But what if I don't get caught and punished—then it's not painful, is it? Well, if you don't get caught and punished the only difference is that it isn't as obvious to you that the evil you did has come back upon you. In reality, though, any time anyone does evil, something far worse than having that same evil done to them *has already happened to them*. When we do evil, *it sickens or kills the best thing in us—the life of God.* Stupid people ("the fool" of Psalm 53:1) think (if they think about it at all) that because they can't see this with their eyes, then it must not be true, or must not matter.

The physical world has laws. For example, two bodies cannot occupy the same space at the same time. My head and a brick wall, for example, cannot both be in the same space at the same time. If I try to break this law, it will hurt me. The spiritual world, the world of our intellect and will, also has rules. The rule of the intellect is truth, and the rule of the will is love. If we break these rules it hurts us.

Why didn't God just make the spiritual world like the physical world—if I break a law I automatically feel pain? Well, He did. But the pain we feel at breaking a spiritual law isn't physical usually, at least not right away. When we break a physical law, we immediately feel physical pain. When we break a spiritual law (love your neighbor), we do immediately feel spiritual pain. But that, precisely, is the problem: it's spiritual. Ever since Adam fell, humans have gotten very, very good at ignoring everything spiritual, including their own spiritual pain. So physical punishment is added to this to make it more obvious to those who only notice physical things. If you poke out someone's eye, the same will be done to you. If you break someone's bones, the same is done to you. This law of strict justice is one of the steps by which God is leading His people to the supreme law of love, which is to "love one another as I have loved you" (John 13:34).

Summary

In this lesson, you have studied the code of reverence in Leviticus. You have seen its connections to the code of holiness. As we are to be holy, so we are continually to keep in remembrance the holiness of God, by revering Him. You have learned the root meanings of the words translated as "curse" and "blaspheme," and have seen how the failure to be enlightened by God and to nourish this enlightenment by the continual remembrance and living out of what God has given is the greatest danger to faith. You have also learned how the law of strict justice given here is a tool by which God is leading the people to revere God and the presence of God in our neighbor, and ultimately to the supreme law of love.

QUESTION

What is the essence of the sixth part of Leviticus?

The essence of the sixth part of Leviticus, the code of reverence, is to remember and revere the things of God as the most important of all things.

LESSON 24

The Code of Redemption of the Land

This will be our final lesson on the book of Leviticus. Throughout these lessons we have been referring to the chart that shows how the parts of Leviticus correspond to the parts of the Tabernacle. We are now on the last part, A' (read "A prime"), which corresponds to the first part, A.

In the last lesson, you learned how the two parts in each pair of the chiasm have a different emphasis. The first part of the pair emphasizes knowledge and things, while the second part emphasizes love and actions. This is to show that we must begin by coming to know God, but we must end by loving Him and acting as He does. As Jesus taught, the goal is not simply to know God, but to BE and ACT like God—"Be perfect, as your heavenly Father is perfect" (Matt 5:48; see also 1 John 3:2, "we shall be like Him"). This also corresponds to the Mass where we first learn about God from the Scriptures, then receive Him in the Most Holy Sacrament of His body and blood, and then are sent forth (*Ite missa est*) to live and do what we have learned and received.

This is why this last portion of Leviticus is all about what the Israelites are to DO when they get to the Promised Land. Parts A and A' correspond to the outer court of the sanctuary because the first deals mainly with sacrifices. The sacrifices themselves are all the products of *the land* (animals and plants or plant-products). Also, you remember, the place where animals are sacrificed is on the altar in the *outer courtyard*. The animal and grain offerings that will take place here represent the fruits *of the Promised Land* God is going to give the people. The outer court is open to the sky and represents *the Promised Land* itself, which in turn represents the whole world, which is meant to glorify God in worship.

This last part of Leviticus is all about how the Israelites are to treat *the Land* that God is giving them, and how they are to treat each other in the Land, so that they remember that *the Land is only* FOR THEM *so that they can be* FOR GOD. This in turn teaches about the purpose of the whole world. What God is doing with Israel is a miniature of what He is doing with the whole cosmos—creating a moving and material "picture" of the invisible realm of eternity, in which His creatures can live and love and worship Him who is their very life. Everything in this last section of Leviticus is to remind the priests and people of Israel of God's absolute sovereignty—He is the Lord and Master of Heaven and Earth. He IS life—and only by adhering to His ways can we hope to share in His life.

There are three basic parts in this last section of Leviticus, which correspond with the three last chapters.
1. Chapter 25 = The Promised Land and the people Israel are God's.
2. Chapter 26 = God's promises (covenant) to His people for their life in the Land.
3. Chapter 27 = The people's promises (vows) to God when they live in the Land

We will deal briefly with each in order.

Ch. 25: The Promised Land and the people Israel are God's

The Sabbath years and the Jubilee years which we read about here teach that this land that God is giving His people is not like the land of other nations. Every seventh year, like every seventh day, is a time of joyful rest. Likewise the year after the "seventh-seventh" year (50th year) was a time of great "jubilee," when everyone who had become separated from their ancestral land would return to it, where all debts were forgiven, where life started over again, as it was in the beginning, with everyone free and in their home place and among their family.

When he read this passage, St. Clement of Alexandria noted that 49 years makes it so that *no one* who lives a normal lifespan will be separated from his ancestral land for his whole life. He will at least be there for part of it. Everyone will get a chance to experience the life God intended for them.

Our word "jubilee" comes the Hebrew word *yobel* which was the ram's horn that was blown on the day of Atonement (Lev 25:9).

Just as the people were commanded in Chapter 18 to *not* be like the other people around them, so the Land that is being given to them is not to be treated like other lands. It is not merely for profit and it is not merely their possession. Hence, they must let it rest, as God did. They must trust God to supply for them in the seventh year while the land rests. The land does not belong to them, but rather belongs to God and those to whom God gives it.

Hence they must give back the land to its original owners every so often as a reminder and reinstatement of this all-important fact. All of this signifies that the Land belongs to the people only so that they can, in this Land, honor the God who gave it to them. This implies that if the land is not being used for its proper purpose, it will be taken away (this point is made explicitly in the next chapter).

Ch. 26: God's promises to His people for their life in the land

After telling them how to live in the Land, God tells them what they can expect if they obey—or disobey. When you read Leviticus 26, you should remember Genesis 2, the Garden of Eden. Although the whole earth was given to Man, Eden was where he first experienced this gift from God, and where he first lived in a covenant of love and obedience with God. Now God gives promises to the People of Israel (seven of them, in fact) that, if the people listen and obey God's statues, then:
1. The land shall yield its increase (Lev 26:4),
2. the trees of the field shall yield their fruit (Lev 26:4),
3. there will be peace in the land (Lev 26:6a),
4. no evil beasts (no serpent?!) (Lev 26:6b),
5. no enemies (Lev 26:7-8),
6. God will make the people "fruitful and multiply" (Lev 26:9),
7. most important, "I will walk among you" (Lev 26:12).

Just as God "sevens" Himself with these promises, so He sevens Himself again in a renewal of the covenant (Lev 26:9).

However, (beginning in verse 14) there is also a very severe and stern warning about what will happen if the people do not obey the statutes God is giving them. (Here these are just a threat; in Deuteronomy 30 they will become a prophecy.) All of the plagues that He cast upon the Egyptians, and even worse (Lev 26:29!) He will cast upon the Israelites. These are a way of showing the people what it is that departing from God and His ways does to them. Following God = life and happiness; leaving God and His ways behind = death and misery.

But even if all of these terrible things come to pass, God opens up a door of hope. First of all, notice that these things are done as discipline and training of God's people to get them to reform, not simply to kill them (Lev 26:23). In Lev 26:40 God also tells the people that even if all of these terrible things happen they can still return to Him. The people can repent, and, after they have atoned for their sins, God will "remember" His covenant. The Hebrew word for "repent" means to "turn around" and to "return." One of the worst results of the sins of the people is that they will be exiled from the

Promised Land. As Adam and Eve were exiled from Eden, and as the Promised Land is a New Eden, so if the people sin, they will be exiled again. But God, being ever merciful, will seek them out again and bring them back. God always hates sin, but He is infinitely patient and merciful with sinners.

In Lev 26:43 God says something that might seem very strange. When it happens that the people are exiled from the Land, then "The land will enjoy its Sabbaths." What this means is that the major temptation of the people when they get into the Land is to "skip" the laws regarding the Sabbath years. They are going to get to that seventh year and be tempted to see that year as a waste of time, instead of seeing it as a time for God. "I could be making money!" "I need to feed my family!" "If I don't work, I'm not going to eat!" Or they won't redeem the land—they won't return it to its original owner.

Think about it. Think about the kind of trust it would take to NOT plant your fields for a year—and that is your only source of food. Think of the kind of trust it would take to NOT worry about where your money, food, clothing, housing, etc. would come from for a whole year. Think about buying a piece of land from someone and then having to just give it back. Now, it's true that the price would be set according to the number of years you owned it before the Jubilee, and it's true that God would provide enough in the years *before* the seventh to last all the way till the harvest in the eighth, but think of how much trust it would take to really believe that and simply stop everything, give everything back, and *spend a whole year devoted to God rather than gain.*

The word for the "liberty" to be proclaimed at the beginning of the Jubilee year (Lev 25:10) at root is the Hebrew word for a kind of bird—the swallow. The people were to be as free as the swallows that swoop around in the sky! The prophet Isaiah would later proclaim a year of "liberty" (Isa 61:1–2) using the same word, and Jesus would later begin His public ministry using the very same words of Isaiah (Luke 4:16–20)!

But what IS this great liberty and freedom? Is it just freedom from work and debt or the freedom to go do what you want for a while?

King David described what this liberty was, using the very same word:

> How lovely is your dwelling place, O LORD of hosts! My soul yearns and pines for the courts of the LORD. My heart and flesh cry out for the living God. As the sparrow finds a home and the swallow a nest to settle her young, My home is by your altars, LORD of hosts, my king and my God! Happy are those who dwell in your house! They never cease to praise you (Psalm 84:1–4)

The Jubilee sets people free like the swallow in order to do what the swallow does—go and live in the house of God, forever singing His praise. The real "work" of creation is the liturgy, which is a Greek word that means "public work." The real work of mankind is the liturgy—to worship God together—so that from the rising of the sun even to its setting, the name of the Lord is praised. So, Lev 26:43 shows that the Sabbath and Jubilee years are the devotion of the best things to God. The curses discussed come from NOT devoting the best to God. The point is this: the worship of God is life, anything else is death.

Jesus would call people to the same trust that God called His people to in the Jubilee years by again pointing them to the birds: "Therefore I tell you, do not be anxious about your life, what you shall eat or what you shall drink, nor about what you shall wear . . . Look at *the birds of the air: they neither sow, nor reap, nor gather* into barns, and yet your heavenly Father feeds them (Matt 6:25-26). Now look at Lev 25:11—in the Jubilee *you shall neither sow, nor reap, nor gather*)!

Jesus was calling people to live a Jubilee year—to take the time that He was there among them to focus their whole life and heart and energy on loving God and being perfect in trusting and worshipping God! Just before this in Matthew's Gospel, Jesus also went to the root of the problem of NOT following the Jubilee year. Why don't people follow the Jubilee year if it's such a great thing? Because, in order to do it, you have to *stop* doing everything else: "You cannot serve both God and mammon (= money, wealth, riches)" (Matt 6:24). St. Paul would later say that "love of money is the root of all evil" for the same reason—because it leads to not keeping the Sabbath. The Sabbath signifies the best and doing the thing that leads one away from that is the root of all evil. *Corruptio optimi pessima.*

This kind of perfection was at least as hard then as it is now, but it is still the perfection to which God calls His people (Matt 5:48).

Ch 27: The People's promises to God when they live in the land

God's focus on His *divine covenant* and His divine fulfillment of it to His people at the end of Leviticus 26 prepare the way for Leviticus 27 with its focus on *human vows* and man's fulfillment of them. Chapter 26 ends with God's promise: here is what I will do if you obey or disobey me. Chapter 27 makes the book of Leviticus end with a statement of what the people will do for God. God has offered, but the people must respond.

These final laws govern free-will offerings and vows to God and the free dedication of people, animals, houses, and lands to God. Once in the land, it will happen that people, for various reasons, will make a free-will offering or vow to God—either for something they hope God will do or for something that God has already done. *Lord, if you will do thus and such for me, or because you have done thus and such for me, then I will do thus and such for you. I will dedicate my servant, house, land, animals, etc., to you.*"

Once they have dedicated (literally "sanctified") something, it is set apart for God for a period of time. But it may happen that they want it back. They can redeem it, that is, buy it back, in the ways stated here. The people can freely offer things to God, but there are some exceptions to what they can offer (Lev 27:26), and to what they can redeem, once it is offered (Lev 27:28).

Thus, just as the book began with free-will offerings, so it ends with freewill offerings. The point of all of this is that God is showing the importance of the people's response to His call. God calls them to be Holy as He is Holy. He calls them to adhere to His commands with their whole heart. He has shown them the way to life. All of this is wonderful, but the people have to respond. Now that they have received the word of God they need to accept it and do it.

Summary

In this lesson you have completed your study of the book of Leviticus. You have learned how the last three chapters of this book show how God gives the land to the people so that the people can be for God—that is, so they can worship God and through this find life. You have learned the meaning and importance of the "Jubilee" year and the "liberty" proclaimed at the beginning of this year. You have learned how the book ends and why it ends this way—with a description of how the people respond to the promises of God. The question of HOW the people will respond to the call of God sets the stage for the next book in the Pentateuch (Numbers), in which the men of Israel will be called to put their lives and the lives of their wives and children totally into God's hands, so that they can enter the Promised Land—less than two years after they left Egypt.

Questions

1. What is the essence of the seventh and final part of Leviticus?
    The essence of the seventh and final part of Leviticus is that the Land is God's.

2. If the Land is God's, why does He give it to the People?
    God gives the Land to the People so that they can have a place to be set apart with God and for God.

3. Of what is the Promised Land a symbol?
    As a symbol, the Promised Land is connected to the whole cosmos, the earth, the garden of Eden, the tabernacle, the Temple, and man's body (especially Christ's). All of these are physical, material places which typify (= are types of) the intimacy of love between God and man to which man is called, which is begun in this life and fulfilled in Heaven.

NUMBERS

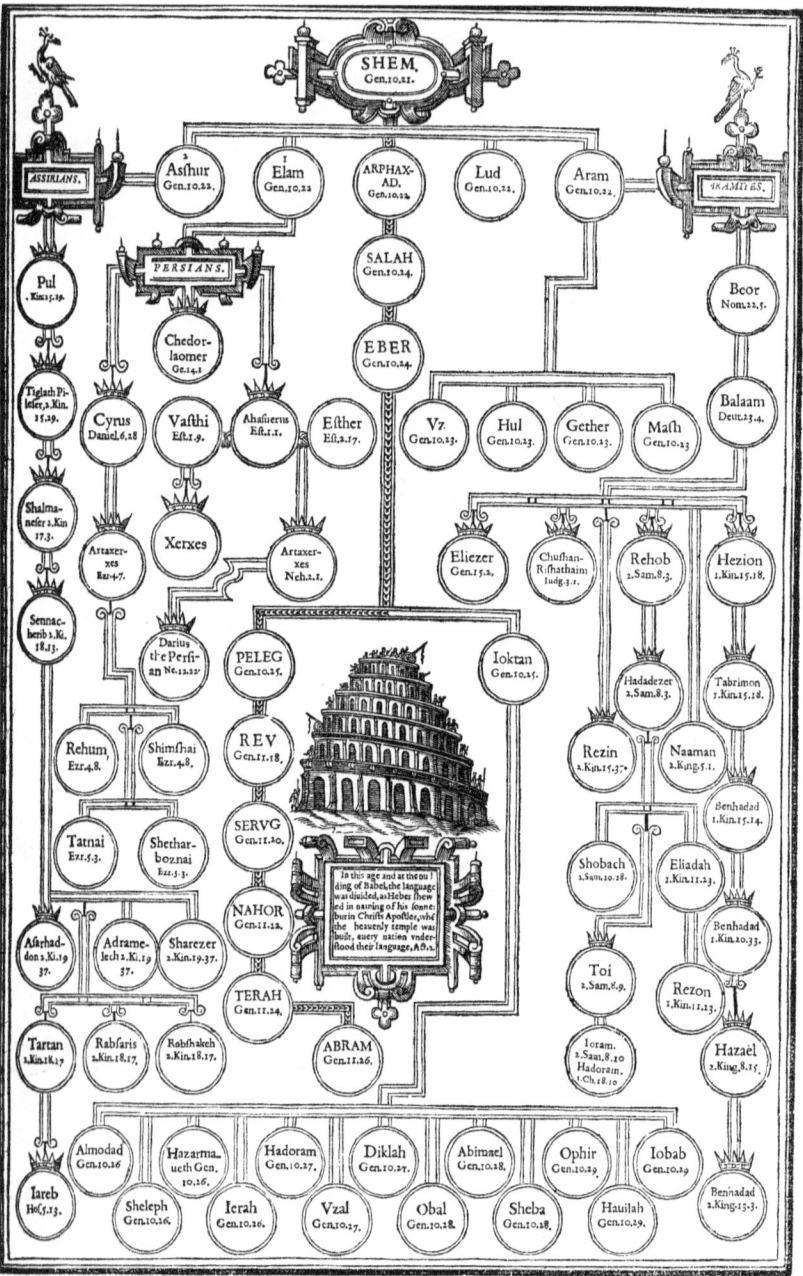

LESSON 25

That's a Lot of Numbers

We are now in the fourth book of the Pentateuch, the book of Numbers. The title "Numbers" comes from the Greek Septuagint (translated from the Hebrew 300 BC) title of the book, which was *Arithmoi* (like the word *arithmetic*), which was later translated into Latin as *Numera* and from thence to English as *Numbers*. The reason for this is that the book records many "numberings" of the people of God. The first and last parts of this book record a census, in which the people are counted. In Hebrew this book is called *Bemidbar*, from the fifth word in the Hebrew text, which means "in the wilderness." This is also a fitting name for this book since it is in this book that the Israelites have to wander, in the wilderness, for forty years. The wandering is, in fact, the central part of this book.

The time of Numbers

At this point in the story, believe it or not, the people have been out of Egypt less than a year. Take a look at the following time table to help you understand the timing of the different parts of the Pentateuch we have read so far.

1. Exodus from Egypt	15th day of 1st Month	Exod 12:2; Num 33:3
2. Arrival at Mt. Sinai	1st day of 3rd Month (6 weeks later)	Exod 19:1
3. The Lord gives instructions for the people and the building of the Tabernacle	Morning of the 3rd day of 3rd month (about one day after arrival at Sinai)	Exod 19:16
4. Completion of the Tabernacle	1st day of the 1st month, 2nd year (fifty weeks post-exodus)	Exod 40:17
5. God's command to count the Israelites	1st day of the 2nd month, 2nd year (52 weeks post-exodus)	Num 1:1

Even though Leviticus took such a long time to get through, it all "happened" between items 4 and 5 on the table above. The Tabernacle was completed less than a year after the Israelites left Egypt. Then Leviticus gives all the instructions for correct worship in that Tabernacle. As you learned already, these instructions are for preparing the people for how to live their life as God's people in the Promised Land. And *now*, just *one year* after they left Egypt, God commands that the people be counted before moving into the Promised Land.

The structure of the book of Numbers

The book of Numbers begins one year (52 weeks) after the Exodus. But it won't end until 40 years after the Exodus, just as the NEXT generation of Israelites are about to enter the Promised Land and so need to be counted, again. You have enough training now that when you read that the beginning and ending parts of the book both have a census, you should expect to find evidence that the book is structured as a chiasm. And indeed it is. But before we get to the chiasm there is one other feature of the book that it will be helpful to know ahead of time.

Numbers is even more difficult than Leviticus!

Numbers sometimes proves even more difficult to read than Leviticus because it frequently goes back and forth between sections that are devoted to laws and sections that are devoted to narratives (the stories that relate what is actually happening with the people, not just laws about what they should be doing). Leviticus stuck to one sort of literature for the most part, but Numbers alternates between different types of literature. Simply knowing this in advance can ease much of the difficulty. Knowing *when* it is going to happen can help even more. Here is when it is going to happen: Narrative (N) and Law (L) alternate in a fairly consistent pattern throughout the entire book, as follows:

Chapters	Law/Narrative
1–10:10	L
10:11–14:45	N
15	L
16–17	N
18–19	L
20–25	N
26:1–27:11	L
27:12–23	N
28–30	L
31:1–33:49	N
33:50–36:13	L

Even more of the difficulty is removed if we keep in mind that this isn't just a random going back and forth. Rather, there are very often important themes and ideas that connect the Law material to the Narrative material that preceded it, or that follows it, or both. So be on the lookout for connections as you read along.

The seven-part chiasm of the book of Numbers

Numbers is now the fourth book of the Pentateuch that we have divided into seven parts, the pairs of which form a chiasm. This can help greatly with your ability to remember the book, its parts, and their meanings, so spend some time on this.

A	Numbers 1–6	Census #1 (for war and worship)
B	Numbers 7–8	Worship
C	Numbers 9–10	Movement toward the Land #1
D	Numbers 11–19	40 years of wandering
C'	Numbers 20	Movement toward the Land #2
B'	Numbers 21–25	War
A'	Numbers 26–36	Census #2 (for entering the Land)

Let's spend a little time on each of the parts of the chiasm.

A and A'—the census

Both of these parts of the book of Numbers begin with a Census. In the first one, God commands that all the men who are old enough to go into battle be counted and then all the Levite men old enough for service in the Tabernacle. The second census is a census of the NEXT generation of Israelites, because the first generation have all died during the forty years of wandering (see part D below).

B and B'—worship and war

We should note this right away: in the first census, God is drawing a connection between what the people are doing in taking over the Promised Land from its sinful inhabitants through warfare, and what the Levites are doing in their service of God in the Tabernacle. This connection is emphasized in these sections. In B the Levites are consecrated for Worship and all of the tribes that were numbered earlier for war are again numbered, along with all of their sacrificial gifts to the Lord for worship. War and worship may seem like the two most opposite things, but in your next lesson you will learn some surprising ways in which God is pointing the way to a very deep truth about the spiritual life of His people in all of this. For now, just ponder what St. Paul said in Ephesians 6:10–12:

> Be strong in the Lord and put on the whole armor of God that you may be able to stand against the methods of the devil. For we are not fighting against flesh and blood but against the world-rulers of this darkness, against the spiritual powers of evil in high places.

After this section of the lesson, we will also be dealing with the difficult question of God's commands to His people to kill all the peoples currently inhabiting the Promised Land.

C and C'—movement toward the Promised Land

After parts A and B have numbered and ordered the people around the Tabernacle and strengthened the people through the worship of God, the people are sent out (just as we are after worshipping God at Mass!) to begin moving toward the Promised Land. C is where the movement toward the land begins. In D movement toward the Land stops and the wandering begins. Then in C' the next generation starts moving toward the Promised Land again.

D—The center: wandering in the wilderness

This section covers three basic things. First God brings the first generation up to the Promised Land and orders them to go in and take it. Second, because they are afraid of fighting the inhabitants, they rebel against God and Moses and want to return to Egypt. Third, because they would not enter into the Promised Land, they are cursed to wander until the fortieth year, when all who sinned in the first generation have died.

The commands to destroy ALL

In Numbers 31 we see God command the army of Israel to kill all the males of the Midianites, which they did (Num 31:7). Then Moses also commands them to kill all the women and male children, leaving only the young girls alive (Num 31:17). Reading this and similar passages in Scripture scandalizes many people. How could God command such a cruel punishment to prisoners of war, defenseless women, and little children?

There are some difficulties in this, but there are also a number of principles to keep in mind when reading these passages which will help you to understand them correctly.

1. God is sovereign

As the absolute Lord and Maker of Heaven and Earth, God has the complete and total right to do as He pleases with all that He has created. As we know very clearly from the first page of the Bible—God did not have to create anything and we don't have a "right" to our existence. It is a gift. Period.

When King Solomon (whom the Bible calls the wisest of men) was writing about the same question we are dealing with, he said:

> For who will say, 'What hast thou done?' Or will resist thy judgment? Who will accuse thee for the destruction of nations which thou didst make? Or who will come before thee to plead as an advocate for unrighteous men? For neither is there any God besides thee, whose care is for all men, to whom thou shouldst prove that thou hast not judged unjustly; nor can any king or monarch confront thee about those whom thou hast punished. Thou art righteous and rulest all things righteously, deeming it alien to thy power to condemn him who does not deserve to be punished. For thy strength is the source of righteousness, and thy sovereignty over all causes thee to spare all. *(Wisdom 12)*

Since the Fall, and the breaking of friendship with God, it is even more true that we do not *deserve* our existence. ALL of humanity comes into existence deserving God's wrath, not His love. (Yes, we still believe this, which is one of the reasons we baptize babies—it's not just a nice ceremony, but is actually *necessary* to put them in a right relationship with God). So, the first point is that, in strict justice, God does not *have* to create or sustain anyone in existence.

2. God is both just and merciful to sinners

We see with Pharaoh an example of how God gives the sinner many, many, many chances to turn away from sin (remember all the plagues). But after a certain amount of rejection of God, the sinner merits the worst of all punishments—that of having the grace of repentance removed from him. Through the abuse of his freedom, the sinner can close himself off from grace. Then the only thing the sinner is able to receive is punishment and destruction.

Back in Genesis, we saw another example of this when God revealed to Abraham what would happen to his descendants. We read that his descendants *"shall come back here in the fourth generation; for the iniquity of the Amorites is not yet complete"* (Gen 15:16). Now (in Numbers) Abraham's descendants are coming back . . . and now the iniquity of the Amorites (among others) has been completed. Israel is the instrument of God's justice upon them.

King Solomon also commented on this point:

> But even these (Canaanites) thou didst spare, since they were but men, and didst send wasps as forerunners of thy army, to drive them out little by little, though thou wast not unable to give the ungodly into the hands of the righteous in battle, or to destroy them at one blow by dread wild beasts or thy stern word. But judging them little by little thou gavest them a chance to repent, though thou wast not unaware that their origin was evil and their wickedness inborn, and that their way of thinking would never change. For they were an accursed race from the beginning, and it was not through fear of any one that thou didst leave them unpunished for their sins. *(Wisdom 12)*

3. Free will and divine Providence are both real

We have already seen from the Book of Exodus that Man is created with a free will. Even though God knows beforehand what we will do, this does not change the fact that our actions are free and that therefore we are responsible for them. God knew before it happened that Pharaoh would "harden his heart" against the command of God, but Pharaoh still really had a choice in the matter. He *chose* not to listen. We can reject God and thereby make ourselves worthy of what comes naturally from rejecting Him who is our life. Destruction and death are the natural result of separating ourselves from God and His will. This is the case with the people God commanded the Israelites to kill.

4. This is a punishment for the sin of the inhabitants of the land

Again, let's look at what Solomon says on this point:

> Those who dwelt of old in thy holy land thou didst hate for their detestable practices, their works of sorcery and unholy rites, their merciless slaughter of children, and their sacrificial feasting on human flesh and blood. These initiates from the midst of a heathen cult, these parents who murder helpless lives, thou didst will to destroy by the hands of our

fathers, that the land most precious of all to thee might receive a worthy colony of the servants of God. (Wisdom 12)

5. This is a warning for the Israelites

The Israelite men had to KILL these sinful people, with their own hands. In doing so, they would have received a very graphic and gruesome lesson about the dangers and effects of sin. As much as it was justice for the Canaanites, it was a very real, stern, unforgettable warning for the Israelites.

6. This is necessary because of Israel's exalted vocation

Even the dullest reader of the Pentateuch can see that the narratives purposefully focus our attention on the ways in which Israel is whiny, stubborn, and prone to idolatry before the time of the conquest. But they also tell us of Israel's exalted calling to be God's firstborn son and a priestly nation. If they were to remain in God's good graces, they needed both the complete isolation from bad influences *and* the graphic "hands-on" lesson given by the slaughter of the Canaanites: "This is what the sin of this people and your own tendency toward sin makes necessary."

The message is: there can be no friendship with sin—it has to be ruthlessly rooted out. This is how the Church Fathers understood these passages in Scripture. The attitude of the Israelites toward the Canaanites should be our attitude toward the devil, sin, and evil generally: kill it, no mercy.

After the Fall and the subsequent downward spiral of humanity in Gen 3-11, God called Abram and promised that by his descendents all the nations of the earth would be blessed. When Israel was formed at Mt. Sinai, God told them that they will be "a kingdom of priests and a holy nation" (Exod 19:6). Thus, the blessing that is to come to ALL nations *depends* in some way on Israel's holiness. The process of separation from other peoples and the killing of the Land's inhabitants was ordered toward the blessing of all nations. So, even in this case, Joseph's insight stands: no matter what evil people may intend, "God intended it for good." God brings good out of every evil.

7. This is only for the Promised Land—and that's it

There is no notion at all of a continued armed conquest that will overtake the whole world. Instead, this is only for a particular place—Canaan—that will be set apart for God's purposes. And the purpose is . . . *blessing* (not armed conquest) of the whole world.

Summary

In this lesson you have learned the Greek and Hebrew names of the fourth book of the Pentateuch, their meanings, and their fittingness as titles for this book. You learned the seven part chiastic structure of the book and the relation of the parts to each other and the whole. Finally you have learned some principles for the correct understanding of those difficult passages in Scripture where God commands the Israelites to destroy their enemies. In your next lesson, you will begin to study the first census of God's people and find out the surprising truth about the "war" that God is waging in the world.

QUESTION

What are the main features of the Book of Numbers?

The seven main features of the Book of Numbers, which form a chiasm, are as follows:

A	Numbers 1–6	Census #1 (for war and worship)
B	Numbers 7–8	Worship
C	Numbers 9–10	Movement toward the Land #1
D	Numbers 11–19	40 years of wandering
C'	Numbers 20	Movement toward the Land #2
B'	Numbers 21–25	War
A'	Numbers 26–36	Census #2 (for entering the Land)

LESSON 26

The First Census of the People

In our last lesson we learned the whole structure of the Book of Numbers, so we are now ready to go into more detail on each of the parts. As you learned in your last lesson, the focus of the first part is the census. This first part has three sections.

1. The first is the census which separates out the men who can go to war (Numbers 1-2)
2. The second is the census which separates out those men who can serve in the tabernacle for worship (Numbers 3-4)
3. The third separates out those men and women who for physical, moral, or spiritual reasons need to be apart from the people. (Numbers 5-6)

You know the routine—we will deal with each in order.

1. Census of men for war: why is God counting the people? (Num 1-2)

Well, He certainly isn't doing it for His own benefit. He who knows the number of the hairs on our heads has no need of a census to figure out how many people He has. No, He is commanding that the people be counted for *their* benefit, because He is about to call them to a new and wonderful role in their relationship with God. It will help them in this new role to know that God has been faithful to His promise to Abraham that He would increase and multiply and become exceedingly numerous. Just as God was faithful to His promise regarding descendants, which the Israelites will now be able to see and literally count with their own eyes, so the Israelites can trust that God will be faithful to the other parts of the promise—in particular, the Land.

From infant to militant

The census is not to count every single man, woman and child in Israel, but only those men, twenty years old and older, who are fit for battle (Num 1:3). The new role that He is calling the men of Israel to be warriors for God.

Prior to this God had told the people that they had only to sit still and the Lord would fight for them (Exod 14:14). The prophet Hosea recalls how "when Israel was a child I loved him and out of Egypt I called my son" (Hos 11:1). But now He is calling them to a new level of maturity. Getting the Israelites OUT of the land of Egypt was completely God's doing. Now God wants the people's participation in His action of getting them INTO the Promised Land. They are being called to participate in and work for the fulfillment of God's promises to them. God has promised, and so they can be certain of victory and God's continued help (Exod 27:28–29), but they still have to go and do it. God does not need their help, but desires their willingness, for only that willingness to put their life totally in the service of God will make them able to receive and keep the gift that God is giving them in the Promised Land, which is ultimately nothing less than the gift of Himself.

Counting the people is also part of bringing them into order as an army, according to their tribes, around the Tabernacle (Numbers chapter 2). The Church Fathers noted with delight that the shape of the army of God as it encamped around the presence of God in the Tabernacle was . . . the shape of a cross! If you stood to the east, looking back toward the Tabernacle, Judah's camp would be the longest arm, Ephraim's the shortest, and Dan and Reuben's almost equal. (See the picture for an idea of how the tribes were arranged and how it might have looked.)

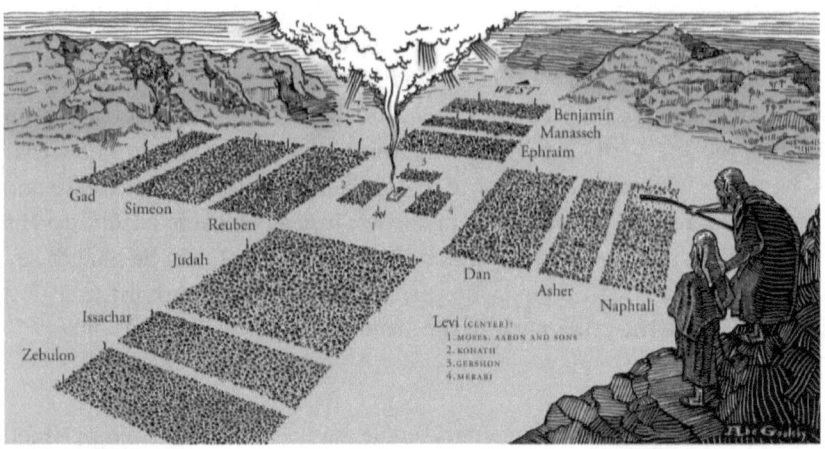

So although this is a real army and they are really going to fight and kill the inhabitants of the Land in punishment for their sins, the army itself—in its very shape—looks forward to the real "weapon" by which God is going to fight and defeat all sin: when His own firstborn Son by nature will take up, not the sword, but the cross, and take upon His own body all of the violence and punishment for all sins ever. The Church militant will continue this work of Christ—going out into battle in the world not with swords and spears but armed with the word of God and the love of God.

Notice that the Levites are not counted in the census for battle, but rather are counted separately for their service in the Tabernacle. Yet there are still twelve tribes. Why? Because Jacob adopted Joseph's two sons—Ephraim and Manasseh (Genesis 48). So each of them count as a tribe. Notice also that the sons of Rachel are the smallest in number and are all in a group to the west, opposite Leah's most important son, Judah, to the east. Moses and Aaron camped near the entrance to the Tabernacle, with the Levites and Kohathites (servants of the Levites in their sacred duties) camped all around it. Note also that Judah has the place of honor—to the east, where the sun rises. We mentioned in your final lesson on Genesis that Ephraim is a type of the Gentiles and Judah of the Jews. The sun rises in Judah, but sets in Ephraim. Think about that for a while...

The total number of men ready for battle comes to over 600,000. And that's just the *men* and only those men over 20 years old. God has certainly been faithful to His promise to give Abraham numerous descendants. The numerology of 6 is important here. Six is the number of man apart from God. This army, apart from God, is not good, but with God it can do all things.

2. Worship (Num 3-4)

The first census is for war but the second is for worship. The Levites are numbered separately from the rest of the people, just as their function as priests sets them apart from the people for the direct service of God in the Tabernacle (Num 3:14). When God saved the firstborn of the Israelites from death in Egypt at that first Passover, they all became HIS in a special way. Now, instead of taking the firstborn of ALL of the Israelites to be priests, God is simply taking one tribe who will all be priests (Num 3:11-13) and serve with different roles at the Tabernacle (Numbers 4). This again points to the purpose of the war—it isn't conquest for possession so much as it is conquest for worship. Remember also that the Levites were first consecrated as priests because in their faithfulness and zeal for God they were willing to kill even their own kinsmen who had turned to idolatry and rebellion (Exod 32:25-29).

3. The others (Num 5–6)

As mentioned earlier, the last section of this first part deals with those who for physical, moral, or spiritual reasons are apart from the people. The physical reasons are diseases and such. You already know how to understand these from your lessons in Leviticus. The moral reasons addressed are first, "any of the sins that men commit by breaking faith with the Lord." The men are commanded to *confess* their sins and to make *restitution* for what they have done. The next moral problem is that of adultery and marital jealousy, in which a woman breaks faith with her husband (or the husband *suspects* that she has). Again the Lord gives directions for how to deal with this problem. This solution strikes some people as being totally unfair to the woman, but it was actually a way of making sure that her husband didn't just kill her or cast her out when he started suspecting her of unfaithfulness. Instead of him or his jealousy deciding the matter, God decides. Finally, there are the vows of the "Nazirites," a word that means "unpruned" because the Nazirites, during the time of their vow, did not cut their hair. The Nazirite vow was taken by a man or woman who wished to "separate himself for the Lord" (Num 6:2). During the time of their vow they would also draw close to God by abstaining from anything having to do with grapes (wine, vinegar, juice, the fruit, the seeds, etc.) as a sort of a fence around the law that prevented drunkenness especially of someone who was in the service of God (remember Nadab and Abihu).

Now that the whole house of Israel has been counted and put in order and swept clean, as it were, this section ends with a beautiful blessing:

> Thus you shall bless the people of Israel:
>   you shall say to them
> "The Lord bless you and keep you,
>   The Lord make his face to shine upon you
>   and be gracious to you
>   The Lord lift up his countenance upon you,
>   and give you peace."
> So shall they put my name upon the people of Israel,
>   and I will bless them. (Num 6:22–27)

Summary

In this lesson you have studies the first part of the book of Numbers. You have learned the purpose of the census for the men and for the Levites, the shape of the arrangement of the people around the Tabernacle and its significance looking forward to Christ. In your next lesson we will see how important it is that the call to worship comes before the call to war.

QUESTIONS

1. What is the purpose of the census in the book of Numbers?

The census in the book of Numbers is to show the people how faithful God has been to His promises to multiply Abraham's descendants and to give them confidence in the new role to which He is calling them.

2. What is the new role to which God is calling the Israelites in the Book of Numbers?

The New role to which God is calling the people in the Book of Numbers is to participate in the fulfillment of the promise of God to give them the Holy Land.

3. Are all the Israelites counted?

Not all the Israelites are counted, but only those men fit for battle or those Levites for the service of God in the Tabernacle.

4. Why does God arrange the tribes around the Tabernacle as He does?

God arranges the tribes around the Tabernacle in the shape of a cross to show them that God is at the center of their whole life and to point toward the fulfillment of God's victory over all sin on the cross of Christ.

Lesson 27

Worship before War

In your last lesson you studied the first part of the Book of Numbers—the first census. You saw the census had two main parts—one counting the men of the tribes of Israel who were ready for war, and the other counting the men of the Levites who would do service before the Lord in the tabernacle on behalf of the people. You will see this same pattern in this lesson's reading—first the tribes of Israel, and then the Levites. Here it becomes even clearer that all of the numbering for war is ultimately ordered toward worship because although the men were numbered for war, the first thing they do once they are numbered is all for worship of the Lord.

Three big events

This second part of Numbers divides into three main events.
1. The offerings that the 12 tribes bring to the Lord (ch. 7)
2. The offering of the Levites (Num 8:1–20)
3. The consecration of the Levites for service in the Tabernacle (8:20–26).

1. The offerings that the 12 tribes bring to the Lord (Num 7)

We just finished the census. The next thing we read about in chapter 7 is a long list of what each of the tribes offered to the Lord. For twelve days, one of the twelve tribes each day offers the following (a shekel is a measure of weight supposedly equal to a certain amount of barely-corns):

- A 130-shekel silver platter (full of flour and oil for cereal offering)
- A 70-shekel silver basin (and full of flour and oil for cereal offering)
- A 10-shekel golden dish full of incense
- 1 young bull, 1 ram, 1 year old male lamb (holocaust)
- 1 male goat (sin offering)
- 2 oxen, 5 rams, 5 male goats, 5 male yearling lambs (peace offering)

The basins and incense would be used in the service of the Lord in the Tabernacle, as would the cereal, holocaust and sin offering. Each tribe offers a total of 21 animals and 21x10 (210) shekels-worth of precious metals for the service of the Tabernacle. The peace offering has the largest number of animals because, as you remember from your first lesson in Leviticus, it was eaten by all the people. And there are a lot of people in each tribe.

Some other things to note here are that Judah (Leah's most important son), once again, is given the place of honor. His tribe goes first. But Ephraim (day seven) and Manasseh (day 8), the sons of Joseph, son of Rachel, also have significant days assigned to them. You should be able to figure out the numerology.

One other striking thing is that Naphtali is usually put last (see Num 2:29; 7:78). His tribe is the rear guard, as it were, of all the tribes of Israel. Since the rear guard is the one that gets attacked first in time of retreat, it's interesting at this point to look ahead in Israel's history and note that Naphtali was the first tribe to undergo attack and exile under the Assyrians (see 2 Kings 15:29). This was the beginning of the end of the nation of Israel. St. Matthew is careful to point out that when Jesus came to restore Israel from its exile He began, of all places, in the land of Naphtali (see Isaiah 9:1–2 and Matt 4:17).

After all of these offerings to the Lord, Moses enters the tent of meeting and hears the voice of God speaking to him from above the mercy-seat between the Cherubim (7:89).

2. The offering of the Levites (Num 8:1–20)

What the Lord says to Moses is for Aaron to set up the lamp-stand in preparation for consecration of the Levites. They are brought into the holy place, washed and shaved, then presented to the people. The people of Israel lay their hands upon the Levites, similar to the way in which the priest was to lay his hands on the head of the scapegoat. The Levites in turn lay their hands on two bulls, one of which is sacrificed as a sin offering, the other as a holocaust. This is for the purification of the priests and the people.

BUT THEN, the Levites THEMSELVES are offered as a "wave offering." The Levites have no inheritance in the Land. All they can offer is themselves and whatever is given to them. They themselves become a living sacrifice to God. God has never been interested in animal or "human sacrifice" as such. All animal sacrifice is just a substitution for human sacrifice, and "human sacrifice" in its true sense is what God wants. God doesn't want a dead animal or a dead human sacrifice. God doesn't want death at all but the fullness of life (John 10:10). God wants a living and loving sacrifice. He wants the human themselves freely offering their complete self up to God. St. Paul in Romans 12:1 wrote to the early Christians in Rome:

> I beseech you therefore, brethren, by the mercy of God, that you present your bodies as *a living sacrifice*, holy, pleasing unto God, your reasonable *service*. And be *not conformed to this world*; but be reformed in the newness of your mind, that you may prove what is the good, and the acceptable, and the perfect will of God. (Rom 12:1)

The Levites are living sacrifices, separated from the ordinary life of this world. They are dedicated to the supernatural life and the service of God. They are a reminder that THIS is the ultimate calling of all Israel and of all humanity. Man was not made for this world, but for the world to come. And the world to come (=God) isn't something we sit around and wait for, like a train; it's something we have to let into ourselves and receive right now, like the air we breathe.

3. The consecration of the Levites for service in the Tabernacle (Num 8:20-26)

Moses and Aaron and the Levites set out to obey the command of God for the Levites. The Levites are consecrated and set apart as living sacrifices to the Lord and assigned a time for their duties. So the twelve tribes of the people have made their offerings to God. But the climax of all of these gifts, the truly best thing that Israel has offered, is the single tribe of the people which has become a living offering to God.

Summary

In this lesson you have studied how Moses makes clear that the purpose of everything God is doing in Israel is worship. From the census of the people for war we move to the list of the offerings of the people for the Lord (worship). From the list of all of the tribes we see the people lay their hands on that one tribe who will be dedicated to the service of the Lord (worship). The total dedication of the Levitical priests as living sacrifices to God is a reminder of the love to which God is calling His people. Strengthened now in worship, the people are ready to start moving toward to the Promised Land.

Questions

1. Why does God command that the Levites be offered as a wave offering?

The Levites are offered as a wave offering to remind God's people that all of them are called to be what St. Paul called "living sacrifices."

2. What does it mean to be a living sacrifice?

To be a living sacrifice means to love the Lord your God with all your heart and all your soul and all your strength.

LESSON 28

The First Generation Prepares to Move

In the last lesson, you studied how the people prepared for moving to the Land by consecrating the Levites as living sacrifices in the service of worship to the Lord. Union with God gives life and joy and strength to people. Strengthened by worship, the people are now ready to move toward the Land. Everything in this third part of Numbers is ordered toward the movement of the people toward the Land.

Passover revisited

Since coming to Sinai after the Passover and Exodus from Egypt, the people had not moved from their camp. Out here in the wilderness, God was forming and reforming His people to prepare them to live the exalted vocation of their life as God's priestly people in the Land Promised to Abraham Isaac and Jacob. It had been about one year since they left Egypt.

The Book of Numbers began: "In the SECOND *month of the second year*" (Num 1:1)—but now the story skips backward to "in *the* FIRST *month of the second year*" (Num 9:1).

You already know that the order of presentation in the Bible is not always strictly chronological. This is one of the places where this is completely obvious. What is not completely obvious is the reason. When the narrative departs from strict chronology, there is some reason for it. What is the reason here?

In this passage, God reminds the people to celebrate Passover (Num 9:2). Why? Because it had been one year and it is just about time for the first celebration of Passover since they left Egypt. God is helping them to form the habit of celebrating this feast each year. Last year no one forgot because the angel of death would kill them if they did forget. Looming angels of death are very good for helping one to remember. This year they don't have the threat of immediate death over their head, so God reminds them. A year ago they celebrated just as they were getting ready to leave Egypt. Now they are celebrating just as they are getting ready to begin moving again—leaving Sinai and moving toward the Promised Land. Passover is, also, the first of all the feasts, so this is a reminder to them to keep each of the seven feasts that God had appointed for them in the law as related in Leviticus. This also points out that they celebrated Passover BEFORE the census. What prepares them to be counted as the army of God is the Passover.

This chapter then relates the story of some men who are ritually unclean because of burying some people who had died. They cannot celebrate the Passover on the correct day, and so the Lord commands them to wait and keep the feast of Passover one month later (Num 9:10-11). One month later is the second month of the second year—in other words, right back where we started in Num 1:1, right before the census. So the people could have left a month earlier, but the Lord wants NO ONE—even the non-Israelites who are living among the Israelites—to be left out of the celebration of the Passover (Num 9:14). Why is this so important? Because the Passover was when death passed over those people marked with the blood of the Lamb, those people who ate the flesh of the lamb. It was also when they passed over from Egypt and slavery into the freedom and joy of a friendship with the God who saved them. And "Christ is our Passover" as St. Paul said (1 Cor 5:7): He, the lamb of God, took upon Himself the punishment of death, and passed over, with us, from death to life, from this world to the Father, to prepare a place for us. But what is the point of telling this story about Passover *here*? In part this continues to develop the thought of the previous chapter, where the Levites become a living sacrifice to the Lord. Passover is when everyone, even the foreigners among the people, becomes a living sacrifice to the Lord. But there is more...

Reminder of Exodus: the people move when God moves (and not when He doesn't)

The next part of Numbers (9:15-23) is a reminder of the end of Exodus where it said that the people never moved until the cloud, the visible presence of God among them, was taken up (Exod 40:36-37). The cloud hasn't moved for a year now. And it's still sitting there. Why? The reason this is mentioned here is to let you know that not only the Israelites, but GOD, is waiting so that those people who weren't able to celebrate the Passover until a month later have duly celebrated it. The God of the universe sits around and *waits for a whole month* so that a couple of guys who had to bury a dead body can celebrate the Passover. If *that* doesn't tell you how important the Passover is, then I give up.

The people are about to begin another "passing over." The first one was from Exodus to Sinai, and it was important. But the second is even more important—it is from Sinai to the Promised Land. On the spiritual level the first Passover is leaving behind the life of sin and entering into the life of grace with God. The second Passover is the completion of the life of grace and entering into the life of glory—the presence of God (the Promised Land).

On the Move (Numbers 10)

The rest of this part of Numbers is all about the People making preparations and actually starting to move. In Num 10:1-10 God commands them to make two trumpets to be used for summoning the people or the leaders for important meetings or celebrations and generally for putting them in order for organized movement. Trying to organize well over a million people and animals without getting anyone lost or stampeded was quite a task, no doubt. These trumpets also recall the feast of trumpets and all the important things it signifies (the work of the Church Militant).

Finally, after all of this preparation, in Num 10:11, it really happens.

> *In the second year, in the second month, on the twentieth day of the month,* the cloud was taken up from over the tabernacle of the testimony, and the people of Israel set out by stages from the wilderness of Sinai; and the cloud settled down in the wilderness of Paran. They set out *for the first time* at the command of the Lord by Moses.

Notice that this happens on the day 20 of the 1st month (Remember the numerology of 20?). The men who celebrated the Passover a month late would have celebrated it on the 14th day of the 2nd month (instead of the 14th day of the 1st month like everyone else). But you also know that they had to celebrate the feast of unleavened bread which comes right afterwards, for seven days. From your study of the feasts, you know that the feast of unleavened bread starts on the 15th day of the month, the day after Passover, and is celebrated for 7 days. Wouldn't that make it the 21st that they should leave on, not the 20th? No, because although Passover begins on the 14th, sunset on the 14th is counted as the beginning of the 15th. So the feast of Unleavened Bread began on Passover.

The Israelites and other ancient peoples often counted days this way because their time was measured by the motion of the sun, moon, and stars (not clocks, which are an artificial imitation of the motion of the sun). When the sun goes down, that particular day is over. Thus, unleavened bread (15th) starts at sunset on the 14th and ends during the 20th. In other words, the border between 14th and 15th is a geometric line—with no thickness—the point where 14 ends IS the point where 15 begins. Therefore it's that point that is the beginning of the count of seven days. We still have regard for this way of measuring time in the liturgy when we celebrate great feast days and Sundays starting on the evening of the day before. If you still don't believe me that the feast of unleavened bread starts on the evening of the Passover, go read what St. Matthew wrote about it in his Gospel (Matt 26:17), which makes it obvious.

The people finally set out, for the first time since they had camped at Sinai (Judah 1st; Naphtali 12th—do you remember why?). This is the last time that Sinai appears in Scripture (with the exception of a brief visit by Elijah), except where someone is simply recalling it as a past event. This is the mountain of the Law. From now on, the People and the Lord with them will be moving toward the mountain of Zion in Jerusalem, where the temple will later be built and the Law fulfilled (see Gal 4:24–25).

Moses is so happy on this joyous occasion of movement toward the Promised Land that he wants *everyone*, even non-Israelites, to come along. In his joy and enthusiasm, he invites his brother-in-law, a non-Israelite, to come with them—promising that all the good God does to them, He will do to him and his people. This is an image of the saints who, far from trying to keep the good that God gives them to themselves, seek only to give it to others. They are so happy about having God that they want everyone to have Him. We love someone when we will what is good for them. The highest good is God and we should seek with all our strength to give God to others.

Hobab, however, is cautious. He had encamped with the people while they were near his own land, but now that they are going to be moving away he does not want to leave behind what is familiar to him. This is a picture of us. We are attracted by the things of God and will stick around as long as we can still be near the things we are more comfortable with. But when the call comes to leave all these things behind—even though a much greater good is promised us if we do—we falter, like the rich young man in the Gospel who preferred his earthly treasure to treasure in Heaven. Moses PLEADS with Hobab to come. The Scriptures do not say whether he went with them or not.

Summary

In this lesson you have learned the importance of the reminder of Passover and have seen all the preparations of the Lord come to fruition in the people's readiness to begin moving toward the Promised Land. Although the Scriptures pass over Hobab in silence, this is a warning to the people of Israel. Will they persevere in seeking the Promised Land? Or will they too, when confronted with leaving all things behind for the promises of God, desire to return to where they came from? We'll find out in your next lesson.

QUESTION

How are the Israelites called to show their love for God?

In preparation for entering the Promised Land the Israelites are called to show their love for God by putting their trust in His promises.

LESSON 29

Forty Years of Wandering

Many people think that God required His people to wander in the desert for forty years after they came out of Egypt. While it is true that the people did wander for forty years, it is equally true that they did not *have* to do so. As you will see in the reading for this lesson, they could have entered the Promised Land less than two years after they left Egypt! In this lesson we are going to study one of the saddest moments in the Exodus—when the people are shown the Promised Land, but do not want it. This is a very important lesson, because, as you already know, the Promised Land is a type of Heaven. The great danger in our spiritual lives is that we can see and desire the Good that God promises, but still turn away from it because we don't want to undertake the self-sacrifice necessary to obtain it. We can sprout up quickly, but if we lack depth, we can wither in the sun (Matt 13:6). The problem with a living sacrifice (remember Num 8:11!) is that it can, if it chooses, crawl off the altar!

Chapter 10 of Numbers ended on a glorious note from the divine perspective—God has formed an enormous army from His people whom He leads by the Ark of the Covenant and the Pillar of Cloud. In Chapter 11 we switch suddenly to the merely human perspective—*the people complained* (Num 11:1). Moses sees the glory of God in their midst and the wonderful plan that God is bringing about through His People (Num 10:35-36). But he's almost the only one to see it. By and large, the people see only their hardship, not the glory to which their hardship is leading them. While one can certainly understand their unhappiness with the situation from a human point of view, the point is just that—they are the one people on earth that were called to have MORE than a merely human point of view. They are supposed to begin to see things as God sees them (Lev 19:2).

In Num 11:4 we learn that when they left Egypt, there were a bunch of other people who were not Israelites, who came out with them—half-Egyptians and others. The Bible calls them by an odd name, usually translated as a "mixed multitude" or "rabble" or "foreign group." The word is actually a form of the same word that Rachel used when she named Joseph back in Gen 30:25, *asaph*, which means "he adds" because she wanted God to "add" another son to her. So here this "added" group probably had connections to Joseph, who, you remember, had children by his wife Asenath, daughter of an Egyptian priest. Thus his sons—Ephraim and Manasseh—were half-Egyptian (re-read Gen 48:8–22, see also Psalm 78, paying attention to what it says about the tribe of Ephraim).

Ephraim is the only one of the tribes to be given a blessing that he will become MANY nations. Remember also that Ephraim is opposite Judah in placement of the cross-shaped camp around the Lord. If you look at the camp as if it were a crucifix, Jesus's head is right where the ark of the covenant is. Jesus's body is where the tribe of Judah would be (the tribe from which He took His human nature). But where is Ephraim? Ephraim is opposite Judah, that is, in the place over Jesus's head. What was over Jesus's head on the cross? All of the Evangelists mention that there was an inscription; Matthew and Luke both mention that it was written "over him" or "over his head" (Mat 27:37; Mk 15:26; Lk Jn 19:19–20). Aside from what was written—"Jesus of Nazareth, king of the Jews"—we also know who had it written, the Gentile overlord Pilate, and that it was written in Hebrew, but also in the two Gentile languages, Latin and Greek. Ephraim, as the part-Gentile who is given a blessing of becoming many nations is the one within Israel who is a type of all of those outside of Israel, that is, the Gentiles. These descendants of Ephraim mentioned in Numbers 11 thought it sounded good to get out of Egypt and came along with the rest of the Israelites. Once they learned how difficult it was going to be, however, they craved the easier life and pleasures of Egypt, forgetting the terrible slavery to which they were subjected there. So they start to complain and the other Israelites follow their lead.

> O that we had meat to eat! We *remember* the fish we ate in Egypt for nothing, the cucumbers, the melons, the leeks, the onions, and the garlic, but now our strength is dried up, and there is nothing at all but this manna to look at! (Num 11:4–6)

As the people were preparing to leave Egypt, Moses had told them:

> *Remember* this day in which you came forth out of Egypt, and out of the house of bondage, for with a strong hand hath the Lord brought you forth out of this place—no leavened bread shall be eaten. (Exod 13:3)

So now, here we are, a year and a half later. God has been feeding them on an extended "no leaven" diet of Manna, to detach (one might say, *detox*) them from Egypt. Now, just when God is about to give them their own land and freedom from oppressors and a prosperous life, what do the people *remember*? They completely forget what God has done for them and they *remember* the tasty morsels they had in Egypt. And they prefer *that* to the freedom of the children of God.

To paraphrase Shakespeare: "Frailty, thy name is human" . . . or perhaps "Ephraim."

The people cry to Moses. They want meat. Moses, under the crushing burden of leading this people, cries out to God (Num 11:10–15). God responds by dividing the task of governing this enormous people among seventy elders, placing some of the spirit that is on Moses, onto them. When they receive the spirit, two of the elders who were not with the rest, begin to prophesy in the camp. Joshua comes running up to Moses, thinking that only Moses should be prophesying. Moses's response is very important:

> Are you jealous for my sake? Would that ALL OF THE LORD'S PEOPLE WERE PROPHETS—That the Lord would put His spirit upon ALL of them! (Num 11:29)

This is not Moses saying that all of the people *had* the spirit of God, but that he *wishes* they all had God's spirit. THAT is the great deep secret of Israel's vocation. They are the firstborn to the nations, the prophet who knows the mind of God and reveals it to the other nations. Moses longs for the same thing the prophet Jeremiah longed for when he prophesied a New Covenant—that ALL, from the least to the greatest would know the Lord and love Him (Jer 31:31–34).

Much of the rest of the book of Numbers will be dealing, in one way or another, with precisely this question: who has the spirit of God, who does not, and how can we tell? Who has the real authority of the spirit of God?

There is an important connection between this incident about God's "spirit" and the next, in which a "wind from the Lord" blows a lot of quail to the camp so the people have the meat that they craved. This connection is lost in English translations. The word for "spirit" and "wind" is the same word in Hebrew: *ruach* [roo-ahk]. Wind = Spirit: this makes sense if you think about it. Wind surrounds us everywhere and rules every aspect of our lives because our every breath depends on it. It IS what we breathe. The wind is also the symbol for spirit because, though it obviously IS, it is invisible, uncontrollable, powerful, yet silent as a whisper (1 Kings 19:12).

For a moment, when it says in Num 11:31 that "a spirit went up from before the Lord," you might think that now the people also are going to receive the spirit. But no, remember how it goes: *quidquid recipitur ad modum recipientis recipitur*. The people are not able to receive the *spirit* of God that gives Moses and the elders the power to be prophets. Why not?—Because they are not interested in being prophets—they want fast-food. The people show their enthusiasm instead for the "wind" that brings them flesh to eat, by spending the next two days gathering in all the quail that they possibly can. As Jesus would later say, "The Spirit gives life, the flesh is of no avail" (John 6:63). Quail is of no avail either.

How different from the daily gathering of the Manna! There each one peacefully took just what he needed for the day, learning the discipline of trust—God will provide for the following day. Here they go out in a frenzy to grab as much as they possibly can—each man making his own hoard—a hoard that would weigh him down and make him totally unable to move any closer to the Promised Land. When man rejects God to choose creatures, it always slows down his progress toward true happiness. If this way of choosing becomes habitual, it leads to death, as it does here. By preferring creatures, one loses everything—even the ability to enjoy the very creatures one chooses over God.

Confusion about the Spirit of God

The people think God's spirit is a matter of the right "wind" blowing in prosperity. Now even Moses's own siblings are confused about the spirit of God. Miriam is mentioned first. She takes a step beyond what the people think—it isn't a matter of the right "wind" blowing around, rather, it is a matter of being a relative of the one who obviously has the spirit (she is Moses's older sister). Aaron takes it a step beyond his sister and thinks that having the spirit is a matter of his high office and ordination. He had spoken for Moses (see Exod 4:14) and was high priest. If anything would seem to qualify a man for the spirit, it would seem to be this. As this incident makes clear, however, neither high office in God's service, nor blood relation is any guarantee of possessing the spirit of God. Rather, what is it that the sacred author here reveals as the only thing that makes the spirit of God dwell in a person? "Now the man Moses was exceedingly meek, more than all men that were on the face of the earth" (Num 12:3).

This is what separates Moses from everyone else, and what makes him able to be the bearer of so great a gift as the spirit of God. God confirms that His spirit is in Moses by saying that even the men who received the spirit that was on Moses are prophets indirectly—God speaks to them in dreams. But Moses is more than a prophet, God speaks to him "mouth to mouth," breathing His very life breath—His Spirit—into Moses, who beholds God.

Miriam, by comparison, is "as one of the dead" (Num 11:12). She is made leprous, but later healed through the intercession of Aaron and Moses. This was apparently enough to teach her and Aaron a lesson, but, as we will see, the people will continue to prefer their own confusion. When we reject what is clear from God, we get the confusion that we have chosen.

The Promised Land—found and then lost again (Num 13–14)

The people reach the borders of the Land of Canaan and God tells them to send spies into the land to see what it is like. He wants one man from each of the tribes to see with his own eyes the faithfulness of God in giving to their descendants the land He promised to Abraham, Isaac, and Jacob—a good and spacious land flowing with milk and honey. These men spend 40 days spying out the land, bringing back some of its produce (such as the enormous grapes depicted in the drawing) and reports about what the land and its inhabitants are like (you should understand the numerology of 40 here). They are happy that it is indeed "a land flowing with milk and honey," but are fearful of the inhabitants of the land, who seem like giants (the descendants of the Nephilim, mighty in doing wickedness, see Genesis 6:4-5). As a result, this army of 600,000 men, which has God on its side and is plenty large enough to take over Canaan, decides that they just can't do it. They can't obey the command of God. It's impossible. They wish they had died in Egypt or in the wilderness (Num 14:2). They think their little ones are going to get killed (Num 14:3). Worst of all, they decide they should just go back to Egypt (Num 14:4). Notice the contrast with Abraham to whom this land was promised. In order to obey God and retain the Blessing he was willing to sacrifice his beloved son Isaac. But here his descendants are unwilling to entrust their children to the God who has led them so miraculously this far.

Only Moses, Aaron, Caleb, and Joshua reject this cowardice and infidelity toward God for what it is. The men are afraid of putting their lives on the line because they don't trust God, pure and simple. But they don't say that. No, they blame their cowardice on their wives and children: "Our wives and our little ones will become a prey!" They say this so that they can look like they are being "prudent," "safe," and "professional." God, however, who sees their hearts, and who isn't all that impressed by safety and professionalism (but rather by trust in Him and faithfulness) says to them:

> None of the men who have seen my glory and my signs which I wrought in Egypt and in the wilderness and yet have put me to the proof these ten times and have not hearkened to my voice, shall see the land which I swore to give to their fathers, and none of those who despised me shall see it.
>
> Your little ones, who you said would become a prey, I will bring in and they shall know the land with you have despised, but as for you, your dead bodies shall fall in this wilderness and your children shall be shepherds and in the wilderness forty years, and shall suffer for your faithlessness, until the last of your dead bodies lies in the wilderness. According to the number of days in which you spied out the land, forty days, for every day a year, you shall bear your iniquity forty years . . .

The men who brought the evil report all die (Num 14:37), but Caleb and Joshua live because they were the only ones who encouraged the people to enter the Land (Num 13:30).

Next morning, the people realize how foolish they have been in not obeying God. They admit: "we have sinned" (Num 14:40). But now they decide to disobey again! Now they want to enter the Land. Of course they do—since their only other choice is wandering in the wilderness until they die. But this is like going to confession and then not doing the penance you have been given. It's a sign that you're sorry you got caught and punished, but not sorry that you sinned. The forty years of wandering is a punishment of justice, but it is also God's mercy—to give the people just what they need in order to truly repent of their sinfulness and hopefully, to pass on to their children a more obedient and courageous spirit. Moses again warns them, but many of them go ahead and try to take the Canaanites on in battle. But God and Moses are not with them, so they are utterly defeated.

"When you enter the Land" (Numbers 15)

Lest the reader despair that the people will ever get it right, and that God will bring His people into the Land He promised, the next chapter is a bit of a break. It is a law-section that is all about what the people are to do when they finally enter the land. Thus, on top of it being a list of laws about sacrifices, it is also an assurance that they will indeed enter the Land. Fittingly, the laws are about making atonement for the sins of disobedience of the people. The chapter ends with a story about a man who broke the Sabbath law of rest. Just as the whole people would not enter into the "rest" of the Promised Land, so this man shows on an individual level the refusal to enter into the Sabbath. Just as all of those who refused to enter the Land will die in the wilderness, so this man who rejects the Sabbath dies in the wilderness. To show the seriousness of sin, God commands the people to stone the man outside the camp. This is followed by a command to make for each man a special tassel and cord for their robe the purpose of which is to remind the people constantly to obey the commands of the Lord.

Rebellions

After this brief reprieve, we are right back in the thick of it in the next chapters. No one wants to listen to God; no one wants to listen to Moses. But you already know that men cannot really reject authority altogether; they just reject one authority in preference for another. Here God, Moses, and Aaron are all rejected and the people choose themselves as the ultimate authority. They say to Moses:

> You have gone too far. For all the congregation are holy, every one of them and the Lord is among them, why then do you exalt yourselves above the assembly of the Lord.

This is a lot of nonsense, and is just the age-old assertion of the serpent: You can live outside of God's authority; God's authority is just to keep you in slavery—you need to break free from it because really YOU can be like God is—controlling everything and everyone else for yourself. Korah (from the tribe of Levi) and Dathan and Abiram (from the tribe of Jacob's eldest son Reuben) become the mouthpieces of the serpent at this point.

Moses (also from Levi) is trying desperately to save the people. He is like a man who knows that the building is on fire and is trying to tell the people in the building that they need to get out. And the people in the building respond by saying: "Who are you to be giving us orders? Go away!" For the serpent, as for the people who listen to him, any command and any authority is just one person trying to enslave another person. This is the only way the devil can understand power. He cannot (or does not want to) comprehend power exercised in truth for love and service, life and joy.

Korah, Dathan, Abiram and their families want to take over the religious rule of the people by taking the priesthood of Aaron for themselves rather then just being the Levitical servants of the tabernacle (Num 16:10). Dathan and Abiram want to take over the political and military rule of the people because they are from the tribe of Jacob's eldest son. They all persist in their insolence and disobedience. As a result God makes the earth open and swallow Korah and his followers, while Dathan and Abiram and their followers are incinerated for despising God and His servant Moses (Num 16:31–35).

The rebellion spreads

First it was Aaron and Miriam, then eleven of the twelve who spied out the land, then Korah, Dathan and Abiram, now, finally, the "whole congregation of the people of Israel murmured against Moses and against Aaron saying: "You have killed the people of the Lord" (Num 16:41). All of this murmuring has been about one and only one thing—who really is the authority here? Who really is in charge of the people of God? Who really has the spirit of God? Miriam thinks it has to do with being related to Moses, Aaron thought it had to do with being high priest, the eleven unfaithful spies think it has to do with their own special knowledge and their own judgment based on that knowledge, Korah thought it had to do with his leadership of the priestly tribe, Dathan and Abiram thought it had to do with their leadership of the eldest son's tribe, now, finally, the people seem to think it has to do with some kind of democracy—they all should be in charge.

From a merely human point of view any one of these claims to authority might seem like a strong claim. But from the truest point of view (God's) the authority that He has chosen—Moses and Aaron—is both the best and also the clearest. The obvious authority is the true authority, but again, if we reject the obvious, we are left with the dubious (at best).

Aaron, the priest chosen by God

Aaron, as a true priest, directed by Moses, helps to avert the plague that God sends on the people for their rebellion. "He stood between the dead and living and the plague was stopped" (Num 16:48). This serves to establish him as the priest whom God has chosen for His people. But if any doubt should remain, God provides another proof. A leader from each of the twelve tribes gives over to Moses his staff with his name engraved on it. These are all placed before God in the Tabernacle. The next day, Aaron's staff has flowered and born fruit, while all the other have remained barren. This miracle firmly establishes Aaron and his sons as the priests of the Lord and the people begin to see their dire need for a God-appointed priest (Num 17:13).

Following this reestablishing of Aaron as the one with the authority of the priesthood, God also gives to him all of his rights and responsibilities as priest (Num 18:1–20), as well as the rights and responsibilities of the rest of the Levites who serve in the Tabernacle (Num 18:21ff). This section ends with God giving further instructions for a special sacrifice—of a red cow, the ashes of which will be used with water as a cleansing from contact with death, and a cleansing from sin. This new sacrifice and all of the statutes about contact with dead bodies are given here both as a practical measure and as a reminder. The people are embarking on a forty year journey that they know will be the death of all of them, twenty years old and older (Num 14:29). If you just count the men (roughly 600,000), and the number of days in 38 years (roughly 14,000), the average number of deaths per day would be a staggering 40 men.

Thus, this brief chapter on a seemingly disconnected topic is really the best we get regarding the forty years of wandering and dying in the wilderness. It is to be a time of death, but also, as this chapter makes clear, a time for the people to be cleansed of their sin (Num 19:9). This forty years of penance, as one might call it, is the pattern for Jesus's forty day fast in the desert before entering His public ministry, and the Church's forty day fast during Lent before Easter.

Summary

In this lesson you have studied the central part of the book of Numbers, which records the finding of the Promised Land and the causes of the forty years of wandering in the wilderness. At its root the causes have all been the same as the cause of the Fall—letting one's trust in God die—rejecting God's obviously good authority in preference for one's own authority. This leads of necessity to confusion, error, and sin. In your next lesson you will see some of the sad and surprising things that happen when even Moses contributes to this confusion and what happens at the end of the forty years of wandering.

QUESTIONS

1. Why did the Israelites have to wander in the desert for forty years?

The Israelites wandered in the desert for forty years because even though they had seen the goodness of the Promised Land for forty days, they would not enter it when God commanded them to do so.

2. Why wouldn't the Israelites enter the Promised Land when God told them to do so?

The Israelites wouldn't enter the Promised Land when God told them to do so because they were afraid of the inhabitants of the Land and were afraid to put their lives in God's hands.

3. Which of the Israelites would die in the wilderness during the forty years of wandering?

All of those who had been counted in the first census of God's army would die in the wilderness during the forty years of wandering.

Lesson 30

Movement Toward the Land, Part 2

In your last lesson, you studied the central part of the book of Numbers, which is called *bemidbar* in Hebrew, which means "in the wilderness." The forty years of wandering in the wilderness are now complete, the old generation that rejected God and the Land died in the wilderness, and the next generation has taken their place. In this lesson we will find out that there are three more important people who will not enter the Promised Land, the most surprising of whom is Moses himself. This next generation still does not trust God with all their heart, but they are making progress toward the Promised Land. In our next lesson, we will see that this new generation, for all its faults, has one very important virtue that their fathers lacked.

The last of those to die outside the Land

Chapter 20 of Numbers begins with the death of Moses's sister Miriam and ends with the death of Moses's brother Aaron. Miriam, the last of all the women to die in the wilderness, represents all of the women who died in the wilderness, and Aaron, all of the men. In the middle, between these two is Moses, representative before God of the whole people who came out of Egypt. Because of what seems like a very minor mistake, He also is told that he will not enter the Promised Land.

The disobedience of Moses

What did Moses do to deserve this? Numbers 20 records how the new generation, like the old one, complains about a lack of water (Num 20:2) and food (Num 20:5). Some things haven't changed from one generation to the next, but there is the significant difference that this new generation desires types of food that come from the agriculture of the Promised Land, rather than food that comes from the agriculture of Egypt (compare Num 11:4-5 with 20:5). This indicates that they still desire the consolations that come from God more than they desire God Himself. But this is a step in the right direction. Their ancestors desired consolations that came from Egypt and all the spiritual and physical slavery it symbolizes. This new generation desires consolations that come from working for God rather than man, though it is still not quite the perfect attitude of spiritual and physical freedom of God's "firstborn son" (Exod 4:22), who is returning home (Luke 15:19).

In response to the complaints, God, rather than punishing them, instructs Moses to help them—another sign that they are actually asking for a good thing:

> Take the rod and assemble the congregation, you and Aaron your brother, and speak unto the rock before their eyes—to yield its water; so you shall bring water out of the rock for them, so you shall give drink to the congregation and their cattle. (Num 20:8)

Moses and Aaron begin to do as God had said. Aaron says, "Listen, please, you rebels, whether from this rock we shall bring forth, for you, water."

Notice that Aaron tells the people to "listen" and not "watch." Since God had told Moses to "speak" to the rock, the people are supposed to be listening to what Moses will say. Moses, the representative of the people and of the old covenant, is supposed to do something rather strange. He is supposed to go and *talk* to this rock. This is not just any old rock, however. It is surprising that this rock is always referred to in Scripture as "THE rock" and not just "a rock." It is also strange that "THE rock" is referred to right at the beginning of the Exodus (Exod 17:6) and here again right at the end of the Wandering. This is part of what led the early interpreters of the Torah, St. Paul among them, to say that The Rock actually followed them through the wilderness (1 Cor 10:1–4)! "And the Rock," St. Paul says, "was Christ."

Here Moses, the representative of the people, is supposed to have a conversation with the rock/Christ, which would look forward to how the Israelites should receive Christ. But instead Moses strikes the rock/Christ, twice. St. Augustine saw in the two strikings, the two beams of the cross. This action prevents Moses (here representing the Israelite people) from entering the Promised Land (here symbolic of the new covenant). So although this action makes him unable to enter the Land, his action nevertheless brings forth an abundance of water for the people, looking toward the grace that flows from Christ's sacrifice on the cross for all peoples.

Move toward the Promised Land

After this incident, we see another reference to all nations as the people begin to move. Just as their ancestor Jacob met with his brother when he returned to the Land, so, as they move toward the land of Edom, southeast of the Promised Land, they meet with the descendants of Esau, the Edomites. You will remember from earlier lessons how Esau is a type of the gentiles. In Scripture they have a double signification—sometimes as those who are outside the covenant and sometimes as those who are called to be inside the covenant. Here they are called to participate, but reject the call. The Israelites proclaim to the Edomites the story of their salvation from Egypt, inviting them in some way to participate, just as Moses did to Hobab, son of Reuel in the chiastic pair to this chapter, back in Num 10:29ff. But these descendants of Esau, remembering the enmity between Jacob and Esau, will not let these descendants of Jacob pass through their land. So the Israelites pass around them to the south.

The death of Aaron

When they arrive at Mount Hor, the Lord reveals that Aaron is to die. He cannot enter the Promised Land because of his rebellion against the command of God at Meribah. His priesthood lasts only until death, and so his son Eleazar takes up the high priesthood in his place. All of Israel mourns for Aaron for thirty days. Just as the old generation has now passed away in the wilderness and the new generation begins to move toward the Promised Land, so the old priest passes away, and a new one takes his place.

Summary

In this lesson you have studied the very end of the forty years of wandering in the wilderness and the beginning of the next generation's movement toward the Promised Land. You have learned the significance of Miriam's and Aaron's death, and the significance of the sin by which Moses also will be kept from entering the Promised Land. The whole older generation has passed away because they refused to entrust their lives and the lives of their children to God. In your next lesson you will see how these very same children, now grown up, will be the ones to do what their fathers were too afraid to do.

QUESTIONS

1. Why does Moses not enter the Promised Land?
   Moses does not enter the Promised Land because he disobeyed God by striking the Rock twice.

2. What does Moses's striking of the Rock symbolize?
   Moses symbolizes the people of the Old Covenant who were called to receive (speak to) Christ (the Rock) but who instead "struck" him, twice, with the two beams of the cross.

3. What does the abundant water that came from the Rock symbolize?
   The abundant water that came from the Rock that Moses struck twice signifies the abundant grace for all people that comes from Christ's rejection by His own people.

Lesson 31

Waging War

In your last lesson, we learned about the last of the older generation to die in the wilderness after the forty years of wandering toward the Promised Land. In this next portion of the book of Numbers, we begin to see the next generation—those who will enter the land—come into their own. They are not perfect, but they are willing to fight for what the Lord is giving them, something their parents would not do. This section is especially devoted to showing both the perfection to which God calls this people and the imperfection to which their own foolishness can lead them. In some ways this next generation is just as disobedient and foolish as their fathers were, but the one important difference, the difference that makes them able to enter, and which made their fathers unable to enter, is their willingness to put their own lives second—and enter into battle with God's enemies.

There are three main parts to this section of Numbers, all of which concern Israel and how it deals with its enemies:

1. The first battles of this next generation (Numbers 21)
2. Balaam's visions of the Army of Israel, (Numbers 22–24)
3. The halting of a plague on the people by the zeal of Phinehas, grandson of Aaron the priest. (Numbers 25)

We will discuss each in order.

The first battles of the second generation (Num 21)

Chapter 21 is all about the first battles of the second generation of Israelites. Back in Numbers 14:31, when this second generation were still little children, God had said to their parents, who refused to fight for what God was giving them: "But your little ones, who you said would become a prey, I will bring in, and they shall know the land which you have despised."

Now those little ones are all grown up. The cause of the forty years of wandering was that the people would NOT FIGHT for the fulfillment of the promises that God made to their fathers (Numbers 14). Once that generation died out (Numbers 20), the very next thing that is recorded is that the next generation of Israel as a whole making a vow to God that they WILL FIGHT, and not only that, but that they will utterly destroy the cities of the enemies of God's people.

> When the Canaanite, the king of Arad, who dwelt in the Negeb, heard that Israel was coming by the way of Aharim, he fought against Israel, and took some of them captive. And Israel vowed a vow to the Lord, and said, "If thou wilt indeed give this people into my hand, then I will utterly destroy their cities." (Num 21:1-2)

How things have changed! Now, instead of having to command the people to enter into battle with God's enemies, the people themselves are pleading with God to let them fight His battle! Moreover, the reason the people are going to fight is to redeem those who were taken captive by a Canaanite king (the Negeb is the southern part of Canaan). As you already know from earlier lessons, redeeming captives and being willing to put one's life on the line for the sake of the well-being of the clan/family was the responsibility of a good firstborn son. In other words, this next generation, even though it is the "second born" generation since Egypt, is acting more like a firstborn should.

Bypassing of the firstborn

As we have seen several times already, God often bypasses the actual firstborn for the sake of another who is (or who will become) more like a firstborn ought to be in his way of acting. Ishmael was born first, but God chose Isaac. Esau was born first, but God chose Jacob. Reuben was born first, but God chose Judah. The first generation out of Egypt was the "firstborn" (Exod 4:22), but it is the second generation that will actually enter the Promised Land.

Some of the Fathers and saints of the church even pointed out that the angels were God's "firstborn" intelligent creatures, but when some of them rejected Him, God created mankind as a "second born" who was to act more like his firstborn ought to. God is sovereignly free to choose whom He will and is not impressed by someone simply because they happen to be born into a certain position or time or nature, or born with certain gifts and abilities. What impresses God is when He sees a son who makes up his mind to be and to act like a true son of God, that is, one who thinks, acts, loves—and hates—as He does. We will see a very important example of this at the end of this lesson with Phinehas, the grandson of Aaron the priest.

Warfare for the sake of worship

The historical reality of these battles points to a deep spiritual truth. So long as mankind exists in a fallen world, he exists on a battlefield. "We fight," St. Paul says, "not against flesh and blood, but against the principalities and powers and the rulers of this present darkness" (Eph 6:12). The earth is the battleground between the demons who have rejected God and good angels who love and obey Him. Human beings are a part of this great spiritual battle and are on one side or the other *whether they are aware of it or not*. As Jesus said, "Whoever is not with me is against me" (Luke 11:23).

The two human armies in biblical battles are the visible side of the invisible battle between good and evil spirits. The only difference is that a bad angel is always bad and a good angel is always good. Humans can be partly good and partly bad; at one time good, at another time bad. Humans change their minds; angels do not. God wants His people to be totally good, while the demons work to make people totally bad. Thus, this battle takes place not just between nations, but also within nations and most especially within each individual human person.

Some people mistakenly think that because in the Old Testament God commands His people to fight while in the New Testament He commands them to love their enemies, there must be two different "gods" and only the God of the New Testament is the real loving compassionate God. This is a very wrong way of reading Scripture.

We can see even in the Old Testament that the wars are all ultimately spiritual in nature, and in the New Testament, that Jesus is every bit as ruthless toward spiritual evil as God was toward His enemies in the Old Testament (for just one example, see Matt 5:29–30). It is also noteworthy that the one time Jesus did violent and warlike actions, it was for what purpose? That's right—it was to prevent the falsification and cheapening of the worship of the true God. Truth, and the true worship of the true God, is most worth fighting for (see Matt 21, Mark 11:17, Luke, 19:46 John 2:14–17). Thus, as we will see in the final part of this section of Numbers, when the people fail to fight as they should, they also fall into false worship. The purpose of this warfare is not for an earthly kingdom or treasure, but so that God may be rightly worshipped. This is clear again in the New Testament where, for example, Zechariah, father of John the Baptist, says in his great hymn the *Benedictus*:

> Blessed be the Lord the God of Israel

For He has come to His people and set them free
He has raised up for us a mighty savior,
born of the house of his servant David (= *the warrior king*)
Through his holy prophets he promised of old
that he would save us from our enemies (= *demons and all who serve their purposes*)
From the hands of all who hate us (= *demons and all who serve their purposes*)
He promised to show mercy to our fathers and to remember his holy covenant
This was the oath he swore to our father Abraham:
To set us free from the hands of our enemies
Free to worship him without fear,
holy and righteous in his sight all the days of our life.

The bronze serpent

Thus, the wars aren't about one people against another people, but rather are about good versus evil. Biblical warfare is about freeing God's people from anything that would prevent them from being "free to worship Him without fear, holy and righteous in his sight." The Book of Numbers makes it very clear that biblical warfare is about good and evil and not about one people or another people. How so? Because God fights even against Israel when they turn to evil. In Num 21:5–9 we see an example of this. The people speak against God and Moses (and the manna), so God sends "fiery serpents" which bite the people and make them die.

The book of Numbers emphasizes the new level of maturity to which God is calling His people. In keeping with this, God is much more severe with the people who complain or sin than in some earlier examples of the same thing. For example:

In Exod 14:10, the people complain that Egyptians will slay them; God responds by opening the Red Sea for them. "I will fight for you…" *But in Num 11:1*, the people grumble about their misfortunes, and God's fire breaks out against them in the camp.

In Exod 15:23, the People grumble about the water; God tells Moses to purify it. *But in Num 11:4*, the People complain about food; God sends quail, and a plague along with it.

Some other examples of the same thing in Numbers are what happen to Miriam when she speaks against Moses (Num 12—leprosy); to the people when they refuse to go in and take the Land; to Korah and his followers when they rebel (Numbers 16—consumed by fire, etc.); and here to the people when they complain, are bitten by the serpents.

God is expecting more from them, and so punishes more when they don't follow Him. But, you should already know from earlier lessons that even God's punishments are merciful. Jesus referred to the incident with the serpents in Numbers when He said: "As Moses lifted up the serpent in the wilderness, so must the Son of Man be lifted up that whoever believers in him may have eternal life" (John 3:14–15).

God makes the punishment fit the crime, but also uses the punishment to heal the crime.

Balaam's visions of the army of Israel (Num 22–24)

As Israel is still learning about God, so now the view switches to the nations around Canaan who are beginning to learn about the God of Israel. Balak is king of Moab and wants a seer he has heard of, Balaam, to come and curse the Israelite army, which is camped out at his front door. He promises Balaam lots of money and honors for doing so. Balaam goes along, but warns the king that he can speak only what the Lord tells him. God isn't happy with Balaam for going—He seems to know that Balaam would really like to curse Israel so that he can get the money and honors from Balak.

On the way, God makes it so that the donkey which Balaam is riding sees the Lord's avenging angel standing in the path, sword in hand. So the faithful donkey keeps leaving the path, finally crushing Balaam's leg against a wall and then laying down to avoid the avenging angel. While Balaam is beating the poor donkey to death for hurting his foot, God gives it the ability to speak: "What have I done to you that you have struck me these three times?"

It is rather hilarious, but Balaam, apparently not noticing how strange it is that his donkey just spoke to him, responds: "Because you have made sport of me! I wish I had a sword in my hand, for then I would kill you." Balaam wishes he had a sword in his hand to destroy the donkey—the donkey who is saving Balaam from the angel—with a sword in his hand—who would destroy Balaam. But then, God allows Balaam to see: the donkey was saving his life the whole time.

The whole story hinges on the idea of true vision. The donkey sees more clearly than Balaam. Once God has opened his eyes, Balaam—an outsider—will see more clearly what Israel's vocation is than Israel itself does. And Israel, in the preceding episode, was saved by *looking* upon the bronze serpent.

In the visions and oracles of Balaam that follow, we receive through him a vision of the holiness, beauty, strength, and exalted vocation of Israel. But Israel itself does not get to see this vision. It seems strange, but the vision that saves Israel is the vision of its own sinfulness, embodied in the bronze serpent. Only if they are convinced of *that* vision first will the vision of their glory do them any good.

Balak and Balaam ascend different high places to offer sacrifice and wait for what God will say. God tells Balaam to bless Israel—over and over again.

Here is the really interesting part: on the last high place, Balaam already knows that God means to bless Israel, so he doesn't go to look for an omen or sign of it. Rather, it says that "Balaam lifted up his eyes, and saw Israel encamping tribe by tribe" (Num 24:2).

Now, wait a minute. You remember from the beginning of the book of Numbers how Israel encamps, tribe by tribe. They encamp in the form of the cross. When Balaam sees this, it says that *the Spirit of God came upon him*. Here he begins to prophesy, not only of Israel's great numbers, or their strength in battle, but of their great beauty and of the exalted state of someone who will be king over Israel, and of the water that will flow from him, and of how all the nations will be gathered in by him. And he says this while looking upon a cross formed by the people Israel. He continues this same prophecy in his last message to Balak saying "a star shall rise out of Jacob and a scepter from Israel" (Num 24:17) that will totally defeat all other nations. This looks forward not only to the great victories of David, king of Israel, but ultimately to the Son of David, Jesus, king of the cosmos, and His victory over everything.

Here the earlier vision of the bronze serpent is transformed. The vision of the sinfulness of Israel becomes the vision of their glory. Notice also that this is now the fourth time Balaam has blessed Israel, one for each arm of the cross. In his first blessing he asked: "Who can count the *fourth part* of Israel" (Num 23:10b—the Hebrew word is also translatable as 'dust clouds', in parallel with the first half of the verse, but the double meaning is intentional). Now he has given four blessings. The remaining three discourses he gives are all about the defeat of Israel's enemies—their first enemy = Amalek (see Exodus 17), their "middle" enemy (Assyria—in 722 BC), and their last enemy (Kittim = Greece, eventually defeated by Rome—see 1 Macc 1:1).

Phinehas (Numbers 25)

This very exalted picture that we receive by means of Balaam's visions and oracles is the divine view of Israel. God sees clearly the mission He has for them and the great plan for the salvation of the whole world through them.

However, in the next chapter, we are no longer looking down upon Israel from a great height, but rather are taken right into their midst, where we see again their unfaithfulness to their exalted vocation. The men of Israel begin to have relations with the women of Moab, who invite them to come to their sacrificial feasts to their false god Baal. The people's complaints at the beginning of this section were about the food that God was giving them: they hated the miraculous manna. Here, they are offered food more to their liking, along with the chance to become slaves to another god. The name "Baal" means "master" or "overlord." Israel has exchanged the God who calls them to be His firstborn son (Exod 4:22) for a god who calls them to be his slaves.

A plague begins, and the people gather by the tent of meeting, weeping for their sin. In satisfaction of His justice, God commands that all the chiefs of the people, the ones who allowed this to happen through approval or through sloth, be "hung in the sun before the Lord"; Moses, in his usual role as mediator of mercy for the people, commands that only those who actually "yoked themselves" to the false god should be killed.

But before anyone can do anything, a man of Israel walks right in front of them all, bringing a Midianite woman, one of those who had led Israel to yoke itself to Baal, into his tent. And it isn't just an ordinary Israelite, but one of the great princes of the people, and she is one of the princesses of her people. This very public display of union between a prince of Israel and a princess of Moab was intended to show that there was now an official alliance between the two peoples, and likewise an alliance with Moab's false god. Phinehas sees all of this and puts an end to it—and the plague is halted. He is praised, not because he killed a Midianite woman, but because he killed an Israelite prince who was publicly sinning with a Midianite princess and attempting to lead the whole people into alliance with a false god. He saved everyone from certain death.

In the Bible, when God commands or conducts a battle, it is always a battle against evil—especially the evil that would separate His people from Him. It is not genocide; it is sin-o-cide. The goal of biblical battles is not a lot of dead people, but a lot of people alive and ready to serve the Lord with their whole heart. To serve God totally is to have life. To fail in this (no matter what else you succeed in) is to have death.

Moderns tend to look at this episode and think that God or Phinehas or both are being extremely small-minded and mean, but this is only because they are not convinced that being connected to God IS LIFE and that being yoked to anything else IS DEATH. Phinehas saw this clearly, acted on it, and is praised by God for doing so. Does this mean that Christians should run around with swords and kill anyone they see sinning? Surprisingly, yes, it does—but only in the way that Christ fulfilled these things. In the new covenant, Christians are to take up and wield the sword of the word, the praise of God, and the spirit of God. These are the weapons with which Christians are to actively confront and defeat sin in themselves and in the world (see Eph 6:17; Heb 4:12; Rev 1:16; see also Psalm 149:6).

Summary

In this lesson, you have studied the sixth part of the book of Numbers, which records the first battles of the second generation of Israelites who came out of Egypt. In their willingness to fight for what God has promised them, this generation goes beyond their fathers. The great visions and oracles of Balaam looking down from above with the vision of God reveal the exalted vocation of God's people. This people is the earthly counterpart to the heavenly angelic armies and its destiny is to conquer the whole world, not through force of arms, but through the cross of Christ, who is the "star that will arise out of Jacob." The story of Phinehas, which closes this section, reveals in a special way the kind of zeal for holiness to which God calls His people. This is the kind of zeal that enables one to enter the Promised Land. In our next lesson, we will complete the book of Numbers, fittingly, with another "numbering" of the people. This time it isn't for war, but rather, for living the life of peace and true worship to which God calls His people when they enter the Promised Land.

QUESTIONS

1. How does the second generation of those in the wilderness differ from the first?

The second generation differs from the first in that they are willing to fight—to put their lives in danger—for the sake of obtaining what God has promised them.

2. What are all battles that God commands or conducts ultimately against?

All battles that God commands or conducts are ultimately against sin and evil and the death and separation from God, who is our life, which comes from them.

3. Why does God often bypass the firstborn in favor of someone else?

God often bypasses the firstborn in favor of someone else who acts more like a firstborn ought to—in particular, in his faithfulness to God.

4. What do the visions and oracles of Balaam reveal?

The visions and oracles of Balaam reveal the holiness, strength, and beauty of Israel in its ultimate vocation to conquer all nations, not through force of arms, but through the cross of Christ.

LESSON 32

Second Census

In your previous lessons on the Book of Numbers, you have learned the seven-part chiasm that is the structure of the whole Book. We have been going through each of these parts one at a time and now we are at the final part. But as you know, in chiasms, the end is like the beginning.

Before we look at the end, then, let's remember the beginning. In the first chapter of Numbers, God commands Moses to take a census for war. The census in Numbers 26 is also a census of "all those who are able to go forth to war" but once it has been accomplished, something new is added that did not take place in the first census. In Num 26:52, just after the second census of all the tribes has been completed, the Lord says,

> To these the land shall be divided for inheritance according to the number of names. To a large tribe you shall give a large inheritance, and to a small tribe you shall give a small inheritance, every tribe shall be given its inheritance according to its numbers. But the land shall be divided by lot according the names of the tribes of their fathers shall they inherit. Their inheritance shall be divided according to lot between the larger and smaller. (Num 26:52-55)

The first census and the second are similar, but they have this important difference: the second census is clearly for the sake of inheritance of the Land. It is taken for granted that this second generation, unlike the first, is going to be willing to fight for what God is giving them, as they have already shown. *Inheritance of the land* is the theme of this last part of the book of Numbers.

Typology: the Promised Land and Heaven

You already know that the Promised Land is a type of Heaven, our true home. It is the "land" to which God is leading His people after their sojourn in this life. The greater and lesser shares of the Land spoken of in Numbers 26 are given according to the greater or lesser number of people in each of the tribes. This points to the reality that our fruitfulness for God—our love for

God and neighbor which brings others to love and serve God—is what determines how much of a "share" of the life of Heaven we will be able to receive.

It comes as a surprise to some people to learn that in Heaven people will have a greater or lesser happiness according to the measure of their love. St. Thérèse of Lisieux was puzzled about this when she was a little girl and her older sister Pauline responded by filling a large cup and tiny thimble with water, then asking "which of the two is more full?" The answer of course, was that both were equally full, though the cup held much more than the thimble. Just so, in Heaven everyone will be perfectly happy, without any room left in them to be filled with more happiness, but some will have a greater capacity for receiving that happiness according to the measure of their love during this life, and at the hour of their death. As Jesus said: "According to the measure with which you measure, so it will be measured back to you" (Matt 7:2; Mk 4:24). And again: "God will repay each man according to his deeds" (Matt 16:27).

Seeking an inheritance in the Land: the daughters of Zelophehad (Num 27)

To show that this second census is all about inheritance of the Land, and not about battles, the next part of Numbers records a plea that comes to Moses from some people who will not be in any of the battles, because they were not in the census—and this, because they are women. These courageous daughters of a man named Zelophehad, who had no sons who could be counted in the census, want to ensure that they will have a place of their own in the Promised Land. What a contrast with Numbers 14! There the men throw away their inheritance and say "Let's go back to Egypt," but here the women say "Give us a holding in the Land!" For the boldness of their desire for God's promises, God takes their side (Num 27:7). The gifts of God are there for the taking, but we have to be confident enough in God's goodness to desire and ask for them. The importance of these women's good desire for God's promises is seen in that the whole book of Numbers ends by speaking about them again. Thus, the daughters of Zelophehad, and their concern for inheritance in the Promised Land, form a sort of picture frame around the other events of this last part of the book of Numbers.

If the "picture frame" formed by the daughters of Zelophehad is about inheritance of the Land, what is the "picture" all about? The picture is essentially a picture of Moses and all that God has done to bring the people to the Land through him. Just after the case of the daughters of Zelophehad, God tells Moses that he will soon die. Because of his impending death, Moses asks God to appoint a man to be leader of the people in his place. God appoints Joshua. Then the book of Numbers presents us with seven more instances, for a total of eight, of how Moses's authority was exercised for the care and guidance of the people so they could inherit the Promised Land. These individual stories, which might seem only randomly connected, show in a beautiful order what will now be expected of Joshua, who will actually lead the people into their inheritance in the Promised Land.

Chapter 29: Communal faithfulness to God

First in importance, of course, comes communal worship. Chapter 29 reviews all of the feasts and sacrifices that the community of the People of God are to keep once they have entered the Land. This is both the purpose of their inheritance of the Land and the main means by which they keep it. If they are faithful to God, then God will be faithful to them. This chapter ends with a section on free-will offerings, that is, sacrifices which are not required but which people can make to God for various reasons. This leads naturally into the next chapter.

Chapter 30: Individual faithfulness to God

Next in importance after communal worship, and closely bound up with it, comes the faithfulness of the individual Israelite to God. This chapter is all about personal vows people make to God and how they are to be kept or revoked.

Chapter 31: Obstacles to faithfulness

Chapter 30 is about faithfulness of the individual Israelite to God. Chapter 31 is a reminder to do away with anything that would be a serious temptation to unfaithfulness. The last time we saw individuals among the people being unfaithful to God was just a few chapters earlier, in Numbers 25 when the daughters of Moab convinced some of the men of Israel to worship Baal of Peor. Here in Numbers 31 we learn that they did this by the counsel of Balaam! Balaam knew that God would not curse the people, so he thought of a way to get the people to bring a curse upon themselves—by being unfaithful to the God who protected them! So he advised the people of Moab (and Midian) to use their women to entice the men of Israel into false worship. Thus here, the men are commanded to kill anyone who presents a serious threat to their faithfulness to the true God. The point is essentially the same as Jesus was making when He said: "If your hand causes you to sin, cut it off," and when He used a whip of cords to drive out those in the temple who were cheapening the worship of the true God. In the next book of the Pentateuch (Deuteronomy) we will see that this same attitude is commanded by God not just toward outsiders, but toward one's own closest clan and family members, even a man's own wife or dearest friend (Deut 13:6ff).

Chapter 32: Perseverance in all trials

When faced with the difficulty of doing all that is necessary to turn away from sin and totally conquer it, our frail human nature recoils. When faced with the immense suffering it involved, even Christ, who was the only one who truly did all that was necessary to eradicate sin, said: "Father, if it is possible, let this cup pass me by" (Matt 26:39). Just so, Numbers 32 is about the temptation to avoid the difficulty of the battle necessary for inheritance of the Promised Land. The tribes of Reuben, Gad, and the half-tribe of Manasseh see good grazing land for their herds just outside of the Promised Land and want to stay there. Moses wants to make sure that they don't think they can get out of their responsibility to go into battle to help their fellow Israelites in the total conquest of the Land. This is also a sort of picture of the communion of saints, the reality of the Mystical Body of Christ. The journey to the Promised Land is accomplished by the whole people, not just individuals. Just as the men of these tribes vowed to help their fellow Israelites, so all the saints are committed to helping us in our struggles. This gives great assurance to the rest of the Israelites that they will be able to do what is necessary to obtain the Promised Land.

Chapter 33: Assurance of God's goodness in the past

To increase this assurance, Moses then recounts all of the stages of the journey to the Promised Land, and all of the battles they have fought in order to arrive there. God has brought them this far, He certainly can bring to completion the good work begun in them. By looking at God's help in the past, the people can be reassured of God's help and goodness in the present. Among other interesting numerical things here are that Aaron the priest dies and is buried after the 33rd move (Mt. Hor), and Moses after the 40th (Mt. Nebo).

Chapter 34–35: Assurance of God's goodness in the present

Moses then announces the borders and division of the goal of the whole journey: Here we are right now—and this is what God is giving you right now—the Land itself. The Land and its borders are apportioned out to each of the tribes while cities are given to Levites and to other vulnerable persons as places of refuge in the Land.

Chapter 36: Assurance of God's goodness in the future

To increase this assurance yet again, and to bring it to completion, this whole series of chapters ends as it began, with the daughters of Zelophehad. Their kinsmen are concerned that if the daughters of Zelophehad inherit Land, but then get married, that their land will pass on to their husbands and will not stay within the tribe. The response from God and Moses is that they should marry men from their own tribe so that each of the tribes will always, from generation to generation, retain its ancestral heritage in the Land.

One of the greatest joys of Heaven will not only be in possessing the highest Good (God Himself), but in knowing with certainty that we cannot lose Him. He will be our inheritance forever. Why is the Land such a good type of the life of Heaven? Because the only thing stable and productive of the things necessary for life and security in this world is a piece of productive land that gives those things necessary for food, shelter, clothing, etc. So here the land remaining in the family is a sign of how in Heaven we will possess God—the One truly productive of all that is Good, and know with certainty that we cannot lose Him.

Summary

These eight instances of Moses's leadership are given here to prepare us for the next and final book of the Pentateuch—Deuteronomy—which is the climax of the whole Torah. It is Moses's farewell speech to the People of Israel before He dies—and also a prelude to the next book of the Bible, the book of Joshua—showing the leadership and works of Joshua. So in this last part of the Book of Numbers, we are reminded of all that *Moses* has done for the people. In the Book of Deuteronomy Moses will remind the people of all that *they* should be doing, for each other and for God, before he leaves them—with a promise that some day God will again raise up a Prophet like Moses to shepherd His people even more mightily than Moses.

QUESTIONS

1. What is the theme of the last part of the Book of Numbers?
   The theme of the last part of the Book of Numbers is inheritance of the Land.

2. Why do some tribes inherit more of the Promised Land than others?
   Some tribes inherit more of the Promised Land than others because they have a greater number of people.

3. What is the typology of the inheritance of the Land according to numbers of people?
   The typology of inheritance according to numbers of people in the tribe is that our ability to receive and enjoy God in Heaven is enlarged according to our love of God and neighbor, by which we lead others to God.

4. What did Jesus say to teach the truth that although all in Heaven are perfectly happy, some have a greater capacity for receiving the infinite Happiness of God?
   To teach the truth that some in Heaven have a greater capacity for receiving the infinite happiness of God, Jesus said: "The measure with which you measure shall be measured back to you."

DEUTERONOMY

LESSON 33

Introduction to Deuteronomy

We are now studying the last book of the Pentateuch. Its Hebrew name is *Debbarim* which means "words" or "things." This is taken from the first line of the book which says: "These are the words/things Moses spoke to the Israelites..." (Deut 1:1). The Greek name of the book, *Deuteronomy*, comes from two Greek words—*deutero* which means "two" or "second," and *nomos*, which means "law." God gave the *first* Law to the people through Moses at Mt Sinai in the book of Exodus, but this book is a *"second* law" which reviews the first law and explains it more plainly, and renews the covenant that God made with the people. The task of *explaining* the law is, in fact, the purpose of this whole book, stated in verse five of the first chapter: *"Beyond the Jordan, in the land of Moab, Moses undertook TO EXPLAIN THIS LAW"* (Deut 1:5).

The Hebrew word for *Law* is *Torah*, which is also the name that is given to the whole Pentateuch. Thus, Deuteronomy is, in a way, not only an explanation of the law given at Sinai, but is also an explanation of the whole Torah, the whole Pentateuch! The Hebrew word for "explain" used here basically means to make something obvious and plain so that anyone could understand it.

Farewell

Deuteronomy is written in the form of a farewell speech of Moses. It is Moses's last words to the second generation of Israelites before he dies and before they enter into the Promised Land. When someone is about to die, they don't waste time talking about unimportant things. Rather, they focus on what is most important. Hence, this last speech of Moses is going to be making the most important things that God has been trying to teach throughout the Pentateuch very obvious. God is the best of teachers. He knows that even when someone has more or less been paying attention to some of the details, it is often the case that they have missed the most important things. Now, in Deuteronomy, it is as if God is saying, through Moses, "If you haven't been paying attention or if you haven't really understood what you have been hearing thus far, PAY ATTENTION NOW, because I am going to tell you what this is really all about!"

Love

Jesus also had His own last words to His disciples before He died and those words focus (especially in John's Gospel) on the importance of LOVE. That is also the focus of Moses's last speech here in Deuteronomy: if you haven't been paying attention, God and what He is doing in the world is all about LOVE. If you don't see that then you don't really get it, and you should start over again until you do get it. St. Augustine taught that anyone, no matter how "learned and clever" they are, who reads Scripture in such a way that their understanding of it does not make people love God and their neighbor has failed to understand it. He knew this was true because of Deuteronomy and the fact that Deut 6:4 is where our Lord points the man who wants to know what the most important commandment of God is. What is it? Love God.

The book of Numbers brought us right up to the brink of entering the promised land. With Deuteronomy, the scriptures force us to pause for a time and reflect upon all that has taken place thus far and also upon all that is about to take place.

In Deuteronomy, it is as if we are between two worlds—the exodus is over but the possession of the Promised Land is still to come. This is a situation not unlike our own lives—free, through baptism, from slavery to sin, but not yet in Heaven—and in Deuteronomy as in our lives, the most important commandment is to love.

Structure of the book of Deuteronomy

Each of the books of the Pentateuch can be divided into a seven-part chiasm. There are other ways to divide up these texts, but this way can be helpful for remembering the most important parts and how they relate to one another. In Deuteronomy, the seven-part chiasm is structured around the important character of Moses. He begins, and ends, and is in the middle of this structure. Stationed around him in the center are statutes regarding judges, kings and priests, and around them statutes for all the people. But here is the really great thing: the central portion of Deuteronomy is not about Moses as such, but is a prophecy foretelling that someone is going to come to Israel—someone who is a "prophet *like* Moses." This prophet like Moses will come and speak the word of God to the people in a way even more profound than that of Moses himself.

In a very simplified form, the structure would look like this:

A—Moses (Deuteronomy 1-3)
    B—All the people (Deuteronomy 4-17:7)
        C—Judges, Kings, Priests (Deuteronomy 17:8-18:14)
            D—Prophet like Moses (Deuteronomy 18:15-22)
        C'—Judges, kings, priests (Deuteronomy 19-26)
    B'—All the people (Deuteronomy 27-30)
A'—Moses (Deuteronomy 31-34)

So think about these things:

- The most important part of the Old Testament is the Torah.
- The Bible's own explanation of what the Torah means is the book of Deuteronomy.
- The essential *command* of the book of Deuteronomy is to love God.
- The central *teaching* of Deuteronomy prophesies the prophet like Moses.

This means that the Old Testament is basically about two things:

1. Love God with your whole heart.
2. Await the prophet like Moses who will give further revelation from God.

Now, the people at that time did not know who the prophet like Moses would be, but they did know that they were awaiting Him, and that when He came, He would teach them the deeper mysteries that God had not yet revealed (see Deut 29:29). In the meantime, their efforts to love God, to choose Him, and to be faithful to His commands above everything else was their best preparation for when the prophet like Moses would come.

Now that we have the general view of Deuteronomy, we will spend the rest of this lesson getting familiar with some of the details of each of the parts of the chiasm.

Part A—Moses explains the Torah: history of the people (Deut 1-3)

In this first part of Deuteronomy Moses undertakes to "explain this *torah*" by reviewing the history of the people from Sinai all the way up to where they are now, just outside the Promised Land. He focuses on the important chapter in the book of Numbers where the people refuse to enter the land and where Moses is also not allowed to enter in the Promised Land. This section ends with Moses making a plea to God to allow him to enter, but he is not allowed to do so. Instead, Joshua is appointed in his place.

Part B—Commands to all the people—I (Deut 4–17:7)

Once Moses has reviewed the history by which the people have come to where they are, and why they should obey the commands of God, this second section begins with Moses calling all of the people of Israel to actually do so—to obey all of the statutes and laws that the Lord has given them so that they can enter in and possess the Land which God is giving them. One of the most beautiful revelations in this part of Deuteronomy is that God did not choose Israel because they were great or wonderful or holy. He chose them simply because He loved them (Deut 7:8). In return the people are to love God the way He loves them. The people will be BLESSED if they keep God's laws, and CURSED if they do not. This section is governed by the commandment Jesus said was the greatest commandment: *"Hear O Israel, the Lord is our God the Lord alone. Therefore you shall love the Lord your God with all your heart and with all your soul and with all your strength"* (Deut 6:4–5). You should memorize this.

Part C—Commands for leaders of the people—I (Deut 17:8–18:14)

This section records statutes for those in authority within the people of Israel. For deciding cases of dispute between people, there are statutes and laws for the Levitical Priests and the judges who will decide what is right and wrong. There are also statutes for the men who will, in the future, be kings in Israel, because they will later be the ones whose authority supersedes that of the priests and judges as decision-makers in Israel. THEY are to know and do the Torah too. After this is a short section on the rights of the priests, not as judges, but as priests. As priests, their authority is even greater than their authority as judges, because as priests they are serving God directly, while in judging cases they are serving the people.

Part D—The prophet like Moses (Deut 18:15–22)

This section brings to a climax those that came before. The priests and judges were given authority in part C to decide difficult cases, but their authority will eventually be superseded by the king's authority when he comes. And even his authority as king is subject to the authority of the priests as priests, who are subject to God. But here, last of all, there is mention of one who will come whose authority will supersede even that of the kings and priests of Israel. He is the "prophet like Moses," whom God will raise up from among the Israelites. This prophet will speak just what God tells Him to. The supreme authority of this great "prophet like Moses" is shown in that God says, *"Him you must heed!"* and *"Whoever will not give heed to my words which he shall speak in my name, I myself will require it of him!"* Thus the authority of judges, kings, and priests are all subject to the authority of God, who will speak directly through this prophet like Moses. This is a prophecy about Christ, who will be the supreme judge, king, priest, and prophet of Israel.

Part C'—Commands for leaders of the people—II (Deut 19–26)

The next section goes back to speaking about statutes for priests and other leaders of the people for the purpose of governing the Israelites in times of peace and in times of war once they have entered the Land (see, for example, Deut 19:17; 20:2, 20:5, 20:8; 21:2, 20:18–19; 22:18; 24:8; 25:1; 26:3).

Part B'—Commands for all the people—II (Deut 27–30)

This section, like part B above, shows Moses addressing ALL of the People, encouraging them to remember and to keep all of the commandments of the Lord. Moses then goes into very great detail regarding the ways in which the people will be BLESSED if they remember and obey the commands of the Lord (Deut 28:1–14) and how precisely they will be CURSED if they do not remember and keep the commands of the Lord (28:15–68). He also tells them that even if they incur the curse through disobedience, they can still repent and return to the Lord, who will receive them and restore them to blessing (Deut 30). The key quote from this part is: *"I have set before you life and death, blessing and the curse; therefore choose life that you and your descendants may live, loving the Lord your God, obeying His voice, and cleaving to him, for that means life to you and length of days, that you may dwell in the land which the Lord swore to your fathers"* (Deut 30:19–20).

Part A'—Moses writes the Torah (Deut 31–34)

In the beginning of Deuteronomy Moses undertook "to explain this torah." Here at the end, now that he has *explained* this torah, it is recorded that "Moses *wrote* this torah." He writes down the Torah so that it can be read and remembered through every generation in Israel. Here (Deuteronomy 32), Moses also recites and records the words of a song that he composes which is all about God, how powerful and good He has been toward the Israelites, and how foolish the Israelites have been not to believe, trust, and love Him with all their heart. God then commands Moses to ascend Mount Nebo to die outside the land (Deut 32:49–50). Before he dies, Moses blesses each of the tribes of Israel by name. The whole book ends with another reference to the prophet like Moses.

> And there has not arisen a prophet since in Israel like Moses, whom the Lord knew face to face, none like him for all the signs and the wonders which the Lord sent him to do in the land of Egypt, to Pharaoh and to all his servants and to all his land, and for all the mighty power and all the great and terrible deeds which Moses wrought in the sight of all Israel.

Thus the book ends with the three most important things:
1. God;
2. His people;
3. The One who is to come who will be a prophet like Moses, uniting God and His people, knowing God face to face, and working great signs and wonders.

Summary

In this lesson you have learned the overall structure of the final book of the Pentateuch. You have learned that this book is an explanation, a "making plain" of the Torah. With all that you have learned in mind, the message of Deuteronomy is something like this:

Love God because he loves you; and even when you fail to love God, He will still love you. He will show you this love by sending you the prophet like Moses, the one who will speak God's words and do signs and wonders before you. This prophet will, like Moses, do the most important action of Moses: lead God's people to the Promised Land.

The last words of the Torah, just as the People are about to enter the Promised Land, show their great longing for the prophet like Moses. Just as Adam and Eve were about to be driven out of their own little promised land, they were promised that someone would come from them who would crush the head of the serpent. Just as the people are about to enter the promised Land, they are promised someone who will lead them even deeper into the mysteries and love of God. This conclusion to the Pentateuch takes us powerfully back to the beginning of the Pentateuch, reminding us of God's original plan—the plan to make a place where God and Mankind can dwell together in love. That is the message, the hope, which, in one way or another is written on every page of the Bible, and hopefully written also on our hearts:

> The Lord your God will circumcise your heart

and the heart of your offspring
so that you will love the Lord your God with all your heart
and with all your soul!
That you may live! (Deut 30:6)

QUESTIONS

1. What is the purpose of the Book of Deuteronomy?
The purpose of the Book of Deuteronomy is "to explain this law (torah)."

2. What is the explanation of this Law?
The explanation of this Law rests on one command and one teaching.

3. What is the one command upon which the explanation of the Law rests?
The one command upon which the explanation of the Law rests is to love God with your whole heart.

4. What is the one teaching upon which the explanation of the Law rests?
The one teaching upon which the explanation of the Law rests is that the Law in itself is not yet the complete revelation of God.

5. What does the Law say about the complete revelation of God?
The Law says that the complete revelation of God will be accomplished with the coming of the Prophet like Moses, who is Christ.

6. What are the main features of the Book of Deuteronomy?
There are seven main features of the Book of Deuteronomy, which form a chiasm as follows:
Part A—Moses explains the Torah: history of the people (Deut 1-3)
* Part B —Commands to all the people—I (Deut 4-17:7)*
*   Part C—Commands for leaders of the people—I (Deut 17:8-18:14)*
*   Part D—The prophet like Moses (Deut 18:15-22)*
*   Part C'—Commands for leaders of the people—II (Deut 19-26)*
* Part B'—Commands for all the people—II (Deut 27-30)*
Part A'—Moses writes the Torah (Deuteronomy 31-34)

LESSON 34

Moses Explains the Torah

In your last lesson you were introduced to the main structure and contents of the Book of Deuteronomy. For the next seven lessons you will be studying each of the parts of the seven-part chiasm of Deuteronomy outlined there.

In this lesson we will study Deuteronomy 1–3. This section begins with Moses explaining the Torah to the Israelites who are about to enter the Promised Land; it ends with Moses recounting how he begged God to allow *him* to enter the Land, but God would not allow it.

In the following recapitulation (= retelling) of the story of the people of Israel from Sinai up to their current time, Moses tells the story of Israel here at the end of the Torah such that it compares to what happened with Adam and Eve at the very beginning of the Torah. This is how all of this historical detail about places and times and movements, and battles, which may seem like anything BUT an explanation of the Torah, really IS an explanation of the whole Torah. THIS is what God is doing from creation onward—He is calling His people who came forth from Him, and who fell away from Him, to do what is necessary to return to Him.[6]

1. God makes a covenant	"The Lord God said to us in Horeb" (Sinai—where the covenant was made). (Deut 1:6)	"And God blessed the seventh day and hallowed it." (Gen 2:3)
2. God gives a mission	"Behold I have set the Land before you, go in and take possession..." (Deut 1:8)	"...to tend the garden and guard it. And the Lord God commanded the man saying "... of the tree of the knowledge of good and evil you shall not eat..." (Gen 2:15–16)

---

[6] This comparison between the people about to enter the Promised Land just on the other side of the river Jordan and the first Man about to enter his own little Promised Land, a place near the river Pishon and a land with much gold back in Gen 2:12 may perhaps have been what led St. Jerome in his translation of the Hebrew of Deut 1:1 to translate the place name *"Dizahab"* as a place with "much gold" (*zahab* = gold). This is only in the Douay-Rheims version, which is based on St. Jerome's translation from Hebrew into Latin.

3. They reject their mission and thus die	"Yet you would not go up, but rebelled against the command of the Lord your God" (Deut 1:26) "Not one of these men will see the good land which I swore to give to your fathers..." (Deut 1:35)	"and she gave some to her husband and he at it." (Gen 3:6) "In the sweat of your face you shall eat bread till you return to the ground..." (Gen 3:19)
4. The future generation will accomplish what the first did not because it has the "militancy" against God's (and their own) enemies necessary for what it takes to accomplish the return	"your little ones, who you said would become a prey ... shall go in there and to them I will give it, and they shall possess it." (Deut 1:39)	I will put enmity between .. . your offspring and hers— He will strike at your head while you strike at his heel. (Gen 3:15)

Moses's retelling of the story of Israel from Sinai to Canaan concludes with Moses begging God to allow *him* to enter the Land. God tells Moses that he cannot enter the Land, but that Joshua will lead the people in.

Since Moses spends the most time on the fourth part and the conclusion, we will also spend the rest of this lesson focusing our attention on them.

Entering the Land: the battles of the second generation (Deut 2:16-3:22)

In this section of Deuteronomy, there are a number of battles recounted. The point of all of them is to show that this second generation is willing to put their own lives in danger for the sake of receiving God's promises (or for the sake of obtaining them for their children). As long as the first generation is still living, God commands them NOT to fight (Deut 2:4-15). When they meet the descendants of *Esau*, they are reminded that God gave even Esau land and descendants, but not a covenant with God. The Israelite's failure was that they desired the land but forgot their covenant with God, which would have made them able to have the Land. When they meet the descendants of *Lot*, they are shown that even these people, outside the covenant, because they were willing to fight people taller and apparently stronger than themselves, had God on their side in the battle (Deut 2:21), as did the descendants of Esau (Deut 2:22). If God can do this for the descendants of one of the potential heirs of *Abraham* (Lot) and for the descendants of one of the potential heirs of *Isaac* (Esau) then *how much more will He do all of this and more for the actual heirs of the covenant*—all of the descendants of *Jacob?!*

What is the meaning of this? It means that all of those who have a relationship with God are saved while those who do not are doomed. Why? Because to be united to God IS life because only God has life of Himself—everything else has life because of Him. The human life we have is only ours because God is the source of it. Our life cannot continue on its own without God. These stories make this more obvious: if you are connected to God, you can live; if you are not, you cannot live. This isn't because God is a power-hungry and won't give you a life all your own. It is because the only way for anyone or anything to have life of any sort is to have it *from God*. Other creatures receive this life simply by being naturally what they are, but man, made in God's image, must receive this life through what is proper to him—that is, through knowledge and free will, through knowing God and freely choosing to love Him.

People get upset when they read that the Israelites killed all of these people because they think God is commanding evil, or that the people made up the command and then said, "God told us to" as an excuse for their bloodthirstiness. Both of these are wrong. These passages need to be read in the light of the whole of revealed truth and reality, not just as if the Bible is reporting these battles for the sake of telling history. The Old Covenant reveals in the flesh what will later be revealed in the spirit in the New Covenant. In the OT the people contend against other people who are God's enemies and are given their land to inherit. This historical reality is a sign of a spiritual reality that is to come later in history, but which has been the plan from the beginning. In the NT we learn that "it is not against flesh and blood that we contend, but against principalities and powers and the rulers of this present darkness," which means the bad angels. In the OT we see the people exacting God's judgment upon the Canaanites and inheriting their land; in the NT we learn that God's people will even judge angels (see 1 Cor 6:2-3) and will inherit the place that the bad angels forsook when they forsook God.

If we are offended by these passages, it is because we are not really convinced of the truth they are teaching—that "it is the spirit that gives life; the flesh is of no avail" (John 6:63). We still think that the life God offers us in the spirit is something altogether unconnected with our physical human life. We hate the idea that our spiritual life and our physical life are so connected that how we live the one can destroy or build up the other. We think: "Sure, those people may have been morally bad, but that's no reason that God should kill them," as if moral evil and physical life have nothing to do with one another. In fact, to die spiritually by rejecting God is a far worse evil than physical death. For all we know, the inflicting of physical death may have been the means by which God brought at least some of these people to Himself. Looking death in the face has a way of getting one's attention and helping one to focus on what truly matters. That is certainly what will happen in the next book of the Bible with Rahab (Joshua 2), the Gibeonites (Joshua 9-10), and, in the New Testament, with the Good Thief (Luke 23). God is the ultimate good father. If He has to put His children through a lot of suffering so that they can be with Him forever, He won't hesitate to do so.

We read in this section about how the Israelites were willing to fight people who were bigger than they were, who were better prepared and better defended than they were. But before any of this, God first commands the Israelites of the second generation to show patience and restraint—by *not* fighting (see Deut 2:16-23). Before they enter into conflict God first tests their motives by commanding them NOT to enter into combat. If the only reason they are going into battle is for love of gain, or for personal glory, or for revenge or any other merely human motive, God does not want that. This is not a war like other wars. This is a war that symbolizes the ultimate war happening in the cosmos between good and evil, between those who reject God and those who receive Him.

Once they have passed this test by avoiding battle with two peoples, God then sends them into battle against two peoples—the people of Sihon, king of the Amorites, and those of Og, the king of Bashan (see Deut 2:24-3:11). These are the first two major battles won by the Israelites of the second generation, which is why they are so much spoken of here, as well as in other passages in the Bible (see for example Psalm 136). These take place just outside the Promised Land and furnish a type of the Church Militant—not in the Promised Land of Heaven yet, but fighting bravely for the reign of God even in this world.

Moses and Joshua (Deut 3:23-29)

Moses, perhaps because he sees what is really going on more than anyone else, ardently desires to participate in the entry into the Promised Land. You can hear the great longing in his prayer to God: "Let me pass over—please!—and see the good Land" (Deut 3:26). But God tells him: "It is enough for you. Do not speak to me again about this."

Many people read this and think that God is still angry with Moses and so will not let him enter. But Moses says that God was angry with him *because of the people*—and the people are still entering! Why is Moses then not able to enter? Because, as we have said before, Moses is himself a symbol of the people and all that they are supposed to be. His (and Aaron's) sin is that they "did not sanctify" God in the sight of the people. This shows what Israel's true vocation is: to reveal God's holiness to all people. Holiness means otherness, not likeness to the gods and fads that everyone else is running after. People should look at Israel and say: "They have something so good, so perfect, so wonderful, that they must have the secret to life. We should pay attention to them." If that was true of the Israelites, all the more should it be true of Christians.

By doing this with Moses, God shows that there is something more to be expected than simply entering into the Land. And Moses is the one most fit to show that. Moses is the one *most* prepared to enter the Land, and that is why he is not allowed to enter the Land. As the symbol of the people, Moses is left outside the Land to signify that there is something more than entering into the Promised Land. We know that the "more" to be expected has to do with the Prophet like Moses and the life of Heaven.

Moses is the one, almost the only one, who went through the exodus and received from it the spiritual truths and graces it was meant to signify and give:

- Moses changed from timidity in doing God's work to courage and endurance.
- Moses began to act as a mediator between God and the people.
- Moses longed to see God's face.
- Moses desired that all the people might be filled with the Spirit of God and be prophets.
- Moses spoke to God as one man speaks to another.

Yet, for all that, Moses could not behold God's face and Moses did not enter the Promised Land—though he passionately longed for both. We know that the Promised Land is a type of Heaven and that the life of Heaven consists primarily in the perfect vision of God "face to face." Thus, the two things that Moses was not allowed to do are both symbols of the ultimate goal of Man. And because Moses is a type of the Old Law, the Torah, He cannot have those things because they are reserved for the New Covenant and the perfect fulfillment of the goal of Man in Jesus Christ, the Son of God, the only one who has seen the Father (Jn 1:18), who is also, as we will see, the prophet like Moses (Deut 18:15).

Instead of allowing Moses to lead the people in, God commands Moses to put Joshua in charge of the people. It is not Moses who leads the people in; it is Joshua. This is a wonderful mystery, since the name Joshua is the Hebrew name translated in the New Testament as "Jesus." Thus is it "Moses" (= he draws out) who draws the people out of Egypt, but it is "Jesus" (= he saves) who leads the people into the Promised Land!

Summary

In this lesson you have studied the first part of the Book of Deuteronomy. You have learned why Moses retells the story of the People from Sinai to just outside the Jordan, why he tells it in the way that he does, and how this truly is an explanation of the Torah. You have gained a deeper understanding of the nature and purpose of the conflicts and combat between Israel and other peoples and the relationship between these battles and spiritual warfare. You have learned more about why Moses could not lead the people into the Land and why God chose Joshua to do so instead. In your next lesson you will study the second part of Deuteronomy where the attention turns from Moses to all that is required for the People to enter in and remain in the Land.

No questions for this lesson.

LESSON 35

"Hear, O Israel!"

In your last lesson we studied the first part of the book of Deuteronomy in which Moses begins to explain the Torah to the people. Now that Moses has reviewed the history by which the people have come to where they are just outside the Promised Land, and why they should obey the commands of God, the second part of Deuteronomy begins with Moses calling to all of the people of Israel to actually do so—*to obey all of the statutes and laws that the Lord has given them so that they can enter in and possess the Land which God is giving them.*

> And now, O Israel, give heed to the statutes and the ordinances which I teach you, and do them; that you may live and go in and take possession of the land which the Lord, the God of your fathers, gives you. (Deut 4:1)

This is a large portion of Deuteronomy which covers the next 13 chapters and it is sometimes difficult to see the order or purpose of all of the words that Moses is speaking here. But this opening call of Moses to the People: "And Now O Israel, give heed . . ." is basically the whole thing in a nutshell. Moses is really just doing one thing: he is trying to get the people to love God, but he does this in a number of ways. If we summarize each of the parts of Moses's speech in this section it looks like this:

Deut 4 = Pay Attention!
Deut 5 = To the Ten Commandments.
Deut 6 = The Ten Commandments = love God with your whole being.
Deut 7 = Love God because God loves you—not because you are big;
Deut 8 = Not because you are powerful;
Deut 9 = Not even because you are righteous.
Deut 10 = But with a supernatural love—so love Him in the same way.
Deut 11 = LOVE God. Loving Him makes you Blessed.
Deut 12 = Loving God means true worship, so get rid of idolatry;
Deut 13 = And of idolaters.
Deut 14-16 = True worship is done by keeping the laws and festivals of the Lord.

Now that we have the basic outline, we will go into a little more detail with each of these parts.

Deuteronomy 4: Pay attention!

In this chapter Moses gives one of the most important reasons for why the people should pay attention to all that he is telling them. It is not only so that they can be blessed in themselves, but also that other peoples may see how good their Law is and be drawn to the True Faith (see Deut 4:6-8). He also begins to warn them here, as he will many times throughout his farewell speech, to *not forget* all that God has done for them and all that Moses has taught them. It is noteworthy that the Bible (New Testament included) is about thirty percent revelation and seventy percent exhortation. What that means is that *some* of the Bible is revealing new teaching, but *most* of the Bible is simply exhorting its listeners *to remember and do what they have already been taught!* Moses warns that if the people forget to do what they have learned they will be destroyed or exiled from the Land. Even in exile, however, if they seek the Lord with all their soul God will forgive them and bring them back (Deut 4:25-31).

Deuteronomy 5: The Ten Commandments

Summoning this new generation, Moses renews the covenant with them. What they are to give their attention and life to remembering and doing is the Ten Commandments.

Deuteronomy 6: The greatest command is to love God with your whole being

All of these commandments are here summed up in the greatest commandment. Jesus called this part of Deuteronomy the MOST IMPORTANT SENTENCE IN THE TORAH. It is still prayed daily by devout Jews and is part of the Church's liturgy of the hours for night prayer at the beginning of Sunday. You should memorize it.

> Hear O Israel: The Lord our God is Lord alone and you shall love the Lord your God with all your heart and all your soul and all your strength! Take to heart these words which I enjoin on you today. Drill them into your children. Speak of them at home and abroad, whether you are busy or at rest.

That we are to LOVE God is a NEW revelation at this point; moreover, the text will go on to specify the reason for our love of God, namely, that He first loved us. God has not been said to love anyone up to this point in Scripture. This, too, is a new revelation. Love between God and Man, though present as a reality from the beginning, has never been stated explicitly. Now it's obvious. We are to love God because God loves us. This joyous relationship of love is the heart of all that God is doing in the world, because it is also at the heart of all that God Himself is in His own being.

Deuteronomy 7: Love God because God loves you—not because you are big.

Why should Israel love God with their whole being? Israel should love God because God loves them. Here Moses begins to explain the reason that God loves Israel, or, perhaps more correctly, the things which are NOT the reason God loves Israel. The conclusion is that God doesn't love Israel for any natural reason. Anyone else would choose a big nation. But here it says that God did not choose Israel because they were a big nation. Really they were among the smallest of nations (Deut 7:7-8).

Deuteronomy 8: Not because you are powerful

Anyone else would choose a powerful nation. God did not choose Israel because it was powerful. In fact, God here warns them against the temptations that wealth and power bring with them. When they have gotten into the land and have had great success in all of their earthly endeavors, He warns: "Beware lest you say in your heart: my power and the might of my hand have gotten me this wealth" (Deut 8:17). All power comes from God. He didn't choose Israel because they were powerful, but to reveal that HE was powerful.

Deuteronomy 9: Not even because you are righteous

Next Moses warns of an even deeper temptation: the temptation to think that God chose and helped the Israelites because they were righteous (Deut 9:4). But God does not love us because we are good. God loves us because HE is good. To reinforce that it is NOT the Israelite's righteousness that caused God to choose them, Moses recounts three of their most unrighteous acts: the molten calf (Deut 9:16), their rebellion against Him at Massah (Deut 9:22), and their refusal to trust God and enter the Promised Land (Deut 9:23). He also recounts the time that they were saved from God's wrath only by Moses's prayer and fasting (Deut 9:25).

Deuteronomy 10: Circumcise your heart

The purpose of all of this is to show that God's love for Israel is a supernatural divine love. He has chosen them out from all the other peoples of the whole earth because of His faithfulness to His promises and really, simply, because He loved them with a love that has no other explanation—not numbers, not size, not power, not even righteousness. The only explanation is

God Himself. Thus, they should return the favor, loving God not in a merely human way (I love you because you give me good things), but in a divine way (I am totally consecrated to you because of what you are). This attitude of total consecration to God is summed up Moses command: "Circumcise, therefore, the foreskin of your heart, and be no longer stubborn!" (Deut 10:16)

Circumcision was the bodily sign by which the Israelite men were set apart from others and consecrated to God. But the more profound way the Israelites should be set apart from others is by the condition of their heart, the seat of all their emotion, thought, conviction, and resolution, which should be totally consecrated to God in love. Remember the first time the word "heart" appears in the Bible—sadly reporting how the evil in man's heart grieved God to His heart (see Gen 6:5-6). Everything God creates seems to have the power to make Him glad ("He saw that it was good"). Only one thing in His creation has a dual power, either to grieve the heart of God, or to make God glad, and that is the heart of man. But man's heart is so dysfunctional at this point that Moses shows by means of this saying that man needs heart surgery, to be cut to the heart, before he can make his heart able to gladden the heart of God.

Deuteronomy 11: Loving God will make you blessed

Here Moses concludes this discourse on divine love by again exhorting the Israelites to love God and keep His commandments and to speak about these things "when you are sitting in your house, and when you are walking by the way, and when you lie down, and when you rise." He even encourages them here (Deut 11:22) to "cleave" to God, the same Hebrew word that was used in Gen 2:24 to speak of how a man leaves his father and mother to "cleave" to his wife. The love between the Israelites and God is to be even more intimate, complete, lasting, and life-giving than the love between husband and wife.

> Behold I set before you this day a blessing and a curse: the blessing if you obey the commandments of the Lord your God which I command you this day, and the curse if you do not obey the commandments of the Lord your God, but turn aside from the way which I command you this day, to go after other gods which you have not known (Deut 11:26-28).

Deuteronomy 12: Love of God means true worship, which starts with no idolatry

Just as unfaithfulness to the marriage bond can destroy a marriage, so unfaithfulness to God can destroy the covenant between God and Israel. To ensure that this doesn't happen, the Israelites are to destroy all places of idolatrous worship from the Land they are entering to possess (12:1-3). Instead, the people must worship in the way and in the place that God decides (12:5).

Deuteronomy 13: True worship also means intolerance of idolaters

Nothing is more important than a right relationship with God. The True worship of God is so precious and important that nothing can be allowed to usurp it: not a prophet (even a prophet who works signs and wonders!), not your brother, your son, your daughter, your wife, your best friend, or an entire city full of people (Deut 13:1-12). If any of these—religious authorities, family, friends, or society—tries to draw a person secretly away from God then they are cursed. "You shall kill him; your hand shall be first against him to put him to death, and afterwards the hand of all the people" (Deut 13:9).

In the New Covenant, we no longer inflict physical death on the one who would draw us away from God, because physical life or death is not what this law is ultimately about, but rather something even more important—spiritual life or death. We should still decisively and totally reject anything that would separate us from God.

St. Paul said basically the same thing in Galatians: "Even if we, or an angel from heaven, should preach to you a gospel contrary to that which we preached to you, let him be accursed" (Gal 1:8).

Jesus also said what amounts to the same thing several times: "He who loves father or mother more than me is not worthy of me; and he who loves son or daughter more than me is not worthy of me" (Matt 10:37). Or again: "Woe to him through whom scandals come. It were better for him if a millstone were hung about his neck and that he were cast into the sea" (Luke 17:1-2). Or again: "If your hand (or foot, or eye, etc.) scandalizes you (that is, impedes your relationship with God), cut it off" (Mark 9:43). Or, most drastically: "The Son of man indeed goes, as it is written of him: but woe to that man by whom the Son of man is betrayed. It were better for him if he had never been born" (Mark 14:21).

Deuteronomy 14-16: True worship, keeping the laws and festivals of the Lord

On the negative side (what they should *not* do), to love God means to get rid of anything that would destroy true worship. On the positive side (what they *should* do), it means to keep the laws and festivals the Lord has established. That is why this section, after prohibiting certain practices connected in some way with the practices and false worship of other nations (Deut 14:1–2), reviews all of the food prohibitions (Deut 14:3–21), food and tithe laws (Deut 14:22–28), Jubilees (Deuteronomy 15), and yearly festivals (Deut 16:1–16). You have already studied these and their deeper significance, but be mindful of the fact that all these things are here explicitly put in the context of the love of God. *That* is what these are all ultimately about.

Having established the deepest basis of Israelite society, which is true worship, Moses begins to speak about the details of the governance of Israelite society in Deut 16:18–17:7. In this section he is still speaking mainly about the duties of the people with regard to their leaders—their judges and the priests. In the next lesson we will see Moses begin to speak regarding the duties of the judges, priests, and kings themselves.

Summary

In this lesson you have studied the second part of the book of Deuteronomy in which Moses addresses the people regarding their duties to God. Their ultimate duty to God is to love Him with their whole life and being, to have a heart totally consecrated to God in love, and to let nothing separate them from the love of God.

QUESTIONS

1. What passage of the book of Deuteronomy did Jesus say was the most important in the whole Torah?

The passage of the book of Deuteronomy that Jesus said was the most important in the whole Torah is Deut 6:4–5, which says: "Hear O Israel, the Lord is our God, the Lord alone. Therefore you shall love the Lord your God with all your heart and with all your soul and with all your strength."

2. Why is the commandment to love God the most important commandment?

The commandment to love God is the most important commandment because loving God makes us most like God.

3. Why does loving God make us most like God?

Loving God makes us most like God because, as Moses teaches in Deuteronomy, God loves His people (Deut 7:8; 10:15).

Lesson 36

The Leaders of the People

Our last lesson covered the commands and statutes for the people regarding all the things they are to do. In this lesson Moses continues his discourse to speak of the duties of the people toward their leaders and the duties of the leaders themselves—the judges, the future king, and the priests. This section ends with a warning NOT to accept or look for any other authorities outside of those that the Lord is giving the people. The only NEW authority that they are to look for is coming in the next section—the prophet like Moses.

Why these three?

You will see that the office of judge is really just a prelude to the office of the King. Since that is the case, the three offices spoken of here and in the next section of Deuteronomy (Deut 18:15-22) are, in order, *King, Priest,* and (next lesson) *Prophet*. These three will influence every aspect of Israelite life and culture. Why did God divide the duties of leadership among these three and why does Moses present them in this order? In this division and order of the leaders we can, from our vantage point in the New Covenant, see here in the Old Covenant a certain faint image of (and thus a preparation for the revelation of) the Holy Trinity.[7]

KING/Father/Creator: The office of kingship is like the Person of God the Father, who is King, as it were, in the Trinity. He is the First Person of the Trinity, without origin and the origin of the other Persons, the Father Almighty, Creator and Ruler of all, the one to whom the Son and Spirit give, in a sense, obedience and glory. So too, the earthly king is, as it were, the creator and sustainer of the nation, who is over all and orders everything in his "mini-creation."

---

[7] In technical theological language, what we are about to say has to do with "appropriations," that is, aspects in creation that have a special resemblance to the ways in which the Persons of the Trinity are distinguished from one another. Since God is one and simple, the Father, Son, and Holy Spirit always act *as one* towards creation, and in this way the Son and Spirit are also kingly, fatherly, and creative; the Father and Spirit are also responsible for redemption; and the Father and Son sanctify, precisely as the one God.

PRIEST/Son/Redeemer: The office of priesthood is like God the Son incarnate, who is the great high priest. He is the mediator between God and His People (Heb 2:17). In the nation, the priest is the one who acts as redeemer of the people—"buying them back" from sin and death, and reinstating them in life with God.

PROPHET/Spirit/Sanctifier: The office of Prophet is like God the Holy Spirit. The Spirit is the one who, as the Creed reminds us, "has spoken through the prophets." The Spirit knows even the deep things of God and reveals them to the prophets. The Prophets, like the Holy Spirit, enlighten people and speak the words of God to them, guiding the work of God on earth and sanctifying the people of God.

The division of this short portion of Deuteronomy is thus a division by duty: the duties of judges/kings, priests, and (next section), prophets, as well as the duties the people have toward these leaders. God wills that the society He is forming in Israel on Earth be a fitting image of the triune *koinonia* ("fellowship") that God Himself is in Heaven.

Judges (Deut 17:8–13)

In God Himself there is a "communion" of Three Persons, the Holy Trinity, which is the exemplar of all human communities. In Israel, which is fashioned "in the image of God," since they are God's firstborn (Exod 4:22), the Lord is also forming a communion/community of human persons. And He is inviting them to be in communion with Him. But in any community of fallen human persons, there arise problems that need to be settled as a result of sin or accident. Here God makes provision for this by appointing judges, or Levitical priests acting as judges, to decide what to do in every case. The people are to abide by the decisions of these men in authority over them. If the case is too difficult to settle in their own town, then they are to go to "the place which the Lord your God will choose." Later, God revealed that this place was the city of Jerusalem, where the temple was and where the king resided. In this way the authority of the judges is supported by the authority of the king and the priests of the Temple and of God Himself. Thus the people in the dispute are to abide by the decision of those in authority over them. Obedience to the authority that God sets in place brings peace, whereas disobedience brings the opposite and thus is punished with death; the death sentence makes more obvious and immediate what the real result of disobedience is.

Kings (Deut 17:14-20)

The King's authority is even greater than that of the judges, or the priests acting as judges. Thus, the king comes next. He also comes *after* judges because Israel was first led, not by a king, but by judges. Later, the office of the judges who were called directly by God to lead the people was replaced by the kings who, ideally, were guided by the prophets. The king has so much authority and power that it could easily be misunderstood and misused. Here, Moses first gives all the reasons why the people should NOT want a king.

First, the people should not want a king just so that they can be like all the nations around them. The whole purpose of Israel is so that they should be NOT like all the nations. If they decide to be like the other nations, then they have forfeited their calling from God.

Second, they should not want a king so that they can have a powerful army to protect them from other nations. This is the meaning of "he must not multiply horses..." (Deut 17:16). God doesn't have anything against horses, but horses were used to pull chariots and chariots were the armored tanks of the time, as was seen in the story of Pharaoh at the Red Sea in Exodus. Horses were war animals, but the people are to trust in God as the protector of Israel, and as High king of Israel.

Third, they should not want a king so that they can have prestige and power with other nations. This is the meaning of telling the king that "he shall not multiply wives for himself" (Deut 17:17). The concern here is not so much polygamy as it is idolatry: "lest his heart turn away." Many kingdoms in ancient times forged alliances by means of marriage for political and economic reasons—to help make each other more powerful and rich. The daughters of the king of one nation would be married to the king of another nation so that their marriage could symbolize the union of the two peoples in some way. The danger is that if the king of Israel has many foreign wives then these will bring with them their foreign gods and false worship. This actually ends up being one of the main reasons that King Solomon's kingdom disintegrated, even though Solomon was called the wisest of men.

Lastly, they should not want a king for the sake of money and riches. God and the wisdom and blessings that He gives to them are to be the wealth of this people, not money.

After all of these warnings for what a king of Israel should not do, and for how the people of Israel are NOT to understand kingship, Moses then goes on to show what a king of Israel *should* do and the real reason the people *should* want a king.

> And when he sits on the throne of his kingdom, he shall write for himself in a book, a copy of this law ... and it shall be with him and he shall read in it all the days of his life, that he may learn to fear the Lord his God, by keeping all the words of them; that his heart may not be lifted up above his brethren and that he may not turn aside from the commandment, either to the right hand or to the left... (Deut 17:18-20)

The king is not primarily to be a leader either in military matters, or international matters, or money matters. Those are the things that all of the other nations' kings are concerned with. Israel's king is to be concerned first and foremost with the Torah. The Torah is the written word of God—the written copy of the same word that brought creation into existence. Thus, the king is to rule his miniature creation by the miniature word of God (the written Torah). Just as the Word of God sustains all of creation, so the Word of God in the Torah will keep the king's little creation in existence and in harmony. The king should rule with wisdom, with the fear of the Lord and the wisdom that comes from God. He is to be a leader in holiness—in revering, learning, loving, and practicing the Torah. God and the wisdom He gives are to be the real rulers of Israel. Leadership in wisdom and faithfulness to the True God are the real reasons that the people should desire a king. The king, as image of God the Father, is to rule by the wisdom that is contained in the word of God.

This passage from Deuteronomy is very important for understanding what happens later in Israel's history when they have judges and then kings (who often do not follow the word of God), and prophets who try to correct and guide them.

Priests (Deut 18:1-8)

As the king is to be concerned with the word of God and ruling the people by God's wisdom, the priest is to be concerned with the sacrifices and maintaining the people's relationship to God. Just as Moses first said what the king should *not* be like, so he begins by saying what the priest should *not* be like: he "shall have no inheritance with Israel" (Deut 18:1).

What does that mean? It means that the priest has only the Lord. Since God is the priest's inheritance (Deut 18:2), the priest is sustained from the sacrifices of all Israel to God, not from his own labor on his own ancestral piece of land. Verses 1–5 are speaking of those Levites who were also formally ordained priests (the descendants of Aaron the Priest, a descendant of Levi), while verses 6–8 are speaking of the rest of the Levites (any male descendant of Levi). Why do the priests get to live off of the sacrifices that everyone else has to work for? The priest, as image of God the Son, has no other work than that of mediating between God and the people. He is one of the people, but he is also something else—the one whose job it is to go *between* God and the people. The Jubilee is a once-in-a-lifetime reminder that possession of the Land is not the real "project" of Israel; the Land itself is an image of their possessing a right relationship with God. However, the priest in Israel is a *constant* reminder to the people of the vocation of all of Israel—that even when they are in the Promised Land, they are still there *sojourning with God* (Lev 25:23).

Israel is God's firstborn son (Exod 4:22), but as Israel is to the other nations, so the Levite priests are to the rest of Israel—they are the redeemers, bringing the people back from death and sin to life with God. The work of the priest is not the work of this world; this is signified by his not having any inheritance in the Land. As Moses also had "no inheritance in the Land," that is, he could not enter the Promised Land so that he could signify something *better* than entering the Land, so too the Levites have no inheritance in the Land so that they can signify the better reality that their work looks toward—the work of bringing God's people into eternal life with God.

Anti-Prophets (Deut 18:9–14)

Now that Moses has outlined the duties of king and priest, and the duties of the people toward them, he prepares for speaking about the nature and duties of the Prophet. As with the king and the priest, however, before he speaks positively of what to expect from a Prophet, he first tells the people what they are *not* to be looking for in a Prophet. This is why, in this section, Moses condemns all practices which would seek to avoid God and manipulate the world of the (evil) spirits for the sake of power or knowledge of the future, or for any other reason. He includes divination, soothsaying, sorcery, charms, mediums, wizardry, and necromancy. All of these are ugly, harmful, worthless, and evil mockeries of true prophecy. By showing what prophecy is *not*, Moses begins to reveal the nature of true prophecy. True prophecy isn't about knowing the future or whether to go into battle, or when the rain will come, or manipulating the forces of nature or the spirit-world for personal benefit. True prophecy isn't about man's petty knowledge and selfish power. True prophecy, as you will learn in your next lesson, is nothing short of a revelation of the mind and will of God. True prophecy can make use of knowledge about the future, or control of the powers of nature or of the spirit, but whatever it makes use of is for the sake of revealing God and thereby calling people to be faithful to Him.

Attempts to gain power through evil practices should remind you of Genesis 6 and the Nephilim, where people attempted the same kind of control over God or nature through evil practices. Moses reveals that just as God sent the flood on the people in Genesis 6 because of these practices, so with the Canaanites: "because of these abominable practices, the Lord your God is driving them out before you" (Deut 18:12). Again, the punishment of the flood or death or exile for the Canaanites makes the consequences of evil actions more obvious and immediate. All evil actions have immediate bad consequences (separation from God), but those consequences are in the realm of our spirit and our relationship with God, things that fallen humanity has gotten very good at ignoring. The exterior and sensible punishment makes the evil more obvious to those who only pay attention to what is clear to the senses.

The final verse of this passage is often translated something like the following:

> For these nations, which you are about to dispossess, listen to soothsayers and diviners, but as for you, the Lord your God has not *allowed [or permitted]* you so to do. (Deut 18:14)

This is not a good translation. It makes it sound as if the only reason the people should not be paying attention to soothsayers and diviners is because God hasn't allowed it. Maybe next week God will change His mind and allow it? No. A more literal (and better) translation of this verse is:

> For these nations, which you are about to dispossess listen to soothsayers and diviners, but as for you: the Lord your God has not thus *given* to you.

It isn't about what God has allowed; it is about what God has not *given*. God hasn't given lousy interpreters of the spirit and pathetic controllers of the world of nature and of the spirit such as the other nations have. God has a gift for His people far better than the dismal and warped imitations the other nations grasp at in their attempts at control. This is an example of how a poor translation can have real consequences. One translation would make you think that the only reason to listen to God is because . . . God said so. Another translation would make you understand that there is a reason you should listen to God. God's commands are grounded in the truth of Himself and the things He created, not in a capricious will.

So what is this gift that God has given? What is this thing, of which all the necromancers, soothsayers, diviners, sorcerers, wizards, and mediums in the world are just perverted fakes? This gift of God, which is a million times better than anything the world has to offer, is . . .

. . . what your next lesson is all about.

Summary

In this lesson you have studied the third part of the book of Deuteronomy. You have learned about the different offices of leadership within the people of Israel, what they are, how many they are, and their relationship to the Persons of the Father, Son, and Holy Spirit in the Trinity. You have learned in particular what a king of Israel should *not* be and what he should be, what a priest should *not* be and what he should be, and also what the people should *not* be looking for in a prophet. In your next lesson, you will study more about what a prophet should be and the amazing gift God is preparing for His people in sending them the Prophet like Moses.

QUESTIONS

1. What are the three main offices through which God leads His people to love Him?

The three main offices through which God leads His People to love Him are the offices of Judge/King, Priest, and Prophet.

2. What is the office of Kingship?

The office of Kingship is the office by which the king acts in the image of God the Father, the Creator, governing the people and leading them with the wisdom of God.

3. What is the office of Priesthood?

The office of Priesthood is the office by which the Priest acts in the image of God the Son, the Redeemer, mediating between God and the people by means of sacrifice.

4. What is the office of Prophet?

The office of Prophet is the office by which the Prophet acts in the image of God the Holy Spirit, the Sanctifier, revealing the will of God to the People and making them holy.

THE HIGH-PRIEST ENTERS THE HOLY OF HOLIES.

LESSON 37

The Prophet Who Is To Come

In your last lesson you studied the third part of the Book of Deuteronomy, which dealt with the offices of leadership among the people Israel—Kings and Priests. You also began to study the office of prophet. In this lesson we will study the central portion of the Book of Deuteronomy which completes what you began to learn about prophecy in your last lesson. It is instruction regarding all prophets and a prophecy about THE prophet like Moses, who will come.

All prophets and THE prophet

In the last lesson, Moses warned the people against all of the perversions of true prophecy that exist *outside* Israel. In this lesson he shows the people what characteristics make a true prophet of Israel, that is, a prophet like Moses (Deut 18:15-19). He also shows how to distinguish between true prophecy and false prophecy *within* Israel (Deut 18:20-22). This important passage is both a way to distinguish between all the true and false prophets who will come later in Israel's history, and it is also a prophecy about One prophet, the greatest of all the prophets, who will come as the fulfillment of Israel's history, and the fulfillment of all the Prophets.

The word "prophet" is how the Greeks translated the Hebrew word *nabi*. The Greek word "prophet" means "announcer" or "speaker." In the Greek Bible it refers to one who announces or speaks for God. It is thought that the Hebrew word *nabi* comes from an ancient word that only appears a few times in Scripture, a word that means "to bubble up" or "to gush forth" or "to pour out."

Here are two sentences in Scripture where this word occurs: "Return to my reproof! Behold! I will *pour forth* for you my Spirit, to make known my words to you" (Prov 1:23). "The words of a man's mouth are deep waters; the fountain of wisdom is a *gushing* stream" (Prov 18:4).

From these examples, we can see that the biblical use of this word shows that a *nabi* is one who has received the word of God from the Holy Spirit and who then becomes an overflowing source of divine wisdom by speaking this word to others. If every man were like a small pool of water, that is, having some wisdom, then a prophet is like a spring of water—the wisdom he receives from God is such that he cannot keep it in—it bubbles up and overflows and gushes forth and waters everything around it—and he receives his water directly from the Source. Thus a prophet is one who receives the wisdom and words of God and who must speak them to others. The prophet Jeremiah even described the word of God that he received not as water, but as a fire in his bones. Every time he spoke these words he got in trouble, so he tried to quit speaking them. But he couldn't because the words of God were so important it was as though they burned inside of him until he spoke them (see Jer 20:7–9).

What are the characteristics that make a true prophet—a prophet like Moses? Here is what Moses says:

> The LORD your God will raise up for you a prophet like me from among you, from your brethren—him you shall heed—just as you desired of the LORD your God at Horeb on the day of the assembly, when you said, "Let me not hear again the voice of the LORD my God, or see this great fire any more, lest I die." And the LORD said to me, "They have rightly said all that they have spoken. I will raise up for them a prophet like you from among their brethren; and I will put my words in his mouth, and he shall speak to them all that I command him. And whoever will not give heed to my words which he shall speak in my name, I myself will require it of him."

When we read what Moses says about the prophet who will come, we see there are four main characteristics of this prophet. (1) He comes from God and (2) he comes from Israel; (3) he represents God before Israel and (4) he represents Israel before God.

1. The prophet comes from God.
   a. *The Lord your God will raise up for you a prophet (Deut 18:15)*
   b. *I [the Lord] will raise up for them a prophet like you (Deut 18:18)*

From this we can see that the prophets in Israel will always come from "the Lord your God." As St. Peter would later say, "No prophecy ever came through human will; but rather human beings moved by the Holy Spirit spoke under the influence of God" (2 Pet 1:21). Prophecy is not some sort of human art of the spirit, but rather is a divine gift.

2. The prophet comes from Israel.
   a. *from your brethren (Deut 18:15b)*
   b. *from among their brethren (Deut 18:18b)*

Only the people formed by God are able to receive the great gift of true prophecy, because it is a gift of the Holy Spirit. Remember that Moses had wished "that all of the Lord's people were prophets!" (Num 11:29). But even among them it is very rare that one receives this gift because the Spirit only comes to the pure of heart. If prophecy is rare it is because purity of heart is rare. Purity has to do with having a single purpose. We say that "this is pure water" when there is nothing but water in the water—nothing else is mixed in. Having a single purpose—to love God (Deut 6:4)—is the purity of heart that makes a person ready to receive the gifts of the Spirit.

3. The prophet represents God to Israel.
   a. *him you must heed (Deut 18:15c)*
   b. *and I will put my words in his mouth, and he shall speak to them all that I command him. (Deut 18:18c)*
   c. *And whoever will not give heed to my words which he shall speak in my name, I myself will require it of him (Deut 18:19)*

The prophet "re-presents"—makes present again—God, among His people. That is why the people MUST listen to the prophet. The words he speaks are not his own words, but God's words, in human language. Thus, whoever does NOT listen to the prophet is not listening to God. The words that the prophet speaks are the human version of the same Word that brought the universe into existence and that sustains it in being. To hate or to ignore this *word* is to hate and ignore life and thus to perish.

4. The prophet represents Israel to God.
   Just as you desired of the Lord your God at Horeb on the day of the assembly when you said, "Let me not hear again the voice of the Lord my God, or see this great fire any more, lest I die." And the Lord said to me, "They have rightly said all that they have spoken." (Deut 18:16-17)

As the prophet represents God to the people, so he also represents the people before God. The prophet is the one who is not afraid, the way the people were, to hear the voice of the Lord and to see His "fire." The people stay back, but the prophet goes in. The prophet endures the "fire" as it were, so that he can receive the word of God. He passes by the cherubim with the flame-sword (Gen 3:24) and brings back fruit from the Tree of Life. The prophet is the one most aware of how terrifying God truly is, but whose ardent desire for God is so great that it overcomes fear.

Who is THE prophet like Moses?

These are the four main characteristics of all prophets, but who is THE prophet like Moses, the one who God promises here to His people? St. Stephen and St. Peter—the first martyr and the first pope—both taught that Jesus is the Prophet like Moses whom God promised to "raise up." He is the one "from among you" whom God "raised up" not only as THE prophet, but also from the dead! (Acts 3:15-26; 7:35-56).

True and false prophets

This section ends with Moses giving a final instruction for how the people are to distinguish between true and false prophets. He has already given something like this earlier in Deuteronomy (Deut 13:1-5). If a prophet comes and tries to lead the people away from God, telling them to serve other gods, then they should put such a false-prophet to death. Here the warning is more intense. The people are called upon to recognize and to discern a prophet who may even speak in God's name, but who is still a false prophet. Of course, if the false prophet doesn't come right out and say, "Hey everyone, I'm speaking in the name of some other god!," how are the people supposed to know if he speaks for God or not?

First of all, remember what came right before this part of Deuteronomy: if the king is on his throne studying the Torah, and the priests are faithfully offering the sacrifices to God, and the people are steering clear of all pagan practices and striving to be blameless before the Lord their God (Deut 18:13), THEN they will be able to discern between true and false prophecy when they see it. They will know the kind of thing that cannot be a word from God. Knowing true from false prophecy is a matter of living life as God intends His people to live it.

Here is a literal translation of the warning in Deut 18:21-22:

> And when you say in your heart 'How do we know *the word* which the Lord has not *spoken*? The prophet who *speaks* in the name of the Lord and that *word* will not be and will not come to pass, THAT is the *word* which the Lord has not *spoken*. In his pride the prophet has *spoken* it. You shall not sojourn with him.

Most translations and commentaries on this passage focus on the idea that the real test for true or false prophecy is whether or not the prophet foretells the future. If that forecasted event doesn't occur, then they can know that this was not a prophecy from God. But this, by itself, would be almost totally worthless for being able to tell who a true or a false prophet was, unless he made a prophecy that was supposed to be fulfilled almost immediately, and then it wasn't. But even then, he or his followers could simply say that they misinterpreted what he had said. Besides, Moses already warned of the possibility that false prophets could do signs and wonders! (Deut 13:1-2). What, then, does this passage mean? How are the people to know a true from a false prophet?

The real focus of the passage is on the italicized words translated as "word" and "spoken." In Hebrew these are all the same word. That word, which you should remember from your first lesson on Deuteronomy, is none other than the word from which the Hebrew title of this book takes its name. And it occurs SEVEN times in this verse.

The point is that any prophetic word that does not, or will not, lead the people to be faithful to the central command and teaching of Deuteronomy, the central "word" or "thing" that all of God's action in the world is about—to love God and give heed to the One God raises up as prophet—cannot be a word from God. THAT is how they tell true from false prophecy. It isn't something as mechanical as just waiting around to see whether or not a foretelling of the future comes to pass. No, this calls for true spiritual insight and a holy life—to be able to see whether the thing that the prophet says even *could be* the kind of thing that would lead people deeper into loving God and the One He will send. If it cannot be that kind of thing, then it cannot be a word that came from God. To follow that kind of prophet would be to "sojourn" away from God and the One like Moses whom He will send. How will a man know if it is that kind of thing? By a holy life. It is the pure in heart who can see God (Matt 5:8). A blind man cannot discern light from darkness—only the man with healthy vision can. So it isn't a matter of reading the headlines to see if something happened or not. It is more like learning a language and knowing it so well that you can tell—"this makes sense." Or better yet, it is like getting to know a person and knowing: this is (or is not) something that fits the language, the words and the deeds, of our good and all-powerful and all-loving God.

Summary

In this lesson, you have studied the central part of the book of Deuteronomy, devoted to the last of the three great leaders of God's people—kings, priests and prophets. You have learned the characteristics of all true prophets in general and of the fulfillment of all the prophets in the Prophet like Moses, namely, Jesus. You have learned that the only way for an Israelite to discern between true and false prophecy in Israel is by holiness of life and by faithfulness to the central command and teaching of the book of Deuteronomy—to love God with your whole heart and await the One He will send. In the next lesson, Moses again addresses all the leaders of the people who will govern the people once they have entered into life in the Promised Land, that is, the life of holiness in loving God and yearning for the One who is to come.

QUESTIONS

1. Who is the one with supreme authority among all prophets, priests, and kings in Israel?

The prophet like Moses foretold in Deuteronomy 18 is the one with supreme authority among all kings, priests, and prophets of Israel.

2. Who is the Prophet like Moses foretold in Deuteronomy 18?

Both St. Peter and St. Stephen identify Jesus as the Prophet like Moses whom God raised up from among his brethren, raised up from the dead, and whom all must heed because He speaks the words of God (Acts 3:15-26; 7:35-56).

3. What enables the Israelites to discern between a true and a false Prophet?

The Israelites can discern a true from a false prophet only by living holy lives in conformity with the central command and teaching of Deuteronomy.

Lesson 38

Social Life and Institutions

In your last lesson, you studied the climax of the Book of Deuteronomy's teaching about the religious life and institutions of Israel. After teaching about kings, priests, prophets, and especially the Prophet like Moses, the book turns now to teaching about the social life and institutions of Israel. These all have the same purpose as kings, priests, and prophets in Israel: the building up of the people of God. The commands given here are for all the people but are the special responsibility of the leaders of the People—to see to it that these laws and institutions are followed. Here are some examples from this section:

> The two parties in the dispute shall appear before the LORD in the presence of the *priests* or *judges* in office at that time. (Deut 19:17)
>
> When you are about to go into battle, the *priest* shall come forward and say to the soldiers... (Deut 20:2)
>
> Then the *officials* shall say to the soldiers, "Is there anyone who has built a new house and not yet had the housewarming? Let him return home, lest he die in battle and another dedicate it." (Deut 20:5)
>
> In fine, the *officials* shall say to the soldiers, "Is there anyone who is afraid and weak-hearted? Let him return home, lest he make his fellows as fainthearted as himself." (Deut 20:8)
>
> Your *elders* and *judges* shall go out and measure the distances to the cities that are in the neighborhood of the corpse. (Deut 21:2)
>
> Then these city *elders* shall take the man and chastise him. (Deut 22:18)
>
> In an attack of leprosy you shall be careful to observe exactly and to carry out all the directions of the *levitical priests*. Take care to act in accordance with the instructions I have given them. (Deut 24:8)
>
> When men have a dispute and bring it to the *judges*, and a decision is handed down to them acquitting the innocent party and condemning the guilty party... (Deut 25:1)

There you shall go to the *priest* in office at that time and say to him, 'Today I acknowledge to the LORD, my God, that I have indeed come into the land which he swore to our fathers he would give us.' (Deut 26:3)

War and peace

The basic division of the many and various laws that follow is a division between laws pertaining to times of war (Deuteronomy 19–21) and laws pertaining to times of peace and the conduct of every day life (Deuteronomy 22–26). We will spend the rest of this lesson looking at these two sections in order.

Laws for war (Deuteronomy 19–21)

Because this section is about how the leaders are to assist and guide in the building up of the people of God, and because war and strife can be major obstacles to the building up of the people of God, the laws that follow in this section have first to do with the causes of war (Deuteronomy 19), then with the conduct of war (Deuteronomy 20), and finally with the effects of war and other sorts of strife (Deuteronomy 21).

Deuteronomy 19—the causes of war

If one man *intended* to kill another, then the community was to enforce justice: what you do to others shall be done back to you. This was to prevent war, because if justice were done immediately by the whole community it would not give the injustice time to fester and so lead to the further and greater evil of all-out war.

Next comes the warning not to move property boundaries, which is the next leading cause of wars. After justice regarding a man's life, comes justice regarding the property that supports his life. Thus moving the boundary markers is another form of attacking a person.

Finally, so that wars are not started willy-nilly whenever anybody chooses to charge someone else with a crime, there must be at least two witnesses and they must be sufficiently serious and sober, knowing that if what they say proves to be false, whatever they were planning to do to their fellow Israelite will be done back to them.

This section concludes with a summary statement of the justice to be practiced in Israel: *It shall be life for life, eye for eye, tooth for tooth, hand for hand, foot for foot.* This is the justice that is the foundation of peace—what you do to others will be done to you—the justice confirmed by Jesus Himself (Mat 7:2).

This justice is a great improvement on excessive and defective laws and practices, which would either do nothing at all, or would take ten eyes for an eye, ten teeth for a tooth, etc. That kind of excessive or defective retaliation and punishment leads to further abuses and eventually, war.

Deuteronomy 20—the conduct of war

As long as the effects of the fall are with mankind, there will be times of war, just as on this side of the grave, our spiritual life will always have times of greater or lesser combat. Thus Moses gives here laws for how the Israelites are to carry out war.

First, war, like everything else, is to be placed firmly in the hands of God's providence. If the Israelites are set against an army much greater and better equipped than their own, they are not to be afraid. After all, they have the greatest secret weapon in the universe—God is on their side (see Rom 8:31).

Second, men whose death in battle would leave their lives unfulfilled in some important way are to go home, likewise with men who are fainthearted. They are all to go home so that they will not demoralize the rest of the army. The effect of this is that it will shrink the army and thus give those who remain even more reason to trust in God and to know that their victory in battle is God's victory (To see an example of this law put into practice, read Judges 7).

Third, when the Israelites approach a city of people dwelling outside of Canaan with whom they are at war, they are first to offer it terms of peace. This is an attempt to avoid war and bloodshed altogether if possible. If the people accept the terms of peace they can avoid death by doing work for the Israelites. In this way they will also come to know and revere and respect the true God through their interaction with the Israelites (see Deut 2:25; 4:6). If they do not accept it, then the Israelites are to besiege the city and kill all the males, but spare the women and children. Against the idolatrous nations of Canaan, the sentence is even more severe because otherwise the Israelites will learn false worship from them instead of them learning true worship from the Israelites (Deut 20:16). At this stage in Israel's development, God is requiring a level of conduct which, though is seems very harsh to us, is far better than that of the other nations with respect to people that they conquered (see Amos 1:13; 2 Kgs 8:12).

This is still short of the perfection that Christ will bring to the law (see Matt 5:17). Many people read this and are understandably confused or scandalized. It doesn't seem that these passages do anything to help build up the love of God and neighbor, which is what all Scripture is supposed to do. They might think something like, "Well, those people were really barbaric and we are much more civilized now, so this part of the Bible really doesn't have anything to say to us." This is false.

St. Paul wrote in 2 Tim 3:16 that *"ALL Scripture is inspired by God and is useful for teaching, for refutation, for correction, and for training in righteousness."* We have already studied how *what is true in the Old Covenant on a physical level is* EVEN MORE TRUE *in the New Covenant on a spiritual level.* Christ does not do away with the Old Covenant command to destroy the Canaanites and everything that breathes in their cities. Rather, it is *fulfilled* in the New Covenant command to eradicate every evil from our souls, to have no pity on anything in our soul that would lead us away from God (Matt 5:30; 18:8; 2 Cor 6:14; Eph 5:11; 6:12).

Deuteronomy 21—the effects of war

The first effect of war is death. So here Moses gives commands regarding what is to be done with the bodies of people who have been killed, not just in war but in any situation—even the situation when no one knows who killed a person. In order that life will be reverenced and the sin of murder atoned for, the people are to pray for the forgiveness of all guilt in Israel (Deut 21:8, see also Gen 4:10).

Those who are not killed in war are often captured instead. The next laws have to do with a woman whose husband, or mother and father, have been killed in war with the Israelites. She herself is a captive of war. If an Israelite man desires to marry her, he can marry her after she has had a month to mourn her loss. She cannot be treated as a slave, as was the case in other cultures, rather she is the man's *wife* (Deut 21:13) and must be treated as such.

Since an Israelite man who goes to war is most often already married, if he finds another woman among the captives that he wants to marry and does so, he will then have two wives. The next law reinforces justice among the two wives and their children. The man is bound to treat his wives and their children according to the law and not according to his whim (Deut 21:15-17).

Since Moses has now dealt with the main situations of strife in society—between peoples, between husband and wife, and between a husband and more than one wife—he now deals with the common situation of strife between parents and children. If a child is persistently obstinate, rebellious, disobedient, and wasteful, his parents have the right to turn him over to the authorities of the community who can decide to stone him to death. Again, we moderns might be horrified by such a thing, but this law too, does not pass away with Christ, but is rather fulfilled. *What is true in the Old Covenant on a physical level is* MORE TRUE *in the New Covenant on the spiritual level.*

This commandment in Deuteronomy reveals the dark side of the fourth commandment. Just as it is the first of the commandments to carry a blessing of long life and happiness with it if it is obeyed (see Eph 6:2), so to persist obstinately in hatred of this command carries the curse of death with it. What the Israelites are commanded to do here with stones physically displays what happens to the soul of any person who breaks this command, and what happens to the spirit of a nation whose children habitually break this command, and whose parents do not work to ensure that their children are brought up in the discipline and instruction of the Lord (Eph 6:2). We might think it terrible that anyone would be killed for any reason, but in fact the only reason anybody continues to exist after rejecting God's commandments is God's mercy and patience, which gives sinners time and opportunity to repent (see 2 Pet 3:9). To reject God is to reject life. That is what sin is, and, as St. Paul says, the wages of sin is death (Rom 6:23)—not because God is vengeful and mean but because only God IS. Everything else has existence only because it is given it from God. Our life comes from God and to separate ourselves from Him is to separate ourselves from life.

In the New Covenant, which fulfills the Old without destroying it, we are now at a point in God's pedagogy of the human race that we no longer make physical use of the sign (obstinate disobedience = stoning, physical death), but rather are to preach, teach, and train in the spiritual reality (obstinate disobedience = mortal sin, death of the soul). Nevertheless, it is important to note that this side of the grave, God retains, by means of the Old Testament scriptures, the *sign*. Just in case we get lazy in our thoughts and works regarding the reality, the image and sign of stoning is ever there to shock us back into the reality of just how bad this sin really is.

Having begun with the death of a person killed unjustly, Moses ends this section by discussing how to deal with the body of a person who was executed by the community according to justice. Even in death, however, the body still bears within it the image of God and therefore is not to be left hanging out to rot, as was sometimes done with criminals in other cultures of the time (for example, Sophocles' tragedy *Antigone* is all about this). This law was referred to in the Gospels as the reason why Christ was taken down off the cross the same day He died (John 19:31). Also, St. Paul referred this law to Christ, who died on a tree (Gal 3:13), thereby taking upon himself the curse of a man killed by the law of his own community.

Thus, as in all things, the fulfillment is in Christ, whom we should imitate. He is the innocent one who underwent the curse of the Law, hanging upon a tree. He is the prince of peace (Isaiah 9:6; Eph 2:14), who defeats the devil in battle (Luke 4, Matt 12:28-30); He is the one who is faithful to His one bride, the church (Eph 5:25), and perfectly obedient to His Father (John 15:10).

Deuteronomy 22-26—peace in the assembly of the Lord

The laws given in this next section on the conduct of life in times of peace are all about the preservation of peaceful life in the nation of Israel and for the building up of the people of God, called here "the assembly of the Lord." The Hebrew word for "assembly" or "congregation" (*qahal*) was translated into Greek as *ekklesia*, Latin as *ecclesia* from which our word ecclesiastical (having to do with the Church) comes. So when we talk about "the people of God" or "the assembly of the Lord" or "the congregation of the Lord," these laws are really about the building up the life of the Church.

The people of God are to help one another (Deut 22:1-4), to avoid anything that disrupts the social order (Deut 22:5) or natural order (Deut 22:6-7), keeping house (Deut 22:8) and field (Deut 22:9-10) safe and productive for the family who remembers the commands of the Lord (Deut 22:12; Num 15:37-41).

Next comes a section on preserving family life by preserving chastity, limiting the damage done by unchastity, and protecting the institution of marriage, the foundation of society and normal life (Deut 22:13-30). The goal of marriage in the people of God is to build up the assembly of the Lord both in terms of the union of love of husband and wife, but also the natural result of this loving union, which is children. Thus, the next section is about who can or cannot be a member in the assembly of the Lord (Deut 23:1-8), followed by a section on conduct of the details of daily life when men have gone out away from the full assembly of the Lord and normal life within it to fight against enemies (Deut 23:9-25). This is followed by a series of laws on various aspects of marriage, justice, mercy, and treatment of the poor and sick (Deut 24 and 25), all ordered toward the health and well-being of the assembly of the Lord. All of the laws that follow are for stopping or limiting evil. Among them are laws which Jesus said were written "because of the hardness of your hearts" and hence do not reflect the full flowering of truth and love that comes with Christ's commands, but which are nevertheless a preparation for them (see Matt 5:17-31).

Deuteronomy 23:9-25—keep yourselves from all evil

It is a great temptation, when leaving the routines of everyday life, to also leave behind normal good habits. Hence this first law forbids anything of the sort: *Keep yourselves from all evil* (Deut 23:9).

The first place this temptation would show itself (perhaps especially without women present to enforce it) is in basic cleanliness. Hence the next laws command the men to keep themselves and the camp clean, which also, of course, applies to all daily life, even when not in camp (Deut 23:10-14).

When a town was under attack, slaves of that town would sometimes flee for help to the opposing army. Hence the next command is for the Israelites to aid slaves who flee to them for help (Deut 23:15-16).

While in the army, men are away from their wives. God forbids Israelite men to have anything at all to do with prostitution at any situation or time (Deut 23:17-18).

The disruption of normal life in the army takes men away from their normal means of earning money and the food they eat. Also, money and food are scarcer when men are not at their farms getting what they need from the land or selling it in markets. Hence the next command takes from this situation and makes the universal command about loaning money or food or anything to fellow Israelites: it should be done free of charge (Deut 23:19-20).

Since battle often brings a man's life in danger, men would often make vows to God of the sort: *If you get me through this alive, Lord, then I promise to do x.* So the next law is about fulfilling vows of any sort in all situations (Deut 23:21-23).

Since armies travel through other people's land, the general rule that follows is that men may eat the produce of the land through which they pass, but they may not gather or harvest more than they can pick and eat immediately (Deut 23:24-25), similar to the way they were to act with regard to the Manna.

Deuteronomy 24:1-5—divorce and remarriage

In any society, the leading cause of disruption and disorder and the evils that flow from them is instability in that institution which is the foundation of all stable societies—marriage. Thus, next comes the law that Jesus said was written because of the hardness of heart of the people: the law regarding divorce. Later in the Old Covenant, it is explicit that God hates divorce (see Malachi 2:16). But even this earlier law shows God's hatred for divorce when it attempts to limit the evil of divorce by forcing the husband to go through a complicated legal process to obtain one. Only the scribes knew how to write in those days, and it would have been an expensive ordeal to obtain a written bill of divorce from a professional lawyer. Money aside, the man could only do this after listening to the counsel of a Scribe of the law, thus giving him the chance to reconsider and change his mind because of the advice of the Scribe. Nevertheless, if he will not change his mind about divorce, then he is to know beforehand that *his decision for divorce is as irrevocable as marriage is supposed to be.* THAT is the real focus of this law—once he has sent his wife away and she becomes the wife of another man, he can never take her back. This law discourages divorce because it is harmful and evil. Jesus simply took this to its conclusion and forbade divorce altogether. It is not an accident that this law about broken marriage is followed by a law which upholds and protects God's original plan for marriage, which is nothing other than happiness between husband and wife and the building up of the full number of the people of God (Deut 24:5; Gen 1:28).

Deuteronomy 24:6–25:19—mercy and justice

The rest of this chapter and the next are various laws ordered toward the practice of mercy and justice, encouraging mercy and generosity toward all those in need (Deut 24:6–25:4, 13–16) and demanding justice toward those who showed no mercy, generosity, or restraint toward others (Deut 25:5–12, 17–19). This is all with the purpose of building up the assembly of the Lord, and preventing its decrease.

Deuteronomy 26—the "Creed of the People of God"

The final chapter of this section can almost be compared to a type of creed for the people of God. Here they are commanded to appear before the Lord and His priest with gifts and tithes to recount aloud, in a liturgical setting before the priest, all of the most important truths about God and His saving acts. They are to worship and rejoice with the other people of God (Deut 26:5–11), and to recommit themselves to following all the commandments of the Lord (Deut 26:16–19), sharing their bounty and joy with others. This jubilant worship before God is the goal of this whole section of Scripture ordered toward the leaders of the people because *that* is the goal toward which the leaders of the people are to be guiding and leading the people of God, the assembly of the Lord.

Summary

In this lesson you have studied the fifth part of the Book of Deuteronomy addressing how the leaders of the people are to guide the people in building up the assembly of the Lord in their faith and commitment to God. In the next section, Moses and the leaders of the People turn again to address the people directly, summarizing and making explicit that their very life depends upon their obedience to the commands of the Lord.

There are no questions for this lesson.

LESSON 39

Blessings and Curses

In your last lesson, you studied the commands by which the leaders of the people were to govern and guide all the people of Israel. In this lesson, Moses and the leaders of the people turn together toward the people of Israel and exhort them, very simply and straightforwardly, to follow and obey and love and do all of these commands.

> Now Moses and the elders of Israel commanded the people saying *"Keep all the commandments which I command you this day!"* (Deut 27:1)

The Hebrew word translated as "keep" is the same one God used when He put the Man in the garden to tend the garden and to *keep* it (Gen 2:15). The word means to do and care for, it also means to guard and protect. The people are to guard this law as their special charge from God. It is that within which they will find life for themselves and friendship with God, as the Man did in the Garden of Eden.

Their life and prosperity in the Land does not depend on political prowess or economic power or technological efficiency. It depends on doing the commandments. As Jesus would later say, "Seek first the kingdom of God and His righteousness [spiritual prosperity] and all these other things [material prosperity] will be added to you besides" (Mat 6:33). We should put first things first, as the saying goes, and God is absolutely First.

Moses commands that when the people cross the Jordan and enter into the Land, they are to set up unhewn stones (symbolic of the earth, the work of God, rather than hewn stones, the work of man) for an altar on Mt. Ebal, to put a layer of plaster on these stones, and to write the words of the law out on these plaster-covered altar stones. *This is the first written Torah and here it is also an altar, an altar which symbolizes the whole Land, and the whole earth.* Thus the Torah—doing the commands of God—is the altar upon which man offers himself to God. The act of sacrificing upon the altar, and the act of doing the commandments of the Law, are shown to be one effort, one command—that of offering both the body and soul completely to God in worship and holy living, of loving God with their whole heart (Deut 6:4). This is a peace offering (Deut 27:7), calling for communion and joy between God and man.

The ceremony of the curses (Deut 27:11-26)

Moses then describes a ceremony that the people are to carry out once they have worshipped on Mt. Ebal. The six tribes which will later live in the northern territory of Israel are to stay at Mt. Ebal, which is to the North, while the six tribes that will live in the South are to depart and go to Mt. Gerizim, just to the South. With the people spread out on the two mountains and the Levites bearing the Ark of the Covenant in the narrow valley between, the two mountain sides become like a huge natural stadium. The Levites shout out curses upon any who would not follow the commands of the Law, and all the people shout back "Amen!" after each one. If you take the time to count them, you will find that there are twelve of them, one for each tribe, as it were, the most important laws for maintaining order within the community of the twelve tribes of Israel.

- Duty toward God comes first (Deut 27:15)
- followed by duty toward parents (Deut 27:16)
- then toward the helpless (Deut 27:18-19)
- then toward the institution of marriage (Deut 27:20-23)
- then toward all human life (Deut 27:24-25)
- then toward doing ALL the words of the law, written on the altar (Deut 27:26)

The blessings and the curses (Deuteronomy 28)

Following the description of this ceremony Moses goes on to list all of the great blessings that will come upon the people if they obey the commandments of God (Deut 28:1-14) and, for a more lengthy period of time, all of the terrible curses that will come upon them if they do not (Deut 28:15-68). Basically, every blessing and good thing imaginable will come upon the people if they obey, and every curse and terrible thing imaginable (or even unimaginable, see Deut 28:61) will come upon them if they do not.

Some of the curses described in detail here are so appalling and dreadful that it will just about make you sick to read them. And that is what they are supposed to do—to reveal to the people the truth that God is the source of every good thing that they desire; to depart from Him is to leave behind everything that is good and desirable and to choose everything that is horrible, painful, and vile.

You should note that the curses divide up into three basic parts, corresponding to the three basic parts of the promise God gave to Abraham—Land, Descendants, Blessing to all nations. Here the curses will come first upon the Land (Deut 28:15-52), then upon the people and their descendants (Deut 28:53-63), and finally, worst of all, what should have been Israel's greatest blessing (to all nations, see Deut 29:10), will instead be turned into a curse and Israel will be overrun by the nations and scattered among them (Deut 28:54-68). The other curses were less than this because at least the people still remained in the Land, just as Adam and Eve remained for a time in the garden after their sin. But then, worst of all, they are exiled from the Land, just as Adam and Eve were driven out of the garden.

A new covenant (Deuteronomy 29-30)

At this point, now that everything has been stated in the clearest possible terms, Moses renews the covenant with the people. This is a covenant *"besides the covenant which he had made with them at Horeb"* (Deut 29:1). It is also a covenant, not just with the people present in that time and place *"but with him who is not here with us this day as well..."* (Deut 29:15). Moses recognizes that even though the people saw the great signs and wonders which God worked for them, they still do not really understand what this is all about (Deut 29:4). He also recognizes that because they do not understand, there is further revelation that currently only God knows (Deut 29:29). Finally, he also recognizes that, despite all of his warnings, the curse is still going to come on the people in the future because of their negligence and disobedience (Deut 30:1).

He encourages them, however, with the promise of this new covenant: when they are in the anguish and exile they chose because of their unfaithfulness to God, they can "return." The Hebrew word for repent in Deut 30:2 also means to turn or "to return." To repent is nothing other than to turn around, to realize you are going the wrong way, and to return to where you should have been all along: to God. When the people repent and return, something new will happen—another and better covenant. The promise and sign of this new covenant in the future is not, as with Abraham, circumcision of the flesh, but circumcision of the heart (Deut 30:6). Whereas God commanded them earlier to "circumcise" their hearts, here, God Himself will work directly to circumcise their hearts (see Deut 10:16; 30:6). Instead of their bodies bearing the sign of their dedication to God, their heart will bear it. It will be visible only to those who have "a mind to understand" (Deut 29:4) what it means to be "cut to the heart" (see Acts 2:37!).

Lest the people should grow despondent at their lack of understanding, Moses then encourages them that even if they do not perfectly understand everything about the great secret plan of God (Deut 29:29), they do understand enough to *do* the law that God has given them.

This is the situation of any young child in a family. They are told, *"Do not play in the street."* However, they often are incapable of understanding the real reason for the commands given to them, commands which often seem strange or pointless to them, but which are, in fact, given to save them from pain and death. Even if they are capable of asking, *"Why can't I play in the street? It's fun!,"* they often are not capable of understanding the answer to their question. Only obedience will save them from death, keeping them long enough from harm so that they can grow to understand the reason for the command *(So that you will not get run over by a car!).* We are in a similar relationship to God, who is Our Father, who wants to preserve our life and keep us from harm so that we can grow up to be with Him forever. Sometimes and for some people *understanding* is impossible, but *obedience* never is. They must know *what* the law is in order to do it, but they do not have to know all of the reasons for the Law.

> For this commandment which I command you this day is not too hard for you, neither is it far off . . . The word is very near you; it is in your mouth and in your heart, *so that you* CAN *do it!* (Deut 30:11-14)

Moses then puts the whole matter once again in the absolutely simplest terms:

> God and his Law = LIFE and all blessing and good (Deut 30:15-16)
> Anything else = DEATH and all curses and evil (Deut 30: 17-18)

Even a little child can understand this.

> I have set before you life and death, blessing and curse; choose life therefore, that you and your descendants may live, loving the Lord your God, obeying his voice, and cleaving to him; for that means life to you and length of days, that you may dwell in the land which the Lord swore to your fathers, to Abraham, to Isaac, and to Jacob to give them (Deut 30:19-20).

Summary

In this lesson you have studied the sixth part of the Book of Deuteronomy, in which Moses again addresses all the people, showing them in clearest terms the blessings that come from loving and obeying God and the curses that come from hating and disobeying Him. Though there is more to be revealed about the secret things of God, the people know enough to know that God is good. Loving and obeying Him is the source of all good for them and really is their very life. In showing this, Moses has simplified the whole message of the Torah into one simple command: love God. In you next lesson, we will study the final part of the final book of the Torah, the final farewell of Moses.

QUESTION

What decision must each Israelite make after hearing Deuteronomy?

Each Israelite is compelled to make the decision recorded in Deut 30:19-20: "I have set before you life and death, blessing and curse; choose life therefore, that you and your descendants may live, loving the Lord your God, obeying his voice, and cleaving to him; for that means life to you and length of days."

LESSON 40

Moses Writes the Torah

This is your final lesson on Deuteronomy, and hence, on the Pentateuch. In previous lessons you have been studying the parts of the Book of Deuteronomy, which is the farewell address of Moses to the people before he dies. In this lesson, you will study the final part of that farewell. All the warnings and exhortations and prayers and pleadings of Moses with the people culminate here at the end of Deuteronomy as Moses prepares to die and leave the people. They will no longer have Moses with them—Moses, who is the living voice of the Torah, as it were. Therefore, in this final part, we will see Moses writing down all of the words of the Law so that the written Torah can be a reminder to the people of how they ought to be living their lives as God's people, and a witness against them if they do not live as they should.

There are four main parts to this final section of Deuteronomy:
1. Moses writes the Torah (Deuteronomy 31)
2. Moses "sings" the Torah (Deuteronomy 32)
3. Moses blesses the tribes of the People (Deuteronomy 33)
4. Moses dies and is buried (Deuteronomy 34)

We will deal with each in order and then reflect briefly upon the whole Pentateuch before completing the course.

Moses writes the Torah (Deuteronomy 31)

Throughout the Book of Deuteronomy, Moses has been speaking the Law to the people, using every form of address and exhortation to encourage and fortify the people for their most important task of keeping the commands of the Lord. The key to what happens now, in Deuteronomy 31, is something that Moses says toward the end of this chapter:

> For I know how rebellious and stubborn you are; behold, *while I am yet alive with you today you have been rebellious against the Lord; how much more after my death!* (Deut 31:27)

This reveals something very important. Moses has been, for the last forty years of his life, the living copy, as it were, of the Torah. Whenever the people needed to know or be reminded of who their God really is, and what

God wanted them to do, it was Moses who instructed them. But now Moses has reached the limit of years that God placed on mankind in Gen 6:3—120 years. Forty years he spent growing up in Egypt, forty years in exile in Midian, and forty years leading God's people in their wanderings to the Promised Land. When God placed this limit on the lifespan of mankind, He said: "My spirit shall not abide with man forever, for he is but flesh."

The Law, under which Israel as the representative of Mankind operated, was a Law that bound "the flesh," that is, the people not yet perfectly united to God in loving service. Moses lives to the full the lifespan given to man by God—but it is a lifespan given as a result of the Fall and decline of Man. The Law commands perfection but does not confer the Spirit of God to fulfill its commands perfectly. Divine action requires a divine power. As Jesus would say, "without me you can do nothing" (John 15:5), or again, "the spirit is willing, but the flesh is weak" (Matt 26:41).

Thus Moses, as the living copy of the Torah, shows the limitation of the Torah, which can lead the people to the Promised Land, so they can see it, but cannot lead them into it. It gives them the highest command (= love God) and even assures them that the command IS possible (Deut 30:11-14), but does not confer the power to actually do it perfectly, which it makes clear (Deut 31:21). Rather, the thing that will make it possible is part of the "secret things" (Deut 29:29) of God that have not yet been revealed. The Torah also looks forward to the coming of a prophet like Moses, who will speak the very words of God and who will make it possible for Man to become something more than merely "flesh," that is, something worthy to have God's spirit in him forever. As with Moses himself (Num 11:29), all the Old Covenant Prophets are constantly looking forward to the time when God will send His Spirit upon His people. (One of the greatest examples comes much later in Israel's history from the Prophet Ezekiel; see Ezek 37:1-14). All of these instances are looking forward to Jesus and His and His Father's sending of the Holy Spirit.

Moses "sings" the Torah (Deuteronomy 32)

So Moses first writes down the words of the Law "to the very end" and deposits them in the Ark of the Covenant (Deut 31:24-26), commanding that the whole thing be read aloud to the people every seventh year. But since that is a LONG reading, with a LONG period of time in between, Moses is also given from God a song to write down and teach to the people. The song IS the Torah in concentrated form—a shorter version of the whole thing.

In it we receive a potent reminder of the main points of the whole of salvation history:
- God *created* the people (Deut 32:6).
- He *chose* them from all other peoples to be His own special possession (Deut 32:7-14, see especially verse 9).
- But they *forsook* Him (Deut 32:15-18).
- In forsaking God the people are severely *punished* (Deut 32:19-27), because this is the only kind of teaching they understand (Deut 32:28-35).
- When they are at their lowest, and seem totally dead, God will *rescue* them and have compassion. This will be accomplished through God's complete power over life and death (Deut 32:36-39).
- God will then take *vengeance* on His people's enemies (Deut 32:40-42), which will lead to all nations *praising* His people, through whom this victory for all humanity was won (Deut 32:43).

Thus, in a small space Moses has given the people in this song
- Creation,
- the Fall,
- Redemption,
- And the final victory of God over all.

It is noteworthy that Deuteronomy shows us Joshua singing this song *together with Moses* (Deut 32:44). Moses led the people to the Promised Land but Joshua will be the one who leads them into it. As we mentioned, the Greek form of the name Joshua is *Jesus*. Moses is a symbol of the Old Covenant, and Joshua of the New. Here the men symbolic of the Old and New Covenant sing together the glorious acts of God for His People and the accomplishment of all of God's plans. In the New Testament, St. John put the two together as well when he said: "*The Law was given through Moses, grace and truth came through Jesus Christ* (John 1:17).

However, because Moses is the symbol for the Old Covenant, he is told that same day that he cannot lead the people in to the Promised Land, but must ascend Mt. Nebo to die because "*you broke faith with me in the midst of the sons of Israel at the waters of Meribath Kadesh, in the wilderness of Zin. Because you did not sanctify me in the midst of the sons of Israel*" (Deut 32:51).

You should remember what Meribath-Kadesh is all about from your lesson on Numbers 20, where Moses struck "the Rock" twice instead of speaking to it before the people Israel. It is fitting that in this Song of the Torah, after which God reminds Moses about the incident with "the Rock" at Meribah, God is referred to as "the Rock" six times (Deut 32:4, 13,15,18, 30, 31). The seventh and last time the title is used, God says that the people will rebel and look to other gods as "the Rock," but that only the Lord is true God (Deut 32:37-39). Thus, Deuteronomy itself makes essentially the same point as St. Paul does in 1 Cor 10:1-4: God/Christ is "the Rock."

Moses blesses the tribes of the people, but where is Simeon? (Deuteronomy 33)

Because he is about to die, Moses does here at the end of the last book of the Torah what Jacob did at the end of the first book of the Torah—he blesses the twelve tribes, looking forward to the future territories and character each tribe will later have in the Land. If you read carefully, you will notice something very interesting in relation to what you just read about "the Rock."

You should notice that one tribe is missing from the list—the tribe of Simeon. The historical reason that Simeon is missing from the list might be because in the future his tribe became linked to the tribe that would later be the tribe of the rulers—the tribe of Judah (see, for example, Josh 19:9; 21:9; Judg 1:3, 17), such that the two were sometimes thought of as one under the headship of Judah. But in light of our earlier reading of "the Rock," we can see that more is yet to come in the New Covenant. In Matthew's Gospel, Jesus says that He will build His Church upon "Rock" that is, on *Petrus* (in Greek). This is where the name "Peter" comes from. Peter, as leader of the twelve Apostles, is the leader of the reconstituted Israel, which is the Church (see Matt 7:24-25; 16:18!), while the Apostle who bore the name of the tribe of Judah (Judas) forfeited any role as leader by becoming the betrayer.

God is the great "Rock" which is the foundation of everything absolutely, but Peter is appointed by God to be the "Rock" on earth, of His Church. Peter was appointed leader of twelve apostles—symbolic of all the twelve tribes of reconstituted Israel. Now, what was Peter's name *before* Jesus gave him this new name? Peter's first name was . . . Simeon (see 2 Peter 1:1).

Moses dies and is buried (Deuteronomy 34)

After completing his life's work of leading the people of God from Egypt to the Promised Land, teaching and exhorting and blessing them one last time, Moses ascends Mt. Nebo, opposite Jericho, to see in a vision the whole of the Land promised to Abraham, Isaac, and Jacob. Once more God repeats that He will cause Moses to see the whole Land in a vision, but that Moses cannot enter it (Deut 34:4). Moses, the living Torah, sees the land of promise but cannot yet enter it. He is buried outside the Land in the valley of Moab in a secret place. Moses is gone, but Joshua has succeeded to Moses's position because Moses laid his hands upon Joshua to confer on him the spirit of wisdom. Joshua, the successor of the living Torah, will lead the people into the Promised Land.

The Past and the Future

The Torah ends looking both to the past and to future; it ends with amazement at all God accomplished through Moses, but also with longing for the prophet like Moses who has been prophesied to come, but has not come yet. In Jewish tradition, the Scriptures are divided up into Law, Prophets, and Writings. The Law is the Torah, or Pentateuch. But the last sentence of the

Torah ends on the note of prophecy and expectancy for a particular Prophet—the one like Moses. Hence, the whole next division of Scripture, from Joshua through the historical books and the minor and major prophets is referred to in Jewish tradition collectively as "the Prophets" (see, for example, Jesus's words in Matt 5:17). Thus, before it even happens, the whole next period of Israel's history—the history set in motion by the writing down of the Torah and the covenant between God and the people to keep the Torah—is already governed by the longing for the fulfillment of the prophecy in Deuteronomy 18 (and 34) about the Prophet like Moses who will come speaking the very words of God and revealing the even deeper secrets of God's plan for the world (Deut 29:29).

The structure and purpose of the Pentateuch

Now that we have come to the end, it is good to reflect for a moment on the basic overall "shape" and purpose of the Pentateuch. Based on what you have learned in this course, there is a very simple way to do this. We saw how each of the books of the Pentateuch can be divided into a seven-part chiasm, and how the central part of each of these is of major importance to that book. Thus if we take the central part of each book of the Pentateuch, we get a five-part chiasm for the whole thing, which looks like this:

A	Genesis	The Promises to Abraham = Creation
B	Exodus	God leads His people out of Egypt = Redemption
C	Leviticus	True Worship: Day of Atonement = Sanctification
B	Numbers	God leads His people to the Promised Land = Vocation
A	Deuteronomy	The Prophet Like Moses = Revelation

In your lessons on Leviticus, you learned that Leviticus is the central part of the Torah—true worship of the true and only God is the axis, as it were, upon which the whole Torah turns. Within Leviticus this belongs especially to the divine intimacy between the high priest and God on Yom Kippur. On either side of this central book are books about a journey. Exodus is essentially a journey away from Egypt to Sinai and Numbers is essentially a journey/wandering from Sinai to the Promised Land.

On either side of these books, we have the first and last books of the Torah—Genesis and Deuteronomy. As God brought the world into being in Genesis by His Word, so here at the end of Deuteronomy the people of God learn again that they are held in being as long as they "cleave" to God (Deut 10:20). As a man leaves his father and mother and cleaves to his wife (Gen 2:24), so Israel, the firstborn son of God, is to leave the land of Egypt where he was born and raised and cleave to God. God breathed life into the man, who thus became a living being; and Moses warns the people, at the end that this Torah is *"no trifle for you, BUT IS YOUR VERY LIFE!"* (Deut 32:47). The promises of *Land, Descendants,* and *Blessing to All,* given to Abraham in Genesis are in process of being fulfilled in Deuteronomy as God brings to the *land* Abraham's numerous *descendants,* and promises them the Prophet like Moses, the one through whom Israel will become in the fullest way a *blessing to all* peoples.

In Genesis creation came forth from God, but the pinnacle of God's creation, Man and Woman, fell and were expelled from Paradise, from the place of perfect peace, love, communion, and happiness with God. This also ended their perfect peace with each other, with themselves, and all of creation. Through the patriarchs and their children, God is drawing mankind back to Himself, back to a blessed land full of hope for peace and communion with God, and blessing for the whole world (Gen 12:3). Mankind is (very) slowly learning that only through perfect communion with God who is the source of all that is good, can there be communion and happiness and peace with one's self, with others, and with the rest of creation. The height and perfection of this communion with God is true worship, the outline of which is sketched in the central book of the Torah, Leviticus.

What next?

Genesis begins with the life of Adam and Deuteronomy ends with the death of Moses, leading St. Paul to say, "Death reigned from Adam unto Moses (Rom 5:14)." But didn't death reign all the way until Jesus defeated it? Why does St. Paul say "unto Moses" instead of "unto Jesus"? Well, first of all, by "unto Moses," St. Paul is saying that death reigned from Adam unto the end of the whole period of the covenant governed by Moses and the Torah— the whole Old Covenant period. But there is also a way that "unto Moses" could mean that something new really did begin to happen after Moses, but what was it? Moses had to die outside the Promised Land. Thus far the reign of death—Moses could not lead the People into the Promised Land. But someone *did* lead them into the Promised Land.

Adam was the Man who first had to leave the Promised Land of Eden and could not reenter it (Gen 3:24). Moses was the man who led the people back to the New Eden, but could not enter it. If death reigned from Adam unto Moses then there is also a way in which death symbolically began to be defeated *by the man who could and did enter the Land and who led the People into that New Eden of the Promised Land.*

Joshua is that man. Joshua is the beginning of the new hope given by the prophecy that ends the Torah. And Joshua, as you know by now is *Yehoshua/Yeshua* in Hebrew, which is "Jesus" in Greek.

Thus, in these three names—Adam, Moses, Joshua, which respectively mean "Man," "Drawn Out," and "Saved"—we have the basic outline of all that has happened in salvation history thus far and of what will be the governing principle of what will happen until the end. God created Man, who fell from grace. In His goodness, God "drew out" Man from slavery to sin, death, and the devil. But separation from evil is only the first step. The completion of God's work demands that Man be not only drawn out from evil, but totally saved from it and from its effects, that is, that evil be utterly defeated and the life-giving goodness of God triumph over all. That triumph begins with Joshua's leadership of the conquest of the Promised Land.

Summary

In this lesson, you have completed the lessons on Deuteronomy and with them, this course on the Pentateuch. You learned the importance of Moses as the "living Torah," as well as the importance of the written Torah, which will serve as a reminder and a witness for the People of God to all that God has done for them and all that He expects of them in return, so that they may have life, loving God and doing His will. You have learned the basic order and outline of the books of the Torah, their relationship to one another, and their relationship to the next part of the Scriptures. You have learned the significance of the names Adam, Moses, and Joshua for understanding in outline the whole of salvation history. Finally, you have learned the governing principle for understanding the next part of the Scriptures: the Prophets.

Question

What is the basic form of the Pentateuch?

As indicated by the central portion of each book the basic form of the Pentateuch is outlined as follows:

A	Genesis	The Promises to Abraham = Creation
B	Exodus	God leads His people out of Egypt = Redemption
C	Leviticus	True Worship: Day of Atonement = Sanctification
B	Numbers	God leads His people to the Promised Land = Vocation
A	Deuteronomy	The Prophet Like Moses = Revelation

www.ingramcontent.com/pod-product-compliance
Lightning Source LLC
Chambersburg PA
CBHW020346170426

43200CB00005B/67